# The European Defence Agency

This volume provides a comprehensive understanding of the European Defence Agency (EDA), the leading EU armaments policy institution.

Despite its critical role in European strategic and military affairs as the key hub of European policy-making in the field of armaments, the Agency has hitherto received very little attention from the academic and research community around Europe. To fill this gap in the literature, the book covers a multitude of interrelated themes and topics. Not only does it provide a detailed analysis and assessment of the Agency's record as the first institution dealing solely with EU armaments policy, but it also links these findings to international relations and European integration theory. Thematically, the contributions go beyond the mere description of achievements, gaps and risks, elaborating on novel themes such as space, offsets, pooling and sharing, and transatlantic armaments relations. The book combines an interdisciplinary approach to the study of European defence with theoretical and ontological pluralism, and seeks to unveil the strategic, industrial, institutional and ideational sources of armaments collaboration and capability development under the aegis of the EDA.

The multi-faceted orientation of the book will be of much interest to students of European security, EU institutions, defence studies, arms control and international relations in general.

**Nikolaos Karampekios** is a research fellow at the Centre for Security Economics and Technology, University of St. Gallen, and. holds a PhD in Technology Policy from the National Technical University of Athens.

**Iraklis Oikonomou** is a political scientist and holds a PhD in International Politics from the University of Wales Aberystwyth.

**Routledge Studies in European Security and Strategy**
Series Editors:
Sven Biscop
*Egmont Royal Institute for International Relations, Belgium*
and
Richard Whitman
*University of Kent, UK*

The aim of this series is to bring together the key experts on European security from the academic and policy worlds, and assess the state of play of the EU as an international security actor. The series explores the EU, and its member states, security policy and practices in a changing global and regional context. While the focus is on the politico-military dimension, security is put in the context of the holistic approach advocated by the EU.

**Tactical Nuclear Weapons and Euro-Atlantic Security**
The future of NATO
*Edited by Paolo Foradori*

**The EU and Military Operations**
A comparative analysis
*Katarina Engberg*

**The EU and Effective Multilateralism**
Internal and external reform practices
*Edited by Edith Drieskens and Louise van Schaik*

**EU Foreign Policy and Crisis Management Operations**
Power, purpose and domestic politics
*Benjamin Pohl*

**EU Foreign Policy, Transitional Justice and Mediation**
Principle, policy and practice
*Laura Davis*

**The European Defence Agency**
Arming Europe
*Edited by Nikolaos Karampekios and Iraklis Oikonomou*

# The European Defence Agency
## Arming Europe

Edited by Nikolaos Karampekios and
Iraklis Oikonomou

LONDON AND NEW YORK

First published 2015
by Routledge
2 Park Square, Milton Park, Abingdon, Oxon OX14 4RN

and by Routledge
711 Third Avenue, New York, NY 10017

*Routledge is an imprint of the Taylor & Francis Group, an informa business*

© 2015 selection and editorial matter, Nikolaos Karampekios and
Iraklis Oikonomou; individual chapters, the contributors

The right of the editor to be identified as the author of the editorial
matter, and of the authors for their individual chapters, has been
asserted in accordance with sections 77 and 78 of the Copyright,
Designs and Patents Act 1988.

All rights reserved. No part of this book may be reprinted or
reproduced or utilised in any form or by any electronic, mechanical,
or other means, now known or hereafter invented, including
photocopying and recording, or in any information storage or
retrieval system, without permission in writing from the publishers.

*Trademark notice*: Product or corporate names may be trademarks or
registered trademarks, and are used only for identification and
explanation without intent to infringe.

*British Library Cataloguing-in-Publication Data*
A catalogue record for this book is available from the British Library

*Library of Congress Cataloging-in-Publication Data*
The European Defence Agency : arming Europe / edited by
Nikolaos Karampekios and Iraklis Oikonomou.
   pages cm. – (Routledge studies in European security and strategy)
   Includes bibliographical references and index.
   1. European Defence Agency. 2. European Union countries–
Military policy. 3. European Union countries–Defenses.
   I. Karampekios, Nikolaos, editor of compilation. II. Oikonomou,
Iraklis, editor of compilation.
   UA646.E92346 2015
   355.8094–dc23                      2014039808

ISBN: 978-1-138-79997-4 (hbk)
ISBN: 978-1-315-75574-8 (ebk)

Typeset in Baskerville
by Wearset Ltd, Boldon, Tyne and Wear

Printed and bound in the United States of America by Publishers Graphics,
LLC on sustainably sourced paper.

**To Eleni and Ilias**
**To Andreas, Smaragdi, Diogenis and Dimitris**

# Contents

| | |
|---|---|
| *List of tables* | x |
| *Notes on contributors* | xi |
| *Foreword* | xv |
| HILMAR LINNENKAMP | |
| *Acknowledgements* | xix |
| *List of abbreviations* | xx |

| | |
|---|---|
| **Introduction** | 1 |
| NIKOLAOS KARAMPEKIOS AND IRAKLIS OIKONOMOU | |

**PART I**
**Theorising the EDA**                                                                 9

| | |
|---|---|
| 1 **Institutionalist approaches to agency establishment** | 11 |
| HELENA EKELUND | |
| 2 **The EDA and the discursive construction of European defence and security** | 27 |
| ANDRÉ BARRINHA | |
| 3 **Brothers in arms? The European arms industry and the making of the EDA** | 43 |
| IRAKLIS OIKONOMOU | |

**PART II**
**The EDA in action**                                                                 63

| | |
|---|---|
| 4 **EU military capability development and the EDA: ideas, interests and institutions** | 65 |
| ALISTAIR J.K. SHEPHERD | |

viii  *Contents*

5  **The EDA and armaments collaboration**                                    84
KATIA VLACHOS-DENGLER

6  **The EDA and the field of research and technology**                      102
ANJA DAHLMANN, MARCEL DICKOW AND
LÉA TISSERANT

7  **The EDA and EU defence procurement integration**                        118
ARIS GEORGOPOULOS

**PART III**
**The EDA, the nation-state and beyond**                                      137

8  **France, the UK and the EDA**                                             139
JOCELYN MAWDSLEY

9  **Germany's limited leadership in the EDA: international
and domestic constraints on defence cooperation**                            155
TOM DYSON

10  **Organisations at war: the EDA, NATO and the European
Commission**                                                                 171
MARC R. DEVORE

**PART IV**
**Broadening the EU armaments policy agenda**                                 189

11  **The EDA and military capability development: making
pooling and sharing work**                                                   191
LAURA CHAPPELL AND PETAR PETROV

12  **The EDA and the development of a European Defence
Technological and Industrial Base: between nationalisation
and globalisation**                                                          207
MARIE-LOUISE CHAGNAUD, CHRISTIAN MÖLLING AND
TORBEN SCHÜTZ

13  **The EDA and defence offsets: trailing after the
Commission**                                                                 225
PETER PLATZGUMMER

*Contents* ix

## 14 The EDA's inroads into space 241
FRANK SLIJPER

## Conclusion: future trajectories and a new research agenda 260
NIKOLAOS KARAMPEKIOS AND IRAKLIS OIKONOMOU

*Index* 266

# Tables

| | | |
|---|---|---:|
| 3.1 | European Advisory Group on Aerospace | 55 |
| 3.2 | List of experts invited by the European Convention, Working Group VIII | 56 |
| 3.3 | LeaderSHIP 2015 group members | 57 |
| 6.1 | EDA R&T projects | 105 |
| 6.2 | Structure of EDA's R&T through CapTechs | 108 |
| 6.3 | Overview of Joint Investment Programmes | 112 |

# Contributors

**André Barrinha** is Lecturer in Politics and International Relations at Canterbury Christ Church University and a Researcher at the Centre for Social Studies, University of Coimbra. He holds a PhD in International Relations from the University of Kent, Canterbury. His main research interests are in the fields of Critical Security Studies, European security, Turkish Foreign Policy and International Relations Theory. He has edited the book *Towards a Global Dimension: EU's Conflict Management in the Neighbourhood and Beyond*, published by the Friedrich Ebert Foundation.

**Marie-Louise Chagnaud** has been working as a research assistant within the International Security Research Division at the German Institute for International and Security Affairs, Berlin since 2012. Besides European defence capabilities within the 'European Defence Monitoring' project, her current work concentrates on European industrial matters and military helicopters. She was previously a consultant in a Berlin-based public affairs agency, responsible for various studies on defence industrial transformation.

**Laura Chappell** is Lecturer in European Politics at the University of Surrey. Her current research focuses on European strategic culture, EU military operations and EU military capability development. Her latest publications include *Germany, Poland and the Common Security and Defence Policy: Converging Security and Defence Perspectives in an Enlarged EU* (2012, Palgrave Macmillan) and 'The European Defence Agency and Permanent Structured Cooperation: Are we heading towards another missed opportunity?' *Defence Studies* (2012, with P. Petrov).

**Anja Dahlmann** is a research assistant at German Institute for International and Security Affairs Research Division 'International Security'. Her fields of research are European defence policy, military robotics and cyber security. She holds a Master's degree in political science from the University of Göttingen.

**Marc R. DeVore** is a Lecturer in International Relations at the University of St. Andrews and holds a PhD from the Massachusetts Institute of

xii *Contributors*

Technology (MIT). DeVore's current research deals with international armaments collaboration, civil–military relations and violent non-state actors. His work has featured in such journals as *Security Studies, Review of International Political Economy, Terrorism and Political Violence, Defense and Peace Economics, Cooperation and Conflict* and others.

**Marcel Dickow** is a Senior Associate and Deputy Head of German Institute for International and Security Affairs Research Division 'International Security' and member of the German Institute for International and Security Affairs cluster 'Armament and Technology'. He is a physicist from the Technical University of Berlin by training. Since 2009, Marcel Dickow has been working on topics such as defence technology, space policy, European defence cooperation, robotics and cyber security. He has led and participated in several third-party funded international research projects.

**Tom Dyson** is Senior Lecturer in International Relations at Royal Holloway, University of London. His research interests lie in European defence and security, and British, French and German defence policy. He is the author of *The Politics of German Defence and Security* (Berghahn, 2007); *Neoclassical Realism and Defence Reform in post-Cold War Europe* (Palgrave, 2010); and *European Defence Cooperation in EU Law and IR Theory* (Palgrave, 2013, with Dr. Theodore Konstadinides).

**Helena Ekelund** is Assistant Professor at the Department of Political Science, Lund University, Sweden. She was awarded her doctorate from the University of Nottingham, UK, where she also worked as a teaching associate. In her doctoral thesis she draws on new institutionalist theory and public administration literature to examine the establishment of European agencies. Her wider research interests include European governance, public administration, European integration and executive politics and governance.

**Aris Georgopoulos** is Assistant Professor of EU and Public Law at the School of Law of the University of Nottingham. He is also Global Governance Fellow at the Robert Schuman Centre of Advanced Studies, European University Institute. He has published extensively on aspects of public and defence procurement. His PhD thesis received a special distinction from the European Group of Public Law.

**Nikolaos Karampekios** is a research fellow at the Centre for Security Economics and Technology (C SET), University of St. Gallen. His interests include security R&D and industrial policy. His work has appeared in *Allgemeine Schweizerische Militärzeitschrift, Military Power Review, Journal of Southeast European and Black Sea Studies* and *Géographies, Géopolitiques et Géostratégies Regionales*. Nikolaos obtained his PhD in EU technology policy jointly from the University of Athens and the National Technical University of Athens.

## Contributors xiii

**Hilmar Linnenkamp** has been an adviser to the Research Division International Security at the Stiftung Wissenschaft und Politik since 2009. His key areas of expertise include international relations, security policy, armaments policy and military sociology From 2008 to 2009, he served as Director of the Armaments Department of the Permanent Representation of Germany to the EU and, from 2004 to 2007, as Deputy Chief Executive of the European Defence Agency in Brussels.

**Jocelyn Mawdsley** is a lecturer in European and EU Politics at the University of Newcastle upon Tyne. She has published widely on European armaments issues, most recently on the A400M project, Franco-British defence relations and the homeland security industrial sector. Her current research concentrates on security technologies and export controls, drones, large states and the CSDP and interpretivism in security studies. She is also coordinating a collaborative research network on CSDP Strategy.

**Christian Mölling** is a research fellow with the International Security Division at SWP – German Institute for International and Security Affairs, Berlin. As a project director, he heads the four-year project 'European Defence Monitoring' that studies the impact of the fiscal crisis on the EU's military and defence industrial capabilities, and advises on future pooling and sharing opportunities. His research and advice focuses on German and European defence policies and industries.

**Iraklis Oikonomou** holds a PhD in International Politics from the University of Wales Aberystwyth. His main research interests are European integration theory, militarisation, and the political economy of EU armaments, space and security policies. Among other publications, he has co-edited the volume *Poulantzas Today*, published by Nicos Poulantzas Institute in Greek.

**Petar Petrov** is Assistant Professor in International Relations and EU Foreign and Security Policy at Maastricht University. His current research focuses on the governance of CSDP, EU crisis management operations and the development of European strategic culture. His latest publication is 'Whose Rule, Whose Law? Contested Statehood, External Leverage and the EU's Rule of Law Mission in Kosovo', *Journal of Common Market Studies* (with D. Papadimitriou, 2013).

**Peter Platzgummer** is a Senior Researcher at the Centre for Security Economics and Technology at the University of St. Gallen and a Visiting Scholar at the Graduate School of Business and Public Policy at the US Naval Postgraduate School. Previously, he was responsible for the development of the Swiss Industrial Compensation Strategy. His PhD thesis focused on the usage of performance management in arms trade offsets in Europe.

**Torben Schütz** is a research assistant within the International Security Research Division at the German Institute for International and Security Affairs, Berlin. Besides European defence industrial capabilities within the 'European Defence Monitoring' project, he works on Unmanned Aerial Systems and German defence exports. Torben's master's thesis focuses on the cooperation between the German armed forces and private security and military firms during ISAF.

**Alistair J.K. Shepherd** is Lecturer in Contemporary European Security in the Department of International Politics, Aberystwyth University. His research focuses on EU foreign, security and defence policies; Europe's role in conflict management; NATO and Transatlantic relations; and national security and defence policies in Europe. His latest publication is 'Transforming ESDP for Global Conflict Management', in R. Whitman and S. Wolff (eds), *The European Union as a Global Conflict Manager* (Routledge, 2012).

**Frank Slijper** is a Dutch economist and research associate with the Transnational Institute who has published widely on arms trade and militarisation issues since the early 1990s. The emerging military face of the European Union has been the focus of a number of his articles, including 'Space: The High Ground of the European Union's Emerging Military Policies' (2011) and 'Hidden Actor: The Democratic Deficit of the European Defence Agency' (2010).

**Léa Tisserant** was an intern in German Institute for International and Security Affairs Research Division 'International Security'. A jurist by training, she holds a Master's Degree in international law and human security from the University of Aix-Marseille, where she wrote a Master's thesis studying the applicability of international law in cyberspace. Ms. Tisserant's research interests are also with military robotics and Franco-German defence cooperation.

**Katia Vlachos-Dengler** is a researcher and defence analyst, holding a PhD in Policy Analysis from the RAND Graduate School. She has published extensively on European defence capabilities, armaments cooperation, the defence industry and the defence implications of the economic crisis. Katia has worked as a researcher at the RAND Corporation and at the National Defence Academy of Austria, and lives in Zurich, Switzerland.

# Foreword

July 12, 2014 marked the tenth anniversary of the European Defence Agency's (EDA) establishment by a Joint Action of the European Union. The agency became operational on October 1, 2004. Within a few months it developed into a respected element of the EU's Common Security and Defence Policy (CSDP) infrastructure, driving forward an ambitious agenda of cooperation in a wide range of issues from research and technology, armaments, military capabilities and defence industrial and market themes. Reputation and relevance grew continually over the years: never before has the EDA been mentioned as intensely as in the European Council's conclusions of December 2013. Much is expected from it in terms of the co-operative agenda of CSDP.

The agency has not, however, replaced the 28 Ministries of Defence of the EU – it rather represents the interests of the agency's 27 Member States (Denmark is not participating) in an attempt to explore the maximum common ground of the 27 'pentagons' in the EU. It is not, therefore, an agency for European Defence, but a European agency for defence (slightly better expressed in its French version 'Agence européenne de défense') supplementing the efforts of its constituent defence establishments at strengthening their collective endeavours.

What is the historical background of the EDA's foundation? And why was such an organisation planted into the Brussels CSDP garden? Three strands explain most of the reasoning. First, at the time of the 2003 Thessaloniki European Council, where the decision to establish the agency was taken, most of the political and military institutions and procedures of CSDP were already in place: the High Representative for Foreign and Security Policy, in persona Javier Solana, was firmly in command, the Political and Security Committe (PSC) oversaw the conceptual and operational aspects of CSDP, military advice and planning lay with the EU Military Committee and the Military Staff – but the determination of the right capabilities and the contribution of technology and armaments to such capabilities were not systematically addressed in the existing structures.

Second, year-long attempts at creating a European Armaments Agency (EAA) had gone nowhere, and the armaments-related activities of the

## xvi *Foreword*

remnants of the defunct Western European Union – the Western European Armaments Group (WEAG) and the Western European Armaments Organisation (WEAO) – were lingering on with little effect. Activities of the Letter-of-Intent (LoI) group of six major arms-producing countries were more procedural than substantial. The WEAG and LoI frameworks had both degenerated into a travelling circus of meetings between Stockholm and Taormina, whilst the only well resourced armaments organisation, OCCAR, was caught up in the contractual management of legacy projects, such as TIGER and A400M. A new approach to forward-looking armaments co-operation appeared necessary.

Third, the European Commission had been trying, since the 1997 Bangemann Report, to acquire a major role in defence industry matters and defence market regulation – with little punch hitherto. Therefore, an intergovernmental initiative to deal with this industry and market agenda imposed itself.

In this situation it was logical to design a place where defence capabilities, technology and armaments issues as well as economic aspects of defence were to be dealt with in a more comprehensive and systematic manner than in ad-hoc meetings of government representatives as was the practice in NATO or the WEU. A permanent working institution, an agency, was to replace, and take over duties from, committees, conferences and consultative bodies. No wonder that the comprehensive approach was built into the initial EDA structure – with its four directorates on 'Capabilities', 'Research and Technology', 'Armaments', and 'Industry and Market'. This organisational design has served its purpose until the end of 2013.

What is EDA's record today – its ambitions and limitations, its successes and unfulfilled promises? The years from 2004 to 2007 were characterised by the efforts to set the agenda and establish internal and external procedures: which subjects to address and how to organise the agency's workstreams; how to deal with its shareholders – the Member States' governments – and stakeholders like the EU Commission, the industry and the defence and security bodies in Brussels. A number of seminal strategies, documents and agreements were conceived and negotiated – with mixed practical results.

Progress and disappointment lay closely together. A Code of Conduct on defence procurement with its procedural instrument of an agency-run Electronic Bulletin Board (EBB) was meant to encourage cross-border procurement – but a sea change towards more competition was not achieved. An ambitious 'European Defence Technological and Industrial Base (EDTIB) Strategy' was negotiated and agreed – but no major collective action was initiated towards the intended industrial consolidation and competitiveness of the European defence industry. A forward-looking 'R&T Strategy' found the consent of all Member States – but only very few joint R&T investment programmes were established. High hopes were

*Foreword* xvii

placed on the EDA's 'Long-Term Vision' document as a guideline for a coordinated 'Capability Development Plan (CDP)' – but the EDA has not to this day found the necessary support from its Member States to transform the CDP into a widely accepted tool informing the multitude of national planning agendas in favour of coordinated efforts at R&T and armaments strategies and decisions.

It was possible, though, to initiate in those first few years several groundbreaking practical cooperations. Examples were the start of a first Joint Investment Programme in Research and Technology, where the usual principle of *juste retour* was replaced by common financing and cross-border competition; the establishment of a Software-Defined Radio project in coordination with the Commission's research programme; the initiative for cooperation in critical areas of future UAV capacities via research on 'Sense and Avoid' as well as 'Beyond Line of Sight' technologies.

Nevertheless, the gap between ambitious strategic objectives and modest implementation at the programme level led to a gradual reorientation of the EDA's working style and, indeed, its agenda. From about 2008 on, a narrower focus on practical projects took hold. Agency success was to be measured more in terms of specific islands of cooperation, and less in terms of conceptual breakthroughs. In addition, more emphasis was being put on closer relations with the European Commission, the European Space Agency or, for that matter, OCCAR. All this is still part of the agency's life today.

A third phase, beginning in 2011, has seen the irritations and challenges of the European-wide financial and debt crisis. This crisis, originating in late 2008, has made itself felt in the defence world with some delay only; but from 2010 on it became clear that enhanced cooperation among EU Member States ought to be part of the ensuing resource-crisis management. Consequently, and by taking up bilateral and multilateral initiatives, EDA is being heavily involved in promoting and catalysing a smart answer to the challenge: it became successful in negotiating a 'Code of Conduct on Pooling and Sharing'. This agreement should become instrumental in mainstreaming Pooling and Sharing in national capability development agendas. The European Council of Heads of State and Government in December 2013 gave this instrument a strong backing.

What, now, is the future of EDA's role, responsibility and likely record? From its inception, EDA has served as a coordinator, a conscience and a catalyst. Three main tasks stand out in, as the military would call it, its customer requirement specification: first, encouraging transparency in capability development and R&T agendas Europe-wide; second, engaging Member States to participate in cooperative projects – whether bi-national or multinational; third, enlightening a common reflection of all Member States on the Commission's defence industrial agenda.

For these ambitious and difficult tasks to be supported by national governments, parliaments and industries it is undoubtedly necessary not only

xviii *Foreword*

to increase and enhance the EDA's visibility and profile – its website and regular publications are already part of this effort – but also to intensify outside academic reflection of its functioning and output. To that, this book is meant to contribute. The agency is facing an enormous political challenge: the EU not only needs to become a stronger partner of the United States within a modified transatlantic relationship but must also recognise, and react to, the challenges stemming from the fundamental redistribution of global power. These strategic changes demand that Europe make full use of all the assets and opportunities available to the EU – including its technological, economic and military excellence. CSDP will only fulfil that promise if collective wisdom meets collective action. The EDA can become the agent of such change.

Hilmar Linnenkamp

# Acknowledgements

The publication of this book would not have been possible without the generous contribution, encouragement and help of a number of individuals. First of all, we would like to thank Professor James W. Davis, Director of the Institute for Political Science at the University of St. Gallen and Chair of the Centre for Security Economics and Technology (C SET). Professor Davis not only offered his wholehearted support and guidance, but also secured financial support for a two-day meeting at St. Gallen where the contributors presented initial versions of their chapters. Also, we extend our sincere thanks to Dr. Hilmar Linnenkamp, former Deputy Chief Executive of the EDA, who agreed to write the Foreword to this volume. Furthermore, we are grateful to the series editors, Professors Sven Biscop and Richard Whitman, as well as to the anonymous reviewers for their insightful comments. We also thank Hannah Ferguson and Andrew Humphrys at Routledge for their exemplary guidance before and during the publication process, as well as Steve Turrington for his meticulous copy-editing services. Last but not least, we are wholeheartedly thankful to all of the contributors to this volume, for getting – and staying – on board this project.

N.K. – I.O.

# Abbreviations

| | |
|---|---|
| 3Cs | Capabilities, Competences, Competitiveness |
| AAR | Air-to-Air Refuelling |
| AET | Agency Establishment Team |
| AFV | Armoured Fighting Vehicle |
| ASAT | Anti-Satellite |
| ASD | Aerospace and Defence Industries Association in Europe |
| C3 | Command, Control, Communications |
| CapTechs | Capability Technology Areas |
| CBRN | Chemical, Biological, Radiological and Nuclear |
| CDM | Capability Development Mechanism |
| CDP | Capability Development Plan |
| CFSP | Common Foreign and Security Policy |
| CNAD | Committee of National Armaments Directors |
| CNC | CapTech National Coordinators |
| CnGE | CapTech non-Governmental Experts |
| CoBPSC | Code of Best Practice in the Supply Chain |
| CoC | Code of Conduct on Defence Procurement |
| CoCO | Code of Conduct on Offsets |
| CoCP | Code of Conduct on Prioritisation |
| COPS | Political and Security Committee |
| CSDP | Common Security and Defence Policy |
| CSR | Common Staff Requirement |
| CST | Common Staff Target |
| C-IED | Counter-Improvised Explosive Device |
| DARPA | Defense Advanced Research Projects Agency |
| DeSIRE | Demonstration of Satellites enabling the Insertion of RPAS in Europe |
| DRC | Democratic Republic of Congo |
| DSP | Defence and Security Procurement (Directive) |
| DTIB | Defence Technological and Industrial Base |
| EAC | European Armaments Cooperation (Strategy) |
| EATF | European Air Transport Fleet |
| EBB | Electronic Bulletin Board |

|  |  |
|---|---|
| ECAP | European Capabilities Action Plan |
| EC | European Commission |
| ECJ | European Court of Justice |
| EDA | European Defence Agency |
| EDRS | European Data Relay System |
| EDRTS | European Defence R&T Strategy |
| EDSIS | European Defence Standards Information System |
| EDTIB | European Defence Technological and Industrial Base |
| EEAS | European External Action Service |
| EFC | European Framework Cooperation |
| EHDP | European Handbook of Defence Procurement |
| EPM | Effective Procurement Methods |
| ESA | European Space Agency |
| ESCPC | European Satellite Communications Procurement Cell |
| ESDP | European Security and Defence Policy |
| ESI | European Synergies and Innovation |
| ESM | Environment, Systems and Modelling |
| ESS | European Security Strategy |
| ESSOR | European Secure SOftware defined Radio |
| ESPRIT | Emerging System Concepts for UAS Command and Control via Satellite |
| EU | European Union |
| EUCLID | European Cooperation Long-Term in Defence |
| EUMC | European Military Committee |
| EUMS | European Military Staff |
| EUSC | European Satellite Centre |
| FASGW | Future Anti-Surface Guided Weapons |
| FP7 | Seventh European Union Framework Programme for Research and Development |
| FYROM | Former Yugoslav Republic of Macedonia |
| GEM | Guidance, Energy and Materials |
| GMES | Global Monitoring for Environment and Security |
| GOVSATCOM | Governmental Satellite Communication |
| GPS | Global Positioning System |
| GSM | Groupe Spécial Mobile |
| HEP | Helicopter Exercise Programme |
| HHG | Helsinki Headline Goal |
| HR/VP | High Representative of the Union for Foreign Affairs and Security Policy and Vice-President of the Commission |
| HSPG | High-level Space Policy Group |
| I&M | Industry and Market (EDA Directorate) |
| IAP | Information Acquisition and Processing |
| IEPG | Independent European Programme Group |
| IPR | Intellectual Property Rights |
| IPTs | Integrated Project Teams |

## xxii Abbreviations

| | |
|---|---|
| IR | International Relations |
| ISAF | International Security Assistance Force |
| ISO | International Standards Organisation |
| ISR | Intelligence, Surveillance, Reconnaissance |
| ISTAR | Intelligence, Surveillance, Target Acquisition and Reconnaissance |
| JIP | Joint Investment Programme |
| JIP-FP | Joint Investment Programme on Force Protection |
| JIP-ICET | Joint Investment Programme-Innovative Concepts and Emerging Technologies |
| JVs | Joint Ventures |
| KOR | Key Operating Rules |
| LoI | Letter of Intent |
| LTV | Long-Term Vision for European Defence Capability |
| MALE | Medium Altitude Long Endurance |
| MANPADS | Man Portable Air Defence Systems |
| MARSUR | Maritime Surveillance |
| MAWA | Military Airworthiness Authorities |
| MIDCAS | Mid-air Collision Avoidance System |
| MILSATCOM | Military Satellite Communications |
| MoD | Ministry of Defence |
| MOD | Ministry of Defence (UK) |
| MoE | Ministry of Economics |
| MSA/MAS | Military Standardization Agency/Military Agency for Standardization |
| MSHT | Materials Standards Harmonisation Team |
| MUSIS | Multinational Space-based Imaging System |
| NAMSA | NATO Maintenance and Supply Agency |
| NATO | North Atlantic Treaty Organisation |
| NEC | Network Enabled Capability |
| NMSSS | NATO Maintenance and Supply Service System |
| NPM | New Public Management |
| NSA | NATO Standardization Agency |
| OCCAR | Organisation Conjointe de Coopération en matière d'Armement/Organisation for Joint Armament Cooperation |
| P&S | Pooling and Sharing |
| PESCO | Permanent Structured Cooperation |
| PGMs | Precision Guided Munitions |
| pMS | Participating Member States |
| R&D | Research and Development |
| R&T | Research and Technology |
| RPAS | Remotely Piloted Aircraft Systems |
| SALIS | Strategic Airlift Interim Solution |
| SATCOM | Satellite Communications |

| | |
|---|---|
| SDO | Standards Developing Organisation |
| SDR | Software-Defined Radio |
| SMEs | Small and Medium Enterprises |
| SoI | Security of Information |
| SoS | Security of Supply |
| SSA | Space Situational Awareness |
| SST | Space, Surveillance and Tracking |
| STANAGs | Standardization Agreements |
| STAR 21 | Strategic Aerospace Review 21 |
| TEU | Treaty on European Union |
| TFEU | Treaty on the Functioning of the European Union |
| THLS | Third Party Logistics Support |
| TLMP | Through-Life Management Plan |
| ToL | Treaty of Lisbon |
| UAS | Unmanned Aerial Systems |
| UAV | Unmanned Aerial Vehicles |
| UCAV | Unmanned Combat Aerial Vehicles |
| UK | United Kingdom |
| UMS | Unmanned Maritime Systems |
| US | United States |
| WEAG | Western European Armaments Group |
| WEAO | Western European Armaments Organisation |
| WEU | Western European Union |
| VBCI | Véhicule Blindé de Combat d'Infanterie [Armoured vehicle for infantry combat] |

# Introduction

*Nikolaos Karampekios and Iraklis Oikonomou*

## Scope

This book is an edited volume about the European Defence Agency (EDA). It is based on an aspiration to provide a comprehensive understanding of the EDA as the leading EU armaments policy institution, given that students of European Union (EU) politics have always been somewhat uneasy when dealing with such issues. Armaments collaboration and policy integration have always seemed too technical and economic in nature, usually seen as a footnote in the grand text of the Common Security and Defence Policy (CSDP); a footnote that will supposedly be authored automatically, through some kind of metaphysical inertia. The EDA has been a victim of this hesitation. Despite its critical role in European strategic and military affairs as the key hub of European policy-making in the field of armaments, the Agency has received very little attention from the academic and research community around Europe. No research monograph on the EDA has ever been published, with the exception of a rather descriptive, policy-oriented report (Spanish Ministry of Defence 2010), and the dozen or so relevant articles that have been produced since its establishment only underscore the discrepancy between the Agency's growing policy impact on areas of previously exclusive national jurisdiction, and the quantitatively limited theoretical and empirical analysis it has received.

The academic treatment of defence and armaments policies in the EU context, including the role of the EDA, may have also been slightly undermined by an intellectual fashion that pictures the EU as a 'civilian' or 'normative' power (see Manners 2006; Orbie 2006). While not directly questioning the validity of such theorisations, we feel that there is a need to balance this notion through a rejuvenation of academic interest concerning the core strategic questions the EU faces today. Such questions involve the conception of the EU's key strategic reflections and priorities, the development of military capabilities and the production of armaments, the technological spillovers to and from civilian technologies, the innovation potential that stems from the increasing interplay between the EDA and the European Commission, and the definition of a general interest through and beyond the multiplicity of national and sectoral interests. In other words, the EDA is a missing link in EU security, defence and armaments policies and, in this sense, it has been rather understudied.

Starting from a well-defined empirical epicenter, the EDA as the institutional nucleus of EU armaments policy, the book proceeds to cover a multitude of interrelated themes and topics. These include among others: novel theoretical approaches to agency formation and armaments collaboration; the political role of industrial actors; capability development in the CSDP framework; technological and research foundations of EU security policy; the past and present of EU armaments collaboration; the formation of an EU defence equipment market; Member States' reactions to EU defence and armaments policies; the development of EU strategic considerations; the agenda of Permanent Structured Cooperation (PESCO) and Pooling and Sharing (P&S) initiatives; and the military use of space. In other words, the book combines a comprehensive approach to the study of European defence with theoretical and empirical pluralism. It moves beyond the mere citation of numbers and technical requirements, to unveil the strategic, industrial, institutional and even ideational sources of armaments collaboration and capability development in the EU, under the aegis of the EDA.

This book bears testament to the idea that armaments policy is a multifaceted endeavour, consisting of technological, industrial and political aspects, which need to be woven together for any such policy to be robust and long lived. Studying the institutional mechanisms set up to enforce the EU's grand policies, the specific 'sectoral' policies, as well as the actors involved, portrays a much richer image of the actual decision- and implementation-policy process. For example, understanding the 'how's' of developing P&S capabilities in areas such as Countering Improvised Explosive Devices (C-IEDs), or the 'why's' of the EDA's engagement with space – in tune with other EU institutional actors – provides invaluable insights into the actual workings of EU policy-making. This logic points to a perspective that focuses on the actual achievements and limitations rather than on mere political declarations and discourse. This kind of *ex post* analysis is further corroborated by taking into account the pressures exercised by the formation of CSDP and the restructuring of the European defence industry, two processes that only now have come to full maturity.

## Methodology

All the chapters are structured around the central themes of the topicality of EDA as the nucleus of EU armaments policy and the interrelatedness of European security, industrial competitiveness and military capabilities. These themes were for the authors to follow up on. Sticking to a set of prearranged themes and rules is one thing, and intervening in the written logic or findings of the authors is quite another. Indeed, we navigated away from attempting to superimpose a certain theoretical argument or position by which each chapter should abide. Instead, we opted for certain questions that needed to be answered and fostered even quasi-conflicting arguments to allow for theoretical pluralism.

Every effort was made to achieve a balance and interplay between theoretical and empirical analysis. An emphasis on theory is reflected in the inclusion of a separate section of the book – the first three chapters of the book have a clear theoretical orientation – as well as in multiple references to strategic, international relations and European integration theory appearing in other chapters. At the same time, all chapters maintain a solid empirical foundation, in the form of a geographical or issue-related focus, covering a broad range of policy aspects – such as Research and Technology (R&T), armaments collaboration, defence procurement and space.

## Structure

Part I is dedicated to alternative theorisations of the making of the EDA, and consists of three chapters. In Chapter 1, Helena Ekelund examines the phenomenon of European agencies and summarises theoretical approaches to agency establishment, with particular attention given to new institutionalist perspectives. To reach a full understanding of the creation and institutional design of European agencies, the author argues, it is necessary to look further than transaction cost arguments and consider also historical contexts and social processes. It is then explained how the three main strands of new institutionalism (i.e. rational choice institutionalism, sociological institutionalism and historical institutionalism) can be used as conceptual lenses for drawing attention to various aspects of the creation of the EDA. Whereas the rational choice institutionalist approach, with its emphasis on functional needs, can contribute to our understanding of why certain tasks and responsibilities are delegated to the EDA, sociological and historical approaches are more useful for understanding the timing of establishment and the institutional design of the agency.

In Chapter 2, André Barrinha argues that the EDA has had a relatively successful story thus far, rising both as a discussion forum between governments, industry and the military, and as a promoter of measures and policies within the framework of defence capabilities development, armaments cooperation, defence market and industrial base, and R&T. Starting from a critical constructivist perspective, Chapter 2 examines how the key political and economic actors in the European defence field discursively justify the agency's existence. The analysis focuses, on the one hand, on the legitimisation of the agency's historical record and, on the other, on its perceived future role in Europe's quest towards the modernisation and integration of both its industry and armed forces. In particular, it sheds light on the continuities and discontinuities between the discourses over the past and those over the future regarding the EDA's role in European defence.

Chapter 3 studies the establishment of the EDA and illustrates the centrality of military–industrial interests in its making. The argument put forward by Iraklis Oikonomou is the following. The setting-up of the EDA stemmed from – and fulfilled – key industrial preferences, representing an institutional transformation driven by the imperative of industrial competitiveness. Not only did the latter rank high among the objectives of policy-makers in the Agency, but also the new institution was subjected to instrumental industrial influence before, during and after its conception. Structurally, the making of the EDA is the institutional outcome of a process initiated by the capitalist restructuring of European arms production. According to the author, this process is embedded in demands for industrial expansion and profitability, rather than limited to capabilities development. Drawing on the notion of the internationalisation of capital, the analysis relates the missions and policies of the EDA to broader industrial trends, suggesting that the entire conception of the EDA has had a strong socio-economic rationale.

Part II deals with the empirical achievements and insufficiencies, the strengths and weaknesses, the declaratory context and the tangible policy output of the Agency. This part comprises four chapters. In Chapter 4, Alistair J.K. Shepherd traces and critically analyses the definitions and development of EU military capabilities since the CSDP's launch in 1999 and since the establishment of the EDA in particular. He does so by providing a three-part chapter structure woven together by the idea of the EU as a military actor, the interests of the Member States, and the institutions that shape CSDP. The first part examines CSDP's formative phase (1999–2004) which saw the establishment of the overarching capability framework, the launch of the first CSDP operations and the significant divisions over the Iraq war. The second part (2004–2009) analyses efforts to consolidate and revitalise EU capability development through the launch of a new Headline Goal, including EU Battlegroups and the EDA. The final section (2009–2014) explores the tensions between the parallel initiatives of the Lisbon Treaty to enhance the prospects for EU-level capability improvement, led by the EDA, and the decentralised moves to enhance capabilities taken on a bi- or multi-lateral framework, such as the Anglo-French Defence Treaty.

Turning to armaments, Katia Vlachos-Dengler starts her analysis in Chapter 5 by highlighting that Member States of both the EU and the North Atlantic Treaty Organisation (NATO) have been cooperating on armaments for decades, both at the bilateral and multilateral level, with varying degrees of success. This long tradition has acquired significant momentum and popularity since the end of the last decade, as it has become not only an economic necessity for most nations but also for the survival of European defence as a whole. Enhancing European armaments cooperation is among the EDA's founding mandates. The EDA has aimed to play an active role in encouraging and facilitating that cooperation with concrete initiatives in areas such as Research and Development (R&D) and cross-border bidding, among others. The chapter analyses the EDA's contribution to armaments collaboration and assesses, to the extent possible, the progress that has been made so far, the lessons learned and the challenges ahead.

In Chapter 6, Anja Dahlmann, Marcel Dickow and Léa Tisserant assert that when it comes to joint procurement and operation of military equipment, the most convenient entry point is common R&T. Thought of as the crystallisation cell of European defence cooperation, the EDA has been trying to implement joint and coordinated R&T from the beginning. Of all common initiatives in the EDA, this has been offering the most promising approach, relatively unaffected by national industry policies and production shares. However, the authors contend that R&T has failed to deliver a common ground amongst Member States so far, because it is strongly dependent on not only national research policy but strategic orientation in defence in general. The lack of a joint European vision in defence has also produced a major backlash in EDA's R&T projects. Nevertheless, the demand of joint military operations has indeed created some successful R&D projects in EDA in recent years. The chapter analyses the political and technical conditions for effective R&T collaboration in the EDA framework by highlighting the completed and ongoing projects.

Following the study of capabilities, armaments and R&D in the context of the EDA, the final chapter of this section, Chapter 7, analyses the EDA's role in the defence procurement integration process. Aris Georgopoulos examines, first, the EDA as an agent for defence procurement cooperation/integration in its historical and political context and identifies its initial goals and aspirations. The chapter then compares and contrasts these aspirations with the policy outcomes that the EDA produced in the last decade in the field of defence market cooperation/integration and analyses the challenging symbiotic relationship of the EDA with the Commission in this area. In particular the chapter examines the EDA's Codes of Conduct on defence procurement and offsets and attempts a preliminary evaluation of their impact and their limitations. The analysis concludes by arguing that the EDA has had a significant legitimising influence on the discussion of defence procurement integration that led to the adoption of the EU Defence and Security Procurement Directive.

Part III focuses on the interaction between the Agency and the Member States, and includes three chapters. In Chapter 8, Jocelyn Mawdsley studies the two largest spending EU Member States on defence procurement and R&D, France and Britain, which share concerns about the future of the European defence industrial base. While the two countries have disagreed from the outset about the design, funding and tasks of the EDA, they have achieved considerable breakthroughs in their bilateral defence cooperation. The chapter looks at the convergences and divergences of French and British armaments policy over the lifespan of the EDA, and the impacts this has had on the ability of the EDA to succeed in its mission. It also considers the consequences for the EDA's policies of the Lancaster House agreements, and looks at the potential for defence industrial consolidation offered and whether this requires the EDA to reconsider its policy agenda. Finally, the chapter explores Franco-British participation in other armaments policy fora, and questions where their institutional preferences lie.

Chapter 9 analyses the role of Germany in the development of the EDA and assesses the extent to which Germany has taken advantage of the opportunities presented by the Agency to 'pool and share' military capabilities/forces and undertake joint procurement with EU partners. Tom Dyson makes use of Neorealist theory to explain the development of German policy toward the EDA (in general) and P&S initiatives (in particular). He finds that German leadership on P&S and collaborative procurement through the EDA has been relatively poor due to the impact of the 'Alliance Security Dilemma'. However, as the European and global balance of power begins to change, the German calculation of the appropriate 'trade-off' between abandonment and entrapment by Alliance partners is beginning to alter in favour of greater European cooperation in defence. As a consequence, the chapter concludes that signs are beginning to emerge of a stronger German role in promoting P&S and collaborative defence procurement projects within the EDA.

In Chapter 10 Marc Devore turns to transatlantic armaments cooperation and the NATO factor. The author's starting point is that cooperation amongst advanced industrial economies has been considered an optimal response to the challenges of weapons cost escalation and the globalisation of the defence industrial supply chain. However, international cooperation has proven exceptionally difficult because the production of armaments is shaped by both market and national security considerations. The EU and NATO have sought to overcome these cooperation problems through the creation of specialised organisations and fora; nevertheless, it is unclear both how European and transatlantic organisations are likely to interact over time and what the comparative advantages of each form of organisation are. The chapter answers these questions by critically examining the extent to which the EU's principal armaments body, the EDA, complements or competes with NATO's armaments committees. In addition, it addresses the overlapping mandates between the EDA and the European Commission, and the ensuing frictions between the two EU institutions.

Part IV of the book aspires to open up the agenda of EU armaments policy, by including some novel and relatively under-studied aspects of that policy. This part consists of four chapters. In Chapter 11, Laura Chappell and Petar Petrov discuss EU military capability development by analysing the work of the EDA and the prospects for practical development of P&S projects as envisaged by the Ghent Initiative in 2010. After the ill-conceived attempt by Member States to operationalise PESCO, whether significant change actually materialises will depend upon how the P&S initiative is implemented in practice. In the context of the financial crisis, several factors pose major challenges. The lack of sufficient political will to practically employ the Battlegroups, together with declining defence budgets and the unwillingness among the Member States to pool capabilities combines with the lack of a fully fledged European strategic culture in security and defence matters. By applying the concept of strategic culture this chapter seeks to analyse these complex dynamics and uncover the possibilities for bringing a new impetus behind military capability development in the EU.

In Chapter 12, Christian Mölling, Marie-Louise Chagnaud and Torben Schütz assess what difference Europe so far has made to the European Defence Technological and Industrial Base (EDTIB). In 2007, Member States inaugurated a strategy to support the EDTIB, aimed to ensure security of supply through gradually integrating the national Defence Technological and Industrial Bases (DTIBs). The Europeanisation of policies and industries, according to this strategy, should lead to a less duplicative, more cooperative defence industrial landscape, supporting Member States' defence needs. The chapter evaluates to what extent a Europeanisation of the empirical field of EDTIB can be observed by assessing the influence the EU has through ideas and institutions on the change in three dimensions: (1) politics: change in national and international policies towards and the polity of the EDTIB; (2) the defence industry; and (3) supply chains and dependencies. Based on this analysis, the chapter pictures potential avenues for the EDA to ensure even more future security of supply.

Chapter 13 discusses the EDA's attempts to curb the the fragmentation of the EDTIB by coordinating the offset practices of its Member States. Peter Platzgummer utilises a descriptive analysis in order to assess how successful the EDA has been in overcoming this fragmentation, also taking note of the negative effects of offsets. The chapter begins by discussing the effects of offsets and provides an overview of offset practices in the EU since the end of the Cold War. Additionally, the Union's and several Member States' efforts towards a common EDTIB before the foundation of the EDA are discussed. The analysis then addresses the EDA's competent department, the Industry and Market (I&M) Directorate, and the relevant initiatives taken – notably the introduction of the 'Code of Conduct on Offsets' (CoCO). The last section concentrates on the period since the introduction of Directive 2009/81 by the European Commission, which constricted offsets definitively to the area of defence and had game-changing effects on national policies.

In the final chapter of the book, Chapter 14, Frank Slijper claims that one of the more successful directions of the EDA so far has been its efforts in the area of space. The Agency is involved in a fundamental change of course with the European Space Agency (ESA), which until recently had stayed away from military work. Furthermore, cooperation with the Commission, NATO and the industry is crucial in the space domain. The EDA has been tasked to federate defence-related space requirements and is currently involved in micro-satellite cluster technology, the spy satellite programme, as well as use of satellites in drone operations. Space has become an essential and integral part of military planning over the past few decades. With no answer yet to the growing risks of rivalry in space, this could eventually lead to military confrontation. This chapter reveals the EDA's involvement in military space-related issues which have remained largely out of the public view so far.

Finally, the conclusion of the book takes stock of the previous chapters, attempting to forecast the parameters shaping EDA's future, and offers avenues for future research.

## References

Manners, I. (2006) 'Normative power Europe reconsidered: beyond the crossroads', *Journal of European Public Policy*, 13(2): 182–199.

Orbie, J. (2006) 'Civilian Power Europe: Review of the Original and Current Debates', *Cooperation and Conflict*, 41(1): 123–128.

Spanish Ministry of Defence (2010) *EDA: Past, Present, and Future*, Madrid: Spanish Ministry of Defence.

# Part I
# Theorising the EDA

# 1 Institutionalist approaches to agency establishment

*Helena Ekelund*

## Introduction

Whilst the European Defence Agency (EDA) is a unique body, in terms of function and configuration, it is part of a wider trend of institutional reform and changes to public management organisation: agencification. This chapter aims to shed light on how the establishment of the EDA can be understood within this context. The chapter builds on the new institutionalist assumption that the form and functioning of institutions 'depend on the conditions under which they emerge' (Przeworski 2004: 527). As different strands of new institutionalism emphasise different aspects of institutional development (Kato 1996), they are not mutually exclusive but can contribute with different insights to institutional analysis. To take advantage of this, the chapter seeks to reach a broad understanding of agency establishment by adopting an eclectic approach to new institutionalist theory. It sets out to fulfil two objectives. First, it provides an overview of the phenomenon of European agencies, and new institutionalist perspectives on agency establishment. Second, it analyses how the creation of the EDA can be understood by using the three main strands of new institutionalism as conceptual lenses.

The term 'agencification' refers to the creation of semi-autonomous bodies that perform public functions at arm's length from central government. The trend to establish agencies is visible in a range of political settings (Pollitt and Bouckaert 2011), and can be seen as a part of a wider shift in public management practices, which has been termed New Public Management (NPM). An increased use of private-sector management tools and principles in public services and an emphasis on results over process are characteristic features of NPM, which seeks to increase efficiency in the delivery of public services. The delegation of functions to agencies is perceived to contribute to efficiency improvements and better results in two main ways. First, by delegating responsibilities to an agency, central government can focus on its core tasks. Second, as expertise is gathered within the agency, the latter can assist with specialised knowledge, thereby contributing to the formulation of better informed policies.

12   *H. Ekelund*

The European Commission (2008) has embraced this line of thought and presents very similar arguments for the creation of agencies at the European level.

The first two European-level agencies, (1) the European Centre for the Development of Vocational Training and (2) the European Foundation for the Improvement of Living and Working Conditions, were established in 1975, but the agencification process really took off in the 1990s, coinciding with the NPM wave in public administration. The trend that started with the Commission seeking opportunities to focus on its key responsibilities by delegating implementation functions to agencies within the former first pillar, spread to the other executive actor, the Council of the European Union, which then began delegating to second and third pillar agencies (Busuioc 2013: 3). The EDA was established in 2004 within the second pillar as a Council agency operating within the Common Foreign and Security Policy (CFSP).

This chapter is structured as follows. First, it will provide an overview of the phenomenon of European agencies. Following this, it will zoom in on the debate on agency establishment and outline how new institutionalist perspectives can be used as conceptual lenses to help us understand three aspects of agency creation: timing, delegated functions and institutional set-up. These lenses are then used to make sense of the empirical findings on the establishment of the EDA. The empirical examination builds on the analysis of documents related to the process and reviews of secondary literature in the form of contemporary commentaries and previous research.

## The phenomenon of European Agencies

Currently, there are around 30 European agencies. Several attempts to classify agencies have been made by public administration scholars in general and scholars working on European agencies in particular (see Ekelund 2012; Groenleer 2009; Thatcher 2011). This literature has shown that agencies come in different shapes and sizes, and fulfil a range of functions. There is no universal definition of the term 'agency', and there is no single classification of agencies (Andoura and Timmerman 2008). A reason for this is that different scholars are driven by different purposes and devise frameworks and classifications that capture the agencies' aspects of interest for the study in question (Hardiman and Scott 2009).

Nevertheless, there are some core features that, most scholars agree, need to be in place for an organisation to be labelled an agency. It should be at arm's length from central government, have a constitution in the form of legislation or formal framework document, be staffed by civil servants rather than elected politicians, and be subjected to performance contracting (Talbot 2004). This means that its performance is measured against set targets, monitored and reported.

Institutionalist approaches  13

There is no single universally endorsed definition of the term 'European agency'. Yet, scholars agree on what they are. As Busuioc (2013: 21) writes, they are 'specialized, non-majoritarian bodies, established by secondary legislation, which exercise public authority and are institutionally separate from the EU institutions and are endowed with legal personality'. Prior to the Lisbon Treaty, a distinction was made between 'Community Agencies', i.e. first pillar agencies, on the one hand, and the intergovernmental second and third pillar agencies on the other. The Treaty of Lisbon abolished the pillar structure and changes to agencies' legal acts have brought these agencies closer together (Busuioc 2013). Yet, when studying agency establishment, it is important to bear this distinction in mind, as agencies within different pillars were set up according to different procedures. As all of these agencies have their own individual founding legislation and were set up to have a degree of independence from the core executive institutions, they can be distinguished from the EU-level temporary bodies called 'executive agencies', which are set up for a limited time at the discretion of the Commission to manage specific programmes.

In the early days of studying European agencies, there was a focus on formal structures (see Chiti 2000; Vos 2000), but now more and more emphasis is given to studying actual practices. Some studies consider agencification in the wider context of a new emerging executive order (Curtin 2009; Curtin and Egeberg 2008). Other studies focus on specific aspects such as accountability of agencies (Busuioc 2013; Curtin 2007), actual level of autonomy (Groenleer 2009; Wonka and Rittberger 2010) and agencies' role in implementation (Groenleer *et al.* 2010).

## New institutionalist explanations of agency establishment

Agencification is an example of institution-building, but it is also a question of delegation. These phenomena have been investigated in a wide variety of contexts. Often, agency establishment is explained through an analysis of functional needs. However, scholars working on European agencies have started to look beyond these functional explanations emphasised by the NPM paradigm. They draw also on organisational theory, and emphasise the need to consider factors such as the wider political situation, contingent events and organisational 'fashion' (Busuioc *et al.* 2012; Ekelund 2010, 2014). This chapter follows in their footsteps by drawing on the three main strands of new institutionalism presented below. This eclectic approach to institutional analysis is selected on the understanding that different new institutionalist perspectives bring different insights. As the different strands focus on different aspects of agency creation, expectations derived from them are not necessarily mutually exclusive. As will be demonstrated, the explanatory power of each strand varies depending on what aspect of agency creation is under consideration.

14    *H. Ekelund*

Rather than being one coherent tradition, new institutionalism encompasses several strands (Hall and Taylor 1996; Kato 1996; Lowndes 1996). These strands share a belief that institutions are political actors in their own right with a degree of autonomy from social contexts and the motives of individuals. Expectations about the future are developed within institutions and, as information is filtered through these institutions, the institutions mediate political action (Cyert and March 1963; March and Olsen 1984; Simon 1978). Within the new institutionalist tradition, one can distinguish three main strands: (1) rational choice institutionalism, (2) sociological institutionalism and (3) historical institutionalism.

Explanations of agency establishment focusing on functional needs are associated with a *rational choice institutionalist* approach. This approach adopts an individualist ontology, and assumes economic rationality, i.e. that relevant actors seek to attain their fixed preferences through strategic interaction (Hall and Taylor 1996: 944; Kato 1996). March and Olsen (1998) have termed this 'the logic of consequentialism'. Agency establishment is explained by a functional logic, i.e. the explanation for the agency is to be found in the functions it is set up to fulfil. This is analytically expressed through principal-agent models and analyses of transaction costs (Epstein and O'Halloran 1999; Tallberg 2002). The approach predicts that agencies (the agents) are established to lower political transaction costs, and delegation takes place when the benefits to the delegating party (the principals) exceed the costs. Costs of delegation are slippage and shirking (Pollack 2003). Benefits of delegation are gathering technical expertise, ensuring credible commitment – some authors speak more specifically of blame-shifting – and increasing efficiency.

*Sociological institutionalism* adopts a 'holist and ideational ontology' (Rittberger 2005: 17), and assumes that rationality is bounded, i.e. rather than assuming perfect objective rationality of humans, we need to understand that human cognitive powers may not be able to grasp all aspects of a situation. As Simon (1978: 8) states, 'in complex situations there is likely to be a considerable gap between the real environment of a decision (the world as God or some other omniscient observer sees it) and the environment as the actors perceive it'. Sociological institutionalists argue that actors follow a 'logic of appropriateness' which means that they 'are imagined to follow rules that associate particular identities to particular situations' (March and Olsen 1998: 151). These rules stem from 'internalized norms and ideas' about what is appropriate in a given situation (Rittberger 2005: 18). Thus, sociological institutionalism argues that agency establishment is a response to socially constructed preferences for this particular organisational form rather than the result of a utility-maximising calculation (McNamara 2002; Pollack 2005; Rittberger 2005). To understand where these socially constructed preferences come from, the wider socio-cultural context must be considered (Jupille and Caporaso 1999). Institutional

*Institutionalist approaches* 15

forms are believed to spread through isomorphic processes that could be either voluntary or coerced (DiMaggio and Powell 1991).

*Historical institutionalism* holds that 'political development must be understood as a process that unfolds over time', and 'many of the contemporary implications of these temporal processes are embedded in institutions – whether these be formal rules, policy, structures, or norms' (Pierson 1996: 126). Contingent events are emphasised over actor preferences. Thus, historical institutionalists go beyond rational calculations and argue that to understand institutional development one must consider the context in which it takes place (Thelen 1999). Importantly, there is a perception that the extent of various actors' influence over the creation of new institutions is determined by power relations built into already existing institutions (Hall and Taylor 1996: 954). From a historical institutionalist perspective institutional development could be explained through analyses of path dependency and 'critical junctures', i.e. 'moments when substantial institutional change takes place thereby creating a "branching point" from which historical development moves onto a new path' (Hall and Taylor 1996: 942).

## New institutionalist predictions for the EDA establishment

Different strands of new institutionalism have different views on rationality and focus on somewhat different aspects of institution building. Thus, it is inadvisable to seek to synthesise them or, indeed, to pit them against each other using methods of hard theory testing (Ekelund 2014). A more fruitful approach involves using the three strands as conceptual lenses that draw attention to three different aspects of agency establishment: (1) timing of establishment, (2) functions delegated and (3) institutional set-up. Whereas these aspects are of course linked, it is useful to separate them for analytical purposes. Below, theoretical predictions derived from the three strands presented above, and evidence needed to corroborate or weaken them, are presented.

### Timing of establishment

As rational choice institutionalism assumes fixed preferences, it cannot be used in isolation to explain the timing of agency establishment. As Hall and Taylor (1996: 953) assert, 'it is not obvious why the actors would agree to a change in existing institutions' given that 'the starting-point from which institutions are to be created is itself likely to reflect a Nash equilibrium'. From the sociological institutionalist logic of appropriateness with its emphasis on institutional borrowing follows the expectation that the EDA establishment would occur around the same time as the creation of organisations with similar institutional structures. To verify this hypothesis, the wider institutional development in Europe must be considered. Historical institutionalism predicts that the timing of the EDA establishment is linked to specific events that led decision-makers down this path of institutional development. To support this expectation, it is necessary to find references pointing to the importance of particular events during the establishment process. Furthermore, it must be possible to argue convincingly that a particular event was of significant importance. To weaken the hypothesis, one must demonstrate that specific events were not significant through the means of counterfactual analysis.

### Functions delegated

Rational choice institutionalism predicts that wishes to lower transaction costs can explain the functions delegated. It is predicted that the agency will be given tasks that require it to become a centre for scientific and technical expertise, that aim to increase efficiency and/or that help ensure credible commitment. Delegation of highly technical tasks requiring specialist expertise to be gathered within the agency itself serves to verify the technical expertise hypothesis. Similarly, competence demands placed on EDA staff and references to the agency as a centre of expertise confirm this expectation. The absence of these factors weakens the hypothesis. Importantly, tasks that involve coordination of technical work carried out by other authorities are not sufficient evidence to verify this expectation. These tasks instead support the expectation that the agency was set up with the aim to increase efficiency. References to streamlining of working methods and similar is also evidence in favour. As it is unrealistic to expect statements opposing increased efficiency, the absence of direct references to efficiency gains weakens the efficiency hypothesis. The presence of regulatory and/or arbitration tasks serves to verify the expectation that an important function of the agency is to ensure credible commitment. By contrast, the absence of such tasks weakens this hypothesis. Sociological institutionalism expects elements of institutional borrowing, i.e. that the agency will be given similar types of functions as agencies in other political settings. To evaluate the accuracy of this prediction, one must consider the decision on tasks in the light of other decisions on delegation to agencies and look for references to other decisions as models. Historical institutionalism predicts previous decisions to inform what tasks to delegate. This hypothesis could be verified or weakened through an analysis of the importance of previous decisions for the outcome in the case of the EDA.

### Institutional set-up

Rational choice institutionalism expects the institutional set-up to reflect a position as a centre of expertise. Highly specialist competence demands on staff would support this prediction, and the absence of explicit demands is evidence against. More significantly, the agency would be expected to have a strong, independent mandate that ensures credible commitment to policy by isolating agency decisions from political pressures. A high level of dependency on other bodies or Member States indicates that credible commitment was not a key concern behind the institutional set-up. Finally, rational choice institutionalism predicts that the institutional design was chosen because it was the most efficient organisational model. Direct references to efficiency gains from the chosen set-up support this hypothesis, and the absence of such references weakens it. Sociological institutionalism predicts that the institutional set-up of the EDA would be modelled on other agencies. This could be verified by direct references to other bodies serving as models, or statements pointing to the desirability of this particular institutional form. The absence of such references and statements serve to weaken the hypothesis. Historical institutionalism expects that previous decisions regarding institutional set-up influenced the decision on the EDA set-up. The explanatory power of historical institutionalism for this aspect could be assessed using the same methods as the expectations on the other aspects.

## Interpreting the EDA establishment through new institutionalist lenses

### Timing of establishment

When the EDA was established in 2004, this signified something new for European cooperation on armaments and defence procurement. However, ideas of an agency were not new. As early as 1978, Egon Klepsch, a member of the European Parliament, proposed the creation of a European armaments agency, and, in 1991, a declaration calling for the establishment of an agency was attached to the Maastricht Treaty. An important reason why these suggestions did not come to fruition was that Britain and other Atlanticist states did not want to limit cooperation to Europe (Grevi and Keohane 2009; Keohane 2004). Unwilling to give up sovereignty over 'the most "national" of all policy areas' (Keohane 2004: 2), Member States had traditionally preferred to keep defence cooperation outside of the European integration process (Schmitt 2004). However, at the Thessaloniki Council Summit in 2003, an agreement was reached and the European Council 'task[ed] the appropriate bodies of the Council to undertake the necessary actions towards creating, in the course of 2004, an intergovernmental agency in the field of defence capabilities development, research, acquisition and armaments' (Council of the European Union 2003a: par. 65). Shortly afterwards, COREPER (Committee of Permanent Representatives in the European Union) 2 set up an ad hoc working group to prepare the creation of the EDA (Council of the European Union 2003b) and in November 2003, the Council created an Agency Establishment Team (AET), tasked with preparing administrative,

18  *H. Ekelund*

financial and legal aspects of the agency (Council of the European Union 2003b; Schmitt 2004).

Without an agreement between Member States the EDA could not have been created. How can we explain the convergence of Member State preferences at this time? In the early 2000s, several agencies were created in the EU, and it is clear that the agency form was popular amongst decision-makers (Ekelund 2010). However, one must remember that the procedure of establishment between first pillar agencies and CFSP agencies is rather different in that the latter is an intergovernmental affair. Would Member States be willing to agree to cooperation in the most national policy area merely because of the popularity of a particular institutional form? Based on the fact that the other two CFSP agencies, the European Union Satellite Centre and the European Union Institute for Security Studies, were set up by incorporating aspects of the West European Union (WEU) into the EU framework (Council of the European Union 2001a, 2001b), whereas this is completely absent from the documents related to EDA establishment, it is unlikely that this was the case. To explain the timing of EDA creation we need to draw on historical institutionalism and consider the wider political context as well as the development of security and defence policy.

Cooperation on foreign and security policy was brought into the EU framework by the Maastricht Treaty and the creation of the intergovernmental second pillar. However, as Heisbourg (2000: 5) asserts, this was widely perceived to be of only 'peripheral importance' at the time. Whilst the Amsterdam Treaty was also seen as modest, Heisbourg (2000) argues that it may have widened the scope for cooperation beyond the original intention. Here, Heisbourg (2000: 5) points specifically to 'the adoption of the Petersberg tasks, the aim of the integration of WEU (a binding military alliance) into the EU, and the objective of European armaments cooperation'. Thus, in line with historical institutionalism, these decisions could be seen as leading decision-makers down a path towards further cooperation. Significant attitude change to defence cooperation allowing for these additions to the Treaty stemmed from events outside of the politics of treaty revision. The Balkan wars of the 1990s were critical in this regard, 'showing how weak European governments were when they tried to act alone' (Keohane 2004: 1). The United Kingdom (UK) became more positive towards European cooperation; Germany opened up to military activity in foreign and security policy alongside civil approaches; and neutral states came to see intervention as an alternative to prevention (Howorth 2001: 767). Importantly, the lack of military capability became apparent (Kaldor *et al.* 2007). Increasing costs, for instance due to more crisis management operations, in combination with budget austerity in Member States are important factors behind this capability problem (Schmitt 2003: 11).

As security cooperation has primarily been an intergovernmental affair, one cannot neglect the preferences and actions of the most significant military powers in Europe: the UK and France. Whereas France traditionally has had a favourable opinion of European defence cooperation, the UK has been sceptical – Chapter 8 provides a detailed analysis of the positions of these two countries. At the bilateral St. Malo Summit in 1998, the states set their differences aside, which came to be of great importance for European cooperation in defence and security (Howorth 2001). Indeed, in its final report for the Convention for the Future of Europe, Working Group VIII – Defence (2002: 4) mentions this summit, together with the Cologne European Summit, as events that 'gave the political impetus and set out the guidelines required for the strengthening of the European security and defence policy'.

The final report of Working Group VIII – Defence was published in December 2002, i.e. a little over a year after the terrorist attacks of 11 September 2001. The report saw the events of 9/11 as signifying the emergence of a new threat that could not be dealt with purely through national frameworks. It also noted that public opinion was favourable to European defence. Although some group members disagreed, later research has shown that 9/11 did indeed form a critical juncture for cooperation on counterterrorism (Argomaniz 2009). Differences in opinion regarding 9/11 aside, Working Group VIII – Defence (2002: 1) argues that 'the way the strategic context has evolved has been an important element in the reflections of the Working Group and the formulation of its recommendations'. One of these recommendations was the establishment of a European Armaments and Strategic Research Agency, an initiative put forward by Dominique de Villepin and Joschka Fischer (2002). Thus, the idea that led to the EDA establishment surfaced during the Convention on the future of Europe. According to Schmitt (2004), 'the idea in mid-2003 was that if approved by the Intergovernmental Conference, [the agency's tasks] would become part of the new EU Treaty'.

However, things sped up as the Thessaloniki Council gave the task to the Council earlier. This can be attributed to the activities of France and the UK. At the bilateral Le Touquet summit in 2003, Blair and Chirac proposed the establishment of 'a new EU defence agency, tasked with encouraging Member States to boost their military capabilities' (Keohane 2004: 2; see also House of Lords 2005). According to Keohane (2004) the emphasis on capabilities set this proposal apart from previous proposals which envisaged an agency similar to national armaments agencies. Whilst capability development was widely perceived to be important (Working group VIII – Defence 2002), this new emphasis was particularly important for the UK as the country opposed an agency that would mainly serve industry whilst neglecting defence needs (House of Lords 2005). The ideas formulated at Le Touquet were taken to the Thessaloniki Summit, where other leaders endorsed them. The fact that leaders agreed to set up a capabilities agency at the time can be explained by the fact that the EU was to take over peacekeeping responsibility from the North Atlantic

20   *H. Ekelund*

Treaty Organisation (NATO) in Bosnia in late 2004. In this context the faltering capabilities posed a substantial challenge. Indeed, as Keohane (2004: 1) remarked at the time, 'Bosnia will be a crucial test of the EU's military mettle', and 2004 was 'a landmark year'.

### Functions delegated

At the time of set-up, the Council specified four 'principal fields' of agency activity: (1) development of defence capabilities in the field of crisis management; (2) promotion and enhancement of European armaments cooperation; (3) working to strengthen the defence technology industrial base and for the creation of an internationally competitive European Defence Equipment Market; and (4) enhancement of the effectiveness of European defence Research and Technology (R&T) (Council of the European Union 2004: art. 5). More specifically, the agency was given the tasks of identifying capabilities requirements, assessing capabilities according to criteria set by Member States, coordinating a range of activities, proposing collaborative activities and projects, identifying best practice, managing projects and pursuing the harmonisation of rules. Since then, the agency's tasks have been extended and specified further by a separate Council Decision (Council of the European Union 2011). However, since the purpose of this chapter is to shed light on the establishment stage, focus will be on the tasks initially delegated to the agency.

Whilst it is stated that staff should be selected 'on the basis of relevant competence and expertise', the founding legislation makes no direct reference to the agency as a centre of expertise (Council of the European Union 2004: article 11). Having said that, it is apparent that the Council expected the agency to draw on expertise already existing in other bodies such as the Western European Armaments Group (WEAG)/Western European Armaments Organisation (WEAO) and the Political and Security Committee (Council of the European Union 2003b), but at the time there was no mention of the agency replacing these. A close reading of the founding document rather shows that efficiency concerns were important when delegating tasks. Coordination is central to the agency's activities. For instance, it was to coordinate joint research activities, harmonisation of military requirement and the implementation of the European Capabilities Action Plan (ECAP) (Council of the European Union 2004: art. 5). The ECAP was agreed by the Member States already in 2001, and one of its main principles was 'enhanced effectiveness and efficiency of European military capability efforts' (Council of the European Union 2001c: 4). Moreover, it was specified that the agency was to work 'for coordination of existing programmes implemented by Member States', and that the Member States could request that the agency assume 'responsibility for managing specific programmes', for instance through the Organisation Conjointe de Coopération en matière d'Armement (OCCAR) (Council of the European Union 2004: art. 5). Given that the agency operates in a largely intergovernmental policy area where policy decisions rely on consensus, it is unsurprising that the agency has not been given regulatory or arbitration tasks in order to secure credible commitment.

No capabilities agency existed in the EU prior to the establishment of the EDA, and the EDA was not given tasks similar to those of national armaments agencies, although commonalities may exist. From a sociological institutionalist perspective one could question whether the increased need for cooperation and development of military capabilities was an objective functional need. Perhaps it is better described as a shared norm. The founding document makes several references to the agency's role in promoting collaboration and developing working relations with other influential actors, which suggests that lesson-drawing was envisaged in the agency's activities. Keohane's (2004: 4) statement that the EDA should 'play a vital role in convincing defence ministers to develop a long-term vision for EU defence' also points to the importance of the EDA's task in promoting shared values.

Regardless of whether the decision to enhance cooperation to improve capabilities was a result of objective necessity or changing norms, the fact remains that once the decision was taken, cooperation became a real need. At an informal meeting in April 2004, defence ministers of the Member States agreed that the EU ought to have 'Battlegroups', defined as 'high readiness forces consisting of 1,500 personnel that can be deployed within ten days after an EU decision to launch an operation and that can be sustained for up to 30 days (extendible to 120 days with rotation)' (European External Action Service 2013). As Keohane (2004) explains, only Britain and France were able to form a battlegroup with any ease in 2004. For many other Member States cooperation was the only option. Thus, one could argue that the emphasis on coordination tasks for the agency is an example of path-dependency in line with historical institutionalist theorising.

### Institutional set-up

Similarly to other European agencies, the EDA has a Board serving as its decision-making body. The Board is 'composed of one representative of each participating Member State, authorised to commit its government, and a representative of the Commission' (Council of the European Union 2004: art. 8). What sets the EDA aside from other European agencies is its dual leadership structure. The EDA is always headed by the High Representative of the CFSP, who is responsible for the 'overall organisation and functioning' (Council of the European Union 2004: art. 7). The agency also has a Chief Executive, whose task it is to implement board decisions and guidelines issued by the Council.

Demands for relevant expertise play a part in the recruitment of staff. Whilst this may give an impression of the agency as a centre of expertise,

## 22   H. Ekelund

this explanation for institutional set-up does not hold. There was no intention of permanently tying these experts to the agency as they are employed on temporary contracts. Some employees are recruited by the EDA itself, others are national experts or EU officials seconded to the agency (Council of the European Union 2004: art. 11). The article on board composition emphasises the political seniority of the members rather than technical expertise per se. Direct references to the agency form as a means to increase efficiency are noticeable in their absence, although the fact that the agency was envisaged as a 'coordinating focus for the existing network of bodies, agreements and competences' (Council of the European Union 2003b: 14) could be seen as an indirect reference. Similarly, in his commentary on the EDA establishment, Schmitt (2004) claims that an agency 'could certainly generate new synergies and increase efficiency', suggesting that we should not dismiss efficiency concerns as a rationale for the choice of institutional set-up. Whilst the agency enjoys legal personality, it does not have a strong, independent mandate. Rather, the agency is to 'operate under the authority and the political supervision of the Council' (Council of the European Union 2004, article 4). The fact that the agency is headed by the High Representative of the CFSP is one manifestation of the agency's obligation to maintain close links with the Council. Moreover, the establishment of EDA was to 'be without prejudice to the competences of Member States in defence matters' (Council of the European Union 2004: art. 2), and was not to affect the competences of the Council's various advisory and preparatory committees. The agency was not given an independent budget for research and procurement. Indeed, Keohane (2004: 5) suggests that the EDA's most important role 'should be political'. Clearly, the institutional set-up of the EDA was not chosen to isolate decisions from political pressures as one would expect when ensuring credible commitment is a goal.

Some aspects of the EDA institutional set-up are similar to those of other European agencies, but the specific set-up is unique. In addition to the dual leadership structure, the EDA is the only agency the board of which 'shall meet at the level of the Ministers of Defence of the participating Member States or their representatives' (Council of the European Union 2004: art. 8). Neither has the EDA been modelled on national armament agencies (Keohane 2004). Thus, the sociological institutionalist hypothesis that the agency would be modelled on other agencies does not hold. However, the agency's institutional set-up may facilitate and encourage learning processes. In its preparatory work the Council emphasised the agency's role in establishing close working relationships with relevant bodies such as OCCAR, WEAG and WEAO 'with a view to incorporate them or assimilate their principles and practices in due course' (Council of the European Union 2003b). The importance of seconded national experts could also be seen as a means to encourage learning by drawing on different national experiences.

Historical institutionalism and ideas of path dependency hold explanatory power for the institutional set-up of the agency. As demonstrated numerous times throughout European integration history, Member States have been reluctant to relinquish sovereignty in defence issues. The fact that the board meets at the level of defence ministers illustrates this intergovernmental emphasis of the agency's set-up.

## Conclusion

This chapter has demonstrated that functionalist accounts of agency creation so commonly used in NPM studies do not hold strong explanatory powers for the establishment of the EDA. To reach a comprehensive understanding of the establishment of this agency – with a focus on timing, functions delegated and institutional set-up – an analysis of the historical context is far more useful. Indeed, historical institutionalism is the strand most apt at explaining all three aspects of the EDA creation considered in this chapter. The other strands may be used as conceptual lenses to throw further light on some aspects.

The timing of the EDA establishment can be explained through analysis of contingent events and path-dependency. The wider security situation, in particular the Balkan wars and the emergence of new threats exemplified by the 9/11 attacks, led to a convergence of Member State preferences in favour of cooperation. Small steps taken in this direction written into the Amsterdam Treaty arguably came to widen the scope for further cooperation beyond the original intention, and the EU take-over of peace-building duties from NATO served as a critical event triggering a need for armaments cooperation.

The EDA was set up with a view to enhance capabilities. Through rational choice institutionalist lenses, the cooperation instigated to fulfil this functional need is seen as a means to increase efficiency. Seen through sociological institutionalist lenses, the need to enhance capability may be socially constructed. Considering the lack of support for the other rational choice institutionalist expectations regarding the EDA's functions, and given the emphasis on the EDA's role in promoting shared values, there is something to be said for the latter interpretation. An objective functional need or a socially constructed one, once the Member States had set the goal to enable the quick launch of Battlegroups, cooperation became necessary. Thus, path dependency has explanatory value for the functions delegated.

None of the rational choice institutionalist hypotheses have much explanatory power with regards to the institutional set-up. Experts are not permanently tied to the agency, and political seniority is emphasised over relevant expertise for board members. Rather than being isolated from political pressures, the EDA is meant to have a political role. Efficiency concerns were not emphasised during the establishment

## 24   H. Ekelund

process, although it was envisaged that the agency could generate synergies. The institutional set-up was not directly modelled on existing armaments agencies or EU agencies. The strongest explanatory factors for the set-up are the tradition of security policy being an intergovernmental field and a shared norm in favour of it remaining so, at least for the time being.

### References

Andoura, S. and Timmermann, P. (2008) *Governance of the EU: The Reform Debate on European Agencies Reignited*, EPIN Working Paper No. 19, October 2008.

Argomaniz, J. (2009) 'Post-9/11 Institutionalisation of European Union Counterterrorism: Emergence, Acceleration and Inertia', *European Security*, 18(2): 151–172.

Busuioc, M. (2013) *European Agencies: Law and Practices of Accountability*, Oxford: Oxford University Press.

Busuioc, M., Groenleer, M. and Trondal, J. (eds) (2012) *The Agency Phenomenon in Europe: Emergence, Institutionalisation and Everyday Decision-Making*, Manchester: Manchester University Press.

Chiti, E. (2000) 'The Emergence of a Community Administration', *Common Market Law Review*, 37: 309–343.

Council of the European Union (2011) 'Council Decision 2011/411/CFSP of 12 July 2011 defining the statute, seat and operational rules of the European Defence Agency and repealing Joint Action 2004/551/CFSP'.

Council of the European Union (2004) 'Council Joint Action 2004/551/CFSP of 12 July 2004 on the establishment of the European Defence Agency'.

Council of the European Union (2003a) 'Thessaloniki European Council 19–20 June Presidency Conclusions'.

Council of the European Union (2003b) '2541st Council meeting – External Relations – Brussels, 17 November 2003', C/03/321, 14500/03.

Council of the European Union (2001a) 'Council Joint Action of 20 July 2001 on the establishment of a European Union Satellite Centre'.

Council of the European Union (2001b) 'Council Joint Action of 20 July 2001 on the establishment of a European Union Institute for Security Studies'.

Council of the European Union (2001c) '2386th Council meeting – General Affairs', Brussels, 19–20 November 2001.

Curtin, D. (2009) *Executive Power of the European Union: Law, Practices, and the Living Constitution*, Oxford: Oxford University Press.

Curtin, D. (2007) 'Holding (Quasi-) Autonomous EU Administrative Actors to Public Account', *European Law Journal*, 13(4): 523–541.

Curtin, D. and Egeberg, M. (2008) 'Tradition and innovation: Europe's Accumulated Executive Order', *West European Politics*, 31(4): 639–661.

Cyert, R.M. and March, J.G. (1963) *A Behavioural Theory of the Firm*, Englewood Cliffs: Prentice Hall.

de Villepin, D. and Fischer, J. (2002) 'Propositions conjointes franco-allemandes pour la Convention européenne dans le domaine de la politique européenne de sécurité et de défense', Secretariat of the European Convention, Brussels, 21 November 2002.

Institutionalist approaches   25

DiMaggio, P.J. and Powell, W.W. (1991) 'The Iron Cage Revisited: Institutional Isomorphism and Collective Rationality in Organizational Fields', in P.J. DiMaggio and W.W. Powell (eds) *The New Institutionalism in Organizational Analysis*, Chicago: University of Chicago Press: 63–82.

Ekelund, H. (2014) 'The Establishment of FRONTEX: A New Institutionalist Approach', *Journal of European Integration*, 36(2): 99–116

Ekelund, H. (2012) 'Making Sense of the "Agency Programme" in post-Lisbon Europe: Mapping European Agencies', *Central European Journal of Public Policy*, 6(1): 26–49.

Ekelund, H. (2010) *The Agencification of Europe: Explaining the Establishment of European Community Agencies*, unpublished PhD Thesis, University of Nottingham.

Epstein, D. and O'Halloran, S. (1999) *Delegating Powers: A Transaction Cost Politics Approach to Policy Making under Separate Powers*, Cambridge: Cambridge University Press.

European Commission (2008) 'Communication from the Commission to the European Parliament and the Council, Agencies: The way forward', COM(2008) 135 final, 11 March 2008.

European External Action Service (2013) 'About CSDP – Military Headline Goals'. Online. Available at: http://eeas.europa.eu/csdp/about-csdp/military_headline_goals/index_en.htm (accessed 25 October 2013).

Grevi, G. and Keohane, D. (2009) 'ESDP Resources', in G. Grevi, D. Helly and D. Keohane (eds) *European Security and Defence Policy: The First 10 Years (1999–2009)*, Paris: EU Institute for Security Studies: 69–114.

Groenleer, M. (2009) *The Autonomy of European Union Agencies: A Comparative Study of Institutional Development*, Delft: Eburon.

Groenleer, M., Kaeding, M. and Versluis, E (2010) 'Regulatory Governance through Agencies of the European Union? The Role of the European Agencies for Maritime and Aviation Safety in the Implementation of European Transport Legislation', *West European Politics*, 17(8): 1212–1230.

Hall, P.A. and Taylor, R.C.R. (1996) 'Political Science and the Three New Institutionalisms', *Political Studies*, 43: 936–957.

Hardiman, N. and Scott, C. (2009) 'Governance as Polity: An Institutional Approach to the Evolution of State Functions in Ireland', *Public Administration*, 88(1): 170–189.

Heisbourg, F. (2000) *European Defence: Making it Work*, Chaillot Papers 42, Paris: Institute for Security Studies.

House of Lords (2005) 'European Union: Ninth Report', European Union Committee Publications.

Howorth, J. (2001) 'European Defence and the Changing Politics of the European Union: Hanging Together or Hanging Separately', *Journal of Common Market Studies*, 39(4): 765–789.

Jupille, J. and Caporaso, J.A. (1999) 'Institutionalism and the European Union: Beyond International Relations and Comparative Politics', *Annual Review of Political Science*, 2: 429–444.

Kaldor, M., Martin, M. and Selchow, S. (2007) 'Human Security: A New Strategic Narrative for Europe', *International Affairs*, 83(2): 273–288.

Kato, J. (1996) 'Review Article: Institutions and Rationality in Politics – Three Varieties of Neo-Institutionalists', *British Journal of Political Science*, 26: 553–582.

## 26   H. Ekelund

Keohane, D. (2004) *Europe's New Defence Agency*, Policy Brief, London: Centre for European Reform.

Lowndes, V. (1996) 'Varieties of New Institutionalism: A Critical Appraisal', *Public Administration*, 74(2): 181–197.

March, J.G. and Olsen, J. (1998) 'The Institutional Dynamics of International Political Orders', *International Organization*, 52(4): 943–969.

March, J.G. and Olsen, J. (1984) 'The New Institutionalism: Organizational Factors in Political Life', *The American Political Science Review*, 78(3): 734–749.

McNamara, K.R. (2002) 'Rational Fictions: Central Bank Independence and the Social Logic of Delegation', *West European Politics*, 25(1): 47–76.

Pierson, P. (1996) 'The Path to European Integration: A Historical Institutionalist Analysis', *Comparative Political Studies*, 29: 123–163.

Pollack, M.A. (2005) 'Theorizing EU Policy-Making', in H. Wallace, W. Wallace and M.A. Pollack (eds) *Policy-Making in the European Union*, 5th edition, Oxford: Oxford University Press: 13–48.

Pollack, M.A. (2003) *The Engines of European Integration: Delegation, Agency and Agenda-Setting in the EU*, Oxford: Oxford University Press.

Pollitt, C. and Bouckaert, G. (2011) *Public Management Reform – A Comparative Analysis: New Public Management, Governance, and the Neo-Weberian State*, 3rd edition, Oxford: Oxford University Press.

Przeworski, A. (2004) 'Institutions Matter?', *Government and Opposition*, 39(4): 527–540.

Rittberger, B. (2005) *Building Europe's Parliament: Democratic Representation Beyond the Nation State*, Oxford: Oxford University Press.

Schmitt, B. (2003) *The European Union and Armaments: Getting a bigger bang for the Euro*, Chaillot Papers 63, Paris: Institute for Security Studies.

Schmitt, B. (2004) 'Progress towards the European Defence Agency', European Union Institute for Security Studies, 1 March 2004. Online. Available at: www.iss.europa.eu/publications/detail/article/progress-towards-the-european-defence-agency (accessed 4 October 2013).

Simon, H.A. (1978) 'Rationality as Process and Product of Thought', *The American Economic Review*, 68(2): 1–16.

Talbot, C. (2004) 'The Agency Idea: Sometimes Old, Sometimes New, Sometimes Borrowed, Sometimes Untrue', in C. Pollitt and C. Talbot (eds) *Unbundled Government: A Critical Analysis of the Global Trend to Agencies, Quangos and Contractualisation*, London: Routledge: 3–21.

Tallberg, J. (2002) 'Delegation to Supranational Institutions: Why, How and with What Consequences?', *West European Politics*, 25(1): 23–46.

Thatcher, M. (2011) 'The Creation of European Regulatory Agencies and its Limits: A Comparative Analysis of European Delegation', *Journal of European Public Policy*, 18(6): 790–809.

Thelen, K. (1999) 'Historical Institutionalism in Comparative Politics', *Annual Review of Political Science*, 2: 369–404.

Vos, E. (2000) 'Reforming the European Commission: What Role to Play for EU Agencies?', *Common Market Law Review*, 37: 1113–1134.

Wonka, A. and Rittberger, B. (2010) 'Credibility, Complexity and Uncertainty: Explaining The Institutional Independence of 29 EU agencies', *West European Politics*, 33(4): 730–752.

Working Group VIII – Defence (2002) 'Final report', CONV 461/02, WG VIII 22, 16 December 2002.

# 2 The EDA and the discursive construction of European defence and security

*André Barrinha*

## Introduction

Created in 2004, the European Defence Agency (EDA) has had a moderately successful record thus far, rising as both a discussion forum between governments, industry and the military, and as a promoter of measures and policies within the framework of its four main areas – defence capabilities development; armaments cooperation; defence market and industrial base; and research and technology. Attached to the creation of the EDA is the notion that in the face of a globalised world and its threats, coordinating efforts regarding the acquisition, research and procurement of defence equipment is the best way to achieve a more efficient European defence. Building on previous work (Barrinha 2010) this chapter examines, from a critical constructivist perspective, how the agency is discursively justified by some of the key actors in the European defence field. By doing so, it attempts to understand the EDA's *raison d'être* within this field.

Following Meyer and Strickmann (2011: 63–65), constructivism has attempted to explain the Common Security and Defence Policy (CSDP) in three different ways: (1) through the understanding of social interaction between relevant actors within the European institutions and between them and Member States; (2) by focusing on strategic and security cultures as crucial factors in explaining the developments in European defence; and (3) by placing a particular emphasis on discourse analysis. This chapter should be understood within the context of this last set of constructivist literature.

In terms of structure, it will start by briefly delving into critical constructivism, justifying its importance within the context of European security research. This will be followed by the contemporary contextualisation of the field, highlighting three particular dynamics that the EDA has to deal with: (1) consolidation; (2) blurring between internal, and external security; and (3) defence budgetary cuts. Given the context, the third section of the chapter attempts to understand the agency's existence within the broader context of Europe's defence by proceeding in three steps. First, it highlights the origins of the agency, then it sets the conceptual

## 28    A. Barrinha

framework and, finally, it looks into how the EDA is more than a mere agency: how it helps to sustain a particular security context that goes much beyond its direct competencies.

## Constructivism, discourse and the study of European defence

This chapter is informed by a social constructivist ontological approach, in which the world that we live in is understood as being constructed and reproduced by human agents (Risse 2004: 160). However, constructivism can be seen through different prisms and different approaches. In this case, the 'version' taken into consideration is what some authors call 'critical constructivism' (Risse 2004) or what Karin Fierke (2007) labels as 'consistent constructivism', an approach that distinguishes itself from the 'middle ground' approach of authors such as Alexander Wendt (1999) by focusing on the importance of language as central to our apprehension of the world, as its epistemological basis. Epistemologically, this constructivist ontology leads to the study of social phenomena not as truth-seeking, in which an actor's discourses are put in contrast with what 'actually happened', but rather as an interpretation of an intersubjectively constructed 'reality' (Klotz and Lynch 2007: 106).

Regardless of the approach one follows in terms of discourse analysis, they all have, as a common notion, the idea that discourse matters, and that it is more than the mere description of a reality (Risse 2004: 164). Indeed, discourse is a constitutive feature of our world, not just an expression of it. According to Jennifer Milliken (2001: 138), there are three main theoretical claims linked to discourse analysis. The first claim tells us that discourses are 'structures of signification which construct social realities' (Milliken 2001: 138). The second claim notes that discourses produce, reproduce and define things, meanings and knowledgeable practices. Finally, the third and last claim is about the play of practice, that is, discourse analysis entails the study of 'dominating or hegemonic discourses and their structuring of meaning as connected to implementing practices and ways of making these intelligible and legitimate' (Milliken 2001: 139). This implies an understanding of language in which it describes our world embedded in other discourses and dependent on an ever, even if slowly, changing context. As put by Ernesto Laclau and Chantal Mouffe (1985: 108):

> The fact that every object is constituted as an object of discourse has nothing to do with whether there is a world external to thought, or with the realism/idealism opposition. An earthquake or the falling of a brick is an event that certainly exists, in the sense that it occurs here and now, independently of my will. But whether their specificity as objects is constructed in terms of 'natural phenomena' or 'expressions

*Discursive construction of European defence* 29

of the wrath of God' depends upon the structuring of a discursive field.

Discourse analysis distinguishes itself from cognitive approaches that try to figure out how people think and perceive (Wæver 2004: 199). It tries to 'find the structures and patterns in public statements that regulate political debate so that certain things can be said while other things will be meaningless or less powerful or reasonable' (Wæver 2004: 199). It draws attention to the communicative resources through which the socio-political sphere is produced and reproduced (Jabri 1996: 90), as well as to the fact that language is not just used to describe politics; it makes it possible (Wæver 2004: 111). It does not claim that there is nothing else than discourse, just that discourse is 'the layer of reality where meaning is produced and distributed', and, as such, it deserves to be analysed (Wæver 2004: 199). This does not mean that material conditions do not matter: they do 'play a key role in making certain courses of action more or less likely, and by doing so, can either spark debates about appropriateness of pre-existing beliefs and norms or reinforce them' (Meyer and Strickmann 2011: 74); however, it is only through discourse that those practices and material conditions are meaningful.

Discourse analysis is weak in finding 'real' motives or intentions (Buzan *et al.* 1998: 177). Nonetheless, besides the advantage of allowing for the possibility to study in depth the production and reproduction of political discourse and practices – the visible, public dimension of politics – by focusing on what is communicated, it also allows for the study of how words can create unintended effects from which it is difficult to get out of, even if one would like to, or even if those words were not deliberate (Wæver 2004: 212), something a cognitive approach would overlook. As summarised by Hannah Arendt (1998 [1958]: 4),

> [t]here may be truths beyond speech, and they may be of great relevance to man in the singular, that is, to man insofar as he is not a political being, whatever else may be. Men in the plural, that is, men insofar as they live and move and act in this world, can experience meaningfulness only because they can talk with and make sense to each other and to themselves.

Discourse is thus fundamental to apprehend the political character of institutions and processes.

In recent years, several authors in the field of Security Studies have focused on the analysis of discourse as a relevant, if not essential, feature within their field of inquiry. Authors such as David Campbell (1998), Ole Wæver (2002), Lene Hansen (2006), Karen Fierke (2001), Michael Williams (2007) or Jeff Huysmans (2006) have highlighted the importance of discourse analysis in their works. In terms of European security literature,

## 30  A. Barrinha

there is also a growing literature focused on discursive approaches (cf. Barnutz 2010; Barrinha and Rosa 2013; Gariup 2009).

The same cannot be said about either the role of defence industries in the European context or the specific role of the EDA. As argued in previous work (Barrinha 2010), that is an important gap in the literature for two main reasons. First, because discourse analysis is fundamental to understand the political implications and meanings of both the European Union (EU) as a political project, and of the defence industry as a sector intimately related to that project. Second, because the specific character of agencies such as the EDA – technical in nature, but political in practice – makes an analysis that emphasises the ideational over the material more pertinent for the understanding of its political influence within the European security field. In that sense, the following section will set the ideational context in which the political construction of the EDA is framed.

## EDA in the context of European defence

Though ample in competencies, the EDA is limited in terms of its budget and human resources. With a budget of just over €30 million and about 120 employees, the EDA faces the additional task of dealing in an area that is still pretty much (mis)understood as an exclusive domain of state sovereignty (Bátora 2009: 1084). In that regard, the EDA closely resembles other EU agencies, such as Europol and Frontex, in that their ideational role largely surpasses their institutional one. As Carrapico and Trauner (2013: 5) highlight regarding Europol, 'with Member States increasingly adhering to Europol's policy recommendations, Europol has expanded its (de facto, *not de jure*) role in EU organised crime policy-making'. Also regarding Frontex, the EU's border management agency, its work in knowledge production through risk-assessment and intelligence reports can 'be seen as securitising practices that contribute to the securitisation of asylum and migration in the EU' (Léonard 2010: 244).

For the EDA, that capacity is even more important; as it is '[s]hort of the ability to act on a par with the regulatory agencies in the EU', it 'has to rely upon a number of alternative procedures supporting intergovernmental networking in the defence sector' (Bátora 2009: 1084). This implies encompassing different ongoing dynamics, namely the push for the liberalisation of the defence industry, the progressive blurring between security and defence equipment and needs, and the different national interests and priorities within the European space, particularly in a time of strong financial constraints.

### The liberalisation agenda

In the United States, the end of the Cold War signalled the need for a significant resizing of its defence industry, leading to the significant reduction in

*Discursive construction of European defence* 31

terms of companies operating in the field. In Europe – with the exception of the UK – it would take longer, but eventually, there was also a merging process between key companies that led to the constitution of a few industry giants, namely BAE Systems and EADS.

This meant that relations between states and industry were further complexified with pan-European companies, such as EADS, sharing the field with 'national champions', and other smaller companies focused on niche sectors, such as Meggitt, Cobham and Racal (Vlachos-Dengler 2002: 15). The discourse was also progressively defined by economic criteria, as defence budgets across Europe were suffering significant cuts. As written by Charles Grant (1997) at the time: 'Whereas it used to be about weapons performance, it now is about economies of scale'.

Even though a market-oriented discourse – and consequent policies and decisions – progressively took hold, that happened in a field in which 'contracts are few but huge, and customers are few but powerful, so market forces do not work' ('Odd Industry Out' 2002). One can thus register this paradoxical evolution in the defence sector in which there has been a progressive push for the liberalisation of what used to be exclusively state-owned national companies – very similar to what has been happening in other economic sectors (e.g. energy, telecommunications, transport) – without the necessary open markets in which these companies could operate, and with a significant public investment in research (Hammarström 2006: 10).

### Blurring the divide between security and defence

Not only is the EDA developing within a context of increasing liberalisation dynamics and market-oriented discourses and policies, but it is also part of the constitution of a security field where the distinction between the external and the internal is less and less clear:

> Defence is sometimes viewed as being military and focused on external security, whereas contemporary homeland security is predominantly internally focussed and civilian. The reality is that divisions are not clear cut. Policing, intelligence and border control customs vary considerably within the EU as does the role of the military in internal security.
>
> (Mawdsley 2011: 11)

Crisis management, technological developments, and the need to seek economies of scale are taking military forces and industries in the direction of homeland security and vice versa, as recognised by the former head of Finmeccanica, Pier Francesco Guarguaglini (2010: 4): 'A peculiar feature of the evolving security dimension is the more and more blurring distinction between homeland and international security, as

## 32   A. Barrinha

well as between civil and military applications'. In Britain and France, recent reviews of their respective strategic documents directly acknowledge those changes (Mawdsley 2011: 11) and within the EU institutions that has certainly become a key motto in how to approach CSDP. According to the former Chairman of the European Union Military Committee, 'Security measures, military as well as civilian, are inextricably linked to strengthening governance structures and economic development' (Syrén 2010: 7).

### Crisis management

As the core business of CSDP, a successful EU crisis management lies, in the words of Catherine Ashton (2010: 5), 'with its ability to combine military and civilian means in support of our [EU's] missions'. In that regard, the Council approved in 2009 a Comprehensive Approach to crisis management that 'underlined the need to identify synergies between civilian and military capability development – in particular referring to the Agency's efforts in the research area' (Weis 2010b: 6). As a consequence, '[t]he Ministerial Steering Board in November launched the European Framework Cooperation (EFC) for Civilian Security, Space and Defence-Related Research with the aim to systematically synchronise R&T investment by EDA, the European Commission and the European Space Agency' (Weis 2010b: 6). Making the EU more efficient in this field is a priority for High Representative Ashton, which means that these 'synergies between civil and military capability development' will certainly be further 'fostered' (Ashton 2010: 6) in the foreseeable future.

### Technological development

This civil–military (civ–mil) discourse on crisis management is, to a large extent, the result of over two decades of European peace operations that have certainly produced lessons learned for all the actors involved, namely regarding the need for a comprehensive approach that goes beyond the military use of force. However, this discourse is equally related to a broader tendency that merges the internal and the external, of which the increasing use of hybrid gendarmerie forces in peace operations is but an example. This pattern is potentiated by technology, with security forces being endowed with the means to undertake 'militarised' tasks, and vice-versa. That is the case with the use of Unmanned Aerial Vehicles (UAVs) and Unmanned Combat Aerial Vehicles (UCAVs, a.k.a. drones). Although designed for military purposes, as a sign of the increasing overlap between internal and external security, there seems to be in the Justice and Home Affairs field a significant enthusiasm for the use of drones, particularly, for border surveillance. A document recently presented by the European Commission proposed the use of the Southern Mediterranean in the framework of the project EUROSUR (Franceschi-Bicchierai 2012) and countries such as Austria are using them for the surveillance of its eastern borders.

In addition to the use of similar equipment and technology by both security and military forces, or related to it, there is the increasing role civilian companies play in the development of technology that is then used by the military sector, as expressed by the British government for whom '[a]dvanced technology development, which was once the realm of Government research organisations, is now carried out almost exclusively in the civil and commercial sectors' (MOD 2012: 38). That is also recognised by the EDA itself when it asserts that technological development is increasingly 'proceeding outside the control of governments and with the commercial sector fully in the driving seat' (EDA 2008: 22).

The liberalisation push is here added by the progressive blurring between external and internal security, creating a context in which companies that produce military equipment find their business either mostly reliant on civilian equipment (such as the case of EADS) or dependent on civilian produced technology (Mawdsley 2011: 17). Be it a cause or a consequence, there seems to be a progressive interest on the part of the industry to further contribute to the blurring between (internal) security and (external) defence.

*Industry interests*

Doctrine changes in crisis management and events such as 9/11 have contributed to the increasing visibility of homeland security. The aforementioned technological developments have allowed industries to increasingly focus on this market, in search for further business opportunities (Sköns and Surry 2007: 346) in a time of dwindling defence budgets. In that sense, blurring the internal and the external has also acquired a strategic interest for companies working in defence.

This industry lobby was quite visible in 2004, when the European Commission asked a Group of Personalities to draft a report on security research. Mostly composed of defence-related industry and officials, the final report 'unsurprisingly [...] contended that there should be no division between military and civilian research and argued for €1 billion per year (minimum) to be spent on security research' (Mawdsley 2011: 13). This would, in their view, allow Europe 'to get a much better return on its defence research investment' (Group of Personalities 2004: 13).

It is in this context of shifting borders between what is defence and security, between what is a sovereign prerogative and a private domain, and between commercial priorities and national interests that the defence field – the privileged ground in which the EDA operates – is faced with an additional dynamic: financial cuts.

## 34 A. Barrinha

### Financial constraints

Defence budgets across the continent have been facing significant cuts, with obvious consequences in terms of both research and defence procurement. This situation is leading to an interrelated discourse in which financial constraints are leading to a disinvestment in Research and Development (R&D) with potentially existential consequences for Europe's defence. In the words of the Chairman of the EU Military Committee, Hakan Syrén (2010: 8), 'low levels of R&D and low renewal rates implies that we are mortgaging the future in ways that raise fundamental questions of leadership responsibilities'.

To this, we should add the value-for-money discourse, in which it is necessary to find alternative ways of investing 'smarter' in the sector. Both discourses have, in turn, contributed to a growing advocacy, on the part of both policy elites and industry, for 'pan-European solutions' (Meyer and Strickmann 2011: 76). This is a context that is certainly favourable to the further development of EDA as both a promoter of this pan-European discourse and the facilitator of its implementation. In the December 2013 European Council, the EDA was invited to undertake a number of tasks such as coming up with suggestions to promote Pooling and Sharing (P&S) in procurement projects among Member States; to prepare a roadmap, together with the European Commission, on the development of industrial standards in European defence and to participate in the creating of a European-wide security of supply regime (European Council 2013).

In short, the EDA nowadays operates in a context that is characterised by the increasing importance of the private sector and liberalisation tendencies, by the progressive lack of clarity regarding what constitutes the (internal) security field and what constitutes (external) defence and by national budgetary constraints that might contribute to facilitate pan-European solutions in terms of arms acquisitions and collaborative development projects. How the EDA has its existence justified within this context is the focus of the following section.

### The EDA and its origins

Though initially proposed within the works of the European Convention, the EDA did not have to wait for the eventually scrapped Constitutional Treaty to come into existence. The Joint Action of 12 July 2004 created the EDA with the explicit aim of helping to improve the EU defence capabilities. It should, in that sense, be a 'capability-driven Agency' (Weis 2010b: 5) supporting 'the Council and the Member States in their effort to improve European defence capabilities in the field of crisis management and to sustain the ESDP [European Security and Defence Policy] as it stands now and develops in the future'. What that exactly meant was –

and arguably still is – a cause for division between Europe's two main military powers – France and the UK. Whereas for Paris, the EDA should focus on the consolidation of a European industrial base, for London, it should help 'improving the military capabilities of Member States' (Guay 2005: 13), namely by creating the conditions for a more open and competitive European market as well as by promoting joint research and training projects between Member States. Regardless of eventual divisions, the EDA was, according to its first Chief executive, established by the Member States 'to be their instrument or tool for taking forward what they begin to sense must be, increasingly, their shared agendas' (Witney 2005).

In that regard, an important dimension of the Agency's work has been the elaboration of voluntary codes of conduct regarding the regulation of the defence market. The first document was approved in 2006 – the Code of Conduct on Defence Procurement that, through the EDA-created Electronic Bulletin Board (EBB), attempted to give more transparency to Europe's defence market. The same year, the Code of Best Practice in the Supply Chain was approved, covering industry-to-industry relations in order to make companies in the sector use the EBB in cases of sub-contracting of services and equipment. Finally, it elaborated the Code of Conduct on Offsets, in 2009, also with the aim of making the defence market more transparent by limiting the form and amount of counter-incentives involved in defence deals. In practice results have been mixed, at best, with companies and Member States still widely engaging in deals outside these codes of conduct.

Again, this is something that should be put into context. Fulfilling the demands inscribed in these codes implies a significant change in the practices of the defence industry, which certainly will not happen overnight. However, by engaging Member States in voluntarily subscribing to them the EDA is contributing to the definition of a behaviour pattern that progressively distinguishes what is acceptable from what is unacceptable. It asserts a Europeanising and liberalisation trend that is progressively set as the norm. For that, the EDA is also sided by the European Commission, increasingly interested in regulating the defence market. This does not mean that both institutions have shared interests when it comes to how this regulation should proceed; it however indicates that they are both pushing towards a similar trend, by adopting a very similar language.

Though still within its first decade of existence, its self-assessment points towards a fast maturing institution that 'has started to produce concrete results to improve European defence capabilities in different areas' (Weis 2010b: 5). Herman Van Rompuy, President of the European Council (2013: 1) at the time, assumes the same position when he says: 'the European Defence Agency is a young institution, but in the eight years since its creation, you have made your mark. Knowing well the challenges of setting up something from scratch, I can say this is no small achievement!'

36   *A. Barrinha*

## Understanding the EDA's *raison d'être*

A quick glance at the EDA's website allows one to see all the areas in which the agency is contributing, in its capability-driven approach towards a more integrated and operational European defence. However, and this is why critical constructivism is important to understand bodies such as the EDA, this only tells us a self-written narrative of its *raison d'être*. It misses the political goals it helps to achieve within the context of European defence and how it contributes to either reify or change the status quo of the context in which it was created and in which it developed. As will be discussed in this section, the EDA is a social agent defined by this double identity of being an EU agency (with all its limitations) and a security and defence actor (with all its ideational possibilities).

### Agency and actor

In order to understand the EDA's existence, this chapter will now proceed in a two-step analysis that goes from the lower to the higher level of generalisation: from the role of the EDA as an EU Agency to the EDA as an agent for change/continuity of a particular security context. The EDA, as an EU intergovernmental agency, is not in a position to impose changes on Member States. However, following the footsteps of agencies such as EUROPOL and Frontex, the EDA is capable of setting common standards that will contribute to the adoption of specific norms and behaviours (Bátora 2009: 1094). In that regard, one could think there is a thin line separating the EDA as an EU agency from the EDA as a security and defence actor. After all, it is a defence agency; therefore, one goes with the other. For this chapter, though, there is an important difference that is reflected in the distinction between its functionalist and its normative dimensions. Regarding the former, the EDA plays a number of expected roles that reflect its competencies as an agency: to conduct research, to propose, to develop, to facilitate, among others. As a defence actor, the EDA fits within a larger European defence field (Williams 2007; Mérand 2010) to which it actively contributes through the discourses it attaches to particular issues and practices. Thus, by looking into what the EDA is for, we end up also gathering pieces of a larger puzzle about European defence in practice.

By acting in the defence field, the EDA is also defined by its security and defence actorness, with the capacity to shape the field, both by its actions and policies, but also by the narratives it constructs and sustains regarding how other actors should behave. The EDA was created within a particular socio-political context; a context that defines what defence is, what the limits of the field are, and what ideological, political and technologically driven best practices should be implemented. As a producer of discourses on itself and on its field, as well as an agent about whom discourses are produced, the EDA contributes to the evolving dynamics – liberalisation, blurring of the internal and the external, and financial constraints – of this broader context.

As argued by Catherine Ashton, 'to be a credible player on the world stage, you need not only will but also the capability to act' (Ashton, in Platteau 2013: 15). The EDA is thus seen as a 'key facilitator and coordinator of efforts in the area of defence capability development' (Ashton 2010: 6) so that the EU can act globally. These are attributes related to the EDA as an agency that reflect larger European defence goals. The EDA is at the centre of a defence Europeanisation process that aims to progressively move this sector from the national to the European level (Barrinha 2010), in all areas – from the procurement policies to the military doctrines in use. As put in the EDA's own language: 'The core role of the EDA is to help governments attain their defence objectives by outlining the efficiency gains that could be a result of doing things together' (Runde 2013: 36).

The Europeanisation of the defence sector can only be successful if articulated with industry. It is thus of utmost importance, in EDA's view, to work closely with these mostly private actors:

> Government has a very special relationship with the defence industry – as customer, regulator, and principal source of research and development funding. But less and less does it remain owner; and, as defence companies move progressively from government to private ownership, and as shareholder funds become increasingly prominent in the control of companies, so one may expect the normal laws of globalised economy to apply; capital will flow to optimise returns.
>
> (EDA 2006: 31)

Following the EDA, it is expected that 'the normal laws of globalised economy' will apply in the defence sector, despite governments' 'special relationship' with the industry (2006: 23). The agency thus operates from the standpoint that defence will increasingly be a private business, while remaining a market entirely financed – and supported – by taxpayers' money. In both cases it is solidly framed in a neoliberal rhetoric (Oikonomou 2006) that reproduces a particular discourse about how the public sphere should be governed, including the defence sector. The – increasingly private – defence industry is seen as a stakeholder of prime importance within the EDA's activities. In the 2010 conference, the President of AeroSpace and Defence Industries Association of Europe (ASD), Pier Francesco Guarguaglini, was, together with Catherine Ashton (recorded), and the already mentioned General Hakan Syrén, the keynote speakers of the event. It is symbolic that there was only one speaker external to the EU and that it was the representative of the defence industries' lobby in Brussels. As argued by Oikonomou (2006: 13), the EDA could, in this regard,

38   *A. Barrinha*

be seen as 'the meeting point and the decision-making centre for the EU military–industrial complex'.

This normalisation is complemented by a discourse focused on the 'strategic' importance of the aerospace and defence industries (ASD 2011b: 2) and on the relevance of constituting a solid European Defence Technological and Industrial Base (DTIB). Ideas such as '[t]he need [...] to accept that the DTIB in Europe can only survive as one European whole, not as a sum of different national capacities' (EDA 2006: 32) are quite common in EDA's documents: not only do they reveal this normalisation, but they link it with the idea that such has to be Europeanised in order to succeed.

For Guarguaglini (2006), to this should also be taken into consideration the EDA's 'fundamental role in building a single defence and security market'. The same idea was more recently expressed by Mr. Guarguaglini's ASD predecessor, Michael von Gizycki when, according to the ASD newsletter, he called for 'more collaborative programmes between Member States' as well advocating 'a leading role for the European Defence Agency in the coordination of these initiatives' (cited in ASD 2011a: 2). That is, the EDA should contribute to the establishment of both a European industrial base and a European defence market. By avoiding all the necessary ethical dilemmas associated with the private ownership of the means to produce heavy military equipment, the EDA creates a legitimate basis for the support of the Europeanisation of both industry and states – of both suppliers and customers. This is nicely summarised by Santiago Secades (2011: 35), an EDA official at the time, when he stated that:

> the EDA is working with governments and industry to reduce the fragmentation and other artificial features of the European defence market, and to develop a research and industrial base that is capable both of meeting Europe's own defence and security needs to the highest standards, and of holding its own in legitimate international competition.

By linking the constitution of both an industrial base and a pan-European market – where it is normal that private actors assume key positions – to the future of European defence, the EDA is establishing an important link between the interests of these private actors and the potential success of European defence and, also, security. In that regard, it becomes increasingly less clear what this European defence is supposed to be as the distinction between its military and civilian dimension is progressively removed from the discourse. Thus, serving European defence is no different from serving European security. As a consequence, the type of market and industrial base the EDA is supposed to help create is also not easily defined.

Since May 2009, the EDA has been working with the European Commission within European Framework Cooperation (EFC) in order to maximise 'complementarity and synergy between defence and civilian research activities' (Mawdsley 2011: 16). This complementarity between defence and civilian research is a common feature in the discourse of EDA's officials. For instance, as argued by EDA's former Chief executive, Alexander Weis, the importance of 'standardisation and interoperability between military and civilian users' is 'growing by the day' (2010b: 6). Ultimately, this close connection between civilian and military activities has important consequences in terms of the work the EDA is supposed to do in the defence field; in effect, not only the EDA's activities go beyond the military sphere, as its aim, its *raison d'être*, seems to largely – and officially – surpass the field.

Finally, this discourse is tied by references to the financial constraints of the sector, which legitimises all the above dynamics. The EDA is presented as aiming to 'deliver best value for money for its Member States and in support of the Common Security and Defence Policy' (Weiss 2010a: 6). The defence budget cuts that are being felt across Europe are used to insert an existential dimension to the discourse leading to the 'natural' conclusion that 'we [Europeans] have no other choice than to cooperate' (Ashton 2010: 6).

## Conclusion

As seen in this chapter, by asking the question 'what is the EDA for', a set of overlapping discourses and dynamics are revealed that point towards a more complex view of what the EDA is and does. If, as argued by the former President of the EU Council, the EDA was to be seen as a facilitator, such an image would paint a portrait of an agency with limited impact in the political environment in which it operates. However, as discussed in this chapter, that is hardly the case. The EDA is at the forefront of a Europeanisation push in an increasingly blurred security and defence field while, simultaneously, 'normalising' the central protagonism consolidated/privatised industry actors play in it. The EDA does all this supported by and supporting an existential discourse that points to the indispensable role it plays, and to the non-existence of viable alternatives (there is no other option but to cooperate) regarding the path that should be traced by EU institutions and Member States alike when it comes to European security and defence. Ten years after its inception, the political discourse associated to the EDA clearly indicates that its importance in the field of European security and defence goes certainly beyond the role of the mere facilitator.

## References

Arendt, H. (1998 [1958]) *The Human Condition*, 2nd edition, London: University of Chicago Press.

ASD (Aerospace and Defence Industries Association in Europe) (2011a) 'ASD at High-Level Seminar on Defence Capabilities', *ASD Newsletter*, 2(6): 3.

40 *A. Barrinha*

ASD (Aerospace and Defence Industries Association in Europe) (2011b) 'Barroso Hails Strategic Value of Aerospace and Defence Sectors', *ASD Newsletter*, 2(6): 2.

Ashton, C. (2013) 'Speech by High Representative Catherine Ashton at the Annual Conference of the European Defence Agency', A 157/13, Brussels, 21 March 2013.

Ashton, C. (2010) 'Keynote Speeches', EDA *Special Bulletin: Bridging Efforts*, 9 February 2010: 5–6.

Barnutz, S. (2010) 'The EU's Logic of Security: Politics through Institutionalised Discourses', *European Security*, 19(3): 377–394.

Barrinha, A. (2010) 'Moving towards a European Defence Industry? The Political Discourse on a Changing Reality and its Implications for the Future of the European Union', *Global Society*, 24(4): 467–485.

Barrinha, A. and Rosa, M. (2013) 'Translating Europe's Security Culture', *Critical Studies on Security*, 1(1): 101–115.

Bátora, J. (2009) 'European Defence Agency: A Flashpoint of Institutional Logics', *West European Politics*, 32(6): 1075–1098.

Bellouard, P. (2011) 'A Success Story of European Cooperation', *The European – Security and Defence Union*, 10(2): 34–36.

Buzan, B., Wæver, O. and de Wilde, J. (1998) *Security: A New Framework for Analysis*, Boulder: Lynne Rienner.

Campbell, D. (1998) *Writing Security: United States Foreign Policy and the Politics of Identity*, Manchester: Manchester University Press.

Carrapico, H. and Trauner, F. (2013) 'Europol and its Influence on European Policy Making on Organised Crime: Analysing Governance Dynamics and Opportunities', *Perspectives on European Politics and Society*, 14(3): 357–371.

European Council (2013) *Conclusions*, EUCO 217/13, Brussels, 20 December 2013.

EDA (European Defence Agency) (2013) *Annual Report 2012*.

EDA (European Defence Agency) (2008) *Future Trends from the Capability Development Plan*.

EDA (European Defence Agency) (2006) *An Initial Long-Term Vision for European Defence Capability and Capacity Needs*.

Fierke, K. (2007) *Critical Approaches to International Security*, Cambridge: Polity Press: 166–184.

Fierke, K. (2001) 'Critical Methodology and Constructivism', in K. Fierke and K.E. Jorgensen, *Constructing International Relations: The Next Generation*, London: M.E. Shape: 115–135.

Franceschi-Bicchierai, L. (2012) 'EU Wants Drones to Spot Illegal Migrants Crossing the Mediterranean', *Wired UK*, 27 July 2012.

Gariup, M. (2009) *European Security Culture: Language, Theory, Policy*, Burlington: Ashgate.

Grant, C. (1997) 'Linking Arms', *The Economist*, 12 June 1997.

Group of Personalities (2004) *Research for a Secure Europe: Report of the Group of Personalities in the Field of Security Research*, Luxembourg: Office for Official Publication of the European Communities.

Guarguaglini, P.F. (2010) 'Bridging Efforts: Connecting Civilian Security and Military Capability Development', EDA Annual Conference 2010, Brussels, 9 February 2010.

Guarguaglini, P.F. (2006) 'Integration of the European Defence Market and Transatlantic Co-operation', Conference on 'High Technology for Italian Development, Jobs and Security', Rome, 18 January 2006.

Guay, T. (2005) *The Transatlantic Defense Industrial Base: Restructuring Scenarios and their Implications*, Carlisle, PA: Strategic Studies Institute.

Hammarström, U. (2006) 'Up and Running', *EDA Bulletin*, No. 3 (December 2006): 10.

Hansen, L. (2006) *Security as Practice: Discourse Analysis and the Bosnian War*, London: Routledge.

Huysmans, J. (2006) *The Politics of Insecurity: Fear, Migration and Asylum in the EU*, London: Routledge.

Jabri, V. (1996) *Discourses on Violence: Conflict Analysis Reconsidered*, Manchester: Manchester University Press.

Klotz, A. and Lynch, C. (2007) *Strategies for Research in Constructivist International Relations*, London: M.E. Sharpe.

Laclau, E. and Mouffe, C. (1985) *Hegemony and Socialist Strategy: Towards a Radical Democratic Politics*, London: Verso.

Léonard, S. (2010) 'EU Border Security and Migration into the European Union: FRONTEX and Securitisation through Practices', *European Security*, 19(2): 231–254.

Mawdsley, J. (2011) 'Towards a Merger of the European Defence and Security Markets?', in A.J.K. Bailes and S. Depauw, *The EU Defence Market: Balancing Effectiveness with Responsibility*, Conference Report, Flemish Peace Institute, Brussels: Drukkerij Artoos: 11–19.

Mérand, F. (2010) 'Pierre Bourdieu and the Birth of ESDP', *Security Studies*, 19(2): 342–374.

Meyer, C. and Strickman, E. (2011) 'Solidifying Constructivism: How Material and Ideational Factors Interact in European Defence', *Journal of Common Market Studies*, 49(1): 61–81.

Milliken, J. (2001) 'Discourse Study: Bringing Rigor to Critical Theory', in K. Fierke and K.E. Jorgensen, *Constructing International Relations: The Next Generation*, London: M.E. Shape: 136–160.

MOD (Ministry of Defence) (2012) *National Security through Technology: Technology, Equipment, and Support for UK Defence and Security*.

'Odd Industry Out', *The Economist*, 18 July 2002.

Oikonomou, I. (2006) 'The EU Politico-Military–Industrial Complex: A New Research Agenda', paper presented at the 31st BISA annual conference, University College Cork, 20 December 2006.

Platteau, E. (2013) ' "Pool it or Lose it" is Becoming a Reality', *European Defence Matters*, 2, pp. 15–17.

Risse, T. (2004) 'Social Constructivism and European Integration', in A. Winer and T. Diez, *European Integration Theory*, Oxford: Oxford University Press: 159–176.

Runde, G. (2013) 'Demand Consolidation is the First Priority', *European Defence Matters*, 3: 36–38.

Secades, S.E. (2011) 'Openness in the European Defence Market and Company Competitiveness', in A.J.K. Bailes and S. Depauw, *The EU Defence Market: Balancing Effectiveness with Responsibility*, Flemish Peace Institute, Brussels: Drukkerij Artoos: 29–25.

Shatter, A. (2013) 'Keynote Address by the Minister for Justice, Equality and Defence', Annual Conference of the European Defence Agency, Brussels, 21 March 2013.

42   *A. Barrinha*

Sköns, E. and Surry, E. (2007) 'Arms Production', in *SIPRI Yearbook 2007: Armaments, Disarmament and International Security*, Oxford: Oxford University Press.

Syrén, H. (2010) 'Keynote Speeches', *EDA Special Bulletin: Bridging Efforts*, 9 February.

Van Rompuy, H. (2013) 'Defence in Europe: Pragmatically Forward', speech by President of the European Council Herman Van Rompuy at the annual conference of the European Defence Agency.

Vlachos-Dengler, K. (2002) *From National Champions to European Heavyweights: The Development of European Defense Industrial Capabilities across Market Segments*, Santa Monica: RAND.

Wæver, O. (2004) 'Discursive Approaches', in A. Winer and T. Diez (eds) *European Integration Theory*, Oxford: Oxford University Press: 197–215.

Wæver, O. (2002) 'Identity, Communities and Foreign Policy: Discourse Analysis as a Foreign Policy Theory', in L. Hansen and O. Wæver (eds) *European Integration and National Identity: The Challenge of the Nordic States*, London: Routledge: 20–49.

Weis, A. (2010a) 'Conference Assessment and Way Ahead. A Word from the Chief Executive', *EDA Special Bulletin: Bridging Efforts*, 9 February 2010: 35–36.

Weis, A. (2010b) 'EDA in 2009', *European Defence Agency Annual Report 2009*.

Wendt, A. (1999) *Social Theory of International Politics*, Cambridge: Cambridge University Press.

Williams, M. (2007) *Culture and Security: Symbolic Power and the Politics of International Security*, New York: Routledge.

Witney, N. (2008) *Re-energising Europe's Security and Defence Policy*, Policy Paper, London: European Council on Foreign Relations.

Witney, N. (2005) 'Role of the Different Actors: Industry, National Governments, European Commission, European Defence Agency', 'Defense 2006' Economist Conference, Paris, 29 November 2005.

# 3 Brothers in arms?

## The European arms industry and the making of the EDA

*Iraklis Oikonomou*

> The European defence industry is emphatic about the need for this Agency.
> (Javier Solana 2004)

### Introduction

This chapter seeks to illustrate the centrality of economic-industrial considerations and arms-industrial involvement in the making of the European Defence Agency (EDA). The argument put forward is the following. The restructuring, consolidation and internationalisation of the European military–industrial capital shifted industrial objectives towards European Union (EU) military–industrial integration. The setting-up of the EDA fulfilled key industrial preferences and represents an institutional transformation driven by the imperative of industrial competitiveness. The latter ranked high among the objectives of policy-makers in the Agency, and the new institution was subjected to instrumental industrial influence before and during its conception. More broadly, the making of the EDA is the institutional outcome of a process initiated by the capitalist restructuring of European arms production. Both complex and contradictory, this process is embedded in demands for industrial expansion and profitability, rather than limited to capabilities development.

The first section provides a brief theoretical overview of the institutionalisation of armaments policy at the EU level, inspired by historical materialist contributions to European integration theory. Then the chapter investigates the politico-economic rationale for establishing the EDA, moving beyond the mainstream rhetoric of capabilities in support of a common European defence policy. The third part relates the creation of the EDA to the interests of the European military–industrial capital and the necessities of military–industrial competitiveness, and highlights the centrality of the arms industry in generating this institutional development. Finally, a short conclusion summarises the findings of the chapter.

The chapter is not concerned with providing an assessment of the Agency's effectiveness, nor does it describe what the EDA has achieved in its ten years of operations. The focal point of the analysis is what the EDA

44    *I. Oikonomou*

was meant to be back in its formative period, around the year 2004; the chapter traces the ideas, aims and logic upon which the Agency was established. Essentially, the orientation of the chapter is politico-economic and historical. This explains why certain arguments are drawn out of unpublished findings from interviews conducted in the period 2005–2007, when the Agency carried the fresh imprints of its original masterminds.

## Theoretical considerations

Historical materialist theory stresses the importance of production in any understanding of the social totality. For Gramsci and neo-Gramscianism, economic life is not subordinated to the political; society remains 'a totality primarily constituted by modes of production' (Gill 1993: 37). The concept of production involves the forces of production and the social relations of production that are, in the final analysis, relations between classes embedded in the production process. Thus, the concept of power is not described in terms of state power only, as in the case of realism. Historical materialism 'examines the connections between power in production, power in the state, and power in international relations' (Cox 1996: 96) and relates them to specific national and internationalised class agents, as well as to the broader national and transnational capitalist structures of production and the state. The realm of production generates a particular social relation: capital. The concept of capital in the Marxist sense denotes a social relationship of exploitation between the owners of the means of production and labour. Out of this relationship comes a particular pattern of 'behaviour': the need for capital to maximise profits, accumulate consistently and safeguard its competitive status (Gill and Law 1988: 83–84). Such a need generates a rationality, which capital can be expected to comply with, but whose policy effects are mediated by internal class contradictions and the role of the capitalist state and supranational institutions.

The particular form of the transformation of the forces of production that is relevant to the development of EU military–industrial policy is the 'internationalisation of production' (Cox 1987: 244). Although the phenomenon of economic internationalisation in arms production has been elaborated elsewhere (Oikonomou 2008), a brief overview of the concept is necessary at this stage. The internationalisation of capital represents a contradiction. On the one hand, it represents the tendency of capital to expand its scope beyond the confines of the nation-state (Mandel 1978: 342). On the other hand, it highlights the tendency of the nation-state, as a superstructural arrangement, to shape and obstruct the development of productive forces. In EU armaments policy, this trend is exemplified by the persistence of national protectionist procurement practices. In this sense, the internationalisation of capital is the expansion of a social relation embedded in the context of the nation-state and subjected to the effects of the transformation of the productive forces. A key driver is the tendency for the average rate of profit to fall, which introduces the export of capital as the 'fundamental and determinant tendency' of the modern capitalist mode of production at the global level (Poulantzas 1975: 42). Arms-industrial restructuring at the EU level is thus integrally linked to changes in the global structures of production.

The internationalisation of capital presupposes the internationalisation of production and denotes the national differentiation in the composition of capital together with a broadening of the territorial scope of production and accumulation. Internationalisation of capital resulting from the consolidation of the arms industry in Europe was a precondition for the generation of both the EU armaments policy and the particular social force that has instrumentally influenced its development, i.e. the internationalised fractions of the European military–industrial capital. Nevertheless, this social force is not passive; it actively responds to internationalisation and feeds this process with further industrial initiatives and consolidation. In other words, the internationalising dimension of production is not simply 'an exogenous structural impact to which actors can only respond', but is interlinked to the conscious activity of the social, class forces it generates (Bieler 2000: 10).

Turning to the theorisation of the EDA as an institution, in this context the intergovernmentalism–supranationalism spectrum is subjugated to the question of societal power and purpose. Institutional form and purpose are only in the last instance interrelated, in the sense that the 'form sets limits to possible contents and vice versa' (van Apeldoorn 2002: 10). Elements of both ends of the spectrum may be justifiably present in EU military–industrial policy integration, without altering the policy's purpose and socio-economic content. No matter which end prevails, this content is defined in the last instance by the interests of the ruling social force, as mediated by the capitalist state and the supranational EU institutional framework. Thus, one may expect elements of different forms of institutional authority to prevail and/or co-exist, according to the specificities of the area of EU armaments policy involved. The EDA is an agency working along intergovernmental lines, while having the Commission among its members and interacting constantly with it. The critical dimension for a materialist understanding of the role of institutions is their purpose, i.e. the actual content and impact of their policy outcome.

Institutions are determined by social relations and at the same time feed into the reproduction of these relations; they represent concretisations of the interests of social classes (Carchedi 2001: 7), while also contributing to the realisation of these interests. Therefore, the autonomy that certain institutions may enjoy is only relative. The quest for institutional autonomy and for an increase in the institution's power over the broader EU system can only exist side by side with the over-determination of the institution's function by the dominant socio-economic interests operating at the EU level. An institutional actor such as the EDA, whose authority is either nascent or heavily contested, strives to strengthen its standing within a given institutional framework – in this case the framework of EU armaments policy-making. Only through this way can an institution safeguard the socio-economic interests that underpin its operations. While bureaucratic considerations do play a role in policy-making, the maintenance and expansion of institutional authority is a precondition for the fulfilment of the socio-economic purpose of the institution. EU institutions are not only outcomes of socio-economic processes, but also active factors that reproduce these processes. The building of institutions contributes to transnational class-formation as much as it stems from it. Economic internationalisation and the respective internationalisation of class structures at the EU level are fed by initiatives such as the formation of the EDA. Such a framework prevents a mechanistic viewing of institutions as passive elements of the superstructure.

## The political economy of the EDA

### *Beyond the capabilities rhetoric*

Mainstream accounts of the creation of the EDA point to a supposed need to address the deficit in EU military capabilities. Hugo Brady and Ben Tonra have suggested that the function of the Agency is to upgrade a common defence policy; 'the EDA's expansive mandate and ambitious development programme ... highlight the priority of making the EDA a critical enabling tool of an effective European Security and Defence Policy' (Brady and Tonra 2005: 2). For the same theorists, there has been a 'logical link', i.e. an apolitical link, between a credible Common Security and Defence Policy (CSDP) and a more integrated European armaments market.

However, the link between military–industrial profitability and defence capability is not as logical as it may seem. Countries that did not maintain any national, competitive, military–industrial base were able to develop fully fledged military capabilities through an effective off-the-shelve procurement policy. Why, to take one example, does the need for strategic airlift have to be fulfilled only through European equipment, if competing alternatives are more efficient? Concerning technology dependence, it remains to be proven that a more competitive European arms industry would maintain a higher level of technological autonomy than a less profitable one in an era of intense technological globalisation. As the case of BAE Systems highlights, often the quest for profitability leads to mergers and acquisitions of foreign companies and the intrusion of foreign markets, such as the US one, thereby cancelling de facto any ideas of 'autonomy'. Besides, such autonomy could be achieved through a state-controlled process, without the presence of the profit motive. It is absurd to claim that technology dependence is an issue when big Member States gear their Research and Technology (R&T) activities to those of the US, as in the case of the Joint Strike Fighter. Thus, the connection between capabilities and competitiveness appears rhetorically reified, as something evident and naturally existing. By leading to a bigger and more controllable market, harmonisation of operational requirements and procurement is a prerequisite not only of capabilities development, but also of the strengthening of the global competitiveness and profitability of the European arms industry.

Therefore, capability development in the context of the EDA and beyond has been inextricably linked to the quest for European military–industrial competitiveness. In September 2006, the EDA agreed upon a set of characteristics of a strong future European defence industrial base. The list included not only technological efficiency and responsiveness to EU defence needs, but also the enabling of arms exports and the promotion of industrial cooperation. Indeed, one is left wondering what arms exports have to do with CSDP capabilities. The proposals put forward included three key industrial demands: (1) the construction of Centres of Excellence; (2) the simplification of intra-Community transfers; and (3) the diminishing of technological dependence from non-EU sources (EDA 2006b). Industrial objectives were thus inserted into the EU agenda under the veil of CSDP.

Since its inception, the EDA has been heavily engaged in the long-term definition of future CSDP capabilities, assuming responsibility for the successful completion of the European Capabilities Action Plan process and launching the Capability Development Plan in 2006. The latter, justified under CSDP operations and requirements, involved the identification of shortfalls from the Headline Goal 2010, the development of long-term capability planning and the establishment of a database of existing military programmes by participating Member States (EDA 2006e). A preoccupation with military capabilities and the definition of the long-term capability needs of the EU is a necessary but not sufficient precondition of the long-term benefit of the arms industry. Consider the following words by the former chief executive of the EDA:

> industry needs not just the right orders tomorrow, but a perspective of the future – the best assessment governments can give them of what will matter for military operations in ten years time, or twenty [...] this has not yet been attempted at the European level, and needs to be.
>
> (Witney 2005a)

Defining future military capabilities means defining the future output of arms production. Due to the monopsonistic nature of the arms market, only states can undertake this task; internationalisation necessitates its fulfilment at the EU level.

## 48   *I. Oikonomou*

### *The socio-economic essence of the EDA*

Regardless of the official rhetoric, the EDA was meant to serve the purpose of maintaining a competitive European arms industry, by achieving higher military spending, closer EU armaments cooperation, joint Research and Development (R&D) and market integration. The European Council (2006: 2) had from an early stage acknowledged 'the Agency's efforts to encourage the participating Member States to spend more, spend better, and spend more together on Defence R&T'. The Agency bridged the two key domains of military policy integration, capabilities development and armaments policy, into a single institutionalised process. It also put in place a meeting point of the three major segments of a European armaments policy – R&D, production and procurement (Keohane 2004: 2) – while adding the identification and harmonisation of requirements and capabilities development in general. In other words, the EDA was envisioned as a tool for the long-term synchronisation of the demand and supply of arms production at the EU level.

The reorganisation of capital and production beyond the nation-state, i.e. the process of internationalisation through mergers and acquisitions at the European level, was the necessary precondition for the facilitation of a more coherent armaments cooperation scheme. In 2001, one could read – even in publications funded by the European Commission – that the 'post-Cold War European defence industry rationalisation … has created the need for governments to respond and adapt their policies and laws to the changed nature of the defence industry, as well as support the restructuring process' (Bauer and Winks 2001: 59–60). This reorganisation forced the governments of the arms-producing states to reconsider their military–industrial policies in order to facilitate the interests of a radically restructured social force. The EDA represented the culmination of efforts to coordinate the internal reorganisation of state policies through an EU institutional body. It was an attempt to promote the internationalisation of the state in the face of increased internationalisation of production and the political pressure exercised by military–industrial capital. Industrial consolidation was not only a source of the EDA, but also one of the anticipated end-results of its operations through programmes that would map existing industrial patterns and provide common industrial solutions. Further consolidation of the European arms industry has been one of the long-term aims of the EDA, especially in the land and naval sectors (Witney 2005b). Therefore, politico-economic trends produced a political outcome that would return to, and have an impact on, production.

Budgetary constraints in Europe helped push internationalisation in the armaments sector. The decline in military budgets is also a key to understanding European armaments cooperation in the form of EDA. All cooperative schemes 'have been the response of sovereign national governments to the growing budgetary, industrial and technological pressures they have each faced' (James 2003: 69–70). Cooperation may lead to greater production efficiency, because the participating Member States (pMS) achieve higher production output and consequently a lower cost per unit of military item. The duplication of prime equipment makes little sense in an era where no single national market in Europe is big enough to sustain the global competitiveness of any industry. Technological progress and the need to incorporate it into modern weaponry manufacturing took its toll in terms of rising costs, coupled with the so-called 'revolution in military affairs' which brought about the application of new technologies, advanced communications systems, information technology and space applications, i.e. with products that are costly in development and production.

What about common procurement? Seeing the EDA become the substitute for national procurement agencies was, and still is, a very improbable outcome in the short to medium term. The persistence of the nation-state and its procurement institutions, the national Ministries of Defence (MoDs) and armament directorates, means that such a transformation would have to overcome severe obstacles, the power of the nation-state and the national economic interests that support it being the two primary ones. Nevertheless, turning the EDA into a procurement agency as the final stage of national armaments policy integration has a strong politico-economic rationale. An EU procurement agency would be in a unique position to take advantage of economies of scale in large-scale arms purchasing (Hartley 2001: 3; Cox 1994). Strategically, such a transformation also makes sense, if the EU is serious about the need for CSDP to achieve true inter-operability and autonomy. There can be no better inter-operability than the one brought about by the use of a single type of equipment and there can be no further strategic autonomy than the one offered by an EU-wide concept of security of supply introduced by a single procurement body. Until that stage is reached, the EDA will act as a catalyst for the increase of European collaborative procurement, i.e. for procurement of military equipment agreed by at least two Member States, mainly via the Organisation Conjointe de Coopération en matière d'Armement (OCCAR). Witney (2005b) expressed his vision: 'Maybe in the future we shall do some management ourselves. At present, however, I see our role as complementary to OCCAR's. We should hopefully generate the cooperative programmes that OCCAR might then manage'. Years later, in 2012, the signing of an administrative arrangement between the two organisations signified the materialisation of this very direction (EDA 2012).

Another mission assigned to the EDA was to ensure that the technological and industrial potential of Central and Eastern European states would remain under the control of European arms manufacturers. Despite the collapse of their arms industry in the early 1990s, these states maintained key niche capabilities at the sub-contracting level (Kogan 2005). In addition, the arms procurement capacity of the newcomers is not negligible and offers real opportunities for European manufacturers. Through specialist workshops and networking, the EDA sought to ensure that Small and Medium Enterprises (SMEs) from the new Member States would link their business to large European prime-contractors, thereby minimising the probability for US arms industry to take over these companies (EDA 2006c). This strategy and the contradictions it entails were revealed through the EDA policy paper on EDTIB adopted in May 2007. There, the defence ministers of the pMS complained over 'the slowness of Western European prime contractors to see the new Member States as places to invest, rather than just sell' (EDA 2007: 5). Overall, a common strategy on the new Member States would have been impossible without a prior grouping together of major industrial actors and state preferences.

### The industrial logic of R&T and the early EDA flagship programs

The early steps of EDA in the area of R&T cooperation highlight further the industrial logic that underpinned its making. Hilary Davies (2004: 272) points to at least three reasons why governments choose to cooperate in R&T: (1) increased cost of high-technology equipment; (2) development of interoperability through R&T cooperation; and (3) cross-fertilisation of ideas and rapid review of results. However, these advantages are obstructed by the lack of common requirements and procurement mechanisms at the EU level. In this sense, CSDP, EDA and R&T cooperation form a conceptual totality. In contrast to previous schemes of armaments cooperation, the EDA does not seek simply to bring together the supply side of the industry, but also to integrate both demand and supply. Also, by allowing top-down coordination and the legitimisation of increased expenditure, the EDA provides advantageous terms of reference for R&T activity, allowing Javier Solana (2006) to urge: 'we should spend more, spend better and spend more together'.

The vision of making an EU equivalent to the US Defense Advanced Research Projects Agency (DARPA) fits well in this context, considering the immense impact DARPA has had on US technological superiority. US supremacy in R&T undermined past European collaborative R&T initiatives. For example, the European Technology and Acquisition Programme was launched in 2001 by the Letter of Intent countries, in order to identify and develop capabilities for future aerial combat systems. This effort was severely injured by the decision of the UK and Italy to join the Joint Strike Fighter programme. In 2006, the total expenditure on R&T by EU Member States was only 1.25 per cent of total EU military expenditure, at approximately €2.3 billion a year (EDA 2006f: 3). France and the UK contributed around 75 per cent of it. While their R&D expenditure in terms of percentage of the overall military budget (13 per cent) was close to that of the US (15 per cent), there were vast disparities between the

## The European arms industry and EDA 51

other EU Member States (Keohane 2004: 3). The EDA was seen as an instrument for the encouragement of more and more homogenised research spending by the countries lagging behind. Encouraging collaborative R&T expenditure is also part of the EDA mission; in 2005, only 12.4 per cent of the value of EU military R&T was collaborative (EDA: 2006d). The development of a European strategy for military R&T formally topped the Council's guidelines for the 2006 EDA work. In early 2006, the first ad hoc project to be developed under the auspices of the Agency was announced, on lightweight radar technology, initiated by France and the UK (EDA 2006a).

CSDP capability requirements and industrial preferences may not always coincide; as the former EDA armaments director pointed out, 'we are driven by capability requirements for ESDP, but at the same time industry is seeking products they can sell in an ever increasing global market. Unsurprisingly these desires do not always align' (Magrassi 2006: 10). In this respect, the joint R&T programmes and the flagship projects that the EDA undertook in the early years of its operation deserve some further attention. The programme on force protection had no apparent linkage to any identified capability shortfall. Instead, it served as a political tool for the initiation of joint R&T investment under industrial pressures. A Member State representative recalled that the project came directly from Witney's office, lacking any interface with capabilities (Interview 6). The 2005 flagship programmes had more to do with the need to maintain technological and industrial parity with the US. The Command, Control, Communications Systems (C3) programme focused on the emerging technology of Software-Defined Radio (SDR) in order to initiate European convergence and cooperation in this area (EDA 2005c). CSDP operations do require modern telecommunications equipment but this requirement need not be facilitated through SDR technology made in the EU. As EDA (2005a: 4) noted, the industry was heavily involved in the drafting of the joint EDA/EU Military Staff study that first underlined the significance of this technological area. Competition with the US is the key; the fear of the EDA was that the technical standards would be set by the US, which would then gain the technological-economic advantages that stem from this (Interview 5) as discussed also in detail in Chapter 10 of this volume. This is irrelevant for the effectiveness of CSDP and crucial for the survival of the European military–electronics industry.

The same observation is valid for the Armoured Fighting Vehicle (AFV) programme. Although some level of AFV interoperability is necessary in order to conduct land-based CSDP missions, this is a long way from assuming that such missions require the emergence of a single type of vehicle produced in the EU. The AFV flagship programme was about the consolidation of demand and supply for AFVs in Europe – and the exploration of synergies for a single future vehicle platform – through the identification of common requirements and future cooperation opportunities (EDA

2005a: 5). According to the EDA, 'consolidation of demand for AFVs in Europe is necessary and urgent – for operational, economic and industrial reasons' (EDA 2005b). Fragmentation of demand and supply has been disadvantageous for the European land industry and allowed the intrusion of the European AFV sector by leading US firms, such as General Dynamics. Eventually, five feasibility projects were proposed by the Armaments Directorate, reflecting both a military and an industrial desire, in parallel to the development of an AFV prototype corresponding to the requirements set by the EDA (Magrassi 2006: 10). The industrial desire prevailed over the military one. For example, Greece participated in the programme with its General Army Staff having only an advisory role. The actual participants were the General Directorate for Defence Armaments and Investments, and three Hellenic defence industries, including two private ones (Interview 7).

Unmanned Aerial Vehicles (UAVs) form another critical area for industrial competitiveness combined with CSDP objectives. The market for UAVs is one of the fastest growing arms markets globally and, given that the US already has a leading position in UAV technologies, the EDA project on UAV was by definition geared towards transatlantic duplication (Interview 3). Furthermore, these efforts were matched by a growing interest by the European military–industrial capital in Unmanned Combat Aerial Vehicles (UCAVs), where a consortium led by Dassault and EADS was at the time developing the 'Neuron' project demonstrator.

### Creating a European market for military equipment

The formation of the EDA was inextricably linked to the drive towards a European defence equipment market. Four years before the establishment of the Agency, Burkard Schmitt (2000: 76) suggested that 'the recent wave of industrial restructuring means that the creation of a European defence equipment market is highly topical'. Increased collaboration in areas such as missile and aircraft production does translate into the relative opening-up of the markets of the producing states, because in these cases the home market became the market of all collaborative participants. However, this is still insufficient, given the limited number of national markets involved in any collaborative programme and the limited scope of these projects, usually restricted to the high-technology end of the arms spectrum. Market fragmentation, i.e. demand fragmentation, is the prevailing reality around the EU. According to Witney (quoted in *The Irish Examiner* 2005):

> unless defence industries, which are still in many cases confined to national markets, are able to break out of those markets and enjoy demand on a more continental scale they will find it increasingly difficult to run profitable and internationally competitive businesses.

Ten years later, not much seems to have changed.

The European arms industry and EDA   53

Competition with US firms has been central in this logic. The US market is a uniform one, without the national disparities and market barriers that dominate the EU. Internationalised capital headquartered in Italy can have no assurances of securing market access to, say, the Greek market, but a US firm headquartered in California can expect US preference for US arms industry as a whole. Competition from the US is strengthened by its respective market size. Uniformity in its market characteristics translates into a huge disparity favouring US arms manufacturers. The 'sheer size of the US market creates economies of scale and supports much higher levels of equipment spend and of R&T, which is critical to the long term' (ASD 2005b: 2). Additionally, analysts have pointed to the need to protect European arms companies from being acquired by the more powerful US counterparts (Algieri and Bauer 2003: 5). Lack of access to the US market for European companies has been a parallel factor necessitating the creation of an integrated European market. The majority of European arms manufacturers, with the notable exception of BAE Systems, cannot enter the US market in the way their US counterparts can enter the European market. For certain European companies, back in the formative years of the EDA, it was felt that the Pentagon's doors were constantly closed (Interviews 1, 2). In 2002, US companies accounted for approximately 50 per cent of the European arms market, while European firms accounted for only 3 per cent of the US arms market (Keohane 2002: 13). This imbalance between the two markets favours US military–industrial capital that can take advantage of both the special political relationship enjoyed between the US and many EU Member States, and US market protectionism.

Cost reduction for the industry is another outcome of market integration. In general, a firm can either opt to participate in foreign bids, or stick to its home market. In both cases, the lack of a single market incurs extra costs for capital. In the first case, companies are forced to pay the extra costs incurred by the complexity of national procurement processes and the need to correspond to their specific requirements and become familiar with national legal-procurement systems. In the second case, companies are faced with a home market production output that is smaller than the European market. Staying confined to a home market is no longer a viable option for an internationalised arms manufacturer. Therefore, in both cases the competitiveness of the industry is sub-optimal, if compared to conditions of a single European equipment market. Of course, this is a qualified observation, applying only to large, internationalised industries. Nationally oriented SMEs may exist only through their attachment to a national market and thus benefit enormously from the lack of a pan-European market. It follows that one of the effects – or even an aim – of injecting competition is to accelerate consolidation, through the gradual elimination of smaller firms with a purely national scope of operations, thereby adding to the size of internationalised capital.

## 54   I. Oikonomou

### European military–industrial capital and the EDA

The analysis established that the EDA has had since its establishment a distinct politico-economic function and orientation. As for its conception, there is no doubt that, formally, the EDA was an intergovernmental initiative. However, industrial state actors and the Commission played an instrumental role in pushing ahead with it. As one EU official stated, 'the EDA is a case of an institution which the corporations pushed for, and the governments did it' (Interview 2). Industrial pressure and involvement during the later stages of the establishment of the EDA was extensive. This was nothing new; the arms industry and the European Defence Industry Group (the umbrella organisation of all the national defence industry associations of the Western European Armaments Group nations) in particular persistently advocated the establishment of a European armaments procurement agency in the mid-1990s (Guay 1998: 149). However, it was only after the completion of the wave of internationalisation and the establishment of CSDP in late 1990s that this advocacy yielded results.

First, arms manufacturers were offered a forum to present their views in the Strategic Aerospace Review 21 (STAR 21), published in July 2002. STAR 21 was an analysis of the EU political and regulatory framework of aerospace by a team set up by the Commission's DG Enterprise. The panel, named the European Advisory Group on Aerospace, consisted primarily of corporate leaders from the arms sector, together with members of the Commission. The Chairmen of EADS, BAE Systems, Thales, Finmeccanica, Snecma and Rolls Royce were all members of the Group. Table 3.1 provides a list of the composition of the European Advisory Group on Aerospace.

The Panel recommended the establishment of an armaments agency, 'responsible for a wide range of activities related to acquisition, common research and development, off-the-shelf procurement' (European Commission 2002: 33). In addition, the Report identified several aspects of what should be a coherent approach to CSDP capabilities and military–industrial competitiveness. These included the increase in European military budgets, the harmonisation of military requirements, the planning of arms procurement, the development of large collaborative demonstrator programmes as part of pooling together R&D projects, and the promotion of the Framework Agreement principles of cooperation at the EU level. Finally, STAR 21 called for the establishment of a European defence equipment market and for an increase in the overall spending for arms procurement in the EU (European Commission 2002: 31–32). All proposals were the outcome of an industry-Commission consensus, confirmed by a press release issued jointly by the European Association of Aerospace Industries (AECMA) and the Commission immediately after the publication of STAR 21, as well as by the extensive meetings between arms manufacturers and the Commission a year later (AECMA-European Commission 2002; AECMA 2003).

*Table 3.1* European Advisory Group on Aerospace

| Institution | Name | Position |
|---|---|---|
| *European Commission* | | |
| DG Enterprise | Errki Liikanen | Commissioner |
| DG Research | Philippe Busquin | Commissioner |
| DG Trade | Pascal Lamy | Commissioner |
| DG Transport | Loyola de Palacio | Commissioner |
| DG External Relations | Chris Patten | Commissioner |
| *European Parliament* | | |
| Committee on Industry | Carlos Westendorp y Cabeza | MEP / Chairman |
| Subcommittee on Security and Defence | Karl von Wogau | MEP / Chairman |
| *European Council* | Javier Solana | High Representative for CFSP |
| *Companies* | | |
| SNECMA | Jean-Paul Béchat | Chairman and CEO |
| EADS | Manfred Bischoff | Co-chairman |
| EADS | Jean-Luc Lagardère | Co-chairman |
| BAE Systems | Richard Evans | Chairman |
| Finmeccanica | Alberto Lina | President and CEO |
| Thales | Dennis Ranque | Chairman and CEO |
| Rolls Royce | Ralph Robins | Chairman |

Source: European Commission 2002: 4–5.

The list of experts invited by the Convention's Working Group VIII on Defence highlighted the centrality of European military–industrial capital in the drafting of the 'defence'-related clauses of the EU Constitutional Treaty. Representatives of the national and European armaments establishment – including senior industrialists from EADS and BAE Systems, the President of the European Defence Industries Group (EDIG), and members of national armaments directorates – dominated the list of experts heard by the respective working group (Broek and de Vries 2006: 22; European Convention 2002b: 26). Ten out of the 13 experts held a position related to arms production, MoDs and the military, while no civil society representative was invited. The Vice-President of EADS called for the establishment of a 'European Security and Defence Research Agency', the President of EDIG advocated a 'Common Armaments Agency' and the BAE Systems representative mentioned the importance of CSDP as a precondition of a successful agency (European Convention 2002a: 1–2). Table 3.2 lists the experts invited by the defence-related working group.

Individual companies were particularly visible in their advocacy of the Agency. Their efforts culminated in an open letter to the European press, signed by the CEOs of EADS, BAE Systems and Thales, which invited EU policy-makers to strengthen their efforts in policy and planning coordination. According to the industrialists, the creation of an EU armaments

## 56 *I. Oikonomou*

*Table 3.2* List of experts invited by the European Convention, Working Group VIII

| Name | Institution/Function |
| --- | --- |
| *EU Staff* | |
| Javier Solana | High Representative for CFSP |
| Rainer Schuwirth | Head of EU Military Staff |
| Carlo Cabigiosu | Former KFOR Commander General |
| Alain Le Roy | Special Envoy of the EU in the FYROM |
| Gustav Hagglund | Chairman of the EU Military Committee |
| Christopher Patten | Commissioner for External Affairs |
| *NATO Staff* | |
| Lord Robertson | Secretary-General of NATO |
| *National armaments directorates/defence ministries* | |
| Laurent Giovacchini | DGA, French MoD |
| Peter Lundberg | Swedish Defence Equipment Agency |
| Alain Richard | Former French Minister of Defence |
| *European arms industry* | |
| Corrado Antonini | President of the EDIG |
| Jean-Louis Gergorin | EADS |
| Anthony Parry | BAE Systems |

Source: European Convention 2002b: 26.

agency 'would take on massive strategic importance for the future of the European defence industry' (BAE Systems *et al.* 2003). The executives also called for an increase in national military budgets, juxtaposing the European level of military investment to the US one. Others publicised their vision of an agency with increased supervisory capacity on a common pool of EU R&D resources, bringing together military research and project management (Bühl 2004: 283).

The Aerospace and Defence Industries Association in Europe (ASD) (2005a: 13) provided extensive input in the discussions over the establishment of the Agency through its EU Working Group. Industrial engagement increased during deliberations at the Agency Establishment Team (AET), when it was clear that intergovernmental consensus was about to initiate a novel scheme of armaments cooperation. AET was a small team and lacked a common doctrine, therefore the arms industry found a fertile ground to establish links through ASD and individual companies (Interviews 4, 5). The formal recognition of ASD and European arms manufacturers as the Agency's consulting partners reflected these close links. The Report by the Agency Establishment Team (2004: 55) openly declared that 'the Agency will consult closely with the ... ASD, as well as directly with European companies'.

The European arms industry advocated a particular EDA, not just any armaments agency. A document published in October 2003 by AECMA on behalf of all three constitutive organisations of ASD set out a detailed account of what the missions, programme and institutional structure should be. The missions of the EDA should include the promotion of harmonisation, the monitoring of capability objectives and commitments, the support of defence technology research, the establishment of a common military equipment market and the strengthening of the European defence technological and industrial base. Moreover, the document asked for a senior figure to act as chair of the agency and for the fast setting-up of the agency (AECMA *et al.* 2003). Indeed, the EDA was placed under the aegis of Solana and established swiftly in 2004. Other proposals from that document topped the agenda at a later stage, such as the creation of technological centres of excellence, i.e. the state-sponsored promotion of the particular strengths of individual firms.

*Table 3.3* LeaderSHIP 2015 group members

| Institution | Name | Position |
|---|---|---|
| *European Commission* | | |
| DG Enterprise | Erkki Liikanen | Commissioner |
| DG Research | Philippe Busquin | Commissioner |
| DG Transport | Loyola de Palacio | Commissioner |
| DG Employment | Anna Diamantopoulou | Commissioner |
| DG Enlargement | Günter Verheugen | Commissioner |
| DG Trade | Pascal Lamy | Commissioner |
| DG Competition | Mario Monti | Commissioner |
| *European Parliament* | | |
| European People's Party | Hans-Gert Pöttering | MEP / Chairman |
| Committee on Industry | Carlos Westendorp y Cabeza | MEP / Chairman |
| *Companies* | | |
| Fincantieri | Corrado Antonini | Chairman |
| Alstorn Chantiers de l'Atlantique | Patrick Boissier | Chairman and CEO |
| Damen Shipyards Group | Kommer Damen | President and CEO |
| Kvaerner Masa Yards | Jorna Eloranta | President and CEO |
| ENVC | Manuel Martins Guerreiro | Chairman |
| Blohm & Voss | Reinhard Mehl | Member of the Executive Board |
| Meyer Werft | Bernard Meyer | Managing Director |
| IZAR | Esther Rituerto Martinez | CEO |
| Odense Steel Shipyard | John Skov Hansen | President |
| IHC Caland | Sjef van Dooremalen | President and CEO |
| *Other institutions* | | |
| European Marine Equipment Council | John Young | Chairman |
| European Metalworkers' Federation | Reinhard Kuhlmann | General Secretary |

Source: European Commission 2003: 4–5.

58  *I. Oikonomou*

The naval shipbuilding industry voiced its support for the Agency in 2003 with the LeaderSHIP 2015 Report, drafted by the High-level Advisory Group. The Group brought together Commissioners, Parliamentarians and industrialists, chaired by the then Commissioner for Enterprise Erkki Liikanen. Some industrial members of the Group were active only in civil shipbuilding, as opposed to Strategic Aerospace Review 21 (STAR 21), where all industrial participants were linked to both civil and military production. This can be explained by the limited degree of consolidation and internationalisation of the naval sector. The Group expressed its support for the creation of the Agency and requested the setting up of a joint procurement agency. Lack of international cooperation and consolidation, diverging operational requirements and fragmented markets formed the basis for the Agency's rationale (European Commission 2003: 25–27). Table 3.3 provides an overview of the Group's members.

These panels were not set up for decorative purposes. Through them, the Commission conveyed a sense of urgency and consensus grounded on the voice of experts and showed that it was not alone in calling for policy reform. Arms manufacturers were delighted to be part of these panels, through which they could develop informal links with policy-makers, shape public objectives and promote their own legitimacy. And as it has been shown elsewhere (Oikonomou 2012: 106–108), industrial support for the EDA continued and culminated in the aftermath of its establishment.

## Conclusion

The chapter highlighted theoretically and empirically how the EDA has had a multi-faceted politico-economic function and identity from the start of its operation, driven by the need to safeguard the competitiveness of internationalised military–industrial capital. However, economic necessities do not translate automatically into political developments. Thus, the chapter illuminated the direct and indirect role that the European arms manufacturers played in the shaping of a formally intergovernmental institutional arrangement. Overall, under the veil of capability development for CSDP purposes, the EU succeeded for the first time in its history to introduce armaments as a legitimate element of its mainstream agenda, permanently, through the establishment of the EDA. In other words, the making of the EDA is the story of the translation of a politico-strategic project (CSDP and its capabilities requirements) into a concrete set of economic outcomes, benefiting a concrete social force – the internationalised European arms manufacturers.

Still, one should not view EU armaments policy and the EDA as a linear, mechanistic process. Inter-state divergences have persisted throughout the ten years of the Agency's operations, fuelled by the lack of a single pan-European industrial base. Moreover, it remains doubtful whether European capitalism as a whole can benefit considerably from the potential for accelerated economic expansion that stems from military spending. The relationship between economic development and military investment is probably the most complex topic in military economics and does not have a clear-cut answer. Keith Krause (1995: 14) suggests that reality is somewhere in between the two extremes of armaments investment as a catalyst and as an obstacle to industrial development. Sectors associated with arms production, such as electronics, naval and aerospace engineering, and telecommunications have indeed a dual-use dimension, and may be nurtured by increased military spending. However, this does not mean that the militarisation of economic activity through increases in the investment in armaments production and development has definite economic benefits for all sectors and for all capital fractions. An overt turn towards a war economy may be resisted by the sectors of productive capital that do not benefit from arms production. Given the current crisis of global capitalism and the risks involved in militarisation and the heightening of inter-metropolitan rivalries, such a turn ought to be resisted by European citizens.

## References

AECMA (2003) *Good Progress towards European Aerospace Policies*, Press Release, 11 June 2003.

AECMA and European Commission (2002) *European Advisory Group on Aerospace outlines way forward for industry*, Joint Press Release, Brussels, 16 July 2002.

AECMA, EDIG and Eurospace (2003) *Position Paper: European Armaments, Research and Military Capabilities Agency*, 17 October 2003.

Agency Establishment Team (2004) 'Report by the Agency Establishment Team', in *EU Security and Defence: Core Documents 2004*, Chaillot Paper 75, Paris: Institute for Security Studies: 50–61.

Algieri, F. and Bauer, T. (2003) 'Defining and Securing the EU's Strategic Defence Interests', *EU Reform/Convention Spotlight*, Bertelsmann Foundation – Centre for Applied Policy Research.

ASD (Aerospace and Defence Industries Association in Europe) (2005a) *Annual Review 2004*.

ASD (Aerospace and Defence Industries Association in Europe) (2005b) 'Response to the European Commission's Green Paper on Defence Procurement', Executive Summary, 21 January 2005.

BAE Systems, EADS and Thales (2003) *Time to Act! Joint Declaration of BAE Systems, EADS and Thales*, 28 April 2003.

Bauer, S. and Winks, R. (2001) 'The Institutional Framework for European Arms Policy Co-operation', in C. Serfati (ed.) *The Restructuring of the European Defence Industry: Dynamics of Change*, Brussels: European Commission, DG Research: 55–76.

Bieler, A. (2000) *Globalisation and Enlargement of the European Union: Austrian and Swedish Social Forces in the Struggle over Membership*, London: Routledge.

Brady, H. and Tonra, B. (2005) 'The European Defence Agency: Serious Opportunity, Daunting Challenge', *CFSP Forum*, 3(1): 1–4.

## 60   *I. Oikonomou*

Broek, M. and de Vries, W. (2006) 'The Arms Industry and the Constitution', London: European Network Against Arms Trade.

Bühl, H. (2004) 'Operational Requirements and Industrial Competitiveness', in K. von Wogau (ed.) *The Path to European Defence*, Antwerp: Maklu: 278–283.

Carchedi, G. (2001) *For Another Europe*, London: Verso.

Cox, A. (1994) 'The Future of European Defence Policy: The Case for a Centralised Procurement Agency', *Public Procurement Law Review*, 3: 65–86.

Cox, R.W. (1996) 'Social Forces, States, and World Orders: Beyond International Relations Theory', in R.W. Cox, *Approaches to World Order*, Cambridge: Cambridge University Press: 85–123.

Cox, R.W. (1987) *Production, Power and World Order*, New York: Columbia University Press.

Davies, H. (2004) 'Defence Research and Technology', in K. von Wogau (ed.) *The Path to European Defence*, Antwerp: Maklu: 265–277.

European Commission (2003) 'LeaderSHIP 2015: Defining the Future of the European Shipbuilding and Shiprepair Industry'.

European Commission (2002) 'STAR 21-Strategic Aerospace Review for the 21st Century: Creating a Coherent Market and Policy Framework for a Vital European Industry'.

European Convention (2002a) 'Summary of the Meeting Held on 4 October 2002', CONV 343/02, 14 October 2002.

European Convention (2002b) 'Final Report of Working Group VIII-Defence', CONV 461/02, 16 December 2002.

European Council (2006) 'European Defence Agency: Council Guidelines for the EDA's Work in 2007', 15184/06, 13 November 2006.

EDA (European Defence Agency) (2012) 'EDA and OCCAR Build Links, Seeking Efficiencies through Cooperation', 27 July 2012.

EDA (European Defence Agency) (2007) 'A Strategy for the European Defence Technological and Industrial Base', 14 May 2007.

EDA (European Defence Agency) (2006a) 'UK–French Initiative on Lightweight Radar Breaks Important New Ground for Defence R&T, EDA says', 24 January 2006.

EDA (European Defence Agency) (2006b) 'Characteristics of a strong future European DTIB', 20 September 2006.

EDA (European Defence Agency) (2006c) 'EDA Hosts Workshop to Help New Member States Benefit from European Defence Equipment Market', 26 October 2006.

EDA (European Defence Agency) (2006d) 'European Defence Expenditure in 2005', 20 November 2006

EDA (European Defence Agency) (2006e) 'EU Governments Launch New Plan to Build Defence Capabilities for Future ESDP Operations', 14 December 2006.

EDA (European Defence Agency) (2006f) 'EDA Bulletin, Issue 2'.

EDA (European Defence Agency) (2005a) 'Report by the Head of the European Defence Agency to the Council', 8967/05, 17 May 2005.

EDA (European Defence Agency) (2005b) 'Steering Board Conclusions on Armoured Fighting Vehicles', 23 May 2005.

EDA (European Defence Agency) (2005c) 'Steering Board sets Direction for Agency's Efforts to Build European Defence Capabilities', 21 June 2005.

Gill, S. (1993) 'Epistemology, Ontology and the "Italian School"', in S. Gill (ed.)

*The European arms industry and EDA*   61

*Gramsci, Historical Materialism and International Relations*, Cambridge: Cambridge University Press: 21–48.

Gill, S. and Law, D. (1988) *The Global Political Economy: Perspectives, Problems and Policies*, London: Harvester & Wheatsheaf.

Guay, T. (1998) *At Arm's Length: The European Union and Europe's Defence Industry*, Basingstoke: Macmillan Press.

Hartley, K. (2001) *The Common European Security and Defence Policy: An Economic Perspective*, UK: House of Lords.

Irish Examiner (2005) 'European Arms Industry to be Opened up to Competition', 21 November 2005.

James, A.D. (2003) 'European Armaments Cooperation: Lessons for a Future European Armaments Agency', *The International Spectator*, 38(4): 59–74.

Keohane, D. (2004) *Europe's New Defence Agency*, CER Policy Brief, London: Centre for European Reform.

Keohane, D. (2002) *The EU and Armaments Co-operation*, London: Center for European Reform.

Kogan, E. (2005) *EU Enlargement and its Consequences for Europe's Defence Industries and Markets*, Paper 40, Bonn International Centre for Conversion.

Krause, K. (1995) *Arms and the State: Patterns of Military Production and Trade*, Cambridge: Cambridge University Press.

Magrassi, C. (2006) 'Interview with Carlo Magrassi', *EDA Bulletin*, 2: 10.

Mandel, E. (1978) *Late Capitalism*, London: Verso.

Oikonomou, I. (2012) 'The European Defence Agency and EU Military Space Policy: Whose Space Odyssey?', *Space Policy*, 28(2): 102–109.

Oikonomou, I. (2008) 'The Internationalisation of the European Arms Industry: Trends and Implications', *Agora Without Frontiers*, 13(4): 362–375.

Poulantzas, N. (1975) *Classes in Contemporary Capitalism*, London: New Left Books.

Schmitt, B. (2000) *From Cooperation to Integration: Defence and Aerospace Industries in Europe*, Chaillot Paper 40, Paris: EU Institute for Security Studies.

Solana, J. (2006) *Keynote Speech at the Research and Technology Conference*, Brussels, 9 February 2006.

Solana, J. (2004) *Summary of the remarks made by Javier Solana, EU High Representative for the CFSP, at the meeting of EU defence ministers*, Brussels, 17 May 2004.

van Apeldoorn, B. (2002) *Transnational Capitalism and the Struggle over European Integration*, London: Routledge.

Witney, N. (2005a) *Bridging the Gap between European Strategy and Capabilities*, Speech at the NDA – Bibliothèque Solvay, Brussels, 12 October 2005.

Witney, N. (2005b) 'Interview with Nick Witney', *NATO Review* (Spring 2005).

## Interviews

Interview 1 with European arms industry executive officer, 29 August 2005

Interview 2 with European arms industry executive officer, 31 August 2005.

Interview 3 with US arms industry executive officer, 14 October 2005.

Interview 4 with European arms industry executive officer, 9 November 2005.

Interview 5 with armaments official, 6 December 2005.

Interview 6 with armaments official, 8 March 2007.

Interview 7 with defence expert, 15 March 2007.

# Part II
# The EDA in action

# 4 EU military capability development and the EDA

## Ideas, interests and institutions

*Alistair J.K. Shepherd*

## Introduction

Capabilities matter. If the European Union (EU) is to live up to its ambition 'to assume increased responsibilities in the maintenance of international peace and security' (Council of the EU 2012: 1), then capabilities, especially military capabilities, are vital. The need for reformed and improved armed forces was a fundamental rationale for the launch of the EU's Common Security and Defence Policy (CSDP) in 1999 and the establishment of the European Defence Agency (EDA) in 2004.

The EDA was set up to 'to support the Member States and the Council in their effort to improve European defence capabilities in the field of crisis management and to sustain the European Security and Defence Policy' (Council of the EU 2004). This has been a significant challenge. The 27 EU Member States that participate in CSDP and the EDA (Denmark having an opt-out of CSDP) have an impressive array of military capabilities and, combined, spend close to €200 billion on defence annually. Hence, the EU as whole has the potential to be one of the leading military actors on the international stage. Nevertheless, the EU and its Member States have also struggled to overcome a number of significant problems that have prevented them from addressing the capability gaps (shortfalls) that prompted the launch of CSDP in 1999. Therefore, 15 years after the launch of CSDP and ten years since the EDA was established, the EU as a whole is still struggling to avail itself of the military capabilities required to undertake the full range of missions it has set itself and to fulfil its ambition to be a 'strategic global actor' and 'security provider'. What is particularly worrying for the EU is that even with the pressures of deep budget cuts, increasing demand for the deployment of armed forces and the American 'pivot' to Asia, there is still only limited evidence of the coordination and cooperation so desired by the EU in the field of military capability development.

This chapter will trace and critically analyse the definitions and development of EU military capabilities since CSDP's launch in 1999 and, in particular, since the establishment of the EDA. It will do so in a three part structure woven together by (1) the idea of the EU as a military actor; (2) the interests of the Member States; and (3) the institutions that shape CSDP. The first section briefly examines CSDP's formative phase, 1999–2004, which saw the establishment of the overarching capability framework (the Helsinki Headline Goal) and the launch of the first CSDP operations. The second section, 2004–2009, analyses efforts to consolidate and revitalise EU capability development through the setting up of the EDA, the launch of a new Headline Goal 2010, including EU Battlegroups, and the 2008 French Presidency. The final section, 2009–2014, explores the various capability programmes and projects the EDA has established as well as the tensions between the parallel initiatives of the Treaty of Lisbon (ToL) to enhance capability development through the EDA, and the decentralised moves to enhance capabilities outside the CSDP framework. The principal problem confronting EU military capability development are the tensions between the ideas, interests and institutions working in and across the EU.

## Formation: ideas, identities and interests in CSDP's military capabilities, 1999–2004

At St. Malo in December 1998 the United Kingdom (UK) and France declared that the EU 'must have the capacity for autonomous action, backed by credible military forces, the means to use them, and a readiness to do so' (*Joint Declaration on European Defence* 1998: para. 2). This declaration launched what became the CSDP and with it a plethora of military capability initiatives aimed at reforming the militaries of the EU Member States. The objective of CSDP was to make the military capabilities of EU Member States more deployable and sustainable and better suited to expeditionary crisis management operations.

### Ideas, identities and interests

This rationale was influenced by the ideas, identities and interests of the EU and its Member States. In particular, it was driven by the EU's failure to prevent the violent disintegration of Yugoslavia: 'our experience of the consequences of conflict has been instrumental in the development of civilian and military crisis management capabilities' (Council of the EU 2004: 4). That the EU had proclaimed the Yugoslav crisis as the 'hour of Europe' significantly damaged EU interests and its reputation as a credible foreign and security policy actor. As contingency planning for military action in Kosovo began in late 1998 it became apparent to UK Prime Minister Tony Blair and French President Jacques Chirac that European states did not have the military capabilities to ensure security even in its own backyard. The missing element of the EU's Common Foreign and Security Policy (CFSP) was seen to be the credible threat or use of force:

'diplomatic action, if necessary, needed to be backed up by military action' (Brok 1999).

The rationale for EU military capabilities was also shaped by the idea of humanitarian intervention. During Operation Allied Force, Tony Blair (1999) made an explicit case for intervention based on the belief that:

> the principle of non-interference must be qualified in important respects. Acts of genocide can never be a purely internal matter. When oppression produces massive flows of refugees which unsettle neighbouring countries then they can properly be described as 'threats to international peace and security'.

As Howorth (2007: 54) argues this resonated with the EU, which was keen to 'write the new normative rules' of crisis management. After all CFSP's objectives included: 'to preserve peace and strengthen international security' (Treaty on European Union 1992).

The EU also increasingly promoted the idea that it had a responsibility for international security: 'Europe should be ready to share in the responsibility for global security and in building a better world' (Council of the EU 2003a). It went on to claim that 'the European Union is particularly well equipped to respond to multi-faceted situations', highlighting that the military would complement political, diplomatic, economic and financial instruments. This was apparent in the European Security Strategy's (ESS) emphasis on 'preventative engagement' through a 'mix of civilian and military instruments' (Council of the EU 2003a). The ESS Implementation Report of 2008 went further; asserting that there is a 'distinctive European approach to foreign and security policy' (Council of the EU 2008a). This approach draws on ideas of a civilian (Duchêne 1972; Whitman 1998) or normative (Manners 2002, 2006) power, pursuing milieu goals rather than possession goals (Wolfers 1962). Hence, the ideas of humanitarian intervention, responsibility and distinctiveness have shaped the EU military capability debate.

Finally, the role of interests is clearly illustrated in the British and French approaches to CSDP and military capabilities. In calling for the EU to have credible military capabilities at St. Malo in December 1998 the UK and France were learning the same lessons from the Yugoslav wars but were driven by different interests. The UK government's support for an EU military capability – a significant change in policy – was driven by its interest in making Europe a more credible partner for the US. Conversely, the interest for France was to make Europe more autonomous from the US. This compromise and ambiguity has continued to shape efforts to overcome EU military capability gaps, both inside and outside of the EDA.

## 68   A.J.K. Shepherd

*Launching CSDP and framing EU military capabilities*

The EU responded quickly to the 1998 St Malo Declaration, agreeing at the Cologne European Council in June 1999 to set up the CSDP (originally called the European Security and Defence Policy (ESDP)), linking it explicitly to the Petersberg tasks: 'Humanitarian and rescue tasks; peace-keeping tasks and tasks of combat forces in crisis management, including peace-making' (Treaty of Amsterdam 1997). The Cologne European Council also proposed the new institutional structures for CSDP: a Political and Security Committee (COPS), an EU Military Committee (EUMC) and an EU Military Staff (EUMS) (European Council 1999a).

The December 1999 Helsinki European Council approved these new structures and put forward the Helsinki Headline Goal (HHG), which continues to provide the overall framework for military capability development. Drawing on the North Atlantic Treaty Organisation's (NATO) peacekeeping missions in the Former Yugoslavia, the HHG declared that the 'member states must be able, by 2003, to deploy within 60 days and sustain for at least one year military forces up to 50,000–60,000 persons capable of the full range of Petersberg tasks' (European Council 1999b). These 60,000 troops were to be supported by the required command and control, intelligence, logistics, combat support, and air and naval assets. It is against this, and subsequent complementary objectives, that the EU's and EDA's efforts to develop the appropriate military capabilities must be judged.

The first step towards meeting the HHG was the November 2000 Capability Commitment Conference, which resulted in EU Member States pledging 100,000 troops, 400 aircraft and 100 ships. This exceeded the HHG; yet to sustain 60,000 troops in theatre for at least a year requires approximately 180,000 personnel. A year later, the Capability Improvement Conference cross-referenced the HHG Catalogue, which detailed CSDP's operational requirements, with the Force Catalogue, which listed the commitments made, concluding that 104 of 144 capabilities had been 'filled', leaving 'just' 40 capability shortfalls. However, of those 40 shortfalls 21 were deemed 'significant' as they included assets vital for undertaking the Petersberg Tasks: force protection; logistics; naval aviation; Precision-Guided Munitions (PGMs); wide-bodied transport aircraft; roll-on/roll-off ships; deployable communications; and ISTAR (Intelligence, Surveillance, Target Acquisition and Reconnaissance). There were also significant qualitative shortfalls in terms of the availability, mobility and flexibility of forces. It is these military capability shortfalls that the EDA was set up to address three years later in 2004.

In the intervening period, the EU established the European Capability Action Plan (ECAP) to address these shortfalls. The ECAP set up groups of national experts to explore options across 19 capability areas from April 2002 to March 2003. At the May 2003 Capability Conference, ten project groups, each headed by a lead nation, were established to develop concrete solutions to rectify the shortfalls; eight of these were later transferred to the EDA when it was established in 2004. Despite the HHG, the capability conferences and the ECAP, improvement in military capabilities was negligible. The 2002 Capability Improvement Chart showed that of the 64 capabilities identified capability gaps, seven had been 'solved' and four improved, leaving 53 unchanged. By 2006, just one additional gap had been 'solved'. Indeed, progress was so poor that the EU stopped making the capability improvement charts publically available.

Despite the continuing and significant capability gaps, the December 2001 Laeken European Council declared an initial operational capability for CSDP. Eighteen months later, in May 2003, it was announced that 'the EU now has operational capability across the full range of Petersberg tasks', while acknowledging that this capability remained 'limited and constrained by recognised shortfalls' (Council of the EU 2003a). Nor did the shortfalls prevent CSDP becoming operational in 2003, with missions in Bosnia and Hercegovina, the Former Yugoslav Republic of Macedonia (FYROM) and the Democratic Republic of the Congo (DRC). While the first two EU military missions, in FYROM and the DRC, received some criticism, they did fulfil their mandates and were significant for EU military capability development. In particular, operation Artemis in the DRC demonstrated the EU's ability to autonomously respond to UN requests for assistance and find temporary solutions to some of its capability gaps. It also heralded a symbolic shift away from the EU's traditional civilian power identity. Finally, 2003 also saw the Franco-British Le Touquet summit call for an EU 'defence capabilities development and acquisition agency' whose role would be to encourage EU Member States to enhance their military capabilities (*Declaration on Strengthening European Cooperation in Security and Defence* 2003). This call was swiftly endorsed by all EU leaders at the June 2003 Thessaloniki European Council, and in July 2004 the EDA was launched.

This formative phase of CSDP from 1999 to 2003 was fundamental in establishing the EU's military capability ambitions and, therefore, the objectives of the soon to be launched EDA. With the HHG unfulfilled by the original target of 2003 a major effort to revitalise military capability development programme began in 2004, to which the EDA was central.

## Revitalisation? Military capability development under the EDA, 2004–2009

2004 was a significant year for efforts to re-energise and refocus efforts to enhance the military capabilities of EU Member States. At the heart of these efforts was the June 2004 Headline Goal 2010 (HG2010), which included: the EU Battlegroup concept, an EU civil–military planning cell, renewed calls for improved strategic lift (air, land and sea), the availability of an aircraft carrier and its air wing and escort, improved communications, quantitative benchmarks for deployability and multinational training, and the establishment of the EDA (European Council 2004).

The military capabilities of which the EDA was to help coordinate the development were reiterated and repackaged in the 2004 British–French–German 'food for thought paper' on developing EU Battlegroups (EU Institute for Security Studies 2005: 10–16). Both the Le Touquet summit and the lessons of Operation *Artemis* influenced this paper. The Battlegroups were to be 1,500 strong battalion sized units, deployable within 5–10 days and sustainable for 30 days, possibly extending to 120 days (European Council 2004). Two of these national or multinational Battlegroups were to be on standby in any six-month period to undertake the full range of Petersberg tasks (Lindstrom 2007). With the introduction of Battlegroups interoperability and availability of personnel become even more important. Ensuring interoperability is a difficult task and it is one where the EDA has a crucial coordinating role to play across all areas from weapons to communications. Equally, ensuring availability of military personnel is problematic, with only 30 per cent of European military personnel able to operate outside their national territory (Whitney 2008: 22). It is imperative that national armed forces are structured, trained and authorised for rapid deployment on overseas conflict management operations. The Battlegroups became operational in 2007 but, embarrassingly for the EU, have yet to be deployed.

The EDA was established by the Council Joint Action of 12 July 2004 to support 'the member states in their efforts to improve the EU's defence capabilities in the field of crisis management and to sustain the ESDP as it stands now and develops in the future' (Council of the EU 2004: Art. 2.1). The four core tasks of the EDA are: (1) developing defence capabilities; (2) promoting armaments cooperation; (3) promoting defence research and technology; and (4) creating a competitive defence equipment market and strengthening the European defence technological and industrial base. Each of these areas had, until 2014, its own directorate. In the domain of military capability development the 2004 Joint Action laid out six key roles for the EDA: (i) identifying future defence capability requirements; (ii) coordinating the implementation of the ECAP; (iii) scrutinising, assessing and evaluating the capability commitments of the Member States; (iv) promoting and coordinating harmonisation of military requirements; (v) identifying and proposing collaborative activities; and (vi) providing appraisals on financial priorities for capabilities development and acquisition (Council of the EU 2004: Art. 5).

The EDA is a small organisation with 120 staff headed by the High Representative for CFSP, who chairs the Steering board made up of the 27 EU Defence Ministers. This gave the EDA the potential to provide the much needed political leadership to push forward military capability development. However, with decision-making retained by the Member States the

EDA has a difficult job to 'convince Member States to harmonise requirements, to agree on specific solutions for specific commonly identified shortfalls, and ideally sign up to multinational programmes, which the Agency can then manage on their behalf' (Biscop and Coelmont 2010: 63). In particular the EDA has struggled to reconcile the tensions between being a European agency with responsibility for identifying, assessing, coordinating and promoting capability developments among its Member States and being an intergovernmental organisation run by those very same countries.

The dominance of the Member States has also led to the EDA being hampered by the Europeanist–Atlanticist divide in European security (Bátora 2009). Both the EU and NATO have sought to transform and improve the military capabilities of European Member States. While there are formal arrangements for cooperation and coordination, such as the EU-NATO Capability Group, the deeper tensions between a NATO- or EU-centric defence capability processes remain, e.g. between the EU's 'Pooling and Sharing' (P&S) and NATO's 'Smart Defence' initiatives. Finally, the intergovernmental nature of the EDA has created problems for the EDA's budget. Already relatively small at €31.6 million in 2014, the EDA's annual budget has been frozen since 2010 when the UK government vetoed a move from an annual budget to a three-year budgetary framework and a 3.8 per cent rise in the EDA's budget (House of Commons 2013; Hennessy 2010). Meanwhile, the nature of armaments policy in the EU, with each Member State wanting to support its own national defence industrial base, is leading to duplication of projects (e.g. for Armoured Fighting Vehicles (AFVs)) and limiting cooperation and coordination of force transformation.

When it was launched, the EDA took over eight of the ECAP projects, however within a year the EDA had reduced its focus to four key capability areas: (1) command, control and communications (C3); (2) strategic airlift; (3) aerial refuelling; and (4) AFVs (Biscop and Coelmont 2010: 63). In addition, the EDA carried out a number of specific studies ranging from software-defined radio to unmanned aerial vehicles and helicopter transport. In fulfilling its remit to identify future defence capability requirements in October 2006 the EDA published its Long-Term Vision for European Defence Capability (LTV). This study provided an overview of the global trends (geopolitical, demographic, economic, technological and military) and outlined the principal challenges for defence (changing role of force and the technological revolution) and CSDP operations (expeditionary, multinational multi-instrument) through to 2030 (EDA 2006a: 6–13). The implications for EU military capability needs strongly reflected CSDP's well-rehearsed shortfalls. The LTV highlighted four principal force characteristics that needed attention within the EU: synergy, agility, selectivity and sustainability (EDA 2006a: 16–19).

Synergy related to joint forces spanning land, air, space and maritime components, but also across a range of new force elements such as UAVs,

C3, precision weapons and stealth, and working with, and drawing on, the capabilities of other actors such as non-governmental organisations and the media. In the realm of agility the LTV emphasised the need for genuine rapid reaction, for tailorable force packages, and deployability. Under the heading of selectivity the EDA stressed the need for the EU 'to be able to graduate and vary the application of force as necessary, and in accordance with legal and political constraints' (EDA 2006a: 18). Specifically, this would mean being able to select the appropriate kinetic and non-kinetic means to generate the required effects. Finally, in the area of sustainability, the focus was on ensuring the access of European forces to the theatre of operation and/or needed facilities, especially logistical support. These characteristics were then translated into the EDAs six Capability domains: command, inform, engage, protect, deploy and sustain (EDA 2006a: 25–28).

In late 2006, building on the LTV, the EDA was tasked to develop a Capability Development Plan (CDP) to provide a systematic, specific and structured approach to EU military capability development and assist Member States in developing national plans (EDA 2006b). The CDP is the overall strategic tool for the EDA and it shapes all the work in the Agency, structured around four key components: establishing the baseline of shortfalls and their priority from HG2010, developing the LTV capability guidance, establishing a database of Member States defence plans and programmes and collecting lessons for future capability development from military operations (EDA 2006b: 2). The CDP was finished 18 months later and endorsed by the Member States in July 2008.

It was made very clear that the CDP 'is not a supranational military equipment or capability plan which aims to replace national defence plans and programmes'; rather it 'is an attempt to address the well documented fragmentation in demand for European military capabilities' and provide 'the picture all member states need to take into account when planning future capability agendas' (EDA 2008a). The key conclusions were the importance of intelligence and information-sharing, flexible and agile responses to a broad range of threats, coordinated inter-agency structures to support the comprehensive approach and recruiting talented and well-qualified personnel for the military. More specifically, the EDA's Steering Board selected 12 capabilities requiring specific action: counter-MANPADs (Man Portable Air Defence Systems); computer network operations; mine counter-measures in littoral sea areas; military implications of the comprehensive approach; human intelligence and training; ISTAR; medical support; Chemical, Biological, Radiological and Nuclear (CBRN) defence; third-party logistics support; Counter-Improvised Explosive Device (C-IED); helicopter availability; and Network Enabled Capability (NEC) (EDA 2008b: 3).

Despite the establishment of the EDA and the approval of the CDP it was clear that improvements in military capabilities across the EU were still hampered by a lack of political will. In 2008 the French Presidency tried to 're-launch European defence', culminating in the December Declaration on Strengthening Capabilities. In addition to reiterating the need to be able to deploy 60,000 troops in 60 days, it outlined more precisely the range of CSDP operations envisaged. In the field of military capabilities, initiatives for force projection, information gathering and space-based intelligence, force protection and effectiveness, and interoperability were launched (Council of the EU 2008a). In renewing support for the EDA, the Declaration again raised the need to explore pooling, specialisation and cost sharing – themes studied in detail in Chapter 11. The French Presidency had also hoped to produce a revised ESS; however, it became clear very quickly that it would be almost impossible to get all Member States to agree a new strategy. Instead, an Implementation Report on the ESS was produced, which, unsurprisingly, stressed the ESS remained work in progress. In terms of military capabilities the report was clear; the EU still needed to be 'more capable, more coherent, and more active ... particularly over key capabilities such as strategic airlift, helicopters, space assets and maritime surveillance (Council of the EU 2008b).

By the start of 2009 the EDA had established itself as the principal forum for discussing military capability development within Europe. It had outlined clearly and concisely the long term capability needs for CSDP through the LTV and CDP. Yet, the EDA was still undermined by the Atlanticist and Europeanist divisions on defence, continuing stalemate over its budget and lack of political will among its Member States to invest collaboratively (if at all) in defence capabilities. In the period 2009–2014 these difficulties were, despite the entry into force of the Treaty of Lisbon (ToL) in December 2009, exacerbated by the global financial crisis and its impact on defence budgets and a move by several Member States to pursue capability development outside of the EDA framework.

## Progress and tensions: capability development in an age of austerity, 2009–2014

### The Lisbon Treaty and capability development

Within the EU 2009 was dominated by the escalating financial crisis and the ToL coming into force, which had the potential to significantly enhance the EU's international role through the dual hatting of the High Representative of the Union for Foreign Affairs and Security Policy and Vice-President of the Commission (HR/VP) and the establishment of the European External Action Service (EEAS). However, for CSDP specifically the ToL was perhaps less significant, as it merely rubber stamped previous developments (e.g. the Solidarity Clause) or formalised already agreed processes (e.g. small groups undertaking operations). Even the Mutual Assistance clause was relatively insignificant as it was caveated by stressing the primacy of NATO for collective defence and 'not prejudicing the specific character of defence policy of certain Member States' (i.e. neutrality). For the EDA the ToL was symbolically significant, bringing it into the EU treaties as a formal EU agency, but practically it made no difference to its roles, tools or objectives.

One aspect of the ToL which raised considerable expectations for revitalising military capability development was that 'member states whose military capabilities fulfil higher criteria and which have made more binding commitments to one another in this area with a view to the most demanding missions shall establish permanent structured cooperation within the Union framework' (Treaty of Lisbon 2007: Art. 42.6). Permanent Structured Cooperation (PESCO) was to allow a group of willing and able states to voluntarily integrate further to enhance their military capabilities, even if other states did not wish to do so. It was envisioned that the EDA would play a crucial role within PESCO through monitoring the performance of the participating Member States in meeting their commitments. Specifically, PESCO outlined five objectives: (1) to approve the level of investment in defence equipment; (2) to harmonise the identification of their military needs through pooling and specialisation where appropriate; (3) to enhance forces availability, interoperability, flexibility and deployability; (4) to address the capability shortfalls identified in the Capability Development Mechanism (CDM); and (5) to take part, where appropriate, in the EDA equipment programmes (Treaty of Lisbon 2007: Protocol No. 10).

However, despite a number of meetings on PESCO through 2010 the hopes that it would reinvigorate capability development were quickly dashed as it was overtaken by the Ghent Initiative and subsequently a number of other bi- and multi-lateral initiatives to enhance military capabilities and by the EDA's push for P&S (see Chapter 11 of this volume). This also meant that a potentially crucial role of the EDA has not, so far, been operationalised.

### Revising the CDP: advances and stagnation in EDA capability development

Within the EU, there is a political struggle over what forum military cooperation should take place in, with role of the EDA at the centre. Once again the views of France and the UK differ greatly. In the UK some senior members of the government advocated withdrawing from the EDA altogether, while French officials continued to support the EDA despite their (and many other states) protectionist policies toward their defence industry. Despite the tensions, the EDA has continued to try and stimulate and coordinate military capability development amongst its Member States. The EDA's main focus of activity through 2010 was updating the CDP, which was endorsed by the Member States in March 2011. They also agreed three sets of 'prioritised actions' informed by short-, medium- and long-term perspectives. The short term (2010–2015) elements derive from the HG2010, the progress catalogue and lessons learned from CSDP operations. The medium term (2016–2024) components draw on the EDA database of ongoing and planned projects and their impact of on capability requirements (EDA 2012a). Finally, the long term factors are taken from the LTV and the EDA's Future Trends analysis which aim to provide a comprehensive analysis for trends beyond 2025 (EDA 2008c, 2012a).

The first group of prioritised actions are the 'CDP Top 10 Priorities', consisting of: C-IED; Medical Support; Intelligence, Surveillance and Reconnaissance; Increased Availability of Helicopters; Cyber Defence; Multinational Logistic Support; CSDP Information Exchange; Strategic and Tactical Airlift Management; Fuel and Energy; Mobility Assurance (EDA 2012a). These ten priority areas reflect many of the CSDP's original military capability shortfalls, as well as the emerging capability trends such as cyber security mentioned in the ESS Implementation Report and the 2010 Internal Security Strategy (Council of the EU 2010). The second group of actions consists of 'Maturing/Mature Actions' where the EDA believes considerable progress has been made: Maritime Mine counter measures; CBRN defence; MANPADs; military human intelligence (EDA 2012a). The final group of actions are known within the EDA as 'Core Drivers/Environments', which relate to cross-cutting capabilities that provide the 'backbone' to CSDP improvement. These areas are: NECs; Radio Spectrum Management; space, and the single European Sky initiative; the Comprehensive Approach (EDA 2012a).

Aside from developing and then revising the CDP the EDA has been trying to simulate actual collaborative capability development. They have launched and completed a number of studies but have not yet been able to contract actual projects in many capability areas. In particular, the EDA has struggled to convince Member States to commit to large-scale expensive capability areas (Biscop and Coelmont 2010: 63). One such capability area is force projection, in particular strategic airlift and air-to-air refuelling (AAR). Strategic airlift has been a fundamental capability shortfall since the launch of CSDP. It was partially, and temporarily, alleviated through a 2006 NATO-led initiative, the Strategic Airlift Interim Solution in which 15 EU Member States (plus Canada and Norway) agreed a renewable contract to charter Russian and Ukrainian Antonov AN124–100 transport aircraft; two on a permanent basis, two more on six days' notice and a further two at nine days' notice (NATO 2006). However, the longer term solution, the A400M, has been mired by delays, technical problems and cost overruns of approximately €7.6 billion (Mawdsley 2013). Several countries, and even Airbus at one point, contemplated scaling down, pulling out of, or scrapping the programme. While the project was reconfirmed in late 2010, the delays meant the delivery date for the first aircraft slipped from 2009 to 2013, with the French Air Force being the first to take delivery in late 2013. However, several states will not be taking deliveries until the second half of the decade. The EDA's main role in this field has been to explore ways to improve military airlift availability among participating Member States (pMS) through better use of current and future assets. This has been pursued through the European Air Transport Fleet (EATF) project, which was set up in February 2008 and resulted in a Letter of Intent (LoI) being signed by 14 states in November 2009 (EDA 2011). In 2012, the EDA ran the first European Air Transport Training exercise to improve interoperability between tactical airlift. However, so far the EDA's role in strategic airlift has been limited to the EATF.

Another strategic capability shortfall is AAR. The EU Member States significant capability shortfall was reiterated during the 2011 Libya operation where the US flew 80 per cent of AAR sorties. The lack of sufficient capability is exacerbated by fragmentation in European AAR capability, with ten different types of aircraft making up the 42 tanker aircraft. Partly driven by the Libya experience, in November 2011 the EDA endorsed AAR as one of 11 P&S initiatives. The EDA's approach to AAR is fourfold: first, to fill the short-term gap through leasing existing platforms or commercial providers, but neither has been taken up; second, to optimise the use of existing capabilities and organisations, specifically through technical and operational clearances to enhance interoperability; third, the EDA has suggested increasing the A400M fleet AAR capability by acquiring additional refuelling kits but, again, no states have yet expressed an interest in this approach; finally, and most significantly, the EDA has sought to increase the strategic multirole tanker transport capability by 2020. Here there is progress with ten Member States, led by the Netherlands, signing a LoI to consider collaboratively acquiring new multirole aircraft with an initial operational capability by 2020. AAR was one of four key capability programmes endorsed at the December 2013 European Council. Ensuring the success of this initiative is crucial as the upgrading of the relatively small and aging AAR capability across the EU is urgent (EDA 2013a).

Another important element in deployability and force projection that the EDA has focused on is the availability of helicopters, running training courses, improving technical interoperability, and undertaking operational test and evaluation for the NH90 transport helicopter. By the end of 2013 149 helicopters, 279 crews and over 8,850 personnel had participated in six live exercises and over 1,000 aircrew from 18 Member States had participated in EDA training courses (Council of the EU 2013: 3). Finally, the EDA runs a future transport helicopter programme, which might see the development of a new European platform.

A second key area of focus for the EDA has been force protection. This activity encompasses the C-IED, counter-MANPADs, Maritime Mine counter measures and CBRN defence projects. The C-IED, a top ten priority capability, has seen considerable success with the procurement and deployment of a C-IED Theatre Exploitation Laboratory. This laboratory allows participating Member States to forensically analyse IED incidents and exploit that information to help identify the IED chain (EDA 2012b) and it has been deployed to Afghanistan since August 2011 as a key component of ISAF's counter-IED strategy. In the other force protection projects the EDA has initiated and completed studies examining national activities and requirements, but they have not yet resulted in any firm contracts for new capabilities. Force protection is of real importance given the increasingly hostile environments CSDP operations may face (e.g. the 2014 Central African Republic mission). An initiative related to force protection and a top ten priority for the EDA, is medical support, which has seen some genuine progress through the Multinational Modular Medical Unit. This 16 Member States project, led by Italy, will provide a flexible field hospital with advanced equipment, staffed by highly trained medical personnel, and aims to reach an initial operational capability in 2015 (Council of the EU 2013: 3).

The third key area of EDA focus is information and communications, specifically NECs which are described as a backbone of CSDP development. In this field EDA projects include the European Satellite Communications Procurement Cell (ESCPC), Maritime Surveillance (MARSUR) and the Multinational Space-based Imaging System (MUSIS). The central objective is information superiority, which is essential to current and future military operations. The ESCPC focuses on pooling the procurement of commercial satellite communication capacity to reduce costs, increase access and improve connectivity (EDA 2012c). The framework contract was signed in September 2012 and is one of the first EDA projects to provide a tangible product towards improving EU military capabilities through the provision of wireless communications between headquarters and theatres of operation. The 2013 European Council also proposed that the EDA, alongside the Commission and the European Space Agency (ESA), start making preparations for the next generation of Governmental Satellite Communication (GOVSATCOM) (European Council 2013: 6) as the current satellites come to the end of their operational lives between 2018 and 2025. The project also aims to overcome the current fragmentation of this capability with five national constellations comprising 12 satellites (High Representative 2013).

The EDA has also made progress in developing MARSUR with 18 pMS signing a Technical Arrangement in October 2012 and having a fully operational network of existing maritime surveillance capabilities going live in 2013 (Council of EU 2013: 4; EDA 2012d). The MUSIS is a longer term project to ensure the continuation of space-based imaging capabilities for defence and security beyond the current systems such as HELIOS, SAR-Lupe and Cosmo-SkyMed. The EDA liaises on behalf of the seven pMS with the Commission and the ESA (Council of the EU 2009: 6). A final EDA project that could fit under the category of information and communications is cyber-defence, which was also highlighted at the December

2013 European Council. A one-year EDA study into the cyber-defence capabilities of Member States, completed in May 2013, found a 'complex and diverse picture' and outlined a range of recommendations for the EU and its Member States (EDA 2013b). The European Council then tasked the EDA (alongside the Commission, Member States and the EEAS) with developing a roadmap for strengthening cyber-defence and cyber-security, in particular through training and exercises and improving civil–military cooperation (European Council 2013: 6). In the meantime the EDA is already conducting an analysis of the training needs, working on cyber-defence situational awareness for CSDP operations, developing a cyber-defence research agenda, calling for proposals for an analysis of threat detection, and drawing on academic work on information protection and cryptology (EDA 2013b).

Other capability areas with potential for progress are software-defined radio (SDR), which has a demonstration project underway, military airworthiness authorities, aimed at harmonisation of national air safety systems and a future unmanned aerial system for tactical intelligence (Biscop and Coelmont 2010: 63). UAVs, or Remotely Piloted Aircraft Systems (RPAS) as the EU designates them, were the lead item of capabilities outlined at the December 2013 European Council. A number of initiatives were proposed including the next generation Medium Altitude Long Endurance (MALE) RPAS, a RPAS user community for the pMS, ensuring close synergies with the Commission on RPAS regulation, and appropriate funding for research and development, with the EDA playing a central role (European Council 2013: 6).

Finally, the European Council (2013: 7) called for 'increased transparency and information sharing in defence planning, allowing national planners and decision-makers to consider greater convergence of capability needs and timelines'. To pursue this and develop greater cooperation it called for the EDA (with the High Representative) to 'put forward an appropriate policy framework' by the end of 2014 (European Council 2013: 7). Despite these calls from the European Council and the progress made in a number of projects run by the EDA, in the most urgent, and often large-scale investments, such as strategic lift, AAR and ISTAR, progress has been limited. This is not the EDA's fault. The organisation is only as effective and successful as its Member States allow it to be. In this context the key issues of political will, budgets and EU versus multinational cooperation resurface.

### Austerity, apathy and America

The period 2009–2014 has seen significant trends at the national, European and international levels, which directly affect the EDA's ability to pursue military capability development. Three particular trends stand out: the global financial crisis and the resulting austerity policies across

Europe, the apathy (even hostility) towards defence spending and further European integration, and the American 'pivot' to Asia. First, austerity policies across the EU have led to sizeable defence budget cuts in many Member States. Between 2006 and 2011 real term defence expenditure fell by €21 billion, about 10 per cent, and fell by a further 3 per cent between 2011 and 2012 (EDA 2013c: 4). While the cuts varied, the overall trend is declining investment in defence. The problem is exacerbated by the almost wholly uncoordinated nature of the budget cuts and military capability decisions across the EU. While budget and spending cuts could and should lead to greater cooperation and coordination and more innovative planning, funding and procurement solutions, this is not happening to the degree required, or in any coordinated manner, nor at the EU level.

This leads to the second trend, apathy (even hostility) to defence spending among the majority of EU citizens. It is politically very difficult to make the case for defence spending in Europe given the widely held perception of a relatively benign security environment (even in the wake of the 2014 Ukraine crisis). When confronted with a list of security challenges including terrorism, cybersecurity, migration and organised crime, the public, perhaps correctly, see a limited role for the military. This is confirmed in opinion polling, which consistently places defence low on the list of priorities for government spending. After the struggles to get the ToL ratified there is also apathy among the public and governments of the EU toward further European integration. This apathy towards EU-level coordination, cooperation and integration is affecting military capability development too. Instead of EDA organised and EU centred capability development initiatives European states are increasingly working bi-, tri- or multi-laterally on capability initiatives. Most prominent among these are the Anglo-French Defence Cooperation Treaty of November 2010, covering a range of cooperation from a joint expeditionary force to common support for the A400M to combat UAVs; the Weimar Triangle of France, Germany and Poland; the Ghent initiative on P&S; and Nordic cooperation. While it could be hoped that some of these initiatives may reinvigorate EU-level military capability development this is not necessarily the case. Crucially, unlike the 1998 St Malo Declaration, the 2010 Anglo-French treaty is not aimed at reinvigorating EU military capabilities. Rather, it is focused on ensuring French and British power projection capabilities and fulfilling their aspirations to remain global powers. The UK has long been disillusioned by the failure of CSDP to improve military capabilities across the EU. By 2010, France too had begun to lose patience, seeing cooperation with the UK as essential to pursue its role in global security and to retain the semblance of a full spectrum of forces.

The third trend is American, specifically the 'pivot' to Asia. The refocusing of US foreign, security and defence policy towards Asia, specifically the Far East, should, like austerity, push the EU states to focus on

## 80    *A.J.K. Shepherd*

European-level cooperation in military capabilities. The air campaign over Libya demonstrated quite clearly that 12 years after Operation Allied Force the European states continued to be immensely reliant on the US for key military capabilities. In particular, ISTAR, AAR and precision-guided munitions were in short supply. With the US reducing its focus on Europe the EU states will have to provide for more of their own capabilities. Yet America's 'Asian pivot' has done nothing to reinvigorate military capability development in the EU.

## Conclusion

In the 15 years since the launch of CSDP and the ten years since the establishment of the EDA, the pace of military capability development in the EU has been disappointing. To date the EU has failed to meet its own military headline goals. While the EDA has been a major innovation it has been significantly hampered by its intergovernmental structure, relatively small budget and the lack of political will amongst its Member States to prioritise military capability development. These problems have been exacerbated by the global financial crisis and the subsequent austerity policies, which impacted negatively on defence expenditure. The effects of these cuts have been exacerbated by the uncoordinated approach toward defence spending and equipment decision across the EU. This has been further worsened by the increasing apathy and hostility to further EU cooperation among many EU Member States.

It is not an entirely negative picture. Collectively, the EU Member States continue to have the potential to be a major military power with extensive capabilities and (combined) a large defence budget. The Member States have also called for the EU to share in the responsibility for global security. This should provide a solid foundation for a CSDP that is more active and capable. Combined with the pressures of austerity and the US pivot to Asia, there should be plenty of scope for EU-level and EDA-led military capability development. With less money to spend on military capabilities and unable to rely on American capabilities in the future, the logic suggests more cooperation, but for now there appears little political appetite for this at the EU level, or even at all. In particular the EDA, or more precisely its Member States, have failed to make significant progress in the crucial areas of deployability, sustainability and ISTAR. Hence, in the EDA's tenth anniversary year, and despite progress in numerous smaller scale projects, the future of the EDA as the home of European military capability development is far from assured. The overarching question as we head into the EDA's second decade is whether and where cooperation on military capability improvement will take place: within the framework of CSDP and the EDA; through NATO, which may re-emerge post Ukraine as the forum for greater defence cooperation; or through bi- and multilateral arrangements such as the Anglo-French Defence Treaty.

## References

Bátora, J. (2009) 'European Defence Agency: A Flashpoint of Institutional Logics', *West European Politics*, 32(6): 1075–1098.

Biscop, S. and Coelmont, J. (2010) *Europe, Strategy and Armed Forces: The Making of a Distinctive Power*, Abingdon: Routledge.

Blair, T. (1999) 'The Doctrine of the International Community', speech to the Economic Club, Chicago, 23 March 1999.

Brok, E. (1999) *Statement on European Security and Defence Identity after the EU Summit in Cologne and the Transatlantic Link*, Committee on International Relations, U.S. House of Representatives, 10 November 1999.

Council of the European Union (2013) 'Report by the Head of the European Defence Agency to the Council', 31 October 2013.

Council of the European Union (2012) 'Council Conclusions on Common Security and Defence Policy', 26 November 2012.

Council of the European Union (2010) 'Internal Security Strategy'.

Council of the European Union (2009) 'Report by the Head of the European Defence Agency to the Council', 13 May 2009.

Council of the European Union (2008a) 'Implementation Report on the European Security Strategy'.

Council of the European Union (2008b) 'Declaration on the Strengthening Capabilities', 11 December 2008.

Council of the European Union (2006) 'Capability Improvement Chart I/2006'.

Council of the European Union (2004) 'Council Joint Action 2004/551/CFSP of 12 July 2004 on the establishment of the European Defence Agency'.

Council of the European Union (2003a) 'European Security Strategy: A Secure Europe'.

Council of the European Union (2003b) 'Council Conclusions: European Security and Defence Policy', 20 May 2003.

Council of the European Union (2000) 'Conflict prevention: Report by the High Representative and Commission', 9 December 2000.

*Declaration on Strengthening European Cooperation in Security and Defence* (2003) Le Touquet.

Duchêne, F. (1972) 'Europe's Role in World Peace', in R. Mayne (ed.) *Europe Tomorrow: Sixteen European's Look Ahead*, London: Fontana: 32–47.

European Council (2013) *Part I paragraphs 1–22 of the European Council Conclusions: Common Security and Defence Policy*, 19 December 2013.

European Council (2004) *Presidency Report on ESDP*, Brussels, 18 June 2004.

European Council (1999a) *Cologne European Council Conclusions*, Brussels, 4 June 1999.

European Council (1999b) *Helsinki European Council Conclusions*, Brussels, 11 December 1999.

EDA (European Defence Agency) (2013a) 'Factsheet: Air-to-Air Refuelling', 20 December 2013.

EDA (European Defence Agency) (2013b) 'Factsheet: Cyber Defence', 19 November 2013.

EDA (European Defence Agency) (2013c) 'Defence Data 2012'.

EDA (European Defence Agency) (2012a) 'Factsheet: Capability Development Plan (CDP)', 23 January 2012.

82    *A.J.K. Shepherd*

EDA (European Defence Agency) (2012b) 'Factsheet: C-IED Theatre Exploitation Laboratory (TEL)', 6 June 2012.

EDA (European Defence Agency) (2012c) 'Factsheet: European Satellite Communications Procurement Cell (ESCPC)', 26 September 2012.

EDA (European Defence Agency) (2012d) 'Factsheet: Maritime Surveillance (MARSUR)', 9 October 2012.

EDA (European Defence Agency) (2011) 'Factsheet: European Air Transport Fleet (EATF)', 19 May 2011

EDA (European Defence Agency) (2008a) 'EU Governments Endorse Capability Plan for Future Military Needs, Pledge Joint Efforts', 8 July 2008.

EDA (European Defence Agency) (2008b) 'Background Note. Capability Development Plan', 8 July 2008.

EDA (European Defence Agency) (2008c) 'Future Trends from the Capability Development Plan', 8 July 2008.

EDA (European Defence Agency) (2006a) 'An Initial Long-Term Vision for European Defence Capability and Capacity Needs', 3 October 2006.

EDA (European Defence Agency) (2006b) 'EU Governments Launch New Plan to Build Defence Capabilities for Future ESDP Operations', 14 December 2006.

EU Council Secretariat (2006a) 'Factsheet: EU Battlegroups'.

EU Council Secretariat (2006b) 'Development of European Military Capabilities: The Force Catalogue 2006'.

EU Institute for Security Studies (2005) *EU Security and Defence: Core Documents 2004*, Chaillot Paper No. 75, Paris: EU Institute for Security Studies.

Hennessey, P. (2010) 'Britain to Veto European Defence Agency Budget Increase', *Daily Telegraph*, 28 November 2010.

High Representative (2013) *Preparing the December 2013 European Council on Security and Defence, Final Report by the High Representative/Head of the EDA on the Common Security and Defence Policy*, 15 October 2013.

House of Commons (2013) *Twenty-eighth Report of Session 2013–14 – European Scrutiny Committee, European Defence Agency*, 22 November 2013.

Howorth, J. (2007) *Security and Defence Policy in the European Union*, Basingstoke: Palgrave.

International Crisis Group (2005) *EU Crisis Response Capability Revisited*, Brussels.

*Joint Declaration on European Defence* (1998) UK–French Summit, St. Malo, 3–4 December.

Lindstrom, G. (2007) *Enter EU Battlegroups*, Paris: EU Institute for Security Studies.

Manners, I. (2006) 'Normative Power Europe Reconsidered: Beyond the Crossroads', *Journal of European Public Policy*, 13(2): 182–199.

Manners, I. (2002) 'Normative Power Europe: A Contradiction in Terms?', *Journal of Common Market Studies*, 40: 235–258.

Mawdsley, J. (2013) 'The A400M Project: From Flagship Project to Warning for European Defence Cooperation', *Defence Studies*, 13(1): 14–32.

NATO (2006) *Strategic Air-Lift Solution (SALIS) Agreement Enters into Force*, NATO Update.

Salmon, T.C. and Shepherd, A.J.K. (2003) *Toward a European Army?*, Boulder: Lynne Rienner.

*Treaty of Amsterdam Amending the Treaty on European Union, The Treaties Establishing the European Communities and Certain Related Acts* (1997) Luxembourg: Office for Official Publications of the European Communities.

*EU military capability development and EDA*  83

*Treaty on European Union* (1992) Luxembourg: Office for Official Publications of the European Communities.

'Treaty of Lisbon Consolidated Versions of the Treaty on European Union and the Treaty on the Functioning of the European Union' (2007) *Official Journal of the European Union*, Luxembourg: Office for Official Publications of the European Communities.

Whitman, R. (1998) *From Civilian Power to Superpower? The International Identity of the European Union*, Basingstoke: Palgrave.

Whitney, N. (2008) *Re-energising Europe's Security and Defence Policy*, Brussels: European Council on Foreign Relations.

Wolfers, A. (1962) *Discord and Collaboration: Essays in International Relations*, Baltimore: The Johns Hopkins University Press.

# 5 The EDA and armaments collaboration

*Katia Vlachos-Dengler*

Promoting and enhancing European Armaments Co-operation is central to the mission of the European Defence Agency to improve European military capabilities.

(Introduction to the European Armaments Co-operation Strategy, EDA undated)

## Objective and scope of this chapter

Enhancing European armaments cooperation is one of the founding mandates of the European Defence Agency (EDA). As a consequence, since its establishment, the Agency has sought to play an active role in encouraging and facilitating this cooperation with concrete initiatives in several areas. The aim of this chapter is to analyse and assess the EDA's involvement in European armaments collaboration – its contributions, shortcomings and challenges. The first part of the chapter provides a brief overview of the historical evolution of European armaments collaboration prior to the establishment of the EDA, highlighting the most influential initiatives and explaining how these initiatives paved the way, gradually, for the EDA to enter the scene. This synopsis is followed in the second part by a description and assessment of the EDA approach: its philosophy regarding armaments collaboration, specific initiatives, contribution and challenges faced.

In terms of scope, EDA activities in the field of armaments collaboration are examined up to the point in time when Pooling and Sharing (P&S) was established as an official policy. The EDA's activities in P&S are the subject of Chapter 11 of this volume.

## European armaments collaboration prior to the creation of the EDA

### Definition and scope of armaments collaboration

The term 'armaments collaboration' refers to programmes where two or more participating states agree to procure (joint acquisition) and fund the production (co-production) and/or development (co-development) of military equipment jointly. In joint acquisition, countries (or even national services) coordinate the procurement of a military system that corresponds to their harmonised requirements or slightly different versions of the same basic platform, depending on particular national requirements and specifications. Cooperative production or co-production is a type of collaboration where firms from one or more of the participating countries manufacture (often under licence) military equipment developed by firms of another partner, mostly based on the latter's national requirements. Co-production is based on an intergovernmental agreement and often implies a duplication of production facilities. Despite the fact that there is centralised development, Research and Development (R&D) costs are not shared among participating Member States (pMS) and technology transfer is limited as most R&D work is completed before the co-production agreement.

In co-development, firms from partner countries collaborate to develop and/or produce military systems, based on harmonised military requirements. This is the most complex version of armaments collaboration but also the one with the most potential economic benefits and savings through sharing of R&D costs and production economies of scale. Collaborative procurement may also extend to through-life support and maintenance of a system that is developed and/or produced collaboratively. This extends the range of potential savings. However, governments of partner countries often insist that at least some part of the system be manufactured by their local contractors. This leads to a fragmentation of the production process, resulting in an inability to fully realize the potential benefits of collaboration (Heuninckx 2008: 125–126).

Finally, states may also collaborate by jointly funding R&D for a specific military system or capability. On modern weapons, R&D is so costly that pursuing 'go-it-alone' policies increasingly is becoming unsustainable and undesirable. Through joint development funding, states can create savings by sharing the fixed development costs and reducing or even eliminating duplication in resources devoted to development.

### The history of European armaments collaboration

European Union (EU) Member States have been cooperating on armaments for decades, starting in the 1950s, in the context of the North Atlantic Treaty Organisation (NATO) and since the 1970s also in the context of the Western European Union (WEU) since the 1970s (Keohane 2002: 29). There have been several versions and incarnations of such cooperation, both bilateral and multilateral, with varying degrees of success. Between the early 1950s and the end of the twentieth century, 59 collaborative defence procurement programmes were launched in Europe (Andersson 2001: 3). Towards the end of the last decade, about 30 to 40 were ongoing, most of them in the aerospace and missile sectors (Heuninckx 2008: 127). Examples of high-profile cooperative programmes in those sectors include the Transall C-160 military transport aircraft, the Tornado fighter bomber, the Eurofighter combat aircraft, the Tiger anti-tank helicopter, the NH-90 military transport helicopter, the Milan, Roland and Hot missile systems and the METEOR medium-range air-to-air missile.

Today, collaborative procurement and joint development constitute an important part of European defence expenditures. According to EDA estimates, in 2011, expenditure on European collaborative defence equipment procurement was 25 per cent of total European procurement expenditure – an increase of almost 12 per cent from the year before. Percentages have been relatively stable for the past five years. In Research and Technology (R&T) expenditure, European collaboration represented 12 per cent of the total (European Defence Agency 2013).

### The rise in popularity of European armaments collaboration after the end of the Cold War

In the 1990s, declining defence budgets and increasing weapons development and production costs made collaboration much more attractive to EU Member States, if not absolutely necessary to reduce costs and increase affordability of military equipment. As a result, the number of collaborative programmes increased substantially, especially within the EU. In fact, after the end of the Cold War, the balance between purely European/EU projects and cooperative ones with the United States – which were roughly equal until then – tipped clearly towards the former (Heuninckx 2008: 128). While some Member States were much more supportive of collaborative solutions than others, the general trend was – and is – increasing.

Despite its popularity, European armaments collaboration faced significant challenges. In most cases, it was fragmented, programme-specific and limited to particular segments of the defence market – mainly aerospace, missiles and defence electronics. Most cooperative projects were organised on a purely intergovernmental, ad-hoc basis and characterised by complex politics, leading to cumbersome, inefficient arrangements and programme structures, delays and cost penalties (Schmitt 2005: 3).

The demand side of the European defence market was mostly fragmented as well, leading to the inefficient duplication of defence industrial production sites across Europe. Many Member States with a significant defence industry considered maintaining and protecting that industry a prerequisite for preserving their national independence and for ensuring that their armed forces are supplied reliably with necessary capabilities.

At the same time, Member States did not make an effort to harmonise their national security concepts, military doctrines, or, their defence, technology and industrial policies. As a result, their capability requirements often diverged significantly, which discouraged collaborative solutions.

This multi-level fragmentation had damaging consequences that became particularly acute after the end of the Cold War. Weapons systems became more complex and their costs increased dramatically, making them unaffordable for most but the big European Member States. At the same time, defence budgets either declined or remained flat throughout the 1990s. This discrepancy between resources and costs had a destructive impact on European military capabilities and deficiencies started to appear when European forces had to participate in crisis management operations – such as in Kosovo and Afghanistan. The limited national resources and lack of investment in future capabilities also took a toll on the competitiveness of European defence firms on the global market.

*Efforts to improve collaboration*

Given these pressures, EU Member States had an incentive to collaborate more effectively in arguments. Their efforts to do that, though multinational, were also fragmented, involving several different institutions, processes and approaches.

In 1991, the WEU Declaration annexed to the Maastricht Treaty stated the requirement to explore options for enhanced armaments cooperation in order to create, ultimately, a European armaments agency (Schmitt, 2003). However, despite honest intentions, efforts to determine a unified view of the nature and scope of such cooperation were weighed down by strong and divergent national industrial policies and procurement processes and significant bureaucratic obstacles. This led to the fragmented approach mentioned above.

Throughout the 1990s, many multinational initiatives were put forward both by NATO and the WEU. NATO had been promoting transatlantic armaments cooperation since the 1950s, while the WEU had done the same within Europe since the 1970s (see Keohane 2002; Schmitt 2005).

The Western European Armaments Group (WEAG), composed of national armaments directors of its Member States, was the largest European structure dealing with armaments cooperation. Its forerunner, the Independent European Programme Group (IEPG), was established as a forum for armaments cooperation in 1976 with the aim of creating, eventually, a European Armaments Agency, and transformed into WEAG in 1993. WEAG members included all EU Member States except Ireland and all European NATO Member States except Iceland. WEAG focused on the areas of requirements harmonisation, cross-border competition in defence markets, strengthening of the European defence technological and industrial base and cooperation in R&T.

In 1996 the members of the WEAG created the Western European Armaments Organisation (WEAO), which although intended to evolve into a European Armaments Agency, was limited initially to a Research

Cell, which promoted cooperation in R&T. Unfortunately, the WEAO's core research programme, the European Cooperation Long-Term in Defence (EUCLID), did not receive any substantial financial or political support from Member States, which limited its effectiveness.

Almost at the same time, in 1996, a programme management agency called Organisation Conjointe de Coopération en matière d'Armement (OCCAR) was created through a joint initiative between France, Germany, Italy and the United Kingdom (UK). OCCAR, which achieved legal status in early 2001, aimed at more efficient management of multi-national collaborative armaments programmes and took over programmes such as the Eurocopter Tiger attack helicopter and the A400M transport aircraft. Despite a much narrower initial scope and limited initial membership compared to the pan-European approach of WEAG/WEAO, OCCAR also had the potential to become a European armaments agency. The organisation was open to participation by European Member States that were involved substantively in collaborative programmes that it managed. Spain and Belgium joined in 2003 and 2005 respectively.

In 1998, the defence ministers of the six major European arms producers (France, Germany, Italy, Spain, Sweden and the UK) signed a Letter of Intent (LoI), which aimed at facilitating the restructuring of the European defence industry. The LoI was followed by a Framework Agreement in 2000, which set the stage for the creation of a legal and political framework for cross-border defence industrial consolidation and covered, among other areas, security of supply, R&T, requirements harmonisation and exports procedures.

However, despite all their efforts, both NATO and the WEU reached their limits in the area of armaments cooperation, partly because their initiatives were not binding on their Member States. Furthermore, neither NATO nor the WEU had the ability to develop common weapons systems or to manage joint programmes. Special, separate bodies had to be set up for that purpose (see below), usually consisting of representatives of the pMS (Keohane 2002: 30). Finally, initiatives were not coordinated or part of a coherent overarching armaments strategy or policy.

Work-share in collaborative programmes was allocated according to the principle of *juste retour* – where national industry received work equivalent to the full amount of its government's financial investment – rather than through market mechanisms. This created even more inefficiencies and fragmentation by distorting competition and causing duplication of technologies. OCCAR tried to change that by adopting a more flexible and systematic approach to *juste retour* where a multi-year/multi-programme 'global balance' is targeted instead of an ad-hoc programme-by-programme application of 'cost-share equals work-share'. Still, *juste retour* persisted for a long time, as Member States were more interested in preserving their national industries, maintaining employment and protecting their technological independence, rather than ensuring the efficiency of European defence programmes (Darnis *et al.* 2007: 25).

Most collaborative programmes had cumbersome management structures, which ensured that national interests were protected, but added to programme cost and complexity. Such programmes were either managed by a lead nation or through an informal, usually weak, intergovernmental decision-making structure. Only later did pMS opt for streamlining that structure by assigning management to an international agency or organisation. However, even that allocation to a centralised agency was usually organised on an ad hoc basis, for political reasons or because there was no European-level body with a coherent policy on armaments collaboration (Heuninckx 2008: 130).

As a result of all these challenges, fragmentation and duplication persisted in the European defence market. There was no overarching strategy, no central body coordinating the different collaborative efforts, no unified political leadership to provide guidance and direction. All these initiatives took place outside the framework of the EU, since up until the mid-1990s, the defence market was deliberately excluded from the European integration process in the context of the Union. Article 346 of the Treaty on the Functioning of the European Union (TFEU) (former Article 296 of the Treaty establishing the European Community or TEU) allowed Member States to exclude the area of armaments from the reach of Community policies on the grounds that essential security interests were at stake – and they used it to interpret those security interests widely. The absence of a binding community framework solidified the fragmentation of the European defence market – demand as well as supply (Mölling and Brune 2011: 9).

### The development of a EU defence dimension

The EU started developing a defence dimension in 1996 through the launch of several Communications on the defence industry. Even though Member States were traditionally reluctant to accept the adoption of a common armaments policy, that started to change towards the beginning of the last decade (see discussion in Schmitt 2005: 6–7).

As of 1999, defence was included in the EU's legitimate areas of competence. The EU had started developing a European Security and Defence Policy (ESDP), which created more favourable conditions for considering a common armaments policy. The European Capabilities Action Plan (ECAP), introduced in 2002, was designed to remedy shortcomings in European crisis-management capabilities and enhance the effectiveness and efficiency of European military capability efforts. Although it did not refer to armaments collaboration specifically, ECAP encouraged the use of multinational options to address European capability shortfalls. The ECAP process illustrated the natural link between a common defence policy,

90   K. Vlachos-Dengler

military capabilities and armaments: a credible policy needs the necessary capabilities and means to back it up; it also requires efficient ways to provide those means.

Moreover, the increasingly common security challenges with which the European defence establishment was confronted following the end of the Cold War led to a progressive convergence of military doctrines and capability requirements. In addition, as military operations became increasingly multilateral, standardisation of equipment became more important. Armaments collaboration seemed like a natural follow-on act to these trends.

Finally, armaments cooperation was deemed a necessity if the European defence industry was to survive, faced with dramatically reduced national budgets and competition from its American, Russian and other counterparts. European companies were already actively consolidating and would ideally need a consolidated demand side and common regulatory framework.

All these factors led to a growing consensus that the EU could be an appropriate framework for a coherent European armaments policy and streamlined armaments cooperation and that it could provide the much-needed guidance and leadership. In the context of its budding involvement in armaments, the EU's Communication, in March 2003, on European Defence – Industrial and Market Issues, suggested a common armaments policy (European Commission 2003). Then, in July 2003, Article I-40.3 of the 'Draft Treaty Establishing a Constitution for Europe' (European Convention 2003) stated that a European Armaments, Research and Military Capabilities Agency would, among others, 'participate in defining a European capabilities and armaments policy'. Among the tasks of that Agency, determined in the same Draft Treaty, would be to 'propose multilateral projects to fulfil the objectives in terms of military capabilities, ensure coordination of programmes implemented by the Member States and management of specific cooperation programmes'.

One month earlier, in June 2003, the European Council of Thessaloniki had opened the way for the establishment of 'an intergovernmental Agency in the field of defence capabilities development, research, acquisition and armaments' (European Council 2003: article IV, par. 65). Promoting armaments collaboration would be among the main tasks of this new Agency. Initially, the Agency would aim at coordinating the existing network of arrangements, groups and organisations in the field of armaments (WEAG/WEAO, OCCAR, LoI/Framework Agreement) and integrating their principles and practices.

Still, there seemed to be a missing link between the armaments phase and the capability development phase of capability generation at the European level. The armaments phase comprises the stages of equipment generation that is research, development testing and procurement. The capability development phase includes planning, set up, organisation and routine management of armed forces, that is training, exercises, but also services that allow building and maintaining of a capability. These two phases were both institutionally and conceptually disjointed and there seemed to be no European-level resources for them; only national ones. However, a link between the two phases is critical for the effective and efficient generation of capabilities and the latter is an essential condition for defence cooperation. What you develop and build jointly, you can operate and maintain jointly (Mölling and Brune 2011: 10).

## The EDA approach to armaments collaboration

### *The EDA's potential to fulfil European needs*

The long European tradition of armaments collaboration acquired significant momentum towards the end of the last decade, when it became not only an economic necessity for most Member States but also for the survival of European defence as a whole. The financial crisis, starting in 2007, put public budgets across the EU under so much pressure, that it became an urgency for Member States to seek ways to save on resources through cooperation. The impact of this crisis was different from that of the end of the Cold War in that this time all Member States were affected, albeit to different degrees, and not only the smaller ones. As a result, while traditionally smaller Member States were the ones more interested in collaboration, the crisis made sure that incentives for such collaboration and for building consensus among Member States became more broadly distributed.

When the EDA was established in 2004, after a decade of negotiations, expectations were high that it would be the ideal forum for cooperation in Europe. After all, armaments collaboration was among its main tasks at its inception. The EDA had the potential to represent that missing link between capability development and armaments. Its agenda, structure and tasks extended across all dimensions of the armaments sector and allowed it to engage in armaments collaboration, as well as capability development, research and technology, and industry and markets.

A key objective of the EDA was to coordinate, optimise and harmonise cooperation between Member States – and that included the armaments sector. It was expected to facilitate cooperation by providing a platform for information sharing (Fuchs 2011). The more openly Member States discussed their issues, problems and needs, the more likely it was that they would find commonalities and opportunities for cooperation. Exchanges of opinions could also lead to a more effective harmonisation of capability requirements. In most cases, Member States participated in the same operations; it was therefore likely that their requirements would converge. Besides providing a forum for such and exchange, the EDA's unique overview of national agendas, requirements and plans would allow it to identify common interests in filling capability needs, common or overlapping requirements as well as potential synergies and therefore opportunities for fruitful collaboration. It could use its overview of national technical capacities to help Member States and their taxpayers get better value for money.

The industry was also pressing for a more integrated European armaments effort. In the fragmented European defence industrial landscape, as defence companies started to consolidate, they reached a point where a more integrated European defence market – a unified demand side – was an essential condition for restructuring to continue. This required the political will to overcome this fragmentation of demand – both at the European level, among countries and at the country level, among services. Through its initiatives, the EDA aimed at bringing down national barriers around defence markets and solidifying the government/political side.

Additionally, the EDA was seen as an ideal vehicle for developing the common European vision that was necessary to increase the efficiency of the process of armaments collaboration, from the identification of opportunities through to the implementation of the programmes. The EDA could use the industry and market expertise it had built from other projects and its perspective of best practices to streamline the process of collaboration and help Member States get their needed capabilities as quickly and cost-effectively as possible.

The EDA is the latest step in almost half a century of efforts at collaboration in military matters; an effort to respond to changed geopolitical circumstances and to cover unmet needs. Given its structure, the EDA must balance multiple roles and priorities simultaneously. Its tasks imply the need to be a powerful integrating and driving force, while its intergovernmental nature and mandate require it to do that while maintaining the confidence and support of its national shareholders.

### The role of the EDA's Armaments Directorate

The Council Joint Action on the establishment of the EDA (Council of the European Union 2004) determined the role of the Agency in armaments cooperation. Its Armaments Directorate is responsible for that role and the tasks it implies. The activities of the Directorate cover two complementary dimensions: some of them are linked to preparing, supporting or managing EDA projects, while other activities are of a more crosscutting or overarching nature, and are aimed at creating the necessary conditions and 'enablers' for improving cooperation among Member States. The Armaments Directorate also supports the Agency's other Directorates as part of the EDA's integrated way of working.

Article 45 of the Lisbon Treaty and the Council Joint Action of 2004 defined the EDA's involvement in armaments collaboration as consisting of the following four tasks: (1) promoting and proposing new multilateral cooperative projects; (2) coordinating existing ones; (3) managing specific cooperative programmes; and (4) identifying and disseminating best practices.

In terms of promoting and proposing new cooperation, the EDA's role 'covers the spectrum from monitoring and reporting, through facilitation to management. The aim must be to seek ways to align requirements, budgets, timeframes, industrial capacity and technologies required to deliver these programmes' (EDA Armaments Directorate website). The EDA acts as a catalyst allowing Member States to pool their resources and expertise and to collectively develop solutions to their capability needs.

In coordinating existing programmes, the focus is on promoting collaboration in every phase of a programme. This includes through-life support and maintenance, which is done mostly nationally, even though it represents an enormous proportion of a weapon's total lifecycle cost. Besides encouraging joint support arrangements, the EDA also identifies opportunities for collaborative solutions in the case of upgrades of major equipment and development of technologies or new subsystems and components for existing weapons systems. Finally, with respect to existing collaborative programmes, the EDA searches potential opportunities for joint replenishment or follow-on acquisitions.

As far as managing specific collaborative programmes is concerned, this can be undertaken either by coalitions of participants or by the EDA acting as a 'proxy customer' on behalf of the actual customers (the pMS) to define cost ranges, time-frames and procurement strategy, among others. The actual management of the contractors through the programme implementation phase could be taken over either by the EDA or OCCAR, depending on the Member States' decision.

Finally, in the context of identifying and disseminating best practice, the EDA's Armaments Directorate supports and facilitates the use of common standards for defence procurement and promotes the standardisation of procurement procedures among Member States. The EDA also tasked a consortium of European research institutes to conduct a study on how to launch a successful cooperative programme. Among the outcomes of the study called 'Cooperative Lessons Learned and Best Practice' was a guide on how to conduct cooperative programmes and a list of recommendations in the areas of requirements, R&T, industrial cooperation, budgets, project management. These included, among others: establishing common requirements; promoting convergence of military doctrines; cooperating on military R&T planning; boosting European defence research programmes; phasing out *juste retour*; coordinating budget procedures; using on-site Integrated Project Teams (IPTs) of national experts; and coordinating national procurement processes (Darnis *et al.* 2007: 29–35).

## 94 K. Vlachos-Dengler

### The Capability Development Plan (CDP) and armaments collaboration

Armaments collaboration ideally starts with a common definition of capability needs, which are then translated into military requirements, for which appropriate collaborative solutions are identified. The EDA is designed and best positioned to do that. In fact, one of the aims of the CDP, which the Agency was tasked to develop, together with its Member States and other EU institutions, was exactly that: to identify opportunities for resource pooling and cooperation. The first CDP, which was endorsed by Member States in July 2008, aimed at providing a systematic and structured approach to building the military capabilities European armed forces required to conduct ESDP operations and at helping Member States develop their national plans and programmes. One of the main goals of the CDP was to identify priorities for capability development and in the process of creating a framework for establishing and prioritising requirements, the CDP would also highlight potential opportunities for collaborative procurement of needed capabilities. Even though not all capabilities needed to be procured cooperatively, the CDP was a first and absolutely necessary step before any kind of armaments cooperation could be undertaken. The EDA complements this deductive, capabilities-determined approach by constantly searching to identify 'targets of opportunity'.

### The European Armaments Co-operation Strategy

The European Armaments Cooperation (EAC) Strategy was formulated by the EDA and approved by its shareholders – the Member States in October 2008. A European policy approach to the armaments sector was seen as the necessary – and missing – link between Member States' future capability needs and their investment in a European Defence Technological and Industrial Base (EDTIB). The EAC Strategy provided a clear statement of intent of the EDA's pMS to promote and enhance more effective and efficient European armaments cooperation in support of the Common Security and Defence Policy (CSDP). A core message of the Strategy was that Member States must seek to maximise opportunities for collaboration and ensure that cooperative options are considered in defence planning – not just in developing new systems, but also in in-service support, upgrading of existing assets as well as other lines of capability development.

The Armaments Cooperation Strategy has three strategic aims, briefly described below (European Defence Agency 2008).

*1 To generate, promote and facilitate cooperative programmes to meet capability needs*
The EDA's role in this respect is to facilitate the translation of Member States' capability needs into concrete cooperative programmes in a structured way. Member States define their needs (and potential opportunities

for cooperation) through the CDP process. The description of identified needs – the result or effect that the users need to develop – called the Common Staff Target (CST), is the main input for the programme Preparation Phase. This is the initial phase of either a new cooperative armaments programme or an activity to sustain an existing capability. The Preparation Phase is a structured way to prepare a future cooperative programme and it starts with a Steering Board decision. This includes reporting on a capability identified as necessary, a declaration of intention by a group of contributing Member States to carry out that Preparation Phase, an offer to other Member States to participate and the creation of a Preparation Group comprising national and EDA personnel.

The EDA, Member States and other stakeholders work together to harmonise requirements to the extent possible and translate CST into a Common Staff Requirement (CSR), which is a concrete set of military requirements across all capability areas, complete with solutions in mind. The latter implies that technological, industrial and economic issues are considered as well, particularly for larger, more complex cooperative programmes. The CSR must be approved by the Member States involved in the programme and included in their national plans. The CSR is included in the Business Case for the project, which is a key outcome of the Preparation Phase. The Business Case is a viability report on the cooperative programme, which is supposed to provide compelling reasons for Member States to pursue it, initially proceeding with further activities and negotiations before committing formally.

The Business Case also includes the Through-Life Management Plan (TLMP), a programme that outlines the scope, time frame, cost, acquisition organisation and participation of the programme. This programme takes a through-life approach by taking into account all phases of the life cycle of a programme (definition, development, production, in-service and disposal), as well as the risks and opportunities related to them. At the end of the Preparation Phase, the Member States decide to launch an ad-hoc programme under the purview of the EDA.

*2   To ensure that investment in the EDTIB is capability-oriented and supportive of future collaborative programmes*
The EAC Strategy highlighted the strong connection between a solid EDTIB and effective armaments cooperation. The latter cannot take place without the former; at the same time, cooperation helps enhance the defence industrial base. This two-way relationship implies the need for transparency and open communication between governments and industry to preserve that mutually beneficial connection.

The EDA's role in that respect is, among others, to facilitate the exchange of appropriate information between the two parties on long-term capability planning on the one side and industrial long-term investment planning on the other. The EDA can also encourage transparency

## 96   K. Vlachos-Dengler

and compatibility of procurement policies and practices, including budgetary planning cycles.

*3   To improve the effectiveness and efficiency of European armaments cooperation*
To achieve that aim, it helps if opportunities for cooperation are identified and acted upon early in a system's life cycle, ideally starting with harmonised needs and requirements. The through-life approach mentioned above is valuable from the start. Furthermore, a common understanding among the actors involved of why and how armaments cooperation should work helps improve implementation. The EDA can contribute to all those aspects. It can help by establishing how the programme Preparation Phase will be conducted and how the different stakeholders (the EDA, Member States and programme management agency) will work together. It can also inspire by identifying and disseminating best practices in cooperative programmes.

In addition to those three strategic aims, several specific actions were identified in order to implement the EAC Strategy. Many of them were for the EDA to undertake. Although some actions were concrete, there were others where it was unclear who would undertake them, how and by when. This vagueness might be due to the fact that it is easier to agree in principle but harder to commit in practice (Heuninckx 2009: 11).

### Flagship initiatives

The EDA has several flagship collaborative projects and programs, some of which are briefly presented below (Mölling and Brune 2011: 26–28):

- The *European Air Transport Fleet (EATF)*, a European framework for enhanced cooperation in military air transport. The aim is to increase EU strategic and tactical airlift capabilities and availability through better use and coordination of existing and future assets.
- The *Helicopter Training Programme*, a series of helicopter exercises, held in France, Spain and Italy since 2009. The exercise programme has delivered training to: 72 helicopters, 152 crews and over 1,800 personnel. Over 50 per cent crews that have participated have subsequently deployed to Afghanistan.
- The *Multinational Space-based Imaging System* (MUSIS), a programme initially promoted by six Member States (Belgium, France, Germany, Italy, Greece and Spain) and coordinated by the EDA since 2009, aiming to develop a space imaging system for defence and security in order to increase Europe's strategic autonomy and strengthen its decision-making capacities in the military field.
- *Software-Defined Radio* (SDR). The six-nation (Finland, France, Italy, Poland, Spain and Sweden) ESSOR (European Secure SOftware defined Radio) project signed in December 2008 was aimed at providing the

basis for development and production of SDR products in Europe to be operational by 2015. It had a total value of more than €100 million.

- The *Maritime Surveillance Networking Capabilities* (MARSUR) programme aimed at the development of Maritime Surveillance networking capabilities, the launch of a programme on Maritime Tactical Unmanned Aerial System (seven contributing Member States) and Maritime Mine Countermeasures (13 Member States).
- The *21st-Century Soldier System*, a programme initiated in 2006 to identify commonalities of requirements among Member States and technological components of a twenty-first century soldier system.
- The *Force Protection* programme on protection of forces in urban environments, involving 20 Member States with a budget of €55 million over three years.

Other important programmes include: Chemical, Biological, Radiological and Nuclear (CBRN); Unmanned Aerial Systems (UAS) Air Traffic Insertion; Military Airworthiness Authorities (MAWA) Forum; Counter-Improvised Explosive Devices (C-IED); Network Enabled Capability (NEC); Third Party Logistics Support (TPLS); Joint Investment Programme on Force Protection (JIP-FP); and Joint Investment Programme on Innovative Concepts and Emerging Technologies (JIP-ICET).

## Assessment of the EDA's contribution to European armaments collaboration before Pooling and Sharing

### Balancing assertiveness and flexibility

Given that the EDA is an intergovernmental organisation active in highly sensitive areas that touch on issues of national sovereignty, there is bound to be debate among its shareholders (the pMS) over the ideal extent and reach of its mandate. While for some Member States, the EDA may have exceeded its mandate, for others, it may not have been using its full potential. For instance, one of the criticisms aimed at the EDA is that it has been content to act as a facilitator – a forum making sense of collaboration – rather than attempting to interpret its mandate more broadly (DeVore and Eisenecker 2010: 9). As in many others areas where it is active, in armaments collaboration as well, it is important for the Agency to find the right balance between being assertive and proactive in pushing for progress and being respectful of national sensitivities, so that it can maintain the support of its shareholders.

In that context, one of the challenges the EDA has faced has been to find ways to develop collaborative approaches to fill European capability gaps through a process that is flexible enough, allowing Member States to preserve part of their sovereignty (discussion based on author's interview with EDA official, May 2013). In order to deal with this challenge, the EDA created different types of collaborative projects or programmes. One category of projects can be launched by the EDA itself. These are called 'EDA projects' and are usually large-scale, broad-participation projects, such as the European Air Transport Fleet (EATF). Another category are 'ad hoc projects'. These are distinguished into Category A, which are 'opt-out' projects, where all Member States participate unless they choose not to; and Category B or 'opt-in' projects, which start with two or more initial contributing Member States and are open to other Member States joining. Both types of ad hoc projects are launched in the framework of the EDA but funded exclusively by pMS. The budget for ad hoc A and B projects signed in 2012 was €33 million (EDA 2012). To get a sense of the magnitude of that, European collaborative defence equipment procurement in 2011 was €7.3 billion (EDA 2013). These different programme options allow the EDA the flexibility to adapt to different strategic priorities, operational requirements and particular interest in a project on behalf of Member States, as well as to the importance and desired 'reach' of each project.

### *Improving the efficiency of European armaments collaboration*

Despite the many challenges it faces, the EDA has played an important role in reducing fragmentation in the European defence market and in contributing to the streamlining of Member States' approach to filling their capability gaps. Even though it is the Member States that ultimately decide whether to invest in and proceed with particular programmes – their national interests and priorities having a major influence on such decisions – the EDA has provided a structure and overall framework for that investment to take place. It has helped highlight commonalities in needs, processes and schedules and has guided Member States towards increased harmonisation of their capability needs and requirements, while proposing joint solutions that can satisfy those requirements.

The benefits of this approach are becoming increasingly tangible and quantifiable. When Member States are presented with evidence of the savings that a particular collaborative approach has already brought or could bring to their budgets, their appreciation of and commitment to the EDA increases.

### *Dependence on champion Member States*

However, even though the benefits for Member States of the EDA's contribution to armaments collaboration become more and more concrete, there is only so much the EDA can do without their support. The EDA is ultimately an intergovernmental organisation whose purpose is to support its Member States. Therefore, its success in achieving many of its goals depends on the commitment of these Member States and their willingness to support its initiatives. Most, if not all, initiatives cannot be pursued without that political will, and support by a particular – 'champion' – nation is essential to their success. Shaping political will – both that of the politicians and of their defence bureaucracies – has always been a challenge for the EDA.

In that respect, two factors have made a difference in how Member States view 'their' Agency (based on author's interview with EDA official, May 2013). The first is the 'institutionalisation' of the EDA at EU level through the Lisbon Treaty (European Council 2007). The Lisbon Treaty elevated the EDA from Joint Action level to Treaty level, which provides it with a much firmer legal base to work from, also in the field of armaments cooperation, making the Agency an official part of ESDP. Second, the fact that the Agency has started providing Member States with concrete initiatives and tangible results. In contrast to its initial years, the Agency has shifted its focus from commissioning studies and producing reports to providing concrete deliverables to its shareholders – from exercises and trainings to software development and platforms for Member States' use. Apart from their contribution in terms of substance, these deliverables also enhance the Agency's visibility and increase its appreciation by Member States. Member States begin to have a more solid picture of the benefits they get from the EDA: their 'return on investment'.

### Small is beautiful?

Compared to previous multinational armaments organisations, the EDA is bigger. It has a substantial staff of over 110, a solid organisation and more substantial institutional resources than most of its predecessor armaments organisations. For instance, IEPG possessed 'a miniscule staff of five' (DeVore and Eisenecker 2010: 7). However, even though comparatively more substantial, the EDA's resources cannot always cover the reach of its mandate. This could put in question its prospects of success in promoting more efficient armaments cooperation and a single European armaments market.

While it may be bigger than its predecessor armaments organisations, the EDA is still small and flexible enough to be able to get things done. Its lack of a rigid hierarchical structure allows for more direct communication and fewer – compared to other European organisations – organisational and bureaucratic barriers to implementing initiatives.

In budgetary terms, the EDA depends on Member States for financing. It is not funded by EU budgets, but by its members in proportion to their Gross National Income. Although the EDA's total budget has been relatively stable at €30.5 million for the last five years, its operational budget is small, limiting its access, reach and room for manoeuvre.

# 100   K. Vlachos-Dengler

## Future prospects

Critics argue that it is far from certain that the EDA as an armaments organisation for Europe 'will succeed at integrating, rationalising and improving the efficiency of European states' hitherto separate industrial bases. Although European defence cooperation is now the responsibility of an agency of the EU, there is little prospect of the defence sector being reshaped by the same forces as have integrated other economic domains so long as defence industries are exempted from EU's jurisdiction' (DeVore and Eisenecker 2010: 12).

The EDA may be bigger than previous armaments organisations, but it is still a small organisation, if one compares it to the national procurement agencies or the defence companies that it is supposed to manage. As an organisation, it will have to somehow solidify its mandate and support from Member States or suffer a life of relative irrelevance due to the inadequacy of its present organisational arrangements.

## References

Andersson, J.J. (2001) *Cold War Dinosaurs or High-Tech Arms Providers? The West European Land Armaments Industry at the Turn of the Millennium,* Occasional Paper No. 23, Paris: Western European Union Institute for Security Studies.

Council of the European Union (2004) 'Council Joint Action 2004/551/CFSP of 12 July 2004 on the establishment of the European Defence Agency'.

Darnis, J.-P., Gasparini, G., Grams, C., Keohane, D., Liberti, F., Maulny, J.-P. and Stumbaum, M.-B. (2007) *Lessons Learned from European Defence Equipment Programmes,* Occasional Paper No. 69, Paris: European Union Institute for Security Studies.

DeVore, M. and Eisenecker, S. (2010) *The Three Ages of Armaments Collaboration: Determinants of Organisational Success and Failure,* Paper prepared for the SGIR Conference, Stockholm, 9–11 September 2010.

European Commission (2003) 'Communication on European Defence – Industrial and Market Issues', 11 March 2003.

European Convention (2003) 'Draft Treaty Establishing a Constitution for Europe', CONV 850/03, Brussels: 18 July 2003.

European Council (2007) 'The Lisbon Treaty'.

European Council (2003) 'Presidency Conclusions, Thessaloniki European Council, 19 and 20 June 2003', 11638/03, Brussels: 1 October 2003.

EDA (European Defence Agency) (2013) 'Defence Data 2012'.

EDA (European Defence Agency) (2012) 'Annual Report 2012'.

EDA (European Defence Agency) (2011) 'Defence Data 2010'.

EDA (European Defence Agency) (2008) 'European Armaments Co-operation Strategy', Brussels, 15 October 2008.

EDA (European Defence Agency) (undated) 'European Armaments Co-operation Strategy'.

EDA (European Defence Agency) Armaments Directorate website. Online. Available at: www.eda.europa.eu/Aboutus/who-we-are/Organisation/Armamentsdirectorate/tasks-and-organisation (accessed 15 June 2014).

Fuchs, B. (2011) 'Q&A: European Defence Agency', *Army Technology,* 19 August 2011.

*EDA and armaments collaboration* 101

Heuninckx, B. (2009) 'The European Defence Agency Capability Development Plan and the European Armaments Cooperation Strategy: Two Steps in the Right Direction', *Public Procurement Law Review*, 18(4): 136–143.

Heuninckx, B. (2008) 'A Primer to Collaborative Defence Procurement in Europe: Troubles, Achievements and Prospects', *Public Procurement Law Review*, 17(3): 123–145.

Keohane, D. (2002) *The EU and Armaments Co-operation*, Working Paper, London: Centre for European Reform.

Mölling, C. and Brune, S.-C. (2011) *The Impact of the Financial Crisis on European Defence*, Study prepared for the European Parliament's Subcommittee on Security and Defence.

Schmitt, B. (2005) *Armaments Cooperation in Europe*, Paris: EU Institute for Security Studies.

Schmitt, B. (2003) *European Armaments Cooperation: Core Documents*, Chaillot Paper No. 59, Paris: EU Institute for Security Studies.

# 6 The EDA and the field of research and technology

*Anja Dahlmann, Marcel Dickow and Léa Tisserant*

## Introduction

This chapter compares the strategic approach of the European Defence Agency (EDA) and their participating Member States (pMS) against the available instruments at hand and their actual results. We will analyse Research and Technology (R&T) tools, their adaption over time, their value for practical cooperation and the impact of such cooperation projects on the greater aim of establishing a more integrated Common Security and Defence Policy (CSDP). In the second section, we will discuss the EDA's R&T approach in the wider scope of European institutions, such as the European Commission (EC). Common projects in space, not only in the R&T field, are of special importance when it comes to the EDA's cooperation with the European Space Agency (ESA); however, Chapter 14 of this book discusses the topic of EDA's space ambitions separately.

The 'enhancement of the effectiveness of European Defence Research and Technology' (Council of the European Union 2004: art. 3.4) is one of the EDA's four main functions as defined in the Joint Action establishing the EDA (Council of the European Union 2004). To reach this goal, the Agency is supposed to promote research on future capability requirements and joint R&T between pMS, to catalyse defence R&T through its own projects and to manage the R&T contracts between pMS. Furthermore, the EDA should cooperate with the EC to 'maximise complementarity and synergy between defence and civil or security related research programmes' (Council of the European Union 2004: art. 3.4.6).

On the way towards more cooperation in European defence, common R&T is the earliest possible entry point, offering synergies and increased efficiency without predetermining too much of a common European industrial policy. Since the creation of the EDA, the European Union (EU) Member States' governments have acknowledged this theoretical standpoint. Instruments have been adjusted over time; positive examples of fruitful cooperation under the EDA's umbrella in the R&T domain underpin the concept. Individual pMS have used the EDA's instruments to stimulate R&T in important technology domains such as Remotely Piloted Aircraft Systems (RPAS) or Force Protection (FP). Although a multiplicity of projects are undertaken with an overall strategy, bald figures of pMS R&T spending tell a different story (Guzelyte 2014). Neither has R&T cooperation become the likely entry point for increased common defence spending, nor have pMS found more communality within their project of a Common Security and Defence Policy (CSDP). At first glance, there appear to be failures, but the picture is much more complex.

The EDA can be credited for its work on multilateral cooperation in the field of R&T. Instruments like the Joint Investment Programme (JIP) and Capability Technology Areas (CapTechs) foster the exchange of states and actors from industry, academia or research centres to improve security and defence research. However, the actual impact of those instruments remains slim, at best. Furthermore, the EDA's relation to the EC appears to be difficult despite the optimistic European Framework Cooperation (EFC) (Maulny and Matelly 2013).

**Historical overview**

Prior to 1990, the creation of most of the armament and defence cooperation organisations in Europe was motivated by the perception of the threat constituted by the other bloc. Since the end of the Cold War, a more commercial and economic approach to such cooperation has been adopted (DeVore 2013). In Europe, intergovernmental cooperation of defence R&T used to be quite selective and on a case-by-case basis. However, some institutions, like the Letter of Intent (LoI), have been created in order to implement a more sustainable cooperative scheme on a voluntary basis between some European states.

The EDA has been created as an EU integrated agency, working for the European common interest. The EDA is an intergovernmental tool of the CSDP. It is seen by some as a governance-based approach to defence cooperation and sometimes perceived as an instance of the 'Brusselization of defence industrial policy' (DeVore 2013). That is to say, the institutionalisation of a cooperative agency in the defence area, such as the EDA, can be explained as a holistic governance-related process. It goes further than a monolithic security-based or financial-based approach to the EDA's creation and institutionalisation process (ibid). The EDA was designed to organise and promote defence cooperation between the EU Member States within the EU's frame, unlike the LoI, which was created by some Member States for their own cooperative purposes.

The EDA was set up at the European Summit in Thessaloniki, in June 2003 and institutionalised by the Lisbon Treaty in 2009. Soon after its creation, the EDA entered into a dynamic cooperative dialogue with other European defence cooperation organisations, such as the LoI and the Western European Armaments Group (WEAG), in order to avoid duplications of

104　*A. Dahlmann* et al.

research. However, R&T cooperation within the EDA was not exempt from difficulties at the beginning of its existence. Enhancing and institutionalising the then too often punctual interstate cooperation in such a core sovereignty area as defence R&T was some kind of a challenge after the adoption of the 2004 Council Decision creating the EDA (Council of the European Union 2004). Practice allowed some changes by adopting an even more pragmatic approach, originating in Monnet's method to European integration.

## R&T projects at the EDA

The EDA creates a framework of cooperation in order to manage its Member States' R&T activities. Accordingly, the EDA's genuine financial resource to stimulate and commission R&T projects remains marginal: in 2012, the EDA contracted 14 R&T studies with a total amount of €2.58 million. The Agency offers pMS a working platform to cooperate with their own financial resources and tries to identify existing shortfalls in future technologies. Because it makes sense to avoid duplications with other European R&T agencies, especially the EC and the European Space Agency (ESA), the coordination function of the EDA is whatever EU Member States are willing to grant to such an intergovernmental agency. Taking into account that R&T projects have to be introduced by pMS or must be accepted by the EDA board, little room for manoeuvre remains for introducing an independent European view on defence R&T.

In general, the EDA offers two different project categories in R&T, giving pMS the flexible opportunity to contribute financially to joint programmes in an effective way and according to their resources and political priorities (Council of the European Union 2004). Category A projects, also called opt-out projects, are initiated by the EDA or at least one pMS, and all pMS are expected to contribute to it. Category B projects, on the other hand, called opt-in projects, are projects that can be selectively joined by a pMS, should they match the state's subjective priorities. Over time the EDA has redefined its projects mechanisms to meet the specific demands of several technology domains: new instruments, such as JIP, take into account the specific development cycles and timeframes of certain emerging technologies and geographic distribution of resources, competencies and effort across pMS. With the overall aim to 'support medium to long term European defence capability needs' (Breant 2013), the EDA has focused on establishing agreed R&T priorities, reducing dependence on non-EU resources, 'contribute to build[ing] a competitive European Technological and Industrial Base (EDTIB), including SMEs and Research Centers' and 'increase synergies, in co-ordination with the European Commission (defence and security research) [and] ESA (critical space technologies)' (Breant 2013). According to the EDA, four perspectives have been taken into consideration to ensure defence R&T matches capability development needs (ibid): (1) capability-driven for

## EDA and the field of research and technology    105

short- and medium-term needs; (2) industrial analysis to master technologies for long-term needs; (3) technology-driven to take care of technical (r)evolutions; and (4) CapTech networks to develop strategic research agendas and technology roadmaps.

The latest data on ongoing R&T projects within the EDA list 12 Category B contracts in 2012 with a total amount of €52.5 million (EDA 2013b). Nine projects have been completed in the same year, representing a total of €7.81 million. The EDA foresees 26 Category B candidate projects exceeding the €100 million range in total. Table 6.1 lists all past and present EDA R&T projects under their official title, acronym and description tags.

Bringing these figures into a context, European R&T spending, national expenditures and collaborative R&T under the EDA umbrella have been decreasing both in absolute and relative terms. According to recent data, Member States reduced their defence R&T budget from €2.66 billion to €1.93 billion from 2006 to 2012 (EDA 2013a: 21). It is a continuous trend which does not seem to have recovered from the 2009 financial crisis. While collaborative R&T spending increased in the run-up to the 2008 banking crash, it was one of the first victims of Member States' austerity policies beginning in 2009. From €412 million in 2008, European collaborative defence R&T was cut in half until 2012 (€139 million). Almost 90 per cent was allocated for national defence R&T in 2012, but only 7.2 per cent in a European cooperation framework. This value is far from the benchmark of 20 per cent of the overall R&T spending across Member States agreed in the R&T Strategy (EDA 2008). So is the total of R&T spending (1.02 per cent in 2012) with regard to overall defence budgets (EDA 2013a).

*Table 6.1* EDA R&T projects

| Title | | Tags |
|---|---|---|
| 1 | Exchange of Information and Scoping Study Concerning Test and Evaluation of Biological Sampling, Identification and Detection Equipment Phase 1 (T&E BIO DIM Phase 1) | Biological, BioEDEP, Test and Evaluation, BIODIM |
| 2 | Unattended Ground Sensor Networks for Large Area (UGELAS) | Surveillance, Reconnaissance, Intelligence |
| 3 | Data Fusion in Urban Sensor Networks (D-FUSE) | Data Fusion |
| 4 | Disruptive COTS Technologies in the IT area (DISCOTECH) | Future Planning, Electronics |
| 5 | Demonstration and Evaluation of System In package Realisation (DeSIRE) | Microprocessors, Electronic Warfare |
| 6 | Electro-Magnetic Signature Reduction (EMSR) | Stealth, EMSR, Electro-magnetism |
| 7 | Embarked Middleware  (EMWARE) | Satellite, Helicopters, Unmanned, Middleware |
| 8 | EU Core Technical Framework Study | Cooperation, Technical |
| 9 | Enhanced Radar Imaging Techniques (ERIT) | ERIT, ISAR, Radar |
| 10 | Cognitive Aspects of Friendly Fire Incidents | Blue-on-blue, Friendly Fire |
| 11 | Scenarios for Multiple Unmanned Vehicle Operations (SMUVO) | Planning, Robots, Unmanned |

*continued*

## 106    A. *Dahlmann* et al.

*Table 6.1* Continued

| | Title | Tags |
|---|---|---|
| 12 | JIP FP Generic Urban Area Robotized Detection of CBRNE Devices (GUARDED) | CBRNE, Unmanned |
| 13 | JIP-FP Multi Sensor Anti Sniper System (MUSAS) | Land, Protection, Sniper |
| 14 | Piezo Electric Transformers in Power Converters for Space and Military Systems (PIETRA) | Transform, Power |
| 15 | Submarine Motions in Confined Waters (SUBMOTION) | Sea, Submarine |
| 16 | Development of Ultra Fast Molecular Diagnostics (UFMD) | Biological, Detection, Molecular |
| 17 | Modular Approach for Combat Management Systems | Control, Command, Network |
| 18 | Networked Multi-Robot Systems (NM-RS) | Unmanned, Robot, Network |
| 19 | Naval Environment Modelling and Electro Magnetic Signature of Surface Radar Targets for Improved Simulations (NEMESIS) | Modelling, Electro-magnetism, Radar |
| 20 | Terahertz for Identification of Improvised Explosive Chemicals (TERIFIEC) | Improvised Explosive Device, C-IED, Chemicals, Land |
| 21 | Surface-mount Technologies for Active Mount Production (STAMP) | Information, Communications, Antenna |
| 22 | Unmanned Ground Tactical Vehicle - UGTV (Phase 1) | Land, Unmanned |
| 23 | Electric Armour for Armoured Vehicles (ELAV) | Armour, Electric, Protect, Land |
| 24 | Huge Network Wireless Connectivity for the future autonomous remote multisensing system (ARMS) | Communication, Connection, Wireless |
| 25 | Layered Architecture for Realtime Applications (LARA) | Security, Communication |
| 26 | European Technology Acquisition Programme (ETAP) | Acquisition, Demonstration |
| 27 | Synthesis Tooling for Antenna Structures (SynTAS) | Antenna, Communications |
| 28 | Duct Mapping | 3D, Duct |
| 29 | Network Enabled Capabilities Study (LOI-NEC) | NEC, Network |
| 30 | European Theatre Network Architecture (ETNA) | Communications |
| 31 | ETICE Firepower 2025 | ETICE, Firepower |
| 32 | Advanced Techniques for Laser Beam Steering (ATLAS) | Laser |
| 33 | JIP-FP Advanced Helmet and Devices for Individual Protection (AHEAD) | Land, Dismount, Helmet |
| 34 | Integrated Detection and Estimation Algorithms (IDEALS) | Sensor, Sea |
| 35 | Functional Integration of Electro-Magnetic Sensors (FIEMS II) | Electro-Magnetism |
| 36 | Polyfunctional Intelligent Operational Virtual Reality Agents (PIOVRA) | Modelling, Computer |
| 37 | Overall Platform Energy Efficiency (OPEE) | Efficiency, Fuel, Energy, Sea |
| 38 | Energy Supply for Unmanned Underwater Vehicle (ESUUV) | Unmanned |
| 39 | Multifunction Optical Reconfigurable Scalable Equipment (MORSE) | Optics |
| 40 | JIP FP Wireless Robust Link for Urban Force Operations (WOLF) | Communication |
| 41 | Synthesis of Nitrocompounds | Nitrocompounds, Chemicals |
| 42 | IR Diffractive and Reduced Cost Optics | Optics |
| 43 | Micro-satellite Cluster Technology | Satellite, Space |
| 44 | Maritime Unmanned Surface Vehicles (MUSV) | Surface, Unmanned, Sea |
| 45 | Technology Demonstration Study On Sense and Avoid Technologies For Long Endurance Unmanned Aerial Vehicles (LE-UAVs) | Air |
| 46 | Space-Based military SAR systems and technologies | Reconnaisance, Surveillance, Resolution, Radar, Space |
| 47 | Assessing European Defence Technology and Industrial Dependencies | Security, Dependency, Independence, Industry and Market |

Source: EDA 2014b.

### The plan: European Defence R&T Strategy

The EDA published an R&T Strategy in 2008, the European Defence R&T Strategy (EDRTS) (EDA 2008). The EDRTS is designed to operationalise the EDA's R&T objectives, aiming at improving European defence capabilities and delivering 'the right technologies in time'. Its implementation was supposed to be carried out in concert with the Capability Development Plan (CDP) and the European Defence Industrial and Technological Base (EDTIB) Strategy. The expected results of the implementation of the EDRTS were an increase of R&T spending up to 2 per cent of all defence expenditure, and a rise of the European collaborative defence R&T spending to a level of 20 per cent of the respective national defence R&T expenditure.

The Strategy's architecture is based on three elements: the Ends, the Means and the Ways. The Ends are the technologies in which pMS are invited to invest, and rely on a list of 22 key technologies (EDA 2008). The Means are objectives pursued in terms of frameworks, mechanisms, processes and structures, in order to improve performance in delivering the Ends. The Ways are roadmaps and action plans designed to implement the Ends and the Means. They indicate clearly the way R&T programmes are connected to operational and industrial capabilities.

On a more general scale, the EDA adopts a capability-driven strategic approach to defence R&T. That is to say, the Agency bases its work and orientations on concrete capability needs. For instance, the EDA chose to orientate the R&T debate on cyber-defence towards resilience-related issues, seen as 'vital' by the agency.

The main orientation of the Agency's strategy, other than the capability-driven approach, involves the upholding of the EU supply chain and the competitiveness of its defence industry – the main objective being to deliver the 'right technology in time' (EDA undated). 'This necessarily needs to include a clear view where strategic dependence from sources outside Europe will require specific R&T efforts to access these technologies in Europe' (EDA undated).

The strategy adopted by the EDA is both a common denominator within the EU and a factor of differentiation. That is to say, the strategy chosen by the EDA, which is directly inspired by Monnet's method of concrete steps, as the implementation of the CapTechs, or the capability-driven orientation and the chosen priorities, show, works as a common denominator in the EU, linking together various politics and pMS' defence priorities. At the same time, this strategy is a factor of differentiation of the Agency by its intergovernmental, voluntaristic and negotiated nature. Projects and programmes attached to a priority, when proposed by a pMS, will clearly represent this state's needs before any general interest.

108   *A. Dahlmann* et al.

### The implementation: the EDA as a moderator and a platform

To fulfil its tasks stated in the Joint Action and the R&T Strategy, the EDA uses two main instruments: CapTechs and JIP. In addition to these, single R&T projects and studies are possible as well. Thus, the EDA promotes R&T in different roles. It can give the impulse for new project and studies, or provide a platform for joint projects of pMS. With regard to the CapTechs, the EDA acts as moderator, bringing together the relevant stakeholders of the respective field.

### CapTechs – technology domains

To organise its R&T work and to promote joint R&T projects between pMS, the EDA established the so called CapTechs: networks assembling experts from governments, industry, Small and Medium Enterprises, and academia to share their technical expertise. The groups are coordinated by governmental coordinators and moderated by an EDA employee. They exist through regular meetings, workshops and other fora, and cover multiple topics in the fields of Information Acquisition and Processing (IAP), Guidance, Energy and Materials (GEM), and Environment, Systems and Modelling (ESM) (EDA 2012: 23–24). Each field is divided into four technology areas, as depicted in Table 6.2.

Since the scrapping of the Agency's R&T division, CapTechs are managed by the EDA's operational directorate for capability, armament and technology. Within this directorate, ad hoc (armament) or integrated development teams (capability) can be created in order to develop a specific project. The Directorate still operates, however, under the guidance of the R&T Directorates of the Ministries of Defence of the pMS. The

*Table 6.2* Structure of EDA's R&T through CapTechs

| Information, Acquisition and Processing (IAP) | Guidance, Energy and Materials (GEM) | Environment, Systems and Modelling (ESM) |
| --- | --- | --- |
| IAP01: Components | GEM01: Materials and Structures | ESM01: Naval Systems and their Environment |
| IAP02: Radio Frequency Sensor Systems and Signal Processing | GEM02: Materials and Structures | ESM02: Aerial Systems and their Environment |
| IAP03: Optical Sensors Systems and Signal Processing | GEM03: Ground Systems and their Environment | ESM03: System of Systems Space Simulation and Experimentation |
| IAP04: Optical Sensors Systems and Signal Processing | GEM04: Guidance and Control | ESM04: Human Factors and CBR Protection |

Source: EDA 2013b: 7.

annual EDA Steering Board in R&T Directors' formation is the main forum where strategic decisions are made. The 2005 R&T Operational Concept, which defined seven Key Operating Rules (KOR), delimited the basic competence areas of the CapTechs (EDA 2005).

The seven KOR are the following (Piquer 2010):

- Capability orientation defines the three main CapTechs domains: IAP related to knowledge; GEM related to engagement; ESM related to Manoeuvre.
- Network centric management relates to the method and accessibility of the EDA's work, EDA's role being there to promote the exchange of information between the CapTechs and to keep the information available and updated online while enabling remote working.
- Transparency through monitoring and reporting proposes an R&T roadmap and a strategy in order to 'establish good communications, monitoring and exchange of information between the Agency, the pMS and the Steering Board', and the Capabilities and Armaments directorate, along with a set of indicators enabling the monitoring of R&T cooperation.
- Embracing valuable existing cooperation and networks by inviting other interested R&T groups and networks to transfer their activities to the EDA, with the aim of centralising the R&T cooperation within the EDA, this rule is in fact addressed to two main R&T structures: the WEAG and the LoI.
- Effective interface with dual-use and civil research, implemented in order to secure synergies with dual-use research and avoid duplication, and eventually give the EDA opportunities to submit R&T priorities in the security field.
- Involvement of industry is an acknowledgement of the role of the industry in the defence R&T cooperation, and in its European bottom-up process within the CapTechs.
- Using EDA contracting capacity for R&T re-enacts the EDA's capacity to contract on behalf of the pMS, showing its supportive role of cooperative defence R&T.

The implementation of the aforementioned KOR enables a better cooperation and wider synergies with the EC and between Member States and the industrials taking part in the EDA's R&T activities, and particularly within its CapTechs (Koblen and Olejník 2011; Piquer 2010).

At the very beginning, the CapTechs contributed less significantly to the EDA's profile. The EDA divided the technology areas among the CapTechs, but this was conducted without sufficient consultation with the pMS or sufficient regard for the organisation of multidisciplinary work (Piquer 2010). Multidisciplinary work is a key organisational concept for the CapTechs, as experts from various backgrounds and different expertise fields are supposed to work together on a common project within the CapTechs. As a result, difficulties appeared when the CapTechs provoked a lack of uniformity and inconsistencies in those very actions. The creation of groups where experts, research institutions and the industry could cooperate, hence, did not come without problems. A repositioning of the CapTechs within the EDA reduced the number of projects launched in the early years.

Attempting to cope with these issues, a new CapTech structure was approved in 2008 by the R&T Directorate Steering Board, following a consensus between the EDA and the pMS. According to this new arrangement, four areas for transversal activities ((1) ground; (2) naval; (3) aerial systems; and (4) aerospace systems) were defined, aiming at facilitating the implementation of multidisciplinary work.

All 12 CapTechs are based on the participation of four types of experts: a CapTech Moderator chairs the meetings and acts as the EDA point of contact for CapTech members; the CapTech National Coordinators (CNC) act as official representatives of pMS and have the task to distribute the information on CapTech activities within their countries; the CapTech Governmental Experts (CGE) contribute as experts to specific topics within the CapTech, and support their CNC in the preparation of tasks and activities for the CapTech; and the CapTech non-Governmental Experts (CnGE) come from various backgrounds (e.g. industry, research organisations, scientific institutes, universities), and can propose R&T projects and studies on a bottom-up basis or to answer a top-down request.

The CapTechs use various means in order to achieve their objectives. For instance, both top-down and bottom-up approaches can be adopted. The top-down approach means the information sharing on national R&T priorities or priorities inspired by other EDA work can be used as a case study to copy, while the bottom-up method implies an evaluation of industrial proposals considered relevant to pMS R&T priorities (EDA 2011b). In addition a number of other means for identifying domains of interest can be exploited. For example, technology watch and assessment can be performed in order to identify R&T areas of importance, groups of interested pMS can be formed on selected topics (thus widening the contribution and consultation of the expert community), and EDA-funded studies, such as the Mid-air Collision Avoidance System (MIDCAS), may be proposed in specific areas.

The range and the width of the collaboration in R&T projects can vary from information sharing, to issuing contracts to industry after a formal call for bids (EDA 2013b: 6).

CapTechs groups can get involved in Category A and B projects providing feasibility studies and experts' advice in cooperation with both EDA and EC. This is made possible under the European Framework Cooperation (EFC). Based on this, CapTechs have successfully launched various programmes and shared results among Member States, leading the way towards the development of new technologies.

Such projects and programmes are adopted with regard to a global R&T strategy. For instance, within CapTech ESM01, Naval Systems and their Environment, is an R&T project on Unmanned Maritime Systems (UMS) are seen as a priority by the EDA, and financed through a JIP. Moreover, in 2012 many of the EDA's R&T projects were concluded (e.g. the projects TELLUS and FARADAYS within CapTech IAP02), their follow-ons being discussed soon afterwards.

### Joint Investment Programmes (JIP)

Category A and B R&T projects follow the *juste retour* principal, while JIP recognise that competition may have an impact on R&T results. Turning away from the *juste retour* principal is a major change in the EDA's R&T policy and brings its effort in tune with the EU's Framework Programme for Research and Development, currently called Horizon 2020, where contracts are awarded on the basis of research excellence.

The biggest portion of Category A projects is conducted under the umbrella of Joint Investment Programmes, although Category B projects can be part of a JIP, too. The name of this instrument stems from the joint financial fund of the particular contributing Member States.

The first JIP dealt with Force Protection (JIP-FP) and was launched in 2007 with a budget of €55 million and the support of 20 Member States (EDA 2013b, p. 15). Other JIPs have been or are conducted on Innovative Concepts and Emerging Technologies (JIP ICET I and II, launched 2008 and 2013 respectively), CBRN Protection within the European Framework Cooperation (JIP CBRN, launched 2012), Remotely Piloted Aircraft Systems within the EFC (JIP RPAS, launched 2012), Unmanned Maritime Systems (JIP UMS, launched 2012) (EDA 2013b: 15–18; 2012: 15, 20). Table 6.3 provides an overview of the JIPs undertaken thus far.

### The assessment: does the EDA's R&T concept work out?

In principle, the EDA's concept and reformed internal structure in the R&T domain is fitted to build up a significant collaborative European R&T sector. The EDA offers well-designed instruments to its Member States which allow for the complexity and diversity of the existing European landscape and its nationally focused user community. In reality, however, neither the financial figures of recent years nor the output in joint capability development prove an effective use of the EDA's R&T instruments. In fact, pMS do play a decisive role in the exploitation of opportunities created with the EDA, because their steering and action defines the scope, the priorities and the impact of the EDAs involvement.

While one can observe an overall reluctance from some pMS (United Kingdom, partly Germany), others (France) demand an extended role and are willing to contribute with further resources. France, for instance,

*Table 6.3* Overview of Joint Investment Programmes

| Name | Launch | Contributing Member States | Budget |
|---|---|---|---|
| Force Protection | 2007 | 19+1<br>Austria, Belgium, Cyprus, Czech Republic, Estonia, Finland, France, Germany, Greece, Hungary, Ireland, Italy, Netherlands, Poland, Portugal, Slovakia, Slovenia, Spain, Sweden + Norway | €55 million |
| Innovative Concepts and Emerging Technologies I | 2008 | 10+1<br>Cyprus, France, Germany, Greece, Hungary, Italy, Poland, Slovakia, Slovenia, Spain, + Norway | €15.6 million |
| Innovative Concepts and Emerging Technologies II | 2012/2013 | 8<br>Austria, Germany, France, Italy, Luxembourg, Netherlands, Poland, Sweden | €5.2 million |
| CBRN Protection | 2012/2013 | 13+1<br>Austria, Belgium, Czech Republic, Germany, Spain, France, Ireland, Italy, Netherlands, Poland, Portugal, Sweden + Norway | €12 million |
| Remotely Piloted Aircraft Systems | 2012 | 8<br>Austria, Belgium, Czech Republic, Germany, France, Italy, Spain, UK | – |
| Unmanned Maritime Systems | 2012 | 10+1<br>Belgium, Finland, France, Germany, Italy, the Netherlands, Poland, Portugal, Spain, Sweden + Norway | €53 million |

insists on the necessity of an EU-level inter-state cooperation in order to allow for a dialogue between states and with the EC. The French government sees defence R&T cooperation as the only way to bring forward some projects, thus insisting on the necessity to improve the French contribution and active cooperation with the EDA and the other pMS (Représentation Permanente de la France auprès de l'UE 2014). However, the actual impact of the EDA's R&T concept is hard to assess due to a lack of transparency, and complete and up to date information.

## The relationship between the EDA and the European Commission

Nowadays, the EDA and the EC present a demonstrative harmony in their agenda and actions. The relationship of these two institutions is largely defined by the EFC. The main interlocutor for the EDA R&T branch is the EC's Directorate-General for Enterprise and Industry; the Enterprise Commissioner is an observer in the EDA's Steering Board (European Commission Directorate-General for Enterprise and Industry 2014). In connection with the Horizon 2020 framework, the Directorate-General for Research and Innovation is another important partner for the EDA's R&T.

However, the allocation of competences was not always clear, resulting in a number of diverging opinions on certain issues. For example, the issue of Intellectual Property Rights (IPR) and their exploitation do complicate their cooperation.

### The plan: frameworks and institutional arrangements

In September 2011, the EDA, the EC and the ESA agreed on the EFC, formalising the will to coordinate their research agendas with regard to dual-use technologies. This approach is implemented by formal consultations, the exchange of information on R&T goals as well as the alignment of R&T agendas and timing (European Commission 2011b). Despite common objectives, the three institutions remain independent with regard to rules, financial instruments and budgets (EDA 2012: 19).

Another strong link between the EDA and the EC is the Enterprise Commissioner's role as an observer in the EDA's Steering Board. He is responsible for the industrial part of defence and space policy in the EU, while R&T is a competence of the Directorate-General for Research and Innovation. This department is involved through the financial leadership on R&T projects within the EC.

The EDA's operational directorate, European Synergies and Innovation (ESI), is an interface between the Agency and other actors in the field of defence policies and technologies, especially the EC. Besides conducting impact and feasibility studies, the ESI is supposed to develop synergies and

114   *A. Dahlmann* et al.

complementarities with other EU programmes. In cooperation with the EC and the ESA, this directorate strives for an enhancement of civil–military cooperation, interoperability and effective R&T spending (EDA 2014a).

The previous European Framework Programme for Research and Development – FP7 (2007–2013) – notably established a committed research theme on security (the European Security Research Programme), which allowed Research and Development (R&D) on security-relevant and dual-use technologies. Under the current Horizon 2020 (2014–2020), not only does a similar theme exists, but also the role of the EDA is much more institutionalised and entrenched in setting the overarching research priorities.

### The implementation: obstacles and achievements

In 2014, the principal issues concerning the relations between EDA and the EC, and particularly concerning their relations on R&T-related issues, are the standardisation and the implementation of the December 2013 Council decisions (European Council 2013). Prior to the Lisbon Treaty of December 2009, the competences of EDA and the EC were defined on a cross-pillar basis, said to have affected defence procurements, standing thus 'in the way of a pan-European armaments policy' (Bauer 2005). A conflict loomed large before the respective competences of EDA and the EC were clearly defined by the Lisbon Treaty.

### Obstacles to R&T cooperation

One problem that hampers cooperative projects of the EDA and the EC is the disparate attitude towards IPR. While the EC allows the authors of studies to make further use of IPR rights, the EDA prefers to retain those rights for itself and, therefore, to be the owner of all study results (EDA 2011a).

Furthermore, the EC is quite restrictive towards funding of military technologies. There are, however, options for dual-use technologies that evolve from the civil sector. The FP7, as mentioned, included security as a research theme, mentioning both civil and defence research (European Commission 2006), while the EFC explicitly restricts cooperation only to dual-use technologies (European Commission 2011b).

Co-funding procedures have been developed only with Horizon 2020. As it is still impossible for the EDA and the EC to jointly contract R&T projects due to conflicting financial instruments, a stronger cooperation and coexistence has been introduced. The lack of harmonised financial procedures between the EDA and the EC remains a major institutional shortfall of the EFC. However, for the Horizon 2020 programme the EC introduced new procedures to streamline R&T:

Simplification in Horizon 2020 will target three overarching goals: to reduce the administrative costs of the participants; to accelerate all processes of proposal and grant management and to decrease the financial error rate.

(European Commission 2011a)

While it is important that the major R&T funder in the EU, the EC, enhances and simplifies its formalities for the Horizon 2020 in order to facilitate cooperation with other institutional players, such as the EDA, different approaches remain.

### Positive examples

Despite problems between the two institutions, they reiterate their willingness to work together closely. Since neither the EDA nor the EC can solve the problems in the area of defence R&T alone – more comprehensive cooperation had already been asked for, particularly by pMS and the Council in 2005 – the demand for stronger coherence has been affirmed by the Council in December 2013 (European Council 2013). This cooperation is implemented on a horizontal basis in both formal and informal ways; for example, EC officials participate in EDA events like the Annual Conference and can be given the status of speaker, like in 2013, when the DG Industry was invited to report on the EDA-EC cooperation in R&T policy.

Space technologies are the only area of actual cooperation between the two institutions since this topic is mostly civilian and therefore less controversial. For example, the Joint EC–ESA–EDA task force on Critical Technologies for European Strategic Non-Dependence is basically limited to space technologies (European Commission 2013: 28, 57) and the search for cooperative EDA–EC projects on the EC's website only refers to several documents related to this task force (e.g. European Commission 2013). Further areas of cooperation are to be expected since both the JIP CBRN and the JIP RPAS are conducted within the EFC (EDA 2013b: 17–18).

### The assessment: do EDA and EC foster a cooperative and comprehensive European R&T policy?

The EU's former partition in pillars was a major obstacle for cooperation between the EDA and the EC from the beginning. Although the Lisbon Treaty overcame the pillar principle, cooperation between institutions of former different pillars remains inefficient due to unchanged financial regulations and instruments. In principal, the institutional convergence and modified arrangements have facilitated synergies or at least coherence between the EDA and the EC. Because direct cooperation is impossible in most cases, complementary action and coordination is in focus.

## 116  *A. Dahlmann* et al.

Nevertheless, issues like the handling of diverging IPR rules, the classification of dual-use R&T, and incompatible financial instruments and regulations shape the picture. In addition, the actual implementation of the unspecific EFC is very narrow. Beyond the scope of the EFC, the EC and the EDA could create common R&T funding procedures in the future. This approach would overcome the institutional gap by delegating specific R&T topics to a joint body with harmonised financial instruments. Such an endeavour remains unlikely however, due to political decisions not to mix up civil/dual-use and military R&T and the respective tasks of the representing EU bodies. While a clear distinction makes sense for certain technology areas and applications, e.g. dedicated weapons systems, some basic research areas, e.g. nano-materials, could profit from a joint EC and EDA approach. In the eyes of the authors, this could only be an acceptable solution when EU Member States reduce their nationally oriented defence policies and R&T strategies in favour of a more coordinated and EDA-focused R&T strategy at the same time.

## Conclusion

The EDA's mission of being the easiest and most convenient entry point into common R&D of technologies has been proven a valid concept. In reality, however, engagement of pMS is decisive not only for implementing the EDRTS but also for facilitating the platform function of the EDA. The EDA proved to be flexible in adapting its instruments to the needs of pMS and the constraints of the defence R&T domain. However, pMS have failed to deliver in this respect due to incoherent national R&T objectives and defence industry policies. The EDA is capable of delivering at least a basic joint picture of the European R&T landscape. It is able to draw a picture of a possible collaborative R&T future. EU Member States should not be afraid of learning the lessons from the EDA's experiences. Strengthening the EDA's role in exploring and implementing more cooperation would be a major step forward for the CSDP of the EU.

## References

Bauer, T. (2005) *Defence Agency vs. Commission? Claims and Realities of a Comprehensive European Armaments Policy Strategy*, Reform Spotlight 2005/06, Bertelsmann Foundation, Brussels, and Centre for Applied Policy Research, Munich.

Breant, C. (2013) 'Science and Technology for Defence: Luxury or Need?', PowerPoint presentation, Brussels: Institut Royal supérieur de défense, 7 March 2013.

Council of the European Union (2004) 'Council Joint Action 2004/551/CFSP'.

DeVore, M. (2013) 'Explaining European Armaments Cooperation: Interests, Institutional Design and Armaments Organizations', *European Foreign Affairs Review*, 18(1): 1–27.

European Commission (2013) *Horizon 2020 Work Programme 2014–2015*.

European Commission (2011a) 'Horizon 2020: The Framework Programme for Research and Innovation', COM/2011/0808.

European Commission (2011b) 'European Framework Cooperation in the Field of Research'.

European Commission (2006) 'FP7 – Tomorrow's Answers Start Today'. Online. Available at: http://ec.europa.eu/research/fp7/pdf/fp7-factsheets_en.pdf (accessed 2 July 2014).

European Commission Directorate-General for Enterprise and Industry (2014) 'Our Network'. Online. Available at http://ec.europa.eu/enterprise/dg/network/index_en.htm (accessed 2 July 2014).

European Council (2013) 'Conclusions of the European Council of the 19 and 20 December 2013, EUCO 217/13'.

EDA (European Defence Agency) (2014a) 'European Synergies and Innovation'.

EDA (European Defence Agency) (2014b) 'Project Search Results in Category Research and Technology'.

EDA (European Defence Agency) (2013a) 'Defence Data 2012 Booklet'.

EDA (European Defence Agency) (2013b) 'Research and Technology'.

EDA (European Defence Agency) (2012) 'Business Opportunities R&T'.

EDA (European Defence Agency) (2011a) 'EDA-funded RT Studies. *R&T Projects User Guide*'.

EDA (European Defence Agency) (2011b) 'Generic CapTech Guide'.

EDA (European Defence Agency) (2008) 'A European Defence Research and Technology Strategy'.

EDA (European Defence Agency) (2005) 'R&T Operational Concept'.

EDA (European Defence Agency) (undated) 'European Defence Research and Technology Strategy'.

Guzelyte, S. (2014) 'National Defence Data 2012 of the EDA Participating Member States', Brussels: EDA.

Koblen, I. and Olejník, F. (2011) 'The Key Role of the European Defence Agency in the Enhancement of European Defence Research and Technology', *Advances in Military Technology*, 6(2): 111–122.

Maulny, J.-P. and Matelly, S. (2013) *Pooling of Defence Research and Development*, Les Notes de l'IRIS, July 2013, Paris: IRIS

Piquer, T.M. (2010) 'Research and Technology (R&T)', in *EDA: Past, Present, and Future*, Spanish Ministry of Defence: 85–124.

Représentation Permanente de la France auprès de l'UE (2014) 'L'Agence Européenne de Défence'.

# 7 The EDA and EU defence procurement integration

*Aris Georgopoulos*

## Introduction

The purchase and the development of weapons and related materiel are activities linked to core functions of the notion of the Westphalian nation state, namely national defence. Yet, at the dawn of the new century major regulatory and policy changes have emerged in this area in the context of the European Union (EU). The process of EU integration in the area of defence procurement reached its regulatory culmination with the enactment of the Defence and Security Procurement (DSP) Directive (European Commission 2009a).

This chapter reflects upon the ten years since the establishment of the European Defence Agency (EDA) and analyses the role of the latter in the process of European integration in defence procurement. The chapter examines the various initiatives undertaken so far by the EDA in the process of Europeanisation of a policy area that has been linked to core functions of the state and, for that reason, based upon a decision-making process carried out primarily at national level. The chapter argues that the contribution of the EDA in the process of European integration in the field of defence procurement has been especially noteworthy. In particular the chapter submits that the EDA played a crucial role in two ways. First, it demystified and rendered more acceptable the deliberation at the EU level of issues pertaining to the design, rules and policies of defence procurement. Second, by doing so it provided additional political 'legitimisation' to the process of integration of European defence equipment market, which led to the enactment of the DSP Directive.

The chapter is organised as follows. Section 2 provides the necessary clarifications regarding the definitions of key concepts. Section 3 places the EDA in its historical and political context and suggests that the EDA should be seen not only as an institutional offspring of political developments in the area of 'high politics', such as the emergence of ESDP, but also an institutional product that incorporates lessons learned from previous efforts of coordination in the area of defence procurement in Europe. Section 4 examines the EDA initiatives undertaken in the area of defence procurement. Then, section 5 discusses their impact on the process of integration in this area, and section 6 presents a synopsis of the argument and some concluding thoughts.

## Preliminary conceptual and terminological clarifications

Before embarking on examining the role of the EDA in the process of European defence procurement/market integration it is necessary to clarify some of the terms used and the relevant signified concepts.

To begin with, the term 'defence procurement' is used narrowly. It refers to the acquisition of goods and services that have been manufactured, used or intended to be used for purely military purposes (Georgopoulos 2004: 21–28; SIGMA 2011: 2). According to this narrow definition, defence procurement covers, for example, the acquisition of fighter jets, frigates and munitions. This can be contrasted with a wider definition of defence procurement covering all acquisitions of goods and services in the defence sector (including, for example, the procurement of food supplies, stationery and clothing). This definition uses a functional criterion that looks at whether the procurement activity – and the relevant goods or services – are connected with the core of what is generally understood as national defence and national security. Defence procurement, in this sense, is often characterised by the complexity of the relevant technologies. According to this definition of defence procurement, the size of the relevant market in the EU was approximately €84 billion in 2012 (EDA 2013a: 12).

Furthermore, the term 'European defence procurement integration' needs to be delimited. European integration is understood as the process of progressive Europeanisation of the relevant policy area and the gradual opening up of national defence markets to intra-Union competition. Europeanisation, in this context, does not mean the replacement of the national by the European; instead, it involves the inclusion of a European layer in a policy area that customarily has been deliberated, formed and carried out at national level. Integration is viewed widely and includes looser forms of coordination of national policies without the imposition of a binding EU framework.

In addition, the concept of integration can be further subdivided into three dimensions: an economic, a legal/regulatory and a political one. The chapter will focus on the examination of the EDA's role particularly on the legal and political dimensions.

## Historical and political context

In order to examine the role that the EDA has played in the process of European integration in defence procurement, it is important to remind ourselves of the historical and political context in which EDA was created and the environment in which it later operated.

120   *A. Georgopoulos*

First, it is worth remembering that the EDA's creation in 2004 was a last-minute deviation from the original plan. According to this plan, the creation of the EDA was part of the changes that were to be introduced by the Constitutional Treaty (Article I-40 (3)). Instead, the Thessaloniki European Council (European Council 2003: par. 65) decided to dissociate in effect the creation of the EDA from the uncertain, at that time, future of the Treaty. The European Council tasked the competent bodies of the EU to create within the course of 2004 the EDA; the latter was subsequently established by a Joint Action (Council of the European Union 2004). Two questions arise in this regard: First, why establish the EDA? Second, why the deviation from the original plan?

With regard to the first question, the following have been considered as the main reasons for creating the EDA (Georgopoulos 2005b: 109): the need for improving European defence capabilities, and the need for streamlining the institutional framework in European armaments cooperation whilst learning the lessons from previous experiences. Let us now look at each point more closely.

First, ever since the Anglo-French St. Malo declaration in 1998, the EU had raised expectations that it would increase its role in the field of defence and security but had failed time and again to match the rhetoric with tangible actions. Particularly in the area of defence capabilities, an alarming gap had been demonstrated between United States' and European armed forces during the intervention in Kosovo. Consequently, concerted action in order to improve defence capabilities in an era of reduced defence budgets was seen by the majority of Member States as a necessity.

Second, efforts for coordinating armaments policies in Europe had been already made outside the legal and institutional framework of the EU, initially under the auspices of the Western European Union (WEU) in the form of the Western European Armaments Group (WEAG) and the Western European Armaments Organisation (WEAO), and later on a plurilateral basis amongst some EU MSs under the Joint Armaments Co-operation Organisation (OCCAR) and the Letter of Intent Initiative (LoI). These efforts had up until that point mixed results. Furthermore, they had created a complex institutional landscape that was characterised by a degree of duplication in terms of aims and resources. The creation of the EDA would assist the streamlining of the institutional landscape in armaments and would bring it by and large under the auspices of the EU. The stated aim of the EDA was to assimilate and incorporate principles and practices or pre-existing organisations (Council of the European Union 2004: Preamble). The activities of the WEAG and WEAO were assimilated by the EDA, and consequently WEAG was dissolved in 2005 and WEAO in 2006.

Third, all of these initiatives seemed to have missed the elusive balance between inclusiveness, on the one hand, and flexibility, on the other. For example, both WEAG and WEAO were in principle inclusive, as reflected by their wide membership (Georgopoulos 2007a: 208) but, as a result, they were cumbersome in moving ahead with the process of European armaments cooperation. On the other hand, OCCAR, which was created initially by the four largest armaments-producing Member States (France, United Kingdom, Germany and Italy) seemed to introduce more flexibility, at the expense of inclusiveness by bluntly excluding Member States with medium- and small-sized defence industrial bases (Georgopoulos 2007a: 210; Mawdsley 2003: 18). The creation of the EDA incorporated the lessons learned from these initiatives. This is demonstrated in particular by the incorporation of two different categories of ad hoc collaborative projects, namely Category A and Category B. The first draws from lessons from the WEAG and in particular of the EUROPA MoU, and the second from OCCAR (Georgopoulos 2005b: 111; Schmitt 2003: 94).

After addressing the question 'why the EDA?', we now turn to the question regarding the deviation from the original plan. There were two main reasons for this (see also Georgopoulos 2005b).

First, the Iraq war had created an unpleasant rift amongst the governments of EU15 with the immediate consequence of the EU, once again, not being able to frame a united and coherent voice in the area of CFSP. Finding a CFSP-related theme or project that would attract the support of the large majority of Member States was deemed a priority. One such theme was identified in the 'lower regions' of the 'high politics' of CFSP and was none other than European defence capabilities and armament cooperation.

Second, in March 2003 the European Commission (2003) reopened the debate about the role of the EU in the area of defence markets with the publication of a defence-related Communication. This document demonstrated the Commission's clear aim to introduce supranational elements in the area, thus strengthening its role. As had been suggested at the time, it was clear that 'more Europe' in the area of defence market was necessary but what was uncertain was where this process of integration would take place – namely under the Community pillar or under the CFSP or in an inter-pillar straddled arrangement – and also what intensity this process of integration would have – particularly with regard to the role of the Commission, the Court of Justice (CJ) and the European Parliament (Georgopoulos 2005a: 560). In other words, the decision of the Member States to dissociate the establishment of the EDA from the uncertain and lengthy ratification process of the Treaty should be seen in a context where all the major European institutional stakeholders were trying to secure their role in the European defence market integration process and influence its direction. Thus, the speedy establishment of the EDA was intended to strengthen the intergovernmental pole in the debate that was about to begin about armaments cooperation and regulation in Europe.

## European defence procurement integration and the EDA

It is suggested that the EDA's role in the process of European defence procurement integration has been important. As shown in section 5, this is true for both the legal/regulatory and the political dimension of the integration process. In order to demonstrate this observation, this part of the chapter will examine some of the initiatives undertaken so far by the EDA that are connected with the area of defence procurement. The aim of the analysis is to highlight their combined effect on the process of European defence procurement integration up to now. The relevant initiatives are the Code of Conduct on defence procurement (CoC), the Code of Best Practice in the Supply Chain (CoBPSC), the Code of Conduct on Offsets (CoCO), the initiatives for Security of Information (SoI), the initiatives in connection to Security of Supply (SoS) and the Effective Procurement Methods initiative (EPM).

### Code of Conduct on defence procurement

EDA's first important initiative in the area of defence procurement was the CoC. The latter was launched on 1 July 2006 and aimed at the introduction of openness, transparency and competition in the European Defence Equipment Market (EDEM).

As with all EDA's defence procurement-related initiatives, the CoC has the following characteristics: it is voluntary, non-legally binding or enforceable, and intergovernmental.

The voluntary character meant that EDA participating Member States (pMS) are not obliged to join the CoC. Furthermore, the pMS that decided to join the CoC are free to withdraw from the regime. For example, Spain and Hungary decided not to join immediately – they did so eventually in 2007 – (Georgopoulos 2008: NA8), Romania decided not to join at all and the UK has considered leaving it in the context of the wider reassessment of its participation in the EDA (Lord Astor of Hever 2010). This is linked also with the intergovernmental nature of the CoC. The non-legally binding nature of the CoC meant that the success of the initiative depended entirely on the willingness and political will of the subscribing Member States. It should be remembered that the CoC is very similar to the 'Coherent Policy Document' adopted in 1990, which set the principles for the creation of EDEM under the auspices of WEAG – which had failed precisely because of the Member States' lack of political will (Georgopoulos 2006a: 51–52, 57–58).

The CoC covers defence procurement contracts that meet the criteria of Article 346 TFEU (former Article 296 EC) and are of a value that exceeds €1 million. Article 346 reads:

1   The provisions of the Treaties shall not preclude the application of the following rules: (a) no Member State shall be obliged to supply

information the disclosure of which it considers contrary to the essential interests of its security; (b) any Member State may take such measures as it considers necessary for the protection of the essential interests of its security which are connected with the production of or trade in arms, munitions and war material; such measures shall not adversely affect the conditions of competition in the internal market regarding products which are not intended for specifically military purposes.

2   The Council may, acting unanimously on a proposal from the Commission, make changes to the list, which it drew up on 15 April 1958, of the products to which the provisions of paragraph 1(b) apply.

The CoC contains also some exemptions (Research and Development (R&D); collaborative procurements; chemical, bacteriological and radiological goods and services; nuclear weapons; nuclear propulsion systems; and cryptographic equipment). Clearly, the exclusion of collaborative procurement from the CoC's coverage means that the regime is aimed primarily at off-the-shelf procurement contracts. From this, it follows that there is a significant overlap between the CoC's field of application and that of the DSP Directive.

This observation means that the two regimes are antagonistic, at least from a legal point of view. Why? Because logically they cannot apply both at the same time (Georgopoulos 2007b: 47). One has to give way to the other, particularly because the CoC is a self-regulatory, non-legally binding (CFSP pillar) instrument whereas the DSP Directive is a legally binding and enforceable (first pillar, internal market) instrument. It is important to note that although the CoC was viewed by some commentators as a potential danger to the *acquis communautaire* (Trybus 2006: 690), the Commission (2005) formally characterised the CoC as a complementary instrument to the DSP Directive since, according to the Commission, they covered different segments of the defence market. It suffices to note that the non-complementarity – from a legal point of view (see Georgopoulos 2006a: 58–59; Trybus 2006: 687–690) – between the two regimes is further evidenced by the fact that the EDA tries to adapt the CoC to the post-DSP directive environment

The most significant practical contribution of the CoC initiative was the creation of the Electronic Bulletin Board (EBB) portal. This was a central portal where subscribing Member States would announce contract opportunities. Centralised publication of these contract opportunities in one portal meant that it would be easier for potential contractors to identify them, instead of having to monitor various national ones as was the case under the WEAG regime. Various kinds of notices were publishable at the EBB (Heuninckx 2009: 47): (1) prior information notices providing general information about future needs of a contracting entity; (2) contract notices inviting the submission of tenders or the submission of requests for participation; (3) contract bidder notices containing the list of contractors that have been selected to participate in a particular procurement process; (4) contract notices identifying the successful contractor; and (5) request for information notices, inviting the industry to send information about a future procurement contract without necessarily launching a procurement process.

The variety of these notices means that the CoC, apart from being a vehicle to improve openness of national defence markets, has been a useful tool for data collection about these markets and the conduct of the relevant national authorities.

The CoC and the EBB have been used more than other similar previous initiatives and in this sense should be judged as more successful. However, as will be mentioned further below, the impact of the CoC on the defence procurement integration process is not based only on the frequency of its use by the subscribing Member States. It should be noted that the EBB portal stopped being operational in its original form in June 2013. Although the EDA website refers to the creation of a new gateway, it is highly likely that this development is also linked with the entry into force of the DSP Directive which requires the publication of defence procurement contract in the Official Journal of the EU and as a result Tender Electronic Daily (TED) is the appropriate online platform.

### Code of Best Practice in the Supply Chain

The CoBPSC was agreed in 2006. The elaboration of the CoBPSC had been announced in the document that established the CoC. Therefore the two codes were conceptually linked from the very beginning, forming integral parts of the EDA's intergovernmental regime on defence procurement. The CoC aimed at introducing competition at the level of prime contractors whereas the aim of the CoBPSC was to introduce greater transparency and competition in the lower tiers of the defence market, namely at the level of subcontractors and by doing so increase the efficiency, quality, timeliness and consistency in the supply chain.

This means that the CoBPSC is not addressed to contracting authorities (public actors) but to the prime contractors (private actors) that are awarded the defence procurement contract. In other words, the instrument aims at affecting the behaviour of enterprises.

In principle, enterprises as market participants are subject to market forces. For this reason, according to economic theory these actors – in our case prime contractors – would take rational decisions in the selection process of their subcontractors aimed at increasing efficiency, lowering costs, improving quality, etc. So, what was the need for an instrument that tried to affect the behaviour of enterprises towards a direction that they were prone to follow anyway?

The answer is the particularities of defence market(s). As opposed to the conditions of perfect competition upon which economic theory is based, the reality in the defence procurement markets is different. These markets are characterised by fragmentation, often upon national protectionist lines, and are by definition monopsonistic (i.e. dominated by one buyer), or at the very least oligopsonistic (i.e. characterised by a small number of buyers). This type of imperfect market competition allows for the preferences of the buyer to be fed into the supply chain of the seller. If these preferences are informed by protectionist intentions, then protectionism will probably contaminate the rest of the supply chain. For this reason, it was agreed that the EDA's intergovernmental regime on defence procurement should address this aspect too.

The CoBPSC shares the same characteristics of the CoC; in other words it is an intergovernmental, non-legally binding and non-legally enforceable instrument.

The CoBPSC was also implemented through an Electronic Bulletin Board platform (EBB2). It should be noted that the EBB2 could be used by prime contractors to advertise subcontract opportunities not only in relation to defence contracts that met the conditions of article 346 TFEU – i.e. contracts that are covered by the CoC – but also for defence-related subcontracts more generally. The CoBPSC was one of the 'carrots' to incentivise compliance (particularly by pMS with medium and small defence industrial bases) in the context of a system with virtually no 'sticks' (Georgopoulos 2006b: NA147).

Like the rest of the intergovernmental regime on defence procurement, the CoBPSC is under review in the aftermath of the DSP Directive.

Despite the stated objective of the CoBPSC about 'influencing behaviour in the supply chain to encourage fair competition at the national level and across the subscribing Member States' (EDA 2006a: par. 5), the latter did not deal with the issue of *offsets* and related practices even though it is through these types of practices that protectionist – or domestic industrial – preferences are fed from the demand side (public sector) to the prime contractor level (private sector) and then diffused into their supply chain, arguably distorting competition. In fact, the term 'offsets' is not mentioned in the CoBPSC at all. Instead, offsets were the subject of another EDA code of conduct discussed immediately below.

### The Code of Conduct on Offsets

One of the areas of the European defence procurement market that all the regulatory initiatives at EU level had refrained from addressing directly up until the relevant EDA initiatives was the treatment of offset practices. The first time that an EU regulatory initiative included offsets as its main focus was the EDA CoCO.

126   *A. Georgopoulos*

Offsets are practices followed in the context of defence procurement whereby procuring States try to safeguard a return of their 'investment' – i.e. the payment given to a foreign defence contractor for the acquisition of defence equipment or related services – for their domestic industry (Georgopoulos 2011: 30). Offset policies can be implemented in a variety of ways and offsets may manifest themselves in various forms. Although there is not a standardised nomenclature or categorisation of offset practices as such, offsets can be categorised as follows (Georgopoulos 2004: 344; 2011: 33):

- Direct offsets: Offset transactions that are directly related to the defence items or services imported by a participating Member State. For example under this category offset practices can take the form of co-production, subcontracting, training, licensed production, technology transfer. The distinguishing factor and principal point of reference for these offset practices is the subject of the main defence procurement contract.
- Indirect offsets: Offset transactions that are not directly related to the defence items or services imported by a procuring government. In turn, indirect offsets are subdivided into:
  - Defence-related indirect offsets. The latter are not linked with the delivery of the contract that forms the subject matter of the main transaction between the procuring government and the foreign contractor but still are to be implemented in the field of defence.
  - Non-defence-related indirect (or civil) offsets. Such offsets are not linked with the subject matter of the main defence procurement contract and are implemented outside of the field of defence.

The aforementioned categorisation is meant to function as schematic representation of what in reality is a more complex typological environment. It may be difficult in practice to place some offset contracts only, or strictly, under one of these categories, because modern defence systems contain technologies that are used in both the defence and civil sectors. These technological crossovers blur the distinction between defence and civil technologies.

The discussion of offset practices generates mixed views and strong emotions. On the one hand, offsets are seen as practices that distort competition in the market. They also raise concerns regarding their lack of transparency and for this reason are seen as a factor that can assist the breeding of corruption in the field of defence. On the other hand, they are viewed as an important tool for the development of domestic defence industrial and technological capabilities, particularly for developing countries. In the context of the EU, offsets also raise questions about their compatibility with EU Law. The legal treatment of offsets in the EU has always been controversial. This is why the contribution of the EDA in discussing

# EDA and EU defence procurement integration 127

offsets more openly and providing a preliminary roadmap for their treatment within the EU must be considered as significant (see also discussion in Chapter 13).

Before the elaboration of the CoCO, the EDA had commissioned an independent study that examined the impact of offset practices on the development of a European defence market. Although the study did not provide conclusive answers, it made clear that these practices are not *a priori* compatible with EU law but from a practical point of view – if used properly – they may prove useful tools for industrial development. Furthermore the study acknowledged that offsets are not only a European phenomenon.

The CoCO came into force on 1 July 2009 (EDA 2011; see also Georgopoulos 2011). The stated aim of the CoCO was the improvement of the competitive conditions in the EDEM and also the promotion of a competitive European Defence Technological and Industrial Base (EDITB).

The CoCO put forward a proposition for dealing with offsets that was based on a constructive and pragmatic approach. This approach recognised that although offsets can create market distortions, they can also work as mechanisms that assist in the creation a level playing field in a market characterised by imperfect competition conditions, particularly if the relevant market is influenced by political considerations like the defence procurement market (EDA 2011: 2). By recognising this reality explicitly the CoCO adopted a more useful stance – as opposed to the doctrinal stance of principle against offsets often articulated by the Commission – that furthered the debate regarding the treatment of offsets. In other words, the EDA through the CoCO, instead of the demonisation of offsets, considered the possibility of using them in a way that supports the EDITB – principle of instrumentality – while attempting to minimise their adverse effects on the development of a fair and competitive EDEM – principle of restraint (Georgopoulos 2011: 35). The EDA in-house study on abatements (EDA 2010; see also Georgopoulos 2011: 37–39) was a tangible demonstration of this constructive and pragmatic approach.

Second, by adopting the aforementioned stance, the EDA managed to convince pMS to materialise the two main principles enshrined in the CoCO, namely transparency and mutual trust. The EDA via the CoCO managed to shed light on a sensitive area often characterised by secrecy. It managed, in particular, to convince pMS to share information about their national offset policies. In this way, Member States became both providers and recipients of the relevant information.

The EDA managed to create an environment of mutual trust for information sharing and, as a result, pMS did reveal substantial information regarding their national offset policies. It is worth mentioning that, like other EDA online portals, the offset portal was accessible not only to pMS but also to the general public.

128   A. Georgopoulos

Like the other pre-DSP Directive initiatives of the EDA, the CoCO has been under review in the aftermath of the enactment and transposition in the national legal orders of the new directive. Although the DSP Directive does not deal with offset practices directly, the Commission has issued a Guidance Note on offsets (European Commission 2009b) where it explicates its strict stance vis-à-vis offsets. The Guidance note is not legally binding but, nevertheless, affects de facto the decision of MSs *whether* and *how* to implement offset policies. Member States are considering whether to continue or alter their offset policies.

### Security of Information

Another aspect of defence procurement where the EDA has played a constructive role is SoI. The latter can function as a trade barrier if standards and processes followed by the various Member States differ significantly. For example, as mentioned in the SoI portal, if there is no bilateral or multilateral agreement or arrangement between Member States, the relevant national contracting authorities can refuse to recognise the security clearance from non-domestic firms. In the context of the internal market this could be considered as a market access barrier that underlines the creation of a competitive EDEM. This is also linked with the observation made earlier regarding the overarching aim of EDA's initiatives in the field of defence, namely the building of trust amongst the pMS. As early as 2006, the EDA (2006b) contributed to the process for improving the environment regarding SoI by agreeing on common minimum standards for ensuring industrial security.

Furthermore, on 1 July 2014 the EDA established an electronic portal where the various national legislations, policies that are linked with SoI can be found. This is particularly important in the post-DSP Directive regulatory environment. It should be remembered that dealing with SoI is one of the priority areas of the new regime.

The EDA has been mandated by Member States to identify ways to remove SoI barriers in defence procurement. Through the exchange of information on national SoI standards and policies the SoI portal constitutes the first step in this process.

### Security of Supply

Another practical yet crucial aspect of the defence procurement market where the EDA has been playing a notable role is SoS. The latter covers cases such as the long-term support of military equipment during its life cycle, the ability to supply forces deployed abroad and to deal with unplanned increases of operational requirement due to unforeseeable events (Heuninckx 2014: 34). Often, SoS considerations have been used to justify national offset policies and other protectionist measures.

Although the DSP Directive (Art. 23) includes provisions on SoS that deal with some legal issues, for example whether SoS considerations may be taken into account as award criteria, it does not provide for a specific plan for dealing with the practical issues linked with SoS – and this is also the case for the Commission's Guidance Note on SoS (European Commission 2009c). In order to understand some of these let us consider the following examples:

- Member State A and Member State B have a surge in the demand for a specific type of munition at the same time. The relevant needs of both Member States are catered for by an economic operator established in Member State A. This economic operator cannot satisfy both unscheduled demands simultaneously. Clearly, Member State A can take measures – for reasons of public interest, national security and so on – to oblige the economic operator established in its jurisdiction to prioritise the needs of Member State A (explicitly or implicitly over those of Member State B).
- Member State A, which disagrees with specific foreign policy decisions and actions of Member State B, decides to block or procrastinate the delivery of munitions by economic operator A established in its jurisdiction to Member State B.

The EDA initiatives in the context of SoS try to fill precisely this gap between the legal treatment of SoS in the defence procurement process and the practical issues that arise in this area.

In particular, the EDA elaborated in 2006 a Framework Agreement for SoS which focused initially on cases of operational urgency (EDA 2006c; see also Heuninckx 2008: 13–15). Following the enactment of the DSP Directive, the scope of the Framework Agreement was expanded (EDA 2013b) to cover also cases of defence acquisitions in peacetime when there is no operational urgency. This enhanced Framework Agreement is supported by the Code of Conduct on Prioritisation (CoCP) which is an instrument that aims to involve the industry in the SoS framework, by establishing a way for the industry to demonstrate its commitment to meet Member States SoS requirements in defence procurement (EDA 2014).

These instruments are supported by an online portal launched in 2011, which aims to enhance transparency and provide useful information about national legislations, policies linked with SoS. As with the initiatives on offsets and SoI, the SoS initiative aims to enhance mutual trust amongst Member States.

### Effective procurement methods

The last EDA defence procurement related initiative is the EPM, launched on 7 July 2011. The EPM is the implementation of a specific task set for

130  *A. Georgopoulos*

the EDA by the Treaty of the EU (Art. 45 (1) (b)), namely the promotion of harmonisation of Member States' operational requirements and the adoption of compatible effective procurement methods. The EPM is linked with – and intended to complement – the wider Pooling and Sharing initiative of the EDA, as discussed in Chapter 11.

In particular, the EPM initiative aims to identify ways, methods and areas where Member States' may consolidate their demand in the context of off-the-shelf procurement, thus achieving economies of scale, reducing duplication and improving interoperability. Areas with such potential for demand consolidation are amongst others transport or logistic support, training, standard vehicles, ammunition, legacy weapon systems and communication equipment (EDA 2012).

After the identification of areas for demand consolidation the EPM initiative could use any of the main options for joint procurement, for example acquisition through a lead nation that procures on behalf of other Member States, the option for procuring through an international body or organisation such as the NATO Maintenance and Supply Agency or OCCAR and the option for the EDA to act as a central purchasing body on behalf of Member States. This possibility is envisaged by the DSP Directive (Rec. 23) and is also supported by the EDA's legal framework (Council of the European Union 2011).

The third option means that the EDA could become a one-stop-shop where the identification, shaping of common demand and actual procurement could take place. So far two pilot EPM case studies have been implemented: Counter-IED Training European Guardian (Luxembourg and Austria), and Basic Logistics Services for the EU Battle Group (Austria, Czech Republic and Germany).

## Contemplating EDA's impact on defence procurement integration

This section tries to elucidate the impact on the legal/regulatory and political dimensions of the European defence procurement integration process. Although these two dimensions are interconnected, an attempt to envisage the impact of EDA's initiatives on either of them separately is considered useful in order to better appreciate EDA's overall contribution in the integration process.

### *Impact on legal/regulatory dimension of defence procurement integration*

From the point of view of the legal/regulatory aspect of integration, a quick glance at the state of play of European regulation in defence procurement may lead to the precipitate conclusion that the impact of EDA's initiatives has been limited. This is because the model of regulation

*EDA and EU defence procurement integration* 131

that these initiatives put forward, namely what could be termed as 'coordinated intergovernmental self-regulation' did not prevail. Instead, it was the 'Community method model' proposed by the Commission initiatives that provided the main framework (DSP Directive) and forum of regulation (first pillar, internal market) in this area.

However, this impression would be utterly misguided. To explain this, let us distinguish three main ways in which the initiatives of the EDA contributed crucially to the legal/ regulatory integration in defence procurement.

First, the EDA initiatives provided important information about the state of play of defence procurement markets in the EU. This information was later used by the Commission to strengthen the case for the adoption of a tailor-made instrument of the first pillar in order to facilitate the functioning of the internal market in defence procurement.

In particular, the contribution of the CoC cannot be underestimated. The information available on the EBB portal showed clearly that despite their earlier pronouncements, Member States left significant parts of their defence procurement contract opportunities outside the CoC's more transparent and more competitive framework. Also, many of the contract opportunities published on the EBB portal concerned goods and services that were not in the list of 1958 which, according to Article 346 (2) TFEU, constitutes the point of reference with regard to the material scope for the application of Article 346 (1)(b) TFEU. Instead, these contracts – for example, military boots – should have been procured according to the public sector procurement directive (European Commission 2004). In other words, in some cases Member States were not only opening their defence procurement markets but also were circumventing their obligations under the public sector procurement directive. This demonstrated vividly the level of misunderstanding amongst some Member States of the limits of Article 346 TFEU exemption.

Furthermore, even in the case of contracts that fulfilled the conditions of Article 346 TFEU, the use of the CoC revealed a paradox that in effect strengthened the argument of the Commission for the adoption of a tailor-made directive in the internal market. If Member States are willing to share publicly through the EBB portal information about sensitive defence procurement opportunities then why not do this through the Official Journal following the usual rules for public sector procurement? Member States could only justify their not using the EU procurement rules by arguing that the public sector directive obliged contracting authorities to use by default the open or restricted procedures. These procedures leave very little margin for discretion to contracting authorities. It is precisely this point that the Commission addressed in its proposal for the DSP Directive in order to alleviate the concerns – and eliminate excuses – of Member States by introducing the negotiated procedure with prior publication, which allows for both flexibility and discretion, as a standard procedure (European Commission 2009a: Art. 25).

132   *A. Georgopoulos*

These observations show that without the EDA initiatives, the collection of information and evidence – sometimes 'incriminating' – by the Commission, relevant for building the case for a DSP Directive, would have been more difficult.

Second, the EDA initiatives had a clear impact on the content and direction of the DSP Directive and the other Commission initiatives. For example, the material scope of DSP directive has been clearly influenced by the Member States' preferences included in the EDA initiatives. In particular, the exemption of collaborative procurement on R&D (Art. 13C) echoes the same exemption found in the CoC. Furthermore the provisions on subcontracting (Art. 21) are heavily influenced by the CoBPSC and the CoCO. Likewise the renewed emphasis on SoI and SoS found in the initiatives of the Commission can be traced back to the relevant EDA initiatives.

Third, the EDA initiatives provide a complementary pathway that assists Member States to implement specific aspects of the DSP Directive framework. This is the case for the SoS and SoS initiatives of the EDA which have been adapted to assist Member States with the application of the relevant parts of the DSP Directive.

### Impact on the political dimension of defence procurement integration

From the perspective of the political dimension of defence procurement integration, this chapter argues that the impact of EDA's initiatives has been fundamental.

First, EDA's creation along with its mandate signalled a move towards more involvement of the EU in the area of defence procurement. More importantly, the EDA had a 'numbing' effect on the reactionary and atavistic reflexes of Member States in the context of defence procurement integration through the deliberation of its soft law instruments and policy initiatives. The EDA is a particular kind of EU Agency. It comes under the CFSP pillar, is financed by pMS, not the EU Budget, and its staff is composed of seconded national officials. The Commission takes part in the deliberations of the Steering Board, but without any voting rights. This environment seems to have created a more fertile ground for the discussion of national preferences and contemplation about the design of policy instruments in the area. In this sense, the use of the various online portals for sharing information amongst Member States showed to the latter that using a more open and transparent European approach in the context of defence procurement activities was not an anathema and perhaps could lead to useful outcomes. Likewise, these exercises provided the Commission with useful information for 'selling' the proposal of the DSP Directive to the Member States.

Furthermore, the EDA managed to create a forum where constructive discussion of the different preferences between Member States with significant domestic defence industrial capacity and those with small- and medium-sized ones could take place without hampering flexibility. Such differences had led to the creation of OCCAR initially as an 'exclusive' club. The setup of the EDA created an environment where all pMS had – or were led to believe that they had – equal stakes in the process. This environment appears to have played a significant role in preparing a more receptive atmosphere for what was to follow, namely the Commission regulatory 'defence package'.

These observations could be supported by a number of facts. For example, although Spain and Hungary decided not to join the CoC initially, they did so a year after. Denmark, which participates neither in the EDA nor in the non-legally binding CoC, voted in the Council of Ministers in favour of the enactment of the legally binding and enforceable DSP Directive.

Through its initiatives, the EDA played a legitimising role of a process of discussion of policy preferences linked with core state functions – the 'tools of national sovereignty' (de Vestel 1998: 197) at the EU level. This legitimising role in effect assisted the successful conclusion of the Commission's initiatives. Although it is difficult to prove the counterfactual, without the existence of the EDA the adoption of the Commission's defence package might not have been certain – or would not have been adopted in the record time in which it was. After all, we have the example of the unsuccessful attempt for a process of moderate harmonisation of defence procurement that the Commission had undertaken in the late 1990s.

Moreover, behind the triumphant words of press releases about the 'harmonisation' of defence procurement in the EU, in reality the DSP Directive leaves many issues 'flexibly unclear' and many questions unanswered. The DSP Directive includes many exemptions and has other aspects that require further clarification. This could be described as a process of 'controlled communitarisation' of defence procurement, where the new regulatory framework is characterised by 'incomplete contracts' that will need to be renegotiated as the integration process progresses. The role of the EDA remains crucial in this regard.

## Conclusion: a look into the future

This chapter examined EDA's role in European defence procurement integration thus far and argued that its impact has been significant. It analysed in particular the contribution of EDA's initiatives in the legal/regulatory and political dimension of this process.

The *prima facie* antagonism between the initiatives of the regulatory and policy initiatives of the EDA and the Commission has had one clear outcome: the furtherance of regulatory and political aspects of integration in defence procurement. The initiatives of the EDA and the Commission could be described as a game of chess where each player responds to the moves of the other and tries to establish an advantage; however, what is important from the point of view of the integration process is not so much the specific moves but the fact that the game is being played. In this regard, the presence of the EDA was key for the game to start and continue.

So, what does the future hold for EDA in the field of defence procurement? We identify four strands where the EDA can continue to play a central role in the post DSP Directive landscape, and a necessary condition for this to happen.

First, the exemption of collaborative R&D procurement from the field of application of the DSP Directive may provide an incentive to Member States to engage in collaborative projects – since, among other advantages, it would guarantee some work sharing for their domestic industry. In such a case, the EDA could play a role in facilitating the coordination of the operational requirements of pMS.

Second, the EDA could in time become a central purchasing body in the area of off-the-self procurement for pMS, initially for simple standardised products and progressively for more sophisticated equipment – depending on the level of coordination of Member States operational requirements.

Third, the EDA could work in unison with the Commission in order to provide more clarity to some important yet challenging policy areas linked with the implementation of the DSP Directive, such as the SoI and SoS.

Fourth, the EDA could play the role of honest broker in the next phases of integration in defence procurement between Member States and the Commission. For example, an area where the EDA ought to act constructively is offsets. The area remains a point of contention between the Commission and some Member States. Another important area is that of standardisation in defence and security procurement.

Nevertheless, all this is based on a necessary condition: the continuing willingness of Member States to engage in further integration in defence procurement. The greater transparency brought by the EDA initiatives led to the strengthening of the Commission's position. Will the realisation of this fact lead Member States to return t their old, more secretive and cautious ways? This is not impossible. If this were to happen then the EDA would become a victim of its own success. A lot will depend eventually on the way that the Commission will enforce the DSP Directive. Perhaps this explains the cautious approach followed by the Commission thus far; it seems that the stakeholders seem to realise that the priority is the continuance of the chess game and not the pronouncement of a precipitous – and thus pyrrhic – victory over the 'opponent'.

## References

Council of the European Union (2011) 'Council Decision 2011/411/CFSP of 12 July 2011 Defining the Stature, Seat and Operational Rules of the European Defence Agency and Repealing Joint Action 2004/551/CFSP', OJ L 183/16.

Council of the European Union (2004) 'Joint Action 2004/551/CFSP of July 12, 2004 on the Establishment of the European Defence Agency', O.J. L245/17.

de Vestel, P. (1998) 'The Future of Armaments Cooperation in NATO and the WEU', in K. Eliassen (ed.) *Foreign and Security Policy in the European Union*, London: Sage: 197–215.

European Commission (2009a) '2009/81/EC of the European Parliament and of the Council of 13 July 2009 on the Coordination of Procedures for the Award of Certain Works Contracts, Supply Contracts and Service Contracts by Contracting Authorities or Entities in the Fields of Defence and Security, and Amending Directives 2004/17/EC and 2004/18/EC', OJ L216/76.

European Commission (2009b) 'Guidance Note on Offsets'.

European Commission (2009c) 'Guidance Note on Security Supply'.

European Commission (2005) 'Communication from the Commission to the Council and the European Parliament on the Results of the Consultation Launched by the Green Paper on Defence Procurement and on the Future Commission Initiatives', COM (2005) 626 final.

European Commission (2004) 'Directive 2004/18/EC of the European Parliament and of the Council of 31 March 2004 on the Coordination of Procedures for the Award of Public Works Contracts, Public Supply Contracts and Public Service Contracts', OJ L134/114.

European Commission (2003) 'European Defence – Industrial and Market Issues: Towards an EU Defence Equipment Policy', COM (2003) 113 final.

European Council (2003) 'Presidency Conclusions', Thessaloniki European Council, 19–20 June 2003, D/03/3.

EDA (European Defence Agency) (2014) 'Code of Conduct on Prioritisation Agreed by Subscribing Member States to the Framework Arrangement for Security of Supply', 15 May 2014.

EDA (European Defence Agency) (2013a) 'Defence Data 2012'.

EDA (European Defence Agency) (2013b) 'Framework Arrangement for Security of Supply Between Subscribing Member States', 9 November 2013.

EDA (European Defence Agency) (2012) 'EPM Fact Sheet', 29 June 2012.

EDA (European Defence Agency) (2011) 'A Code of Conduct on Offsets Agreed by the EU Member States Participating in the European Defence Agency', 3 May 2011.

EDA (European Defence Agency) (2010) 'Abatements: A Pragmatic Tool to Facilitate the Development of European Defence Equipment Market'.

EDA (European Defence Agency) (2006a) 'The Code of Best Practice in the Supply Chain', 15 May 2006.

EDA (European Defence Agency) (2006b) 'Steering Board Decision No. 2006/18 on Security of Information between Subscribing Member States (sMS), which Set Certain Common Minimum Standards on Industrial Security'

EDA (European Defence Agency) (2006c) 'Steering Board decision 2006/17 on a Framework Agreement for Security of Supply between Subscribing Member States (sMS) in Circumstances of Operational Urgency'.

Georgopoulos, A. (2011) 'Revisiting Offset Practices in European Defence Procurement: The European Defence Agency's Code of Conduct on Offsets', *Public Procurement Law Review*, 20: 29–42.

Georgopoulos, A. (2008) 'Comment on the Recent Developments in European Defence Procurement Integration Initiatives', *Public Procurement Law Review*, 17: n/a.

Georgopoulos, A. (2007a) 'The European Armaments Policy: A Conditio Sine Qua Non for the European Security and Defence Policy?', in N. White and M. Trybus (eds) *European Security Law*, Oxford: Oxford University Press: 199–222.

Georgopoulos, A. (2007b) 'The Commission's Interpretative Communication on the Application of Article 296 EC in the Field of Defence Procurement', *Public Procurement Law Review*, 16: n/a.

Georgopoulos, A. (2006a) 'The European Defence Agency's Code of Conduct for Armaments Acquisitions: A Case of Paramnesia?', *Public Procurement Law Review*, 15: 51–61.

Georgopoulos, A. (2006b) 'European Defence Agency: The New Code of Best Practice in the Supply Chain', *Public Procurement Law Review*, 15: n/a.

Georgopoulos, A. (2005a) 'Defence Procurement and EU Law', *European Law Review*, 30: 559–572.

Georgopoulos, A. (2005b) 'The New European Defence Agency: Major Development or Fig Leaf?', *Public Procurement Law Review*, 14: 103–112.

Georgopoulos, A. (2004) *European Defence Procurement Integration: Proposal for Action within the European Union*, PhD Thesis, Nottingham University.

Heuninckx, B. (2014) 'Security of Supply and Offsets in Defence Procurement: What's New in the EU?', *Public Procurement Law Review*, 23: 33–49.

Heuninckx, B. (2008) 'Towards a Coherent European Defence Procurement Regime: European Defence Agency and European Commission Initiatives', *Public Procurement Law Review*, 17: 1–20

Heuninckx, B. (2009) 'The European Agency Electronic Bulletin Board: A Survey after Two Years', *Public Procurement Law Review*, 18: 43–66.

Lord Astor of Hever (2010) House of Lords Debate, 28 October 2010, c315W.

Mawdsley, J. (2003) *The European Union and Defence Industrial Policy*, Bonn International Center for Conversion, Paper 31.

Schmitt, B. (2003) *European Armaments Cooperation: Core Documents*, Chaillot Papers No. 59, Paris: EU Institute for Security Studies.

SIGMA (2011) *Defence Procurement*, Public Procurement Brief 23, September 2011.

Trybus, M. (2006) 'The New European Defence Agency: A Contribution to a Common European Security and Defence Policy and a Challenge to the Community Acquis?', *Common Market Law Review*, 43: 667–703.

# Part III

# The EDA, the nation-state and beyond

# 8  France, the UK and the EDA

*Jocelyn Mawdsley*

## Introduction

France and the UK have long been portrayed as being at opposite ends of the spectrum of EU views on armaments cooperation (Walker and Gummett 1993). Schütze (1976), for example, in an analysis that remains relevant, suggested that there are divisions between those states who feel that governments should regulate the arms market with a light hand, and allow firms to shape the market-led constellations of cooperation that emerge in response to military needs (the 'economic liberals' often equated with the UK), and those who believe that armaments cooperation must serve the cause of European political integration (political functionalists often equated with the French). For the former, being able to procure advanced military equipment at the lowest possible cost is the primary motivation, and so United States (US) participation is acceptable, whereas for the latter European Union (EU) autonomy is politically important. Giovacchini (2004) points to another long-lived disagreement between the two states, namely whether armaments cooperation should have its primary goal as increasing military capabilities (UK), or whether armaments cooperation should be an important way of meeting industrial and technology policy goals (France). In short, for analysts like Giovacchini (2004), it was unsurprising that the two would have different levels of ambition for the fledgling European Defence Agency (EDA).

Within the scope of an institutional analysis of Member States and their specific relations with the EDA, the argument that France and the UK have profoundly different attitudes to European armaments cooperation holds up well. However, it rapidly loses traction when the wider picture of European armaments cooperation is considered. This chapter intends to make two main arguments. First, that British and French attitudes to the EDA show continuity with their historical stances on European armaments cooperation, and how that has been understood and internalised in their national contexts, rather than changed. Moreover, both sets of attitudes are more complex than the literature often suggests. Second, that Britain and France are more alike than they are different in their policy behaviour

140   *J. Mawdsley*

on armaments cooperation. The chapter will argue that what distinguishes Britain and France from other EU states (with the partial exception of Germany) is that both understand armaments production to be an important part of their national systems of innovation (Edquist 1997). Or, as the French defence economist Serfati (2001) argues, armaments production forms a 'meso-system' of the national economy, which despite budget cuts since the end of the Cold War and pressures of privatisation and globalisation, remains a core part of national technological and industrial policies. While most literature on the Common Security and Defence Policy (CSDP) notes that British and French defence budgets, and in particular spending on procurement and research, massively outstrip their fellow EU Member States, the wider systemic economic rationale is rarely analysed. For France and the UK, armaments matter. It is this conviction that underpins their intensive bilateral defence cooperation since the signing of the 2010 Lancaster House Treaties, which at first seems so at odds with French rhetoric on the EDA (Kempin *et al.* 2012). The establishment of the EDA did not resolve the basic contradictions and tensions that had dogged cooperation within the Western European Armaments Organisation (WEAO). The long-standing tension between the interests of the large arms producing states and small states with mainly niche or supply chain interests, which derailed the WEAO and forced the development of the Organisation Conjointe de Coopération en matière d'Armement (OCCAR) and the Framework Agreement is also evident within the EDA (Mawdsley 2008), and on this matter Britain and France continue to hold similar views, particularly since the A400M project (Mawdsley 2013). The chapter argues in short that the EDA – and thus the CSDP – has not had a transformative impact on British and French narratives on armaments cooperation.

This argument therefore runs counter to the mainstream academic literature on the CSDP, which has emphasised initially the potential for, and more recently the reality of, elite socialisation and policy learning through the day-to-day interactions of those involved in CSDP to transform national security identities. Meyer (2006), among others, has drawn on the strategic culture literature to claim that deep-rooted differences between Member States need not inhibit EU defence cooperation. This optimism is often extended to the EDA (Meijer 2010), and indeed CSDP scholars' assumptions about the EDA fit well with much of the more recent but rather sparse literature on European armaments cooperation. Much analysis has tacitly or overtly assumed a quasi neo-functionalist process of European integration in this field (Guay 1998; Guay and Callum 2002) even if they are critical of the move (Jünemann and Schörnig 2002), making the assumption that as the EU moves into this policy area, and institutionalises cooperation, it will become the obvious arena for regulation, cooperation and policy-making. It is important to mention though that the EDA and indeed armaments cooperation, along with other material factors in CSDP, remain under-researched in the literature, and so claims about elite socialisation in this field are largely untested empirically (Meyer and Strickmann 2011).

This chapter, using an interpretivist framework, seeks to suggest that the longevity of individual projects, coupled with a comparative lack of political scrutiny, means that national narratives about the rationale for armaments cooperation are both long-standing and largely unchallenged by the EDA, and thus key to understanding contemporary policy dynamics. It will first briefly discuss how an interpretivist reading understands the relationship between national traditions and transformative discourses. The chapter will then draw on a process tracing methodology to show how British and French ideas about *l'Europe d'armement* have developed. It will propose that at the moment of the founding of the EDA, there was a Franco-British convergence in ideas about the rationale for the EDA, but not on its institutionalisation or tasks. The final section will consider the extent to which ten years of the EDA have challenged these national narratives, and why bilateral cooperation perhaps is proving more transformative.

## Interpreting British and French choices

The idea that the CSDP might operate as a transformative discourse where national strategic cultures are concerned is an important part of the constructivist arguments made about the emergence of an EU strategic culture. While broadly sympathetic to the constructivist claims about the potential of the CSDP as a transformative discourse, this chapter attempts to investigate why, in the specific field of armaments cooperation, British and French interests, identities and traditions are not apparently being transformed. This is not to say that the arguments in favour of EDA-sponsored EU armaments cooperation are not compelling, but, as Radaelli and Schmidt (2004: 370) point out, 'a discourse, however "good" or compelling in its arguments, however successful in its co-ordinative and communicative interactions, can nevertheless fail if certain policy actors with veto power remain unconvinced'.

This chapter considers the national narratives about armaments cooperation, suggesting that as the rationale for cooperation long predates the EDA, it is important to understand how and why the original choices were made, and how patterns of interaction on cooperation might solidify into traditions. What this section wishes to argue is that in both countries the defence policy communities have developed webs of beliefs or traditions about European armaments cooperation, sometimes consisting of competing narratives, which are mediated through the organisational culture of the national Ministry of Defence (MoD). Crucially, because British and French meso-systems of armament development and production form a subset of national governance, and actors move between policy-making and production throughout their careers, in this

142   *J. Mawdsley*

case these narratives are transmitted more broadly to both public and private sectors (Bevir *et al.* 2013; Kolodziej 1987). The role of traditions and beliefs is particularly important when considering whether or not CSDP discourses might be transformative in nature, because military organisations are usually thought to be resistant to change.

The framework for analysis draws heavily on interpretivist work and in particular work on tradition, dilemma and change. Traditions might be usefully thought of as 'a set of understandings someone receives during socialisation' (Bevir *et al.* 2003: 11). Security traditions therefore might be understood as inherited beliefs about security institutions, strategic history and practice, in this instance as relating to armaments cooperation. As Berger (1996: 326) suggests assimilation and socialisation into these traditions takes place, 'they [cultures] are transmitted through the often imperfect mechanisms of primary and secondary socialisation and are under pressure from both external developments and internal contradictions'. The multiple beliefs held by an individual or policy community may, however, be competing with each other. Equally, looking at attitudes through the prism of tradition does not rule out change.

In particular, if we accept the human capacity for agency as outlined above, accepting a new belief involves posing a dilemma for or asking questions of the existing web of beliefs. Where EDA is concerned, it can be viewed as a potential new belief system that led British and French policy-makers to ask questions about their existing belief system as manifest in their respective national traditions on armaments cooperation. But how did these narratives develop?

## *L'Europe d'armement*: British and French historical interpretations

### *France*

Post-Second World War France needed to reconstruct its armaments industry and used substantial quantities of US military aid to do so. Krause (1992: 128) points out that between 1945 and 1955 France received more than twice as much US military aid than any other North Atlantic Treaty Organisation (NATO) member and that this accounted for about half of France's defence spending. This largesse allowed the French to re-establish independent weapons production capacities for all weapons systems and in particular to generously subsidise aircraft production. In other words, it enabled the French to re-establish their pre-war understandings of armaments policy rather than adjusting to a new reality. As Kolodziej (1987: 3) put it, 'making arms, conventional and nuclear, is now woven deeply into the fabric of France's scientific and technological establishment, industrial plant, business practices, governing process – even its cultural mores'.

*France, UK and EDA* 143

For France the procurement and manufacture of arms has been viewed as crucial to independence in defence and foreign policy for centuries and their importance, both as a symbol of national independence, and as an economic resource must not be underestimated.

France's first considerations of European cooperation in the armaments field came as part of the discussions surrounding the ill-fated European Defence Community and what should succeed it after the French parliament failed to ratify the treaty in 1954. For France, the primary policy goal was to deny West Germany the means for any future political or military domination of Western Europe, which came quickly – after it became clear that French political opinion could not accept a European army – to mean control of armaments. Calandri (1995: 41) argues that France also wanted to make use of residual German scientific and technical expertise in armaments as well as benefiting from the finance available from West German economic resurgence. Paris therefore proposed that the Western European Union (WEU) should include a supranational armaments agency. Arguing that Germany and the Benelux countries were too strategically exposed to host military production sites, the proposal was that production should be carried out in the South of France and French North Africa. The agency would also have had control over the distribution of US military aid. Unsurprisingly, given Britain's aversion to supranationalism, the overt discrimination against Germany and Benelux countries in favour of French economic interests and Italy's reliance on American finance in its armaments industry, the plan found little support. It is, however, worth mentioning as it reveals several characteristics of French attitudes to armaments cooperation: first, they were willing to compromise their autonomy, if control over Germany was ensured and, second, their concept of a Europe of armaments was one presupposing a directorial role for France.

From the mid 1950s, France regarded collaboration with West Germany in particular, and other European countries, in the field of armaments development and production as a way to maintain its self-sufficiency in the field and to reinforce French autonomy from the US. There does not appear to have been any intention on the French side to treat Germany as an equal partner. Rather, French policy-makers saw Germany as playing a subordinate role in planning and production but contributing an equal share of the cost (Serfati 1996).

De Gaulle's distrust of American involvement in Europe and his belief in national defence led not only to French withdrawal from NATO's integrated military command, but also to the development of an independent nuclear force. These decisions also helped reinforce the consensus among French politicians that France should produce its own weapons (Serfati 1996: 18–21). France's withdrawal from the integrated military command and planning system of NATO had some serious impacts on potential European armaments collaboration. Other European NATO members formed the Eurogroup in 1968 to better coordinate West European defence efforts, and to try to improve the competitiveness of their defence firms. The French viewed the new group as too close to NATO and so refused to join, weakening the efforts. France agreed to join a successor group the Independent European Programme Group (IEPG) on its formation in 1976, but as Schütze (1976: 343) points out acerbically the question for France's partners in the IEPG was whether France was prepared to accept that 'this armaments group was a multilateral concern and not just a method of financing its own interests'. Moreover, the IEPG had another major weakness caused by French sensitivities about coordinated planning. Although, like the Eurogroup, it tried to foster cooperative efforts on the production of equipment, it did not inherit the Eurogroup's EUROLONGTERM project which was trying to harmonise military concepts and doctrines and would have helped move collaboration to much earlier in the planning process (Burrows and Edwards 1982: 53–54).

By the 1980s France had begun to retreat from its stance on defence autonomy and to express desires for more independent defence capabilities for Western Europe instead, although the change was less substantial that it looked. Taylor (1984: 27) points out the French shift in position was largely driven by two factors: a fear of a more independent West German security policy and a French budget crisis that meant armaments collaboration was even more necessary, if French defence firms were not to face large cuts. France's vision for a Europe of defence bore and still bears a startling resemblance to French national goals. In this sense, the dilemmas facing the French have produced incremental shifts in the French narrative on armaments cooperation rather than titanic changes.

Kempin (2001) argued that the most influential French security discourse on European integration believes that the European integration process will culminate in a state which will resemble the French state. This permits the transfer of security powers from France to the EU, but only to an EU which has internalised French republican values and the need to actively represent and defend them globally. As the defence of France is tied to the defence of Europe, it is necessary for the EU to become militarily capable. For the purposes of this chapter, this means that for France to cede power over armaments policy to the EDA, then this must be on French terms and the EDA's armaments powers and ambitions – and thus those of the EU – must match those of France. If the EDA is judged to have failed to do this, then on both counts the rationale for French involvement loses its strength.

### Britain

Britain's defence industry emerged from the Second World War not only intact but also technologically advanced. As Krause (1992) points out, in some areas like jet engines it was even possibly more advanced than the

US. Britain, unlike France or Germany, had the ability to produce the entire range of weapons systems, including nuclear weapons. Surprisingly, however, the UK accepted the necessity of institutionalised European armaments cooperation much earlier than the French. Duncan Sandys' 1957 Defence White Paper admitted that Britain's then defence commitments were financially and politically unsustainable, which posed a dilemma that fundamentally transformed the previous British policy of autonomy, to one of accepting that interdependence might be necessary. The White Paper pointedly asserted that 'no European state is now wealthy enough to carry alone the burden of both atomic and conventional arms' (MOD 1957). Britain went on to present their plans for interdependent arms production in April 1958 to NATO ministers and, after procedures had been established, set out concrete plans for cooperation in a number of areas in 1960 (Draper 1990). Why then has Britain got the reputation of being the reluctant European when in fact it was ahead of France in recognising the necessity of interdependent European armaments cooperation?

There are four reasons. First, between 1953 and 1957 when the French were proposing a supranational armaments agency, establishing ties with West Germany, or indeed leading the first NATO collaborative project (the *Breguet Atlantique* maritime patrol aircraft) the British government was in a weak position to take part in, or even vigorously espouse collaboration. As Draper (1990: 15–16) points out, the UK defence budget was cut by a third in real terms between 1953 and 1957 and any Whitehall protagonists of collaboration were hampered by Treasury fears of the unknown and inter-service rivalries.

Second, even before 1950, Britain had been engaged in substantial weapons standardisation efforts with the US and Canada. This tripartite work, known as the ABC Agreement, involved substantial exchanges of defence information, and the agreement prevented Britain from sharing this with other European NATO states without a US waiver, and even stopped UK participation in European cooperative efforts to define criteria for weapons production in the 1950s (*The Economist* 1957).

Third, and perhaps most importantly, the British were not at the same stage of thinking in the late 1950s as its potential European partners. The other West Europeans wanted to build up their defence industries, to draw level with the US on technologies like guided missiles, and national prestige was at stake. The British, who were more technologically advanced and had realised the impossibility of keeping up with the US, showed little understanding of these motives. Their bilateral offers of assistance were often tactless; for example, offering production under licence deals to the West Germans, without understanding that this failed to meet German demands for equality in the alliance. The relationship with France was particularly plagued by this lack of mutual understanding ('Cordiality without Entente' 1957). While throughout the 1950s discussions were held between the

146  *J. Mawdsley*

British and the French about armaments cooperation, real progress was blocked by the issue of British superiority in ballistic missiles and nuclear research. The French desire for independent nuclear weapons, for example, was viewed as economically wasteful by the British, given the deficiencies that were clear in West European land army capabilities.

Finally, while Britain was genuinely concerned about WEU military capabilities and so accepted the need to cooperate on conventional arms within Europe, and had persuaded the US to agree to this, its forays into promoting European cooperation often had less than pure motives. While Britain was at the forefront of efforts to formalise procedures for armaments cooperation in the WEU in the late 1950s, it was generally agreed that its underlying motive was to undermine the trilateral Franco-Italian-German arms pool established in 1957, which it feared would be detrimental to British interests (O'Driscoll 1998).

These issues have persisted. The UK was consistently more worried about economic efficiency than its partners, encouraging competitive procurement at home, and the consolidation and privatisation of its industry, and the abandonment of unviable collaborative projects. Indeed, a constant thread in British involvement in European armaments collaboration has been its efforts to make multinational procurement projects more efficient (Mawdsley 2013). Its closer relationship with the US has continued to be viewed as proof of its ambivalence by its European partners. Britain did, however, take part in a number of successful collaborative armaments projects like Tornado and Trigat. It has consistently pushed the issue of burden-sharing and the need to collaborate, and has provided leadership in multilateral fora on armaments cooperation, especially when the French refused to cooperate. Moreover, on projects like Eurofighter, Britain did show a willingness to compromise its own interests in a way that France did not. The British discourse on European armaments cooperation has always been one of pragmatic engagement, rather than a commitment to a European autonomy from the US, which it regards as undesirable, viewing cooperation as a way to save money that could then be used to strengthen European military capabilities more broadly. It would not risk damaging its own military capabilities through reliance on less committed states, so as with France autonomy is something not to be surrendered lightly. For the CSDP discourse to be transformative for the UK, it would need to offer a certainty that other European states were now as serious about military power as the British, and prepared to invest in it, and the EDA would need to be able to deliver.

## EDA's establishment: convergence and divergence

The 1990s saw renewed interest from both France and the UK in European armaments cooperation as a response to the multiple pressures of increasing technology costs, defence expenditure cuts following the end of the Cold War and increased international competition from a consolidated US defence industrial sector. Frustration at smaller states' refusal to abandon protectionist practices, such as *juste retour*, within the WEU institutional framework for armaments cooperation, led the larger states to set up modalities that protected their interests. The Framework Agreement – efforts to make European defence industrial consolidation easier – and OCCAR, a multinational defence procurement agency to manage collaborative projects, are the two most notable innovations of this period. Both fitted well with the established British and French narratives on armaments cooperation. Indeed the 1990s saw considerable convergence between the two states on matters of national armaments policy. France moved noticeably to reduce the directorial role of the state in armaments policy with key privatisations (Lazaric *et al.* 2011), while Britain accepted that a wholly laissez-faire approach was unsustainable.

However, neither initiative could help to tackle the central problem for the British and French of an overall lack of military capabilities amongst European states. While they were concerned for different reasons – the French wanting strategic autonomy for the EU vis-à-vis the US, while the British wanted to prevent the Americans from abandoning NATO in frustration at free-riding by Europeans – both had found the EU's inability to act decisively during the violent break-up of the former Yugoslavia unacceptable. As is well known, their bilateral summit at Saint-Malo in 1998 found sufficient common ground on the military capabilities issue to see the two states start what became the CSDP. The CSDP is sufficiently ground-breaking in terms of its potential to transform European defence policy-making that it should have posed a dilemma for British and French policy elites. The question is whether it did transform their national narratives on armaments cooperation.

Given their focus on military capabilities, and a mutual distrust of the European Commission's plans for regulation of the armaments sector, it is unsurprising that an institutional intergovernmental structure for EU armaments cooperation was acceptable to both states. The Fischer/de Villepin Joint Proposals to the Convention on the Future of Europe and the UK counter-proposal for a Capabilities rather than an Armaments Agency from November 2002 do show, however, that at the planning stages Britain and France had quite different ambitions for the structure (Schmitt 2003). A 2003 bilateral defence summit allowed basic common ground to be found. The resulting Franco-British statement made it clear that they wanted OCCAR and the Framework Agreement to remain relevant within the new framework, showing that both continued to see the interests of large arms producing states as paramount. Subsequently agreed within the Convention on the Future of Europe and established in the 2003 Thessaloniki declaration, the compromise EDA represented the common ground between Britain and France, namely their agreement that the EU needed to improve its military capabilities (Schmitt 2003).

148 *J. Mawdsley*

Behind the unanimity of these declarations there were areas of real disagreement from the start between not just Britain and France, but other states as well. The starting phase of the Agency showed that states held divergent views on its role. Zecchini (2004) reported that Berlin and Rome argued for a minimalist version, little more than a coordination office, while Paris wanted a fully fledged armaments agency defining a common armaments strategy. The British government took a middle of the road approach arguing for the agency to help national Ministries to harmonise and develop EU military capacities, which was eventually supported by Berlin (Zecchini 2004). There was also some disagreement over the participation of third countries in the work of the Agency, which shows the disagreement over the extent to which European autonomy should be privileged remained extant. France and some other Member States had argued that all decisions about the involvement of other countries in the agency, such as the US, non-EU NATO members like Norway and Turkey, should be unanimous rather than carried by a majority. Britain, which resisted, succeeded in securing an arrangement under which a Member State can only block the participation of a third country by resorting to an 'emergency brake' on majority decisions. Similarly, the level of autonomy granted to the Agency was a hot issue. France, which is keen for a European military capability that is not dependent on NATO and long in favour of creating big European military industrial champions, managed to get agreement for the agency to launch projects autonomously (Giovachini 2004). But Britain, which saw the Agency more as a lobby group or broker to enhance defence capacities in close cooperation with NATO, won a guarantee that defence ministers would decide the financial framework by unanimity, which essentially has given a British veto over the expansion of the EDA's mandate through financial restrictions. The current British government has used this power since being elected, to hold the EDA budget at 2010 levels, citing public spending cuts across Europe as its rationale (House of Commons 2013). Britain was less successful though in its efforts to give the EDA the role of auditing Member States' military commitments (House of Lords 2004). Finally, realising that the first head of the EDA would have a crucial shaping role, Britain and France battled over the post with the UK's Nick Witney eventually being appointed (Zecchini 2004). But after ten years of the EDA, are these Franco-British differences still so stark, and has the EDA's performance transformed their national narratives on armaments cooperation?

## Ten years of the EDA: continuity or change for French and British narratives?

The story of British and French engagement with the EDA is interesting. Both states are frustrated with the failure of their EU partners to make meaningful progress on military capabilities, but their public reactions to the EDA's role in this have been very different. This final section will discuss their different responses to the EDA, then will consider their broader stances on bilateral armaments cooperation, before considering whether the CSDP has had a transformative effect on their national narratives on armaments cooperation.

Britain's attitudes to the EDA have always been pragmatic. It was viewed from the beginning as a means to an end – improving military capabilities – rather than a political goal. To that extent British support for the EDA and the CSDP in general has always been contingent on its success in reaching those goals and its general utility. It is fair to say that the British have found EDA – and the CSDP – disappointing, quite simply because it has failed to make meaningful progress to closing the military capability gaps listed in the Headline Goal. Jordan and Williams (2007) argue that British disillusionment came very quickly, with the UK blocking an expansion of EDA personnel three years after its inception. According to the House of Commons European Scrutiny Committee (2013) 'the UK approach has been pragmatic – broad, active engagement, participation in some projects but not all, maintaining budgetary discipline and encouraging the Agency to focus on where the Agency could best add value'. Less diplomatically, O'Donnell (2011: 3) says that even before Labour left office

> the UK had decided that the European Defence Agency – which was struggling to get EU Member States to work more closely together – was a waste of money. The MoD had started trying to reduce the agency's budget and refused to take part in many EDA projects.

While the 2010–15 Conservative/Liberal Democrat Government's initial complete opposition to membership softened, with the then EDA head, Claude-France Arnauld, being regarded as more effective than her predecessors, the coalition government constantly reviewed British membership, and used its blocking powers to hold the EDA budget at 2010 levels, thus weakening the ability of Britain to play a constructive role.

France has taken a very different approach to the EDA, continuing to be an engaged and supportive Member State, but it shares British frustration with the CSDP and the failure to improve military capabilities. For some French commentators, the French decision to rejoin the NATO integrated command structure in 2009, following the frustrating experience of the 2008 French EU presidency when they were unable to make progress on ambitious plans for the CSDP, marked French abandonment of its efforts to recreate French defence at the EU level (Irondelle and Mérand 2010). Further disappointment over the CSDP and the Libya and Mali crises was to follow. Certainly, the French now seem resigned to the limitations of the EDA, despite the appointment of a French national, Claude-France Arnauld, to lead the Agency. The proceedings of the 9th

150   *J. Mawdsley*

French summer defence conference, for example, claim the EDA 'can be used as a catalyst, a facilitator of ideas or a forum' to further cooperation, but seem to accept it will not be a fully fledged armaments agency (Teissier and de Rohan 2011: 16). Indeed the current French preference is for OCCAR to manage any procurement projects (Teissier and de Rohan 2011: 16). That said, even at the height of optimism about the EDA, Lundmark (2004) argued that France had clearly defined areas, where European cooperation was not deemed feasible (most notably in the nuclear area and on foreign acquisition of French defence firms), suggesting that perhaps the French always supported only a limited transfer of powers.

In sum, while France is considerably more enthusiastic about the EDA than Britain, the EDA is not really an institution that is able to address the real concerns of the big states' agenda on armaments cooperation, as expressed in the Framework Agreement. There is not sufficient commonality in Member States' needs to agree on policies or projects quickly, and there is a lack of enthusiasm on the part of most states to improve military capabilities to enable the type of high-intensity security missions deemed necessary by Britain and France. Both appear to have learnt from the A400M project that cooperation with partners who do not share these ambitions is frustrating, leading them away from EU-level solutions (Gomis 2013; Mawdsley 2013). In the meantime the acceptance of the 'defence package', the first EU efforts to regulate the defence market, means that the Commission is becoming much more active in the field. France and Britain are both wary of Commission interference. While others share their industrial concerns, with Italy calling for more to be decided within the Framework Agreement group rather than at EU-27 (Kington 2011), Britain and France have a level of agreement on threats and responses and the type of Defence Industrial and Technological Base (DITB) needed to underpin this analysis that is not shared with other EU states. Hence, both states have turned increasingly to each other to try to fill the gap.

### Bilateral cooperation

The November 2010 Lancaster House agreements committed France and the UK to extending the cooperation between their armed forces and to joint development of their nuclear weapons technology. While budgetary constraints certainly play a role in the Franco-British cooperation, the level of cooperation perhaps marks the biggest challenge to both states' narratives on armaments cooperation. Jones (2011) argues that these agreements marked a step change in the level and depth of cooperation between the two states, particularly in the novel field of nuclear weapons cooperation. What is interesting is that this bilateral Franco-British cooperation has entered fields that Lundmark (2004) had argued were deemed unthinkable for France to Europeanise. Alongside the agreement on the establishment of a joint expeditionary force, various agreements on

Pooling and Sharing were made, such as an integrated carrier strike force – subsequently endangered by British procurement decisions on fighter jets – and sharing training and maintenance of their A400M fleets. For this chapter, however the most interesting aspect of the cooperation is on armaments policy. Here the two states concentrated on what are acknowledged as key future technology fields, and set up industrial cooperation deals that have the potential to change the EU defence industrial landscape (Kempin *et al.* 2012).

Franco-British cooperation has a distinct industrial policy rationale, namely the rationalisation of defence industrial capacities. This can be seen most clearly in the missile sector where a 'One Complex Weapons Industry' concept has been established, with the aim of rationalising the industrial assets of the missile sector in both Britain and France, to achieve 30 per cent savings. In May 2013, France finally gave the formal agreement to proceed with a Franco-British deal with MBDA on Future Anti-Surface Guided Weapons. As Tran (2013: 15) points out, this 'would formalize a mutual interdependence between Britain and France in weapon technology'. While less politically straightforward, cooperation between the two states, agreed in January 2014, on development of an Unmanned Combat Air Vehicle (UCAV) could also have a substantial impact on the European defence industrial landscape if successful. There has also been a marked increase in exploring the possibilities of procuring the other's defence industrial products, such as the British interest in Nexter System's truck-mounted CAESAR 155 mm artillery system and the *véhicule blindé de combat d'infanterie* (VBCI) 8×8 infantry fighting vehicle, or the French interest in BAE Systems' Terrier combat engineering vehicle and the Watchkeeper surveillance drone (Chuter and Tran 2014). Perhaps most interestingly, it was Germany rather than Britain or France, which blocked the proposed merger between EADS and BAE Systems in 2012, whereas France and the UK were reported to be closer to agreement, suggesting that trust has developed between the two states.

In sum, while the path of Franco-British armaments cooperation is far from politically straightforward, it has the potential to considerably alter the defence industrial landscape in Europe. It is significant for the EDA because major decisions are being taken about future technologies and defence industrial consolidation outside the EDA. It is cooperation at a qualitatively and quantitatively different level, than what is being carried out through the EDA.

What does this mean for French and British national narratives on armaments cooperation? The chapter has argued that the CSDP has failed to act as a transformative narrative for either Britain or France. For the French, while they remain supportive of the EDA and its initiatives, the EU's CSDP remains too far removed from their vision of a *Europe puissance*, a re-creation of French defence power at the EU level, for them to risk ceding control over their DITB. For the British, CSDP and the EDA have

## 152 *J. Mawdsley*

not been able to deliver the kind of improvement in European military capabilities that would legitimise their active participation according to their national narrative on armaments cooperation. Where the two narratives currently seem to meet on common ground, and where transformation seems possible, if politically very challenging, is in their bilateral cooperation, not the CSDP or EDA.

## References

Berger, T. (1996) 'Norms, Identity and National Security in Germany and Japan', in P. Katzenstein (ed.) *The Culture of National Security: Norms and Identity in World Politics*, New York: Columbia University Press: 317–356.

Bevir, M, Daddow, O. and Hall, I. (2013) 'Interpreting Global Security', in M. Bevir, O. Daddow and I. Hall (eds) *Interpreting Global Security*, London: Routledge: 1–16.

Bevir, M., Rhodes, R. and Weller, P. (2003) 'Comparative Governance: Prospects and Lessons', *Public Administration*, 81. Repaginated online version available at: http://escholarship.org/uc/item/1bz222w3: 1–35 (accessed 6 May 2013).

Burrows, B. and Edwards, G. (1982) *The Defence of Western Europe*, London: Butterworth Scientific.

Calandri, E. (1995) 'The Western European Union Armaments Pool: France's Quest for Security and European Cooperation in Transition, 1951–1955', *Journal of European Integration History*, 1(1): 37–63.

Chuter, A. and Tran, P. (2014) 'Artillery Experiment Shows Deepening UK–French Ties', *Defense News*, 21 June 2014.

'Cordiality without Entente' (1957) *The Economist*, 16 March 1957: 920–921.

Draper, A. (1990) *European Defence Equipment Collaboration: Britain's Involvement 1957–87*, Basingstoke: Macmillan.

Edquist, C. (1997) 'Introduction', in C. Edquist, (ed.) *Systems of Innovation: Technologies, Institutions and Organizations*, London: Pinter: 1–35.

Giovacchini, L. (2004) 'L'Agence européenne de défense: un progrès décisif pour l'Union?', *Politique Étrangère*, 1/2004: 177–189.

Gomis, B. (2013) *Entre Londres et Berlin: le difficile rééquilibrage stratégique français et son impact sur la Politique de Sécurité et de Défense Commune (PSDC)*, Notes de la FRS 20/2013, Paris, Fondation pour la Recherche Stratégique.

Guay, T. (1998) *At Arm's Length: The European Union and Europe's Defence Industry*, Basingstoke: Macmillan.

Guay, T. and Callum, R. (2002) 'The Transformation and Future Prospects of Europe's Defense Industry', *International Affairs*, 78(4): 757–776.

House of Commons (2013) 'European Scrutiny Committee: First Report of Session 2013–14', London: HMSO.

House of Lords (2005) *European Defence Agency, House of Lords European Union Committee 9th Report of Session 2004–05*, HL Paper 76, London: The Stationery Office.

Irondelle, B. and Mérand, F. (2010) 'France's Return to NATO: The Death Knell for ESDP?', *European Security*, 19(1): 29–43.

Jones, B. (2011) *Franco-British Military Cooperation: A New Engine for European Defence?*, EUISS Occasional Paper 88, February 2011, Paris: EU Institute for Security Studies.

Jordan, G. and Williams, T. (2007) 'Hope Deferred? The European Defence Agency after Three Years', *RUSI Journal*, 152(3): 66–71.

Jünemann, A. and Schörnig, N. (2002) *Die Sicherheits- und Verteidigungspolitik der "Zivilmacht Europa": Ein Widerspruch in sich?*, HSFK-Report 13/2002, Frankfurt: Hessische Stiftung für Friedens- und Konfliktsforschung.

Kempin, R. (2001) *France's Discourses on NATO since the Kosovo War*, COPRI Working Paper 27/2001, Copenhagen: COPRI.

Kempin, R., Mawdsley, J. and Steinicke, S. (2012) *Entente Cordiale: Eine erste Bilanz französisch-britischer Zusammenarbeit in der Sicherheits- und Verteidigungspolitik*, DGAP-Analyse 10, August 2012.

Kington, T. (2011) 'Anglo-French Deal Upsets Neighbors: Germans, Italians Warn of '2-Tier Europe', *Defense News*, 13 June 2011.

Kolodziej, E. (1987) *Making and Marketing Arms: The French Experience and its Implications for the International System*, Princeton, Princeton University Press.

Krause, K. (1992) *Arms and the State: Patterns of Military Production and Trade*, Cambridge: Cambridge University Press.

Lazaric, N., Mérindol, V. and Rochhia, S. (2011) 'Changes in the French Defence Innovation System: New Roles and Capabilities for the Government Agency for Defence', *Industry and Innovation*, 18(5): 509–530.

Lundmark, M. (2004) *The Integration and the Non-integration of the French Defence Industry*, Report FOI-R–1291—SE, Stockholm: Swedish Defence Research Agency.

Mawdsley, J. (2013) 'The A400M Project: From Flagship Project to Warning for European Defence Cooperation', *Defence Studies*, 13(1): 14–32.

Mawdsley, J. (2008) 'European Union Armaments Policy: Options For Small States?', *European Security*, 17(2–3): 367–386.

Meijer, H. (2010) 'Post-Cold War Trends in the European Defence Industry: Implications for Transatlantic Industrial Relations', *Journal of Contemporary European Studies*, 18(1): 63–77.

Meyer, C. (2006) *The Quest for a European Strategic Culture: Changing Norms on Security and Defence in the European Union*, Basingstoke: Palgrave Macmillan.

Meyer, C. and Strickmann, E. (2011) 'Solidifying Constructivism: How Material and Ideational Factors Interact in European Defence', *Journal of Common Market Studies*, 49(1): 61–81.

Ministry of Defence (1957) *The 1957 Defence Review: Ministry of Defence*, Defence White Paper: Outline of Future Policy, Cmnd. 124, London: HMSO.

O'Donnell, C. (2011) *Britain and France should not Give up on EU Defence Co-Operation*, Centre for European Reform Policy Brief, London, Centre for European Reform.

O'Driscoll, M. (1998) 'Les Anglo-Saxons, F-I-G and the Rival Conceptions of "Advanced" Armaments Research and Development Co-operation in Western Europe, 1956–58', *Journal of European Integration History*, 4(1): 105–130.

Radaelli, C. and Schmidt, V. (2004) 'Conclusions', *West European Politics*, 27(2): 364–379.

Schmitt, B. (2003) *The European Union and Armaments: Getting a Bigger Bang for the Euro*, Chaillot Paper 63, Paris: EU Institute for Security Studies.

Schütze, W. (1976) 'Möglichkeiten und Grenzen der westeuropäischen Rüstungszusammenarbeit', *Europa-Archiv*, 10/1976: 337–346.

Serfati, C. (2001) 'The Adaptability of the French Armaments Industry in an Era of Globalization', *Industry and Innovation*, 8(2): 221–239.

## 154  *J. Mawdsley*

Serfati, C. (1996) *Les Industries Européennes d'Armement: De la Coopération à l'Integration?*, Notes et Études Documentaires 5042 (1996–17), Paris: La Documentation Française.

Taylor, T. (1984) *European Defence Cooperation*, Chatham House Papers 24, London: Routledge.

Teissier, G. and de Rohan, J. (2011) 'Proceedings of the 9th Summer Defence Conference of the National Defence and Armed Forces Committee of the French National Assembly and the Senate Committee for Foreign Affairs, Defence and Armed Forces: States-Industries From Urgent Operations to Major Programs', Rennes, 5–6 September 2011.

Tran, P. (2013) 'France OKs Joint Missile Development with UK', *Defense News*, 6 May 2013.

Walker, W. and Gummett, P. (1993) *Nationalism, Internationalism and the European Defence Market*, Chaillot Paper 9, Paris: Western European Union Institute for Security Studies.

Zecchini, L. (2004) 'Le Britannique Nick Witney prend la direction de l'Agence européenne de l'armament', *Le Monde*, 29 January 2004.

# 9 Germany's limited leadership in the EDA

## International and domestic constraints on defence cooperation

*Tom Dyson*

## Introduction

As the state with the largest GDP in the European Union (EU), Germany is the leading contributor to the EDA's budget. However, this financial support for the EDA's activities is not matched by a lead role in promoting the four main tasks of the organisation: (1) developing defence capabilities; (2) promoting defence research and technology; (3) promoting armaments cooperation; and (4) finally, creating a competitive European defence equipment market and strengthening the European defence, technological and industrial base (EDA undated). Germany's role in the EDA has been limited and is described by Nick Witney, the former Chief Executive of the EDA (2004–2007) as 'modest ... an average pupil in the class' (Interview 1). This lack of German leadership in a key element of the defence component of the European project is surprising given Germany's strong commitment to the overall process of European integration (Patel 2012). Furthermore, the need for Europeans to take greater responsibility for their own security has been increasingly evident during the post-Cold War era. Recent developments at the international and domestic levels make the work of the EDA in strengthening Europe's military autonomy particularly important, creating an imperative for Germany to pursue deeper European cooperation in the field of military capabilities and armaments policy.

The first of these developments is the 'pivot towards Asia' in the United States' (US) defence and security policy. Since the end of the Cold War the US has sought to expand its influence outside Europe in areas of the globe which are central to its strategic interests (Hyde-Price, 2007: 83–86). The economic and military rise of China since the turn of the century has led the US to focus on bolstering its presence in the Asia-Pacific region in particular (O'Hanlon 2012). However, the ability of European states to respond to the changing strategic priorities of the US on a unilateral basis is undermined by the second major development of recent years: the austerity measures associated with the economic slowdown in Europe which have led to significant cuts to European defence budgets (Brune *et al.* 2010).

156   *T. Dyson*

The North Atlantic Treaty Organisation (NATO) has launched Smart Defence in an attempt to provide an Atlantic Alliance alternative to the EU's Ghent Framework for Pooling and Sharing (P&S) military capabilities. However, Smart Defence is unlikely to get off the ground. First of all, as outlined above, NATO's credibility is being drawn into question by the US 'Asia pivot' in defence. Second, Smart Defence has been used by the Americans as a means to try to encourage its European NATO partners to purchase US armaments (Biscop 2012: 1307). NATO efforts at P&S are therefore likely to fall short given the presence of strong national defence industries in European states, which exert a high level of political influence in national capitals. In short, there is a particularly strong imperative for Germany – and other EU Member States – to undertake stronger defence cooperation through the EU's Common Security and Defence Policy (CSDP). It is vital that Member States make progress on the core tasks of the EDA, if they are to maintain their power and influence at the international level (Witney 2011: 7).

This chapter will seek to explain the paradox of why, despite compelling imperatives to use the EDA, Germany has been so reticent to take advantage of the opportunities for cross-national defence capability cooperation and defence industrial collaboration presented by the institution. The chapter will begin with a brief examination of Germany's role in the development and work of the EDA since its establishment. It will then analyse the international and domestic factors which have driven German policy toward the EDA. Drawing on Neoclassical Realist international relations (IR) theory, the chapter will argue that Germany faces a common incentive with other European states to undertake a process of 'reformed bandwagoning' on US power.

However, the level of European convergence around 'reformed bandwagoning' is characterised by a significant level of differentiation. The chapter argues that Germany policy towards the EDA is affected by nuanced variation in Germany's 'external vulnerability' that creates incentives for Germany to safeguard its national strategic autonomy in defence and security. Furthermore, it is argued that our expectation of Germany's role within the EDA should be limited due to the presence of an 'Alliance Security Dilemma' within CSDP that inhibits states from undertaking P&S initiatives which impinge on national sovereignty in defence. Finally, the chapter finds that domestic factors, including the impact of the domestic armaments industry, German 'strategic culture' and the institutional structures of the federal state have also led Germany to fail to undertake a greater level of collaboration with its European partners in defence policy.

## Germany's role in the development and work of the EDA: limited leadership

Germany played an important role in the establishment of the precise institutional remit of the EDA following the June 2003 Thessaloniki

European Council. The European Council had left significant room for manoeuvre concerning the role and powers of the EDA, having simply proposed a joint action to 'create an intergovernmental agency in the field of research capabilities development, research, acquisition and armaments' (European Council 2003). In the negotiations of the project team that was charged with designing the institutional structure of the EDA and establishing its exact remit, Britain and France were divided (Interview 2). France wished for the agency to have a strong legal and financial remit to promote European armaments cooperation. Britain, on the other hand, wanted the EDA to remain intergovernmental and adopt a looser facilitative role in developing Europe's military capabilities. Germany played an important role in ensuring that the British position won through and that the organisation had a relatively limited set of powers and budget (Interview 2).

Germany was particularly interested in the potential for the EDA to act as a focal point for European states to coordinate their Research and Technology (R&T). Germany has a relatively low spend on R&T as a component of its defence budget when compared to other major European military powers and saw in the EDA an opportunity to help make up for this shortfall (Interviews 2 and 3). However, Germany was unable to turn these plans into leadership on R&T. Germany had to be cajoled and 'shamed' into the first Joint Investment Programme (JIP) of the EDA in 2007 following leadership from the French and Polish (Interview 2).

Germany has participated in several important EDA projects; however, these are limited in number given Germany's relative power and the expectations generated from Germany's financial contribution to the EDA. It has been particularly active in defining European defence capability requirements in the following areas: the category B Biological Detection Identification Monitoring Equipment Development and Enhancement Programme; the category B Project Maritime Mine Counter Measures; the category B Future Interoperability of Camp Protection Systems Project; the Counter-Man-Portable Air Defence Systems Project; the Maritime Surveillance Project; and the Helicopter Training Programme (Interviews 3 and 4).

While there has been some German activity in developing European military capabilities and R&T, its role in two other core tasks of the EDA – armaments cooperation and creating competitive European defence equipment market, and strengthening the European Defence, Technological and Industrial Base (EDTIB) – has been more muted. The EDA's Industry and Market Directorate has been active in developing ideas about how Europe can strengthen its defence industrial base and enhance R&T. Yet the ability of Member States to invoke TFEU Article 346, which states that the procurement of equipment and services of vital interest to national security is exempted from EU procurement rules, allows states undermine the creation of a truly competitive defence equipment market

158    *T. Dyson*

within the EU. The European Court of Justice (ECJ) and the European Commission rather than the EDA will be the key actors in eroding the ability of European nations to protect their national armaments industries (Dyson and Konstadinides 2013: 86–112). However, for reasons explored later in this chapter, it is unlikely that Germany will play a lead role in encouraging the Commission and ECJ to play a proactive role in this area.

Hence this brief overview of German EDA policy demonstrates that while Germany has not taken a back-seat role in the work of the organisation, it has provided only limited leadership. From the inception of the EDA Germany was keen to limit its powers and budget (Interview 2). Furthermore, Germany's national defence procurement processes continue to take precedence over international collaboration. When viewed within the context of the urgency of remedying Europe's collective military deficits, Germany has not provided leadership within the EDA that is commensurate with its economic and political weight and it has failed to use the organisation in a coherent manner to identify the possibilities for joint capability development. The remainder of this chapter examines a variety of international and domestic variables which have fostered this limited leadership by Germany, using Neoclassical Realist IR theory to shed light on the relative importance of these different variables.

## Understanding German EDA policy: the opportunities and constraints of the international system

This section will analyse German policy toward the EDA by exploring the insights of Neoclassical Realist IR theory which, it is argued, provides a compelling and parsimonious account of the relative importance of systemic and domestic level variables, while retaining a significant measure of theoretical flexibility to integrate a wide-range of intervening domestic variables. The section will, however, begin with an analysis of the insights of Neorealist IR theory that forms a central foundational tenet of Neoclassical Realism.

Neorealist IR theory argues that states inhabit a competitive international system (Waltz 1979). The absence of a higher authority above the state creates a high level of mistrust and suspicion of the actions of other states. States must therefore focus on maximising their relative power in order to guarantee their security (Waltz 1979: 118). However, according to Waltzian Neorealism, the level of conflict and cooperation in the international system is a function of the distribution of material power (the 'balance of power') (Waltz 1979: 170–171). However, as Walt (1985) demonstrates, states also balance against threat. A state with aggressive intentions and offensive capabilities that is of greater geographical proximity forms a more pressing danger than the dominant state in the international system.

Despite the gradual shift toward a multipolar system following the increasing ability of the BRIC states (Brazil, Russia, India and China) to

*Germany's limited leadership in EDA*  159

translate their economic power to military power, Europe is situated in a systemic context characterised by unipolarity, but that is characterised by balanced multipolarity at the regional level. This power distribution creates a favourable context for collaboration as the West European great powers (Britain, France and Germany) are subject to relatively similar pressures from the balance of power. While some Neorealists argue that this context creates an incentive to begin balancing US power (Posen 2006), the insights of Stephen Walt's 'balance of threat' theory suggest that Europe is undertaking a process of bandwagoning on US power (Cladi and Locatelli 2012; Dyson and Konstadinides 2013). Although the US may emerge as a threat to Europe over time as it attempts to strive for global hegemony, it is, over the short to medium term, a useful ally in tackling more immediate common opponents. Security challenges including Iran's nuclear programme, managing the re-emergence of Russia, international terrorism and failed states are all challenges which do more to unite than to divide Europe and the US (Art *et al.* 2005/2006: 192).

Hence European states have undertaken a reform of their Cold War bandwagoning on the US (Dyson 2010a). This process of reformed bandwagoning is focused on avoiding abandonment and entrapment by the US. In order to mitigate the threat of abandonment European states have strengthened NATO through defence capability and force generation initiatives. They have also contributed to US strategic goals by participating in International Security Assistance Force (ISAF). At the same time, European states have hedged against entrapment by the US by developing CSDP as a means to 'go it alone' in the event that the US is not able or willing to assist the Europeans with security challenges within their geopolitical neighbourhood (Dyson 2013).

Like the other West European great powers, Germany is subject to these common forces which have spurred the development of the EU's CSDP as the key pillar in the process of reform of Europe's Cold War bandwagoning on the US. However, while the balance of threat provides an incentive for Germany and other EU Member States to begin to consider how they can collaborate in defence, the Alliance Security Dilemma places significant limitations on the scope and depth of cooperation (Snyder 1984: 461). The problem of striking the appropriate balance between the threat of abandonment or entrapment by alliance partners is a feature of all military alliances throughout history (Press-Barnathan 2006: 271; Snyder 1984: 461).

While entrapment in the policy decisions of alliance partners presents a risk for Germany and other EU Member States, this problem is more pronounced in NATO due to the significant power differentiation between the US and its NATO partners. However, this fear of entrapment is mitigated by the intergovernmental nature of CSDP and NATO which permit a high level of strategic autonomy. Rather, abandonment by alliance partners is the greatest problem. As Snyder illustrates, abandonment can be

160    *T. Dyson*

manifested in a number of ways: 'the ally may realign with the opponent; he may merely de-align, abrogating the alliance contract; he may fail to make good on his specific commitments, or he may fail to provide support in contingencies where his support is expected' (Snyder 1984: 466). The threat of abandonment is a vital factor in understanding the reticence of Germany – and other European states – to challenge the intergovernmental nature of CSDP.

However, in the light of the strategic challenge of US disengagement from Europe, the balance in the trade-off between the fear of defection and cooperation in European defence is weighted too far in favour of the perils of defection. Germany, like Britain and France, is failing to take advantage of the possibilities to coordinate its defence reforms and defence budget cutbacks with European partners and to proceed with pooling and sharing projects which would not fundamentally affect the ability of European states to undertake operations should certain partners abstain (Biscop 2012: 1307).

In short, in contrast to the neo-functionalist dynamic identified by Constructivists that views the EDA as a product of social processes of elite socialisation and the 'Europeanisation' of national foreign, defence and security policies (Meyer 2005), a Neorealist perspective understands CSDP and the EDA as a result of the balance of power and threat. The extent of cooperation within the EDA is dependent on the convergence pressures exerted by these material systemic forces. The institution is a key element of EU Member States' attempt to hedge against abandonment and entrapment by the US as part of the 'reform' of their bandwagoning on US power. At the same time, cooperation is inherently limited by the Alliance Security Dilemma. Yet while these systemic forces create a measure of convergence around 'reformed bandwagoning' a significant measure of differentiation remains, which, as the following section highlights, has important implications for Germany policy toward the EDA.

## Variance in external vulnerability and German EDA policy

One of the main factors that undermines the ability of Germany and other Member States to use the EDA to pool and share capabilities and foster a more efficient European defence sector is the differentiation that persists in the extent to which they view CSDP – and therefore the EDA – as a means to decouple Europe from the US security guarantee. France views CSDP as a mechanism to place France at the forefront of a predominantly European security order, while the UK is unwilling to countenance any developments within CSDP which may fundamentally challenge the centrality of NATO (O'Donnell 2011). Germany has adopted a 'bridge-role' in European defence between British Atlanticism and French Europeanism (Dyson and Konstadinides 2013: 155). As a consequence, a strong German leadership role within CSDP and the EDA is unlikely, for while

Germany is committed to defence cooperation in both organisations it will not undertake measures which call into question the role of the US in underpinning the European balance of power (Interviews 5 and 6).

These differences in the Atlanticisation and Europeanisation of Member States – and the level of national strategic autonomy they wish to maintain – derive from nuanced variations in their geographical position and external resource dependencies. Variance in external vulnerability fosters a significant level of contestation between Member States in their fear of abandonment or entrapment by particular alliance partners and therefore in the extent to which they are willing to embed their defence and security policies within CSDP, NATO or prioritise national strategic autonomy.

For example, the UK's high dependency on the US for influence in areas vital to the UK's strategic interest, such as the Middle East, and its reliance on the US for military technology transfers have fostered a greater level of commitment to NATO than many other European nations (Keylor 2006: 306). France, while adopting a more Atlanticised defence and security policy in recent years, remains strongly committed to develop a greater level of European military autonomy. The fundamental driver of French 'Europeanism' in defence is the particularly intensive security dilemma fostered by its geographical position (Cole 2001: 10; Sutton 2007: 109). France is highly vulnerable to German power and has been invaded five times since the inception of the First Republic in 1792. Consequently, French policy-makers have a strong motivation to ensure that France is the predominant military power in Europe and maintains its relative military advantage over Germany. Germany's 'bridge-role' is a result of her vulnerable geographical position in the European *Mittellage* and the consequent need to maintain strong relations with France, Russia, the UK and the US.

The backseat role played by Germany in the Libya crisis and French-led intervention in Mali also provides an excellent example of how variance in external resource dependency impacts on Europe's capacity to establish common responses to security challenges within its geopolitical neighbourhood. France and Britain framed their interventions in Libya and Mali as humanitarian intervention and part of the fight against international terrorism. However, there are vital material interests at stake in North Africa for the UK and France. Both states face a future of declining oil supplies from the North Sea and require access to new secure supplies. With Africa's largest remaining oil reserves, Libya is in an excellent position to supply the UK and France over the medium term (Dyson and Konstadinides 2013: 156–170). Germany, on the other hand, has been looking eastwards – to Russia and Soviet successor states – to fill the gap in energy supplies that will come about in the context of the depletion of North Sea oil. It therefore has little strategic interest in North Africa and little incentive to become involved in military operations in the region (Dyson and Konstadinides 2013: 156–170).

162   *T. Dyson*

This variance in external vulnerability has a very important implication for German policy toward the EDA. It means that Germany is keen to maintain a significant level of freedom of manoeuvre in security and defence policy. Germany is, therefore, unwilling to enter into pooling and sharing arrangements which may exert greater pressure for it to become involved in military operations which are peripheral to its national interests (Interviews 4, 6, 7 and 8).

## Domestic variables and German EDA policy: material interests, strategic culture and institutional misfit

A focus on the impact of systemic-level variables can only provide a partial understanding of Germany's modest role within the EDA. Domestic factors are also important in reducing the willingness of the Federal Republic to take advantage of the opportunities afforded by the EDA to create greater efficiencies in defence spending. Hence we must turn to the insights of Neoclassical Realism to fully understand Germany's role in the EDA. While arguing that the balance of threat is the main independent variable shaping foreign, defence and security, by integrating the insights of Classical Realist thought, Neoclassical Realism has the flexibility to account for the intervening impact of a wide-range of domestic-level variables (Rathburn 2008). These variables include ideology, domestic material power relations and institutional design and management, all of which have impacted German EDA policy and slowed German convergence with the process of 'reformed bandwagoning', as this section will demonstrate.

First, an objective assessment of the advantages of cross-national collaboration is undermined by the presence of a strong domestic armaments industry that is averse to the loss of market share that could arise should Europe develop a more open system of tendering for military procurement (Interviews 1, 2 and 3). The presence of frequent important regional elections makes it particularly difficult for German Defence Ministers to create greater efficiencies in defence procurement through European collaboration. Furthermore, as a consequence of the high-profile of the German *Länder*, powerful regional politicians emerge within the two major political parties (the CDU/CSU and SPD). A significant number of post-Cold War German Defence Ministers – notably, Volker Ruehe (1992–1998), Rudolf Scharping (1998–2002) and Karl-Theodor zu Guttenberg (2009–2011) – had an eye on reaching the position of Chancellor (Dyson 2007, 2011a). Upsetting important figures within their political parties from Germany's north coast and Bavaria by sanctioning European initiatives which may have had a negative outcome for industry within these regions was, therefore, anathema (Interviews 2 and 3).

As a consequence, the political lobbyists who work on behalf of the German defence industry are very influential. There is an expectation within the German defence industry that German politicians will prioritise their interests over any savings which can be made by looking for collaborative European alternatives (Interviews 2 and 3). The Bundestag's Budgetary Committee is an especially important institutional venue where the interests of the German defence sector are represented through politicians with vested political interests in the north of Germany and Bavaria. Any procurement projects which will involve expenditure of over €25 million have to be sanctioned by the Bundestag's Budgetary Committee. On several occasions attempts by the German Ministry of Defence (MoD) to push ahead with joint work in the EDA have been frustrated by politicians within the Budgetary Committee who are acting in the interests of German industry. These politicians have stalled German participation in European projects by awarding a contract to different supplier, or raising so many questions about a project that it effectively thwarts the MoD's attempts to locate it within the EDA (Interview 3).

The desire of German politicians to avoid European initiatives which may harm the domestic DTIB has also limited the ability of Germany to reduce the fragmentation of European defence industry. In October 2010, Chancellor Merkel blocked the merger of BAE Systems and EADS and in doing so, spurned a significant opportunity to create a defence industrial giant that would foster greater efficiency in Research and Development (R&D) and be capable of competing more effectively at a global level. Merkel's opposition was primarily a consequence of her perception of Germany's limited influence within the corporate governance structures of the new company and the potentially negative implications of this paucity of influence for the future job security of the 50,000 EADS employees in Germany (Milmo *et al.* 2012).

The second major domestic factor undermining German participation in the EDA lies in the presence of a strongly institutionally and societally embedded ideological commitment to the use of force only in self-defence, or what a number of scholars have identified as a German 'strategic culture' (Dalgaard-Nielsen 2006; Longhurst 2004). In the immediate post-war era German Chancellors were driven by the twin imperatives of attaining regional and international support for reunification and of ensuring the Federal Republic's moral and political rehabilitation in the international community after the Second World War (Cole 2001: 11–12). As a consequence, German policy-makers developed a non-threatening security narrative that emphasised the use of force only in self-defence and a commitment to multilateral approaches to foreign, defence and security policy. Over the post-war period this security narrative became embedded within German society and the institutions of German defence and security by the end of the Cold War and has come to form a 'culture of restraint' in German attitudes toward the use of military force as a tool of foreign policy.

Policy-makers have sought to refashion this security narrative in the context of the post-Cold War imperative of expeditionary military operations

164   *T. Dyson*

(Dyson 2007, 2010b: 163–197). However, this process has proved highly difficult in the context of the federal state, where frequent regional elections reduce the windows of opportunity to make bold, electorally unpopular changes to defence and security policy, slowing the pace of defence reform (Dyson 2011b: 545–567). As a consequence, Germany faces significant problems in translating its economic power to military power and is a laggard in burden-sharing not only within the CSDP and the EDA, but also within NATO.

The 'culture of restraint' is given institutional expression by the German constitution that restricts the ability of the core executive to initiative military operations by requiring the Bundestag to sanction overseas troop deployments. This undermines Germany's capacity to burden-share by slowing the pace at which troops can be deployed as part of the Battlegroups as well as raising the fear amongst Germany's alliance partners that Germany may not be able to gain Parliamentary support for joint operations, thereby sharpening the Alliance Security Dilemma.

The final factor at work in restricting Germany to limited leadership within the EDA is a lack of 'institutional fit' between the structures of the German MoD and the EDA. Until the recent structural reforms to the Bundeswehr and German MoD undertaken by current Defence Minister Thomas de Maizière (2011–2013), the main point of contact for the EDA was within the MoD's Armaments Directorate. This institutional set-up gave the individual Service Chiefs of the Army, Navy and Air Force a high level of influence over armaments planning (Interview 3). As a consequence, national planning processes have dominated international armaments planning. Furthermore, the quick decision-making processes of the EDA contrast with the MoD, whose budget is set far in advance by Parliament and there is very little leeway to move money between the various sub-budgets of the MoD. This lack of flexibility makes it very difficult to respond to initiatives within the EDA and is one of the reasons why Germany was so reticent to become involved in the first JIP on Force Protection (Interview 3).

## The future of Germany's role in the EDA

While this chapter paints a rather pessimistic picture of international and domestic structural constraints on German policy toward to the EDA, there are grounds for optimism that Germany will play a more active leadership role within the organisation over the short to medium term. The recent reforms to the Germany MoD should help to overcome some of the impediments to a more active German role in capability development. The main point of contact for the EDA has now been brought into the MoD's Political Division. The Division for International Armaments within the Political Division now has the responsibility to coordinate the various experts at the Armaments Directorate and identify where collaborative international armaments projects can take place. This is likely to foster a much more proactive process of identifying the possibilities for international, rather than national procurement (Interview 3).

Nevertheless, the Political Division faces a difficult task in persuading the Armaments Directorate of the benefits of collaborative European initiatives. Many staff within the Armaments Directorate have been left with a negative impression of multinational post-Cold War defence procurement projects such as the NH-90 and Tiger Helicopter projects, where poor project management and the lack of a design freeze led to delays and overspend. As a consequence, key figures within the Armaments Directorate are disinclined to view the EDA and the Organisation Conjointe de Coopération en matière d'Armement (OCCAR) in a favourable light (Interview 3).

A further institutional change in the MoD that will open up opportunities for a stronger German leadership role is the reduction of the power of the individual service chiefs under de Maizière's reform, as the General Inspector now has overall responsibility for decision-making on defence procurement. While it is too early to make definitive conclusions about the impact of this empowerment of the General Inspector it is likely to help foster a more objective assessment of capability requirements and consideration of the possibilities for collaborative procurement or pooling and sharing.

However, a number of the fundamental problems at the higher political levels remain which thwart Germany from taking full advantage of the EDA. First, Germany's national defence industry remains a powerful vetoplayer through its power within the Bundestag's Budgetary Committee. While the ability of Member States to protect their national armaments industries is growing more limited in the context of economic downturn, the political incentives for sustaining national defence industries in Germany are particularly acute due to the impact of the German federal system and regional concerns on defence politics. As a source within the CDU noted: 'like Britain has its Atlanticism and France its Europeanism/national strategic autonomy in defence, so our national defence industry is sacrosanct' (Interview 8).

Second, as Germany begins to become more comfortable exerting its materialist national interests following the Eurozone crisis, it will be less willing to sacrifice its national interests in order to be viewed as a good Alliance partner. Germany's growing assertiveness will sharpen the impact of variance in Germany's external vulnerability on its policy toward CSDP and the EDA. While this does not mean that Germany will 'go it alone' in military operations, it does point to an increased likelihood that Germany will adopt a position of national strategic autonomy on abstaining from missions which do not affect its national interests and be more vociferous in intra-Alliance bargaining. Related to this second factor is the Alliance Security Dilemma which will also limit Germany's willingness and ability to

166   *T. Dyson*

initiate P&S arrangements within the EDA. The recent German defence reform launched by de Maizière outlines Germany's intention to maintain a broad range of military capabilities at the expense of sustainability ('breadth before depth'). As a consequence, Germany remains very sceptical of any P&S arrangements which may fundamentally compromise its military capabilities in key areas.

There are, however, signs that Germany is increasingly becoming a focal point for bilateral cooperation with Benelux and Nordic nations in pooling and sharing, as demonstrated by the 30 May 2013 German–Dutch memorandum of understanding on defence cooperation. However, unlike the Franco-British Lancaster House Treaties of 2010, this bilateralism does not pose a threat to the EDA. Despite Germany's greater proclivity to unilateral rejection of participation in military operations, the ideologically embedded tendency to multilateralism in German defence and security policy continues to reduce the willingness of policy-makers to countenance any cooperative arrangements which might fundamentally compromise the 'bridge-role' in defence and German relations with the UK and France. Hence there is a broad consensus across the main political parties and the core executive that any bilateral cooperation should ideally eventually be brought under the auspices of the EDA (Interviews 6, 8, 9 and 10).

Finally, the Chancellor's Office and MoD as well as elements of the CDU/CSU *Bundestagsfraktion* have begun to attempt to push through reforms to the process of military deployment which will help create a greater level of certainty amongst Germany's alliance partners about German contributions to pooling and sharing arrangements. Following Germany's undermining of a common European position on the Libya crisis and extremely limited involvement in Operation Unified Protector, the Chancellor's Office came under pressure from the Obama administration to reform the Bundestag's role in sanctioning overseas troop deployments (Interviews, 5, 6 and 11).

The Chancellor's Office's response was to allow high-profile defence experts within the CDU/CSU *Bundestagfraktion*, notably Roderich Kiesewetter and Andreas Schockenhoff, to develop plans to reform the process of parliamentary approval (Interviews 5, 8 and 11). The so-called 'Schockenhoff/Kiesewetter Paper' was released on 30 May 2012. Amongst other proposals, the paper suggested that Parliament would grant approval to the executive in advance for multilateral operations under CSDP (Schockenhoff and Kiesewetter, 2012). This proposal met with a significant level of opposition from the SPD and other parties in the Bundestag (Interviews 7 and 12). However, these proposals resurfaced in the CDU/CSU September 2013 federal election programme and, despite SPD opposition, there is no commitment in the coalition agreement to protect the rights of Parliament in respect to mandating troop deployment. Hence, reforming the Bundestag's role in multilateral troop deployment may well emerge once more as a theme in the 2013–2017 legislative period.

## Conclusion

The chapter finds that, in accordance with the insights of Neorealism, Germany is slowly emerging as a stronger regional leader on CSDP, with positive implications for German EDA policy. The Asia pivot and austerity measures are creating ever more powerful incentives for Germany to take a leadership role on behalf of the process of Europe's process of 'reformed bandwagoning' on US power, of which CSDP and the EDA are central elements (Dyson 2013). Yet, as Neorealism predicts, the Alliance Security Dilemma and variance in external vulnerability act as a limit on the extent to which Germany will be willing to pool and share military capabilities and erode its national defence industrial capacity. However, Neorealism is only of limited use in explaining German EDA policy. Domestic interests also play a very important intervening role in slowing the transmission of systemic imperatives into domestic policy response. It is, therefore, Neoclassical Realism which has the greatest analytical leverage in understanding German policy within the EDA.

In the context of variance in external vulnerability and the Alliance Security Dilemma the EDA faces a difficult task in attempting to increase German involvement with its activities. These difficulties will be compounded by the scepticism within the German MoD and the individual services of the Bundeswehr about the ability of cross-national procurement projects to deliver projects on time and within budget. As recent Franco-British defence cooperation has illustrated, much recent defence cooperation in Europe has proceeded on a bilateral basis. This presents a threat to the EDA – and to Europe's capacity to meet the challenge of US strategic disengagement from Europe. Not all Europe's capability deficits can be tackled through bilateral cooperation. Deficits in key strategic enablers, such as precision-guided munitions and future military satellites, will require broader cross-national collaboration that will also necessitate the involvement of Germany. The EDA will provide an ideal institutional venue for such projects. However, the EDA must work to reassure actors within the German defence establishment that it will not repeat the mistakes of past collaborative ventures, which although not undertaken under the auspices of the EDA, weaken the credibility of the institution within the German defence community. The EDA should also look to work with partners outside the MoD. Germany has been a consistent champion of the European project and the EDA may find important supporters within an SPD-run Foreign Ministry willing to champion German leadership on behalf of multilateral responses to Europe's capability deficits.

## References

Art, R., Brooks, S., Wohlforth, W., Lieber, K. and Alexander, G. (2005/2006) 'Correspondence: Striking the Balance', *International Security*, 30(3): 177–196.

168    *T. Dyson*

Biscop, S. (2012) 'The UK and European Defence: Leading or Leaving?', *International Affairs*, 88(6): 1297–1313.

Brune, S.-C., Cameron, A., Maulny, J.-P. and Terlikowski, M. (2010) 'Restructuring Europe's Armed Forces in an Age of Austerity', *SWP Comments*, 28 November 2010.

Cladi, L. and Locatelli, A. (2012) 'Bandwagoning, Not Balancing: Why Europe Confounds Neorealism', *Contemporary Security Policy*, 33(2): 264–288.

Cole, A. (2001) *Franco-German Relations*, Harlow: Pearson.

Dalgaard-Nielsen, A. (2006) *Germany, Pacifism and Peace-Enforcement*, Manchester: Manchester University Press.

Dyson, T. (2013) 'Balancing Threat, Not Capabilities: European Defence Cooperation as Reformed Bandwagoning', *Contemporary Security Policy*, 34(2): 387–391.

Dyson, T. (2011a) 'Managing Convergence: German Military Doctrine and Capabilities in the 21st Century', *Defence Studies*, 11(2): 244–270.

Dyson, T. (2011b) 'Condemned Forever to Becoming and Never to Being? The Weise Commission and German Military Isomorphism', *German Politics*, 20(4): 545–567.

Dyson, T. (2010a) 'Defence Policy: Temporal and Spatial Differentiation within Reformed Bandwagoning', in K. Dyson and A. Sepos (eds) *Whose Europe? The Politics of Differentiated Integration*, Basingstoke: Palgrave Macmillan: 322–343.

Dyson, T. (2010b) *Neoclassical Realism and Defence Reform in Post-Cold War Europe*, Basingstoke: Palgrave.

Dyson, T. (2008) 'Between International Structure and Executive Autonomy: Convergence and Divergence in British, French and German Military Reforms', *Security Studies*, 17(4): 725–774.

Dyson, T. (2007) *The Politics of German Defence and Security: Policy Leadership and Military Reform in the Post-Cold War Era*, Oxford: Berghahn.

Dyson, T. and Konstadinides, T. (2013) *European Defence Cooperation in EU Law and IR Theory*, Basingstoke: Palgrave.

EDA (European Defence Agency) (undated) *Mission*. Online. Available at: www.eda.europa.eu/Aboutus/Whatwedo/Missionandfunctions (accessed 22 May 2013).

European Council (2003) *Proceedings of the Thessaloniki European Council, 19 and 20 June 2003*.

Farrell, T. (2005) 'World Culture and Military Power', *Security Studies*, 14(3): 448–488.

Hyde-Price, A. (2007) *European Security in the 21st Century: The Challenge of Multipolarity*, Abingdon: Routledge.

Keylor, W. (2006) *The 20th Century World and Beyond: An International History Since 1900*, Oxford: Oxford University Press.

Klein, B. (1988) 'Hegemony and Strategic Culture: American Power Projection and Alliance Defence Politics', *Review of International Studies*, 14(2): 133–148.

Longhurst, K. (2004) *Germany and the Use of Force: The Evolution of German Security Policy 1990–2003*, Manchester: Manchester University Press.

Meyer, C. (2005) 'Convergence towards a European Strategic Culture', *European Journal of International Relations*, 11(4): 523–549.

Meyer, C. and Strickmann, E. (2011) 'Solidifying Constructivism: How Material and Ideational Factors Interact in European Defence', *Journal of Common Market Studies*, 49(1): 61–81.

Milmo, D., Connolly, K. and Willsher, K. (2012) 'Angela Merkel Blocks BAE/EADS Merger over Small German Share', *Guardian*, 10 October 2012.

O'Donnell, C. (2011) 'Britain's Coalition Government and EU Defence Cooperation: Undermining Britain's Interests', *International Affairs*, 87(2): 419–433.

O'Hanlon, M. (2012) *Getting Real on Defence Cuts*, Brookings Institution, 22 July 2012.

Patel, K. (2012) 'Germany and European Integration since 1945', in H. Smith (ed.) *The Oxford Handbook of Modern German History*, Oxford: Oxford University Press: 775–795.

Posen, B. (2006) 'The European Security and Defence Policy: Response to Unipolarity', *Security Studies*, 15(2): 149–186.

Press-Barnathan, G. (2006) 'Managing the Hegemon: NATO under Unipolarity', *Security Studies*, 15(2): 271–309.

Rathburn, B. (2008) 'A Rose by Any Other Name? Neoclassical Realism as the Logical and Necessary Extension of Structural Realism', *Security Studies*, 17(2): 294–321.

Schmitt, O. (2012) 'Strategic Users of Culture: German Decisions on Military Action', *Contemporary Security Policy*, 33(1): 59–81.

Schockenhoff, A. and Kiesewetter, R. (2012) 'Europa's sicherheitspolitische Handlungsfähigkeit stärken: Es ist höchste Zeit', 30 May 2012. Online. Available at: www.andreas-schockenhoff.de/download/120611_GSVP-Papier.pdf (accessed 3 June 2013).

Snyder, G. (1984) 'The Security Dilemma in Alliance Politics', *World Politics*, 36(4): 461–466.

Sutton, M. (2007) *France and the Construction of Europe: The Geopolitical Imperative, 1944–2007*, Oxford: Berghahn.

Walt, S. (1985) 'Alliance Formation and the Balance of World Power' *International Security*, 9(4): 3–43.

Waltz, K. (1979) *Theory of International Politics*, Reading, MA: Addison Wesley.

Witney, N. (2011) *How to Stop the Demilitarisation of Europe*, European Council on Foreign Relations Policy Brief 40, November 2011.


## Interviews

Interview 1, Nick Witney, former Chief-Executive of the EDA, London, 9 May 2013.

Interview 2, Dr. Hilmar Linnenkamp, former Deputy Chief-Executive of the EDA, 2004–2007, Berlin, 24 May 2013.

Interview 3, Division for International Armaments, Political Department, German Defence Ministry, Berlin, 29 May 2013.

Interview 4, EU Branch/Force Generation EU, German Defence Ministry, Berlin, 24 February 2012.

Interview 5, Chancellor's Office, Berlin, 1 August 2012.

Interview 6, Defence and Security Policy Division, German Foreign Ministry, Berlin, 9 March 2012.

Interview 7, Frau Elke Hoff, MdB, FDP Bundestagsfraktion, Member of Bundestag Defence Committee, Berlin, 11 September 2012.

Interview 8, Office of Roderich Kiesewetter, MbD, CDU/CSU Bundestagsfraktion, Berlin, 29 May 2013.

Interview 9, Hans-Peter Bartels, MdB, SPD Bundestagsfraktion, Berlin, 21 February 2013.

Interview 10, Joachim Spatz, MdB, FDP Bundestagsfraktion, Berlin, 8 November 2012.

Interview 11, Dr Patrick Keller, Foreign and Security Policy Coordinator, Konrad Adenauer Stiftung, Berlin, 23 July 2013.

Interview 12, Mathias Martin, Koordinierender Referent der AG-Außenpolitik, SPD Bundestagsfraktion, Berlin, 22 August 2012.

# 10 Organisations at war

## The EDA, NATO and the European Commission

*Marc R. DeVore*

## Introduction

For many the European Defence Agency's (EDA) creation in 2004 represented a turning point in Europe's development as a foreign policy actor. Although they spend roughly half as much on defence as the United States (US), the European Union's (EU) 27 Member States possess some of the world's most competitive defence industries and would become a defence industrial superpower if they integrated their defence procurement processes. However, despite the compelling reasons for integration, years of inadequate cooperation preceding the EDA's creation raised the spectre that Europe's atomised defence industries could, barring significant reforms, be gradually driven out of business. Considering both the hopes vested in the EDA and the negative consequences should it fail, the EDA's creation was regarded as a pivotal moment.

Because of the EDA's unique character as the EU's first and only decision to create an agency dedicated to defence industrial matters, scholars generally treat the Agency as a sui generis entity whose prospects and performance should be judged only with respect to the dynamics that led to its creation. For example, Catherine Hoeffler (2012) explains the EDA's emergence as a product of states' strategies for protecting their defence industries during a period of declining budgets. In another vein, Seth Jones contends that the need to 'softly' balance against the United States' power is driving the EDA's growth (Jones 2007). Others argue that the EDA is symptomatic of a broader trend towards the 'Europeanisation' of security issues (Mérand 2008). Even pessimistic scholars, such as Jozef Bátora, contend that divergences between stakeholders constitute the only serious threat to the EDA (Bátora 2009).

Regardless of which factors that each of these scholars asserts will determine the EDA's fate, what prior analyses share in common is their treatment of the EDA as a unique actor seeking to achieve integration in a domain – armaments – where they view cooperation as a recent phenomenon. Unfortunately, such a focus omits the fact that the EDA was created in an environment already crowded with pre-existing institutional actors

(DeVore 2012, 2013). The North Atlantic Treaty Organization (NATO) has, for example, promoted transatlantic and European defence industrial integration since the late 1940s. Within this context, three NATO organisations – the Committee of National Armaments Directors (CNAD), NATO Standardization Agency (NSA) and NATO Maintenance and Supply Agency (NAMSA) – were all large, established entities at the time of the EDA's creation.

In addition to NATO's position in Europe's defence industrial landscape, the European Commission also sought for years to position itself in this domain. Although EU treaties explicitly prevent the supranational Commission from playing a role in defence, defence industries' reliance on dual-use technologies and markets created the ambiguity necessary for the Commission to enlarge its role as the custodian of the integrated European market to encompass the defence industrial domain. For example, if the Commission was barred from regulating weapons procurement practices, it could challenge Member States' policies when it came to the public procurement of civilianised variants of military systems (Blauberger and Weiss 2013). Likewise, even though it could not directly finance defence Research and Development (R&D) projects, the Commission could support research into technologies with both civilian and military applications (Mörth 2003).

Previously unexplored, historic institutionalist scholarship provides powerful reasons for anticipating that the EDA's emergence within a field populated by other institutional actors will powerfully shape the organisation's future. The set-up costs associated with creating specialised organisations and the learning effects associated with those organisations' development create incentives for states to invest more in existing organisations rather than entrusting cooperation to new bodies. For these reasons, new organisations such as the EDA will struggle to impose themselves in domains where dynamic international cooperation is already occurring under the aegis of an existing body. Consequently, new organisations, such as the EDA, should find themselves compelled to focus on those aspects of their mandates that are not contested by competing entities.

To examine inter-organisational dynamics in the defence industrial field, this study examines the EDA's interactions with NATO and the European Commission. To preview the conclusion, the robust nature of NATO institutions for setting technical standards and providing maintenance support for weapons systems led members to support their further development. As a consequence, the EDA's activities gradually focused on those domains where NATO cooperation had either failed or never been attempted. In several domains, such as defence market regulation, the EDA found itself in competition with the Commission over whether intergovernmentalism or supranationalism will prevail. In short, the institutional environment within which the EDA was created fundamentally constrains the Agency's efforts to fulfil its broad mandate.

## Origins of the EDA

The EDA's creation was a logical response on behalf of the EU's Member States to dynamics confronting them since the Cold War. On the one hand, the growing cost of developing weapons systems, combined with declining defence budgets, meant that European states' defence industrial bases depended increasingly on international defence industrial cooperation. However, existing armaments organisations – the Western European Armaments Group (WEAG) and NATO – appeared incapable of fostering the levels of international defence industrial cooperation needed for European defence industrial bases to survive. Meanwhile, the push to create deployable EU military forces after Europe's failure to manage the Yugoslav Wars shed light on capacity shortfalls afflicting European armed forces. The decision to create the EDA – a centralised agency under the EU Council's direct control – was a response to these challenges.

In principal, Europe could potentially become a defence industrial superpower. With an aggregate defence budget of over \$200 billion, the EU's Member States collectively spend significantly more on defence than China, Russia or India (DeVore and Jones 2011). Moreover, Member States also possess some of the world most competitive defence industries, accounting for 27 per cent of the world arms export market, meaning that they lag slightly behind the US, but export more weaponry than Russia or China (DeVore and Jones 2011). However, despite European defence industrial strengths, the post-Cold War era has challenged Member States' defence industrial autonomy.

One reason for this challenge lies in evolving weapons technologies. Originating in the civil economy, developments in digital electronics and material sciences are driving weapons costs upwards at a rate far faster than economies are growing (Buzan and Herring 1998). Indeed, the costs of producing combat aircraft, warships and tanks have increased 6–10 per cent annually (Kirkpatrick 2004). To make matters worse, European defence budgets have progressively fallen since the Cold War (Biscop 2005). Together, these escalating weapons costs and declining defence budgets are eroding the scale-economies Europe's defence industries need to remain competitive.

Europe had been particularly hard hit by these dynamics because the EU is not a unitary state with a single defence budget, but rather individual Member States that allocate their defence budgets with little coordination amongst them. Consequently, duplications abound in R&D projects and manufacturing lines, with Member States manufacturing 11 models of armoured personnel carriers, three types of combat aircraft, and four classes of submarine (Briani 2013). Such duplication has had deleterious effects on industries' competitiveness since individual states cannot produce enough weapons to achieve adequate scale economies

174   *M.R. DeVore*

(Hartley and Martin 1993). To make matters worse, project duplication means that far too large a proportion of Europe's limited defence budgets has been spent on traditional categories of weaponry, leaving too little for investment in such innovative capabilities as precision strike technologies and drones (DeVore 2010; Giegerich and Nicoll 2012).

At the same time as the division of European defence industrial activities along national lines has undermined European industries' ability to produce cutting-edge systems, post-Cold War realities drove Member States to develop collective intervention capabilities. Europe's failure to manage Yugoslavia's collapse between 1991 and 1999 cast a painful light on Member States' lack of deployable military forces (Robinson 2001). Europe's Yugoslav debacle and the recognition that NATO could not be relied upon when American security was not threatened prompted European leaders to develop EU assets to manage military interventions. This process began when the British and French governments agreed to create an EU rapid response capability in 1998, continued with EU Council ratifying an EU rapid response force of 60,000 personnel in 1999, and was further institutionalised with the Council's development of political and military crisis management institutions in 2001 (Weiss 2011).

The process of creating these military units and deploying ad hoc forces on more limited military operations has revealed a host of military capability gaps (Bono 2011). To both rectify these military shortcomings and address their defence industrial deficiencies, Member States agreed to create the EDA in 2003. Within this context, the EU Council's Thessalonica Council defined the Agency's broad mandate in the following terms:

> This agency ... will aim at developing defence capabilities in the field of crisis management, promoting and enhancing European armaments cooperation, strengthening the European defence equipment market, as well as promoting, in liaison with the Community's research activities where appropriate, research aimed at leadership in strategic technologies for future defence and security capabilities, thereby strengthening Europe's industrial potential.
>
> (European Council 2003)

To accomplish this, Member States endowed the EDA with greater organic resources than any previous European armaments organisation had possessed. Whereas organisations preceding the EDA possessed miniscule staffs, ranging from 16 for the WEAG to 48 for the Organisation for Joint Armament Cooperation (OCCAR), the EDA was provided with a staff of 80 (subsequently 110) (Interview with Hilmar Linnenkamp). Moreover, the EDA was allocated an annual budget of $30 million (EDA 2013).

Nevertheless, despite its resources, the EDA would face formidable challenges. Foremost amongst these is the reality that the Agency's mandate was never exclusive by nature, meaning that the EDA had to struggle with

Organizations at war   175

other organisations to carve out a role for itself. Consequently, the EDA has had great difficulty imposing a role vis-à-vis NATO and the European Commission.

## NATO and the EDA

NATO has long constituted one of the most formidable obstacles to the EDA's imposing itself as Europe's key defence industrial actor. NATO has initiated a wide range of defence industrial initiatives since its creation in 1949. NATO's defence industrial track record has been mixed, with notable successes and failures, and many European members resent the preponderant voice of the US within the organisation. Nevertheless, NATO had established institutions specialised in many activities the EDA intended to undertake. For example, the NATO Standardization Agency's (NSA) and its precursors had been developing common equipment standards since 1952, the NATO Maintenance and Supply Agency (NAMSA) had long coordinated pooled maintenance support for European weapons systems, and NATO's Eurogroup existed as a forum for European states to develop weapons collaboratively.

Unfortunately for the EDA, pre-existing institutions possess inherent advantages over new competitors. The reason for this is that four interrelated factors – (1) set-up costs; (2) learning effects; (3) coordination effects; and (4) adaptive expectations – create incentives to invest in pre-existing international organisations rather than create new ones (North 1990; Pierson 2004). Because establishing organisations entails high set-up costs, including headquarters facilities, technical assets and personnel, governments are incentivised to work with existing organisations rather than create new ones. Furthermore, learning effects, including the gradual improvement of bureaucratic routines and employee skills through 'learning by doing', enable mature organisations to outperform new ones under *ceteris paribus* conditions (Nelson and Winter 1982). Coordination effects occur when the attractiveness of institutions increases as a function of the number of actors using them. Because states' willingness to use an organisation grows with time, coordination effects encourage states to reinforce, rather than replace organisations. Moreover, states' tendency to adapt their actions and expectations to existing organisational frameworks creates further incentives for them to invest in the physical and human assets needed to render them efficient.

When set-up costs, learning and coordination effects, and adaptive expectations are significant, a policy area will experience positive feedback. Once this occurs, the role and efficiency of existing organisations will expand, leaving little room for new entrants. Consequently, powerful theoretical reasons exist for anticipating that new organisations – the EDA – will fail in domains where existing organisations – NATO – are active.

The advantages of extant organisations over new entrants are nowhere greater than in the domain of standards-setting for weapons systems.

NATO's efforts at standards-setting date back to 1952, when policy-makers created the Military Standardization Agency (MSA) (renamed the Military Agency for Standardization (MAS)). Despite early disagreements between states advocating distinct standards, the MSA's organisation into boards specialised in terrestrial, naval and aeronautical matters, and a host of issue-specific working groups enabled the organisation to adopt 400 Standardization Agreements (STANAGs) within four years (Huston 1984: 220–222). Although early STANAGs focused on mechanical issues, such as ammunition calibres, it gradually expanded the scope of its work to electronic standards and battlefield communications systems (Mockos 1983).

While the Cold War's conclusion saw many question NATO's utility, NATO's standardisation role nevertheless progressively grew. Indeed, the inter-operability challenges raised by military interventions and digital communications drove European states to rely increasingly on the MAS (formerly MSA) as the only body with a track record of setting interoperability standards (Pedersen 2007). Because of its growing workload and responsibilities, NATO's Member States reorganised and reinforced the MAS as the NSA, providing it with a larger staff and new digital tools (Ferrari 1995).

Meanwhile, the network effects generated by NATO standardisation grew as the alliance expanded from 15 to 28 members, and as non-members such as Israel, Sweden and Switzerland began to adopt NSA standards in their armaments projects to appeal to broader export clienteles. Consequently, NATO's standardisation efforts have expanded dramatically, with over 2,000 STANAGs currently in force, employed by over 13,000 industrial and military actors (Aksit 2012). On a regular basis, over 400 committees meet under the NSA's auspices to develop new standards or update existing ones (Beckman 2006).

The continued growth in NATO standardisation effectively foreclosed the EDA's efforts to stake out a role for itself in this domain. This may appear surprising at first glance because the creation of common European technical standards has been at the core of European reflections on defence industrial integration since before the EDA's creation. Indeed, EU standardisation efforts can be traced back to the Commission-sponsored Sussex Study of 1999, which listed standardisation as the foremost domain where the EU should play a defence industrial role (ASD-STAN 2009: 39–40). Consequently, the WEAG and the Commission had modest standardisation initiatives underway at the time of the EDA's creation, with each organisation planning to expand work in this domain.

The EDA's attempt to develop a role in standardisation began in 2005 when it took over and expanded upon the WEAG's existing standards-setting initiative. The resultant EDA standards institution, the Material Standards Harmonisation Team (MSHT), aimed to first compile a database – the European Defence Standards Information System (EDSIS) – of technical standards employed in Europe as a preparatory step for developing new standards (Wilkinson and Kopold 2007). Similarly the EDA also

Organizations at war   177

took over, in 2011, the Commission's project of developing a European Handbook of Defence Procurement (EHDP) listing national defence acquisition procedures (Jendrossek and Runge 2011).

The EDA's leadership planned to use these projects as a platform establishing itself as a standards setting forum. The editorials opening the new EDA journal, the *European Defence Standardization Journal*, proclaimed this ambition by asserting that common standards would give European industries a competitive advantage akin to the one provided by the EU-level agreement on mobile phone standards in the early 1990s (the Groupe Spécial Mobile/GSM standard) (Pitts 2007). Furthermore, the growing importance of commercial standards and new digital interoperability challenges appeared to provide an opportunity for the EDA to carve out a role for itself (Otterbach 2007).

Nevertheless, despite NATO's shortcomings, the NSA's procedural efficiency and the well oiled machinery of its technical working groups led European members to improve and expand the NSA, rather than invest resources in the EDA's standardisation efforts. Indeed, due to personnel shortages, the compilers of EDSIS and EHDP adopted large numbers of NATO STANAGs (Veita 2009). As a result, the EDA found itself in the ironic role of diffusing NATO standards to the EDA's non-NATO members. Meanwhile, NATO's NSA expanded its activities to include cooperation with civilian standards-setting organisations, adapting commercial standards to NATO needs and encouraging commercial bodies to employ NATO standards (Urbanovsky 2006).

Pre-existing NATO standards and the NSA's ability to progressively expand its role deprived the EDA of opportunities to establish an independent standards-setting role for itself. Indeed, by 2009, Europe's defence industrial lobbying group, the Aerospace and Defence Industries Association (ASD) – a group that stood *a priori* to gain from robust European technical standards – concluded that NATO's hegemonic standards-setting role would persist, arguing:

> A similar position as that of ISO (International Standards Organization) in the classic economic environment is today still held by NATO in the defence and defence economic environment, although NATO is not a traditional supranational SDO [Standards Developing Organization], but an international military alliance. NATO took very early in its existence to a certain form of standardization from a need for interoperability between the military forces of its member nations. NATO has achieved over the years and for several reasons, a status of quasi-recognition as an international standards developer from the classic civilian SDOs.
>
> (ASD-STAN 2009, 29–30, emphasis added)

The EDA tacitly recognised its failure to play a significant standards-setting role when it suspended the Agency's *European Defence Standardization Journal* in 2011.

178   *M.R. DeVore*

While the EDA failed to carve out a role for itself in defence standards-setting, the Agency's efforts were even more abortive when it came to logistics. Within NATO the idea of achieving cost-savings by maintaining equipment via a common agency gave birth to the NATO Maintenance and Supply Service System (NMSSS) in 1958. This organisation's objective was 'to maximize in times of peace, crisis and war the effectiveness of logistics support to armed forces of NATO states and to minimize costs' (NMSSS Board of Directors 1958). In practice, the NMSSS functioned via Weapon Systems Partnerships whereby groups of states specified the support they desired for a weapons system, and the NMSSS' staff then negotiated and managed contracts. To manage component stockpiles, NMSSS members invested in 82,000 m² of warehouse facilities (Visine 1975: 19–21).

In the 1960s the NMSSS was reformed as the NATO Maintenance and Supply Agency (NAMSA). Along with this change in appellation, members invested resources so that NAMSA could support Southern European members (1969–1972), maintain guided ('smart') weapons (1967–1975) and manage a facility dedicated to European F-104 fighters (1965) (Visine 1975: 25–64). Since the Cold War, external military interventions have driven NAMSA's continued growth. For example, when states that hitherto concentrated on territorial defence sent contingents to the Balkans and Central Asia, they turned to NAMSA to supply their forces with food, munitions and equipment (Maynard 2009).

Because of NAMSA's predominant role providing NATO's European members with logistics support, EDA's leaders faced insurmountable obstacles to staking out a role in this domain. Indeed, when EDA officials argued that the organisation should develop logistics and maintenance capabilities, member governments ignored them, preferring to support NAMSA's expansion instead (Larran 2009). Consequently, NAMSA's role in operational logistics has grown since the EDA's creation, generating an annual turnover of €1.4 billion. Moreover, NAMSA's expanding capabilities prompted 12 non-Member States to sign partnership agreements with the organisation and encouraged many EU Members States to use the organisation to support operations conducted either independently or under the EU's ambit (Larran 2009).

While NATO precluded the EDA from playing a role in logistics and standardisation, the new Agency was more successful at supplanting NATO as a forum for collaborative armaments projects. Although NATO had long encouraged collaborative armaments projects, its efforts had never succeeded to the degree expected and its institutions remained weak in this regard. NATO's first such institution, the Armaments Committee, was dissolved in 1966 after its market-based approach failed because states systematically withdrew from projects when their national champion firms were denied production contracts (Huston 1984: 192–195).

The Armaments Committee was succeeded in 1968 by a very different NATO structure – NATO's Eurogroup. This organisation sought to

Organizations at war 179

improve NATO's European members' ability to identify opportunities to collaborate and to reduce the difficulties of initiating projects by providing a platform for meetings between European defence procurement directors and expert groups (Eurogroup 1972). Once two or more members agreed to launch a collaborative project, Eurogroup's legal structures permitted them to incorporate their endeavour as a subsidiary NATO agency – with an independent legal personality – capable of contracting with defence firms (Draper 1990: 44–80).

Over decades of activity, Eurogroup facilitated an extremely slow increase in collaborative European projects. For example, the percentage of European budgets dedicated to collaborative projects rose from 5 to 15 per cent between 1965 and 1990 (Tucker 1990; Vandevanter 1964). Nonetheless, the track-record of European collaboration under Eurogroup was resoundingly negative. Many projects were cancelled, at great cost, because firms disagreed over work-share arrangements and armed forces clashed over requirements (Moravcsik 1993). Moreover, firms extracted excess profits by insisting on the duplication of industrial functions and economically inefficient contracting procedures whenever projects were carried through to completion (DeVore 2011). Consequently, collaborative projects failed to generate the hoped-for scale-economies and R&D savings.

Because of its disappointing results and negligible specific assets, NATO states had few incentives to invest further in Eurogroup. Therefore, contrary to their behavior vis-à-vis NSA and NAMSA, Europe's NATO members gradually transferred Eurogroup's functions to new organisations of an exclusively European character. This process occurred in two steps: with Eurogroup's functions first being transferred to the Western European Armaments Organization (WEAO) in 1996 and, then, these same functions were re-transferred from WEAO to the EDA in 2005 (Grigoleit *et al.* 2005).

As demonstrated above, NATO's past endeavours weighed heavily on the EDA's development. At its creation, EDA proponents viewed the Agency as the organisation that would oversee European defence industries' integration, rationalisation and collaboration. These ambitions were reflected in the EDA's mandate. However, the EDA's core tasks overlapped with NATO's pre-existing activities in three domains: standards-setting, pooled logistics and maintenance, and fostering collaborative armaments projects. Ultimately, the early institutionalisation of NATO cooperation in two of these domains stymied the EDA's efforts to carve out niches for itself. Indeed, the EDA was only more successful in the domain of collaborative armaments projects, where NATO's persistent inability to efficiently manage multinational armaments projects highlights the intractable nature of the problem and pyrrhic nature of the EDA's inter-institutional victory (Mawdsley 2013).

## The European Commission and the EDA

The EDA's failures vis-à-vis NATO forced the Agency to concentrate on residual missions, where inter-organisational competition was initially less intense. These missions included promoting defence market integration, encouraging collective solutions to 'capability gaps' and, as discussed, fostering collaborative projects. However, the EDA's responsibility for fulfilling even these missions has been contested by the European Commission. Dissatisfied with the EDA's intergovernmental approach, the Commission successfully extended its supranational mandate to cover market integration through its instrumental use of the European Court of Justice (ECJ) and its employment of pressure tactics vis-à-vis member states.

In light of the EDA's standardisation and logistics failures, the most important domain where the Agency could still define a crucial role for itself was that of market integration. Because defence markets were exempted from the treaty provisions governing the European common market, defence procurement processes had not been subjected to supranational regulation by the Commission. However, the declining competitiveness of Europe's fragmented defence industries convinced EU governments that some form of market integration was necessary. The EDA's leadership saw this need, combined with the Agency's intergovernmental character, as offering it an opportunity to establish its central role in European defence industrial matters.

The EDA sought to integrate defence markets by developing codes of conduct and other forms of 'soft' regulation. Within this context, the EDA formulated agendas and mediated between governmental and corporate stakeholders to forge agreements on non-binding, intergovernmental codes of conduct. Although the codes were voluntary in nature, EDA policy-makers would monitor compliance and publicise breaches of their mandated procedures. The EDA's leadership anticipated that 'naming and shaming' Member States that violated the codes would generate intergovernmental 'peer pressure' to adhere to the codes' new norms (Hammarström 2008).

Consequently, the EDA negotiated a series of codes in rapid succession, including the 2005 *Code of Conduct on Defence Procurement*, the 2006 *Code of Best Practice in the Supply Chain* and the 2008 *Code of Conduct on Offsets* (Stärkle 2010: 132–138). These codes promised transparency in contracting criteria and non-discrimination in terms of suppliers' nationality. The EDA complemented its codes with an Electronic Bulletin Board (EBB), where it encouraged members to advertise defence contract tenders. Agreement on these codes and the EBB's inauguration prompted an EDA official to enthuse that a 'silent revolution' was underway, heralding the EDA's emergence as an essential defence industrial actor (Hammarström 2008: 91).

However, the EDA's market integration role proved as transitory as its ambitions in standards-setting and maintenance. In this case it was European

*Organizations at war* 181

Commission ambitions, rather than NATO, that frustrated the EDA (Mörth 2003). The Commission had long sought to extend its authority to the defence field in spite of the treaty articles (most recently, Article 346 of the 2007 Lisbon Treaty) limiting its prerogatives. Consequently, the Commission pleaded in 1996–1997 for authority to regulate defence markets (European Commission 1996, 1997). Governments, however, wanted to keep the supranational Commission out of defence matters, which they argued should remain the purview of national authorities and whichever intergovernmental forums they preferred.

Undeterred, the Commission adopted an indirect approach to extending its authority. Rather than plead its case to member governments, the Commission now enlisted the ECJ. By arguing that government procurement practices frequently violated the letter of the Lisbon Treaty's Article 346 and by prosecuting the cases where such violations were most apparent, the Commission instrumentalised the ECJ to apply pressure on Member States. Within this context, two ECJ rulings – against procurement in Spain and Italy – compelled governments to negotiate a 'procurement directive' with the Commission. The Commission's implicit threat was that, in the absence of an accord, the ECJ would integrate European defence markets through an unpredictable accumulation of case-based jurisprudence (Blauberger and Weiss 2013: 1126–1132).

Consequently, the European Council, comprised of Member States' representatives, passed the so-called *Defence Procurement Directive* on 13 July 2009 (EU 2009). Although the *Defence Procurement Directive* (hereafter, *Directive*) bears a superficial verisimilitude to the EDA's 2005 *Code of Conduct on Defence Procurement* (hereafter, *Code*), the two documents differ fundamentally in both their spirit and in the institutions empowered to oversee the markets' integration. For example, while the EDA's *Code* is non-binding and general, the Commission's *Directive* is obligatory and highly specific, laying out in excruciating detail – the document is 61 pages in length versus four for its EDA counterpart – regulations applicable to every form of defence contract. Moreover, because of its greater specificity and obligatory character, the *Directive* superseded the EDA's 2005 *Code* as the core document for defence market integration.

Furthermore, while the EDA's *Code* (Provision C) specified that an intergovernmental EDA steering board would 'monitor' adherence with the document's provisions, the *Directive* (Articles 75–79) empowered the Commission to 'implement' and 'scrutinise' compliance. For the longer term, the *Directive* granted the Commission the right to periodically assess 'whether the defence equipment market is functioning in an open, transparent and competitive way' (Article 79; EU 2009). Thus, by dictating the *Directive's* enforcement provisions, the Commission supplanted the EDA as the body that would gradually eliminate intra-European defence industrial trade barriers.

While the Commission's *Directive* superseded the EDA's *Code*, at least the thrust of the Commission's effort resembled that of its intergovernmental

182   *M.R. DeVore*

predecessor. Such was not, however, the case when it came to defence offsets – a topic explored in detail by Chapter 13 of this volume. Offsets are conditions placed on foreign suppliers by importing governments whereby the former must 'compensate' the latter for contracts by providing 'offsetting' benefits. Offsets may take a variety of forms, including technology transfers, counter-trade arrangements or subcontracting components. Traditionally, governments employed offsets to garner domestic support for arms imports and force multinational corporations to do business with smaller states' defence industries (Mikkola *et al.* 2013).

The EDA tacitly recognised defence offsets' importance for small and medium European Member States in its non-binding 2008 *Code of Conduct on Offsets*. Within this context, the EDA sought to simultaneously preserve and reform offsets, arguing that properly conceived offsets could play a positive role. Consequently, the EDA's *Code of Conduct on Offsets* exhorted Member States to greater transparency in offset practices and to employ offsets only to 'develop [defence] industrial capabilities that are competent, competitive and capability driven' (EDA 2011). Although governments recognised that the *Directive* would require modification of the EDA's offset policy, they failed to recognise the depth to which the Commission's view diverged from the EDA's. This ambiguity was reinforced by the *Directive*'s omission of any discussion of offsets (Shanson 2010). For this reason, it surprised many when the Commission stated its position that all offsets are illegal, baldly stating that:

> Offset requirements are restrictive measures which go against the basic principles of the [EU] Treaty, because they discriminate against economic operators, goods and services from other Member States and impede the free movement of goods and services. Since they violate basic rules and principles of primary EU law, the [Defence Procurement] Directive cannot allow, tolerate or regulate them.
>
> (European Commission undated)

By categorically opposing offsets, the Commission staked out a position starkly opposed to the EDA's. It admitted as much when it argued that 'the application of the Code [the EDA *Code of Conduct on Offsets*] does not of itself make offset requirements compatible with EU law' (European Commission undated).

Armed with the *Directive*, the Commission coerced members into accepting its position on offsets, rather than the EDA's permissive guidelines. To this end, the Commission threatened Greece with prosecution by the ECJ in 2010 because the Greek offset requirements for a $29 million naval tender contravened EU procurement regulations (European Commission 2010). Despite Greece's conforming to the EDA's *Code of Conduct on Offsets*, it bowed to the Commission's threats by amending its contract award procedures. Following on the heels of the signature of the *Directive*, the

Organizations at war 183

outcome of the Greek case cemented the Commission's primacy in dictating how Europe's defence markets will be integrated (Campos *et al.* 2012).

In sum, after losing to NATO in the domains of standardisation and logistics, the EDA competed with the Commission to integrate defence markets. The EDA's approach of 'soft' regulation through non-binding codes of conduct yielded immediate results between 2005 and 2008. However, the Commission soon overtook and supplanted the EDA. Having long sought to extend its regulatory jurisdiction over the defence industrial sector, the Commission pressured member governments with legal action by the ECJ. Ultimately, this tactic bore fruit in the 2009 *Defence Procurement Directive*, which the Commission exploited to unseat the EDA as Europe's principal defence industrial integrator.

A careful examination of the Commission's activities reveals the deliberate nature of its efforts to circumscribe the EDA's role. In the *Directive*, the Commission consciously omits mention of prior EDA efforts at market integration, thereby denying it even the status as a precursor to the Commission's initiatives. However, while rejecting the EDA's market integration ambitions, the Commission implicitly left the door open for the Agency to play a role in fostering collaborative armaments projects and the acquisition of 'pooled' assets. Consequently, the *Directive* (explicitly Articles 11–13) excluded multinational armaments projects and procurement by international organisations from its purview. By writing these exceptions into the Directive, the Commission signalled its willingness for the EDA to play a role in these residual domains.

## Conclusion

As demonstrated above, the inter-organisational competition shaped the EDA's fate. Upon its creation, the EDA's founders planned for the organisation to oversee a wide range of defence industrial activities. From the setting of technical standards to the integration of markets and the promotion of collaborative projects, the EDA was supposed to improve arms production processes and coax states to improve their armed forces' interoperability. Through centralised logistics/maintenance and the collective resolution of capability gaps, the EDA was also designed to obtain greater value from Europe's stagnant defence budgets.

However, rather than blossoming into the powerful Agency originally envisioned, the EDA has developed along truncated lines. The primary reason for this disjuncture between the EDA's original mandate and its modest achievements can best be sought in the inter-organisational conflicts that pitted the EDA against two rivals – NATO and the Commission.

The EDA was thwarted in two of its core missions by NATO, whose agencies had developed standards-setting and logistics capabilities long before the EDA's foundation. Because of set-up costs, learning and coordination effects, and adaptive expectations, these agencies – NSA and

184 *M.R. DeVore*

NAMSA – benefited from high degrees of positive feedback even after the EDA's creation. Consequently, European Member States preferred to path-dependently invest in expanding NATO agencies, rather than bear the start-up costs required to equip the EDA to manage international defence industrial standards-setting and logistics/maintenance contracting. As a result, even the EDA's high-profile efforts to carve out a standards-setting niche for itself via the European Defence Standards Information System (EDSIS) and EHDP resulted only in the further diffusion of NATO technical and procedural standards.

While thwarted at standardisation and logistics/maintenance by NATO, the EDA's efforts to integrate European defence markets were nullified by the Commission's actions. With an existence that long pre-dated the EDA's creation, and with more numerous and more experienced staff, the Commission outmanoeuvred the EDA to become the arbiter of an integrated European defence industrial base. Key to the Commission's success was its tactic of coercing member governments to accede to its demands by threatening action on the part of the ECJ. In this way, the Commission imposed a *Defence Procurement Directive* on Member States that both deprived the intergovernmental EDA of its prerogatives and nullified the non-binding agreement on defence offsets that it had negotiated.

The EDA's setbacks vis-à-vis both NATO and the Commission relegated the EDA to two residual elements of its mandate: encouraging collaborative armaments projects and resolving military capabilities gaps. Unfortunately, these missions will likely prove difficult to accomplish.

Judging by the historic record, fostering collaborative projects is a thankless endeavour. As Andrew Moravcsik (1993) suggested, collaborative armaments projects are frequently terminated when an industrial partner calculates that its commercial interests would be better served by a national project. More recent research suggests that even states' credible commitments to persevere with collaborative projects have detrimental side-effects, as corporations exploit states' perceived unwillingness to cancel collaborative projects to extract excessive profits (DeVore 2011).

Consequently, it should come as little surprise that the EDA's efforts to encourage collaborative projects have foundered. Indeed, the EDA's widely publicised goal of convincing Member States to collaborate on armoured vehicle and frigate designs, rather than pursuing national programmes, failed to produce results. As a result, the EDA refocused its collaboration efforts on modest objectives. At present, these are limited to a Software-Defined Radio (SDR) project and network-enabled warfare studies (Stärkle 2010, 128–129). The Agency has also recurrently proposed air-to-air refuelling, satellite communication, drone and cyber defence projects. However, the EDA's meagre budget and competing national funding priorities have delayed the implementation of these proposals, despite consistent rhetorical support for them (Witney 2013).

Besides this difficult task, the other domain left to the EDA is that of steering the improvement of European defence capabilities. Although Europe collectively dedicates formidable resources to defence, the fragmentation of its efforts has resulted in numerous capability gaps, which have been apparent whenever European states have deployed forces. To this end, the EDA launched its Capability Development Plan (CDP) – endorsed by Member States in 2008 – aiming to provide a systematic approach for building common capabilities necessary for multinational interventions (Heuninckx 2009). However, although the EDA identified and publicised capability gaps, declining defence budgets and inflexible national procurement priorities meant that few, if any of these shortcomings have been resolved (Witney 2013).

To make matters worse, the EDA's efforts to cajole governments generated resistance because, in the EDA's founding Chief Executive's words, 'national defence bureaucracies are naturally inclined to view most Agency activities as intrusive' (Witney 2008). The changing nomenclature of the EDA's efforts to address European capabilities gaps, with the term 'pooling and sharing' becoming *de rigeur* since 2010, has resolved little. Fundamentally, the EDA lacks the centralised budgetary resources needed to purchased 'pooled' resources and lacks the authority needed to make 'sharing' more than cosmetic. Consequently, with the exception of a handful of modest initiatives, the EDA's efforts to address capability gaps have failed to markedly improve Europe's military ability to resolve problems in the continent's vicinity.

In short, ten years have passed since governments created the EDA to forge Europe's disparate defence markets and industries into a defence industrial powerhouse. Compared to its initial objectives, the EDA's accomplishments are modest and its prospects sombre. Competition from more established and better resourced organisations is the primary reason for the EDA's disappointing performance. Within this context, NATO precluded the EDA from establishing itself in standards-setting or logistics/maintenance, while the European Commission supplanted the EDA as the integrator of European defence markets. The two roles left to the EDA – fostering collaborative armaments projects and coaxing governments to address capabilities gaps – are inherently difficult to accomplish, which explains the absence of inter-organisational competition for these missions. As a result, the EDA has unsurprisingly disappointed its proponents, instilling an atmosphere of resignation amongst even the Agency's most fervent supporters.

## References

Aksit, C. (2012) 'The Importance of NATO Standardisation', *Defence Procurement International* (Summer 2012): 1–3.

ASD-STAN (2009) *Study into the Role of European Industry in the Development and Application of Standards*, Brussels: ASD-STAN.

186  *M.R. DeVore*

Bátora, J. (2009) 'European Defence Agency: A Flashpoint of Institutional Logics', *West European Politics*, 32(6): 1075–1098.

Beckman, L. (2006) 'Standardization within NATO', *Defence Standardization Program Journal* (January–March 2006): 14–25.

Biscop, S. (2005) *The European Security Strategy: A Global Agenda for Positive Power*, Aldershot: Ashgate.

Blauberger, M. and Weiss, M. (2013) ' "If you can't beat me, join me!" How the Commission Pushed and Pulled Member States into Legislating Defence Procurement', *Journal of European Public Policy*, 20(8): 1120–1138.

Bono, G. (2011) 'The EU's Military Operation in Chad and the Central African Republic: An Operation to Save Lives?', *Journal of Intervention and Statebuilding*, 5(1): 23–42.

Briani, V. (2013) 'Armaments Duplication in Europe: A Quantitative Assessment', CEPS Policy Brief 297: 3–5.

Buzan, B. and Herring, E. (1998) *The Arms Dynamic in World Politics*, Boulder: Lynne Rienner.

Campos, L., Nelson, A. and Teare, P. (2012) *An End to Offsets in European Defence Trade?*, Reed Smith, June 2012.

DeVore, M. (2014) 'International Armaments Collaboration and the Limits of Reform', *Defence and Peace Economics*, 25(4): 415–443.

DeVore, M. (2013) 'Explaining European Armaments Cooperation: Interests, Institutional Design and Armaments Organizations', *European Foreign Affairs Review*, 18(1): 1–28.

DeVore, M. (2012) 'Organizing International Armaments Cooperation: Institutional Design and Path Dependencies in Europe', *European Security*, 21(3): 432–458.

DeVore, M. (2011) 'The Arms Collaboration Dilemma: Between Principal-Agent Dynamics and Collective Action Problems', *Security Studies*, 20(4): 624–662.

DeVore, M. (2010) 'A Dangerous Utopia: The Military Revolution from the Cold War to the War on Terror', in G. Lawson, C. Armbruster and M. Cox (eds) *The Global 1989: Continuity and Change in World Politics*, Cambridge: Cambridge University Press: 219–242.

DeVore, M. and Jones, L. (2011) *U.S. National Defence Acquisition and Budgetary Policy in an International Perspective*, Monterey: NPS Acquisition Research Sponsored Report Series.

Draper, A. (1990) *European Defence Equipment Collaboration: Britain's Involvement, 1957–87*, London: Macmillan.

EDA (European Defence Agency) (2013) 'Finance'. Online. Available at: www.eda. europa.eu/Aboutus/how-we-do-it/Finance (accessed 1 December 2013).

EDA (European Defence Agency) (2011) 'A Code of Conduct on Offsets Agreed by the EU Member States Participating in the European Defence Agency', 3 May 2011.

EU (European Union) (2009) Directive 2009/81/EC of the European Parliament and of the Council of 13 July 2009, *Official Journal of the European Union*, 20 August 2009.

European Commission (2010) 'Public Procurement: Commission Calls on Greece to Amend Procedure for Awarding Supply Contract for Submarine Battery Kits', 24 November 2010.

European Commission (1997) 'Implementing European Union Strategy on Defence-Related Industries', COM(97) 583, 4 December 1997.

## Organizations at war 187

European Commission (1996) 'The Changes Facing the European Defence-Related Industry, A Contribution for Action at European Level', COM(96) 10, 24 January 1996.

European Commission (undated) 'Directive 2009/81/EC on the Award of Contracts in the Fields of Defence and Security – Guidance Note, Offsets', Directorate General Internal Markets and Services.

European Council (2003) 'Presidency Conclusions', 20 June 2003.

Eurogroup (1972) 'Communiqué Issued by the Defence Ministers of Eurogroup', 23 May 1972.

Ferrari, G. (1995) 'NATO's New Standardization Organization Tackles an Erstwhile Elusive Goal', *NATO Review*, 43(3): 33–35.

Giegerich, B. and Nicoll, A. (2012) 'The Struggle for Value in European Defence', *Survival*, 54(1): 53–82.

Grigoleit S., Kersten, G., Müller, S., Schulze, J., Sondermann, M. and Thorleuchter, D. (2005) *European Defence Agency (EDA) im europäischen Kontext*, Munich: Frauenhofer Institut.

Hammarström, U. (2008) 'A Strong European Defence Industry: What Needs to be Done', *RUSI Defence Systems*, 11(1): 90–93.

Hartley, K. and Martin, S. (1993) 'The Political Economy of International Collaboration', in R. Coopey, M. Uttley and G. Spinardi (eds) *Defence Science and Technology: Adjusting to Change*, Chur: Harwood: 171–205.

Heuninckx, B. (2009) 'The European Defence Agency Capability Development Plan and the European Armaments Cooperation Strategy: Two Steps in the Right Direction', *Public Procurement Law Review*, 18(4): 136–143.

Hoeffler, C. (2012) 'European Armament Co-operation and the Renewal of Industrial Policy Motives', *Journal of European Public Policy*, 19(3): 435–451.

Howorth, J. (2007) *Security and Defence Policy in the European Union*, Houndsmills: Palgrave.

Huston, J. (1984) *One for All: NATO Strategy and Logistics through the Formative Period (1949–1969)*, Newark: Delaware University Press.

Jendrossek, J. and Runge, E. (2011) *The European Handbook for Defence Procurement (EHDP): The Future Reference for 'Best Practice' in Selecting Defence Procurement Standards*, DIN-Mitteilungen, August 2011.

Jones, S. (2007) *The Rise of European Security Cooperation*, Cambridge: Cambridge University Press.

Kirkpatrick, D. (2004) 'Trends in the Costs of Weapon Systems and the Consequences', *Defence and Peace Economics*, 15(3): 259–273.

Larran, M. (2009) 'CSDP Logistics: Can NAMSA Help?', *European Security Review*, 47: 1–3.

Mawdsley, J. (2013) 'The A400M Project: From Flagship Project to Warning for European Defence Cooperation', *Defence Studies*, 13(1): 14–32.

Maynard, G. (2009) 'Untangling the Web', *Defence Management Journal*, 46: 40–41.

Mérand, F. (2008) *European Defence Policy: Beyond the Nation State*, Oxford: Oxford University Press.

Mikkola, H., Anteroinen, J. and Lauttamäki, V. (2013) *The Changing European Defence Market: Will the New European Defence Market Legislation be a Game-Changer for Finland?*, Helsinki: Finish Institute of International Affairs.

Mockos, R. (1983) *NATO Tactical Group C3: Interoperability is Not Enough*, Cambridge: Harvard CIPR.

188   *M.R. DeVore*

Moravcsik, M. (1993) 'Armaments among Allies: European Weapons Collaboration, 1975–1985', in P.B. Evans, H.K. Jacobson and R.D. Putnam (1993) *Double-Edged Diplomacy: International Bargaining and Domestic Politics*, Berkeley: University of California: 128–167.

Mörth, U. (2003) *Organizing European Cooperation: The Case of Armaments*, Lanham: Rowman & Littlefield.

Nelson, R. and Winter, S. (1982) *An Evolutionary Theory of Economic Change*, Cambridge: Cambridge University Press.

NMSSS Board of Directors (1958) *NMSSS Charter*, 21 May.

North, D. (1990) *Institutions, Institutional Change and Economic Performance*, Cambridge: Cambridge University Press.

Otterbach, S. (2007) 'The Materiel Standards Harmonization Team: A View from the Chairman', *European Defence Standardization Journal*, Autumn: 4.

Pedersen, J. (2007) *Interoperability Standards Analysis*, Arlington: NDIA.

Pierson, P. (2004) *Politics in Time: History, Institutions and Social Analysis*, Princeton: Princeton University Press.

Pitts, N. (2007) 'Editorial', *European Defence Standardization Journal*, Autumn: 1.

Robinson, P. (2001), 'Misperception in Foreign Policy Making: Operation "Deliberate Force" and the Ending of War in Bosnia', *Civil Wars*, 4(4): 115–126.

Shanson, L. (2010) 'GICC Conference Review: European Commission Engages with Offset but Dare not Speak its Name', *Countertrade and Offset*, 28(22): 3.

Stärkle, G. (2010) *L'Agence européenne de défense: Régime juridique, organisation et realisations*, Brussels: Bruylant.

Tucker, J. (1990) 'Partners and Rivals: A Model of International Collaboration in Advanced Technology', *International Organization*, 45(1): 83–120.

Urbanovsky, C. (2006) 'NATO Framework for Civil Standards,' *Defence Standardization Program Journal* (January–March 2006): 11–13.

Vandevanter, E. (1964) *Coordinated Weapons Production in NATO: A Study of Alliance Processes*, Santa Monica: RAND.

Veita, L. (2009) 'NATO and MSHT: Complementary Working, *European Defence Standardization Journal*, 2: 10–11.

Visine, F. (1975) *La NAMSA ou La Logistique 'A la Carte', 1958–1975*, Luxembourg: NAMSA.

Weiss, M. (2011) *Transaction Costs and Security Institutions: Unravelling the ESDP*, London: Palgrave.

Wilkinson, D. and Kopold, H. (2007) 'Managing the Use of Standards for the Acquisition of Defence Materiel', *European Defence Standardization Journal*, Autumn 2007: 3.

Witney, N. (2013) *European Defence Summit: It's Groundhog Day Again*, European Council on Foreign Relations Policy Brief, 27 November 2013.

Witney, N. (2008) *Re-energising Europe's Security and Defence Policy*, Brussels: European Council on Foreign Affairs.

## Interviews

Interview with Hilmar Linnenkamp, EDA Deputy Chief Executive 2004–2007, 17 March 2010.

# Part IV

# Broadening the EU armaments policy agenda

# 11 The EDA and military capability development
## Making pooling and sharing work

*Laura Chappell and Petar Petrov*

## Introduction

Despite the financial crisis, Member States still have international responsibilities to fulfil, particularly those with a high international standing. Meanwhile a number of operations both under the European Union (EU) as well as the North Atlantic Treaty Organisation (NATO) have underlined that EU Member States suffer from a shortfall in core capabilities such as Air-to-Air Refuelling (AAR) and command and control. In this respect tools such as Pooling and Sharing (P&S) could allow the Member States to do more with less whilst being able to increase interoperability. However, the success of such initiatives depends on whether Member States are willing to pursue capability development within the EU as well as the ability of the European Defence Agency (EDA) to act as a motor in this field. This chapter seeks to analyse the prospects for the practical development of P&S projects as envisaged by the Ghent Initiative in 2010. It will do so by assessing the implementation of the initiative to date as well as underlining where the pitfalls lie. In particular the economic crisis could be used not only to reinvigorate defence capability collaboration but also as a reason to cut defence budgets and procurement programmes without then working collaboratively with other Member States to produce the necessary items. The idea here is that Member States still need to invest money to pool and share. This brings about the second pitfall – that of political will. As the EU Battlegroups have shown, developing capabilities does not mean an increased willingness to use them. The economic crisis could mean that political willingness even to develop capabilities could be lacking.

Our aim is to ascertain the support among key Member States for P&S as well as how the EDA has been managing the project. In a second step we seek to understand why certain procurement and training initiatives under P&S are chosen and what role the EDA has in bringing together a strategic vision concerning projects. To analyse this we utilise European strategic culture as an analytical approach. Within it we show that there is a clash in vision concerning in which forum to produce capabilities, which in turn means that P&S is based on a case by case basis rather than being shaped by any overall strategic vision. However, some hope is emerging not least because the individual cases sometimes emerge as a result of lessons learnt from operations – though not always EU ones. Thus the Member States, through this piecemeal process, are beginning to understand the types of operations it will be involved in and where capability gaps are emerging within this. A desire to work through the EU to solve these gaps also indicates an increasing preparedness to see the EU as an appropriate forum for capability development and in turn a defence actor. This could indicate that some of these conflicting visions are being overcome, leading in time to a more developed European strategic culture which bases defence capability development on when, where and with whom the EU wishes to use force.

## Strategic culture and a clash of vision for European defence

Strategy is a central aspect of capability development, as a top-down approach underlines which capabilities a security community needs to procure or where gaps lie. A key component shaping EU Member States' approaches to this is strategic culture and in particular whether a European strategic culture is emerging to direct a common EU response regarding capability development. The absence of a developed European strategic culture results in Member States looking to the national level and to their own individual strategic cultures to assess which capabilities they wish to acquire or continue to maintain. Indeed, whether the EU holds a strategic culture is contested with Meyer (2006) and Cornish and Edwards (2005) underlining that some form of strategic culture is emerging, whilst Rynning (2003) and Baun (2005) argue against any such formation. This reflects the theoretical stance that these authors take underlining the constructivist and rationalist versions of strategic culture as epitomised by the debate between Gray (1999: 55) and Johnston (1995: 35–36) concerning whether the link between attitudes and behaviour can be broken to produce a falsifiable version of strategic culture. We side with Gray and the constructivist version of strategic culture and therefore strategic culture is seen to shape the view of a security community (whether the Member States or the EU) concerning when, where and how to use force rather than give a ranked list of preferences. Therefore it marks some courses of action as appropriate whilst other options are ruled out.

Strategic culture can be defined as 'the beliefs, attitudes and norms towards the use of force held by a security community which has had a unique historical experience' (Gray 1999: 51–52; Chappell 2010). However, how do these beliefs, attitudes and norms form? Strategic culture usually emerges over a lengthy time period unless a critical juncture should occur. This underlines that any European strategic culture will not be fully developed, as the Common Security and Defence Policy

(CSDP) was only created in 1999 and has been active since 2003, although we can argue that the EU's strategic culture could date back to the European Economic Community's inception as a 'peace project' (see Biscop and Norheim-Martinsen 2011: 74). This raises the question concerning the degree of convergence which is required to form a fully fledged European strategic culture. Meyer (2006: 7) underlines that 'a European strategic culture is not taking the place of national strategic cultures, but it should be conceived of primarily as the increasing institutionalisation of those ideas, norms and values that are sufficiently shared at the national level'. This highlights the idea that a European strategic culture sits above national ones. However, this leaves little room for institutions at the EU level to shape a potential European strategic culture or to offer a platform to fast track the creation of one. It is here that the EDA could have a role to play as a motor, not only in enhancing Member States military capabilities but also in shaping when they are used by creating expectations and peer pressure.

Whilst strategic cultures, once fully formed, are stable, they can be subject to change in response to the external environment, although this is not automatic. In essence changes can create windows of opportunity although these require a champion or a motor for change to seize this and transform strategic culture. Dramatic change, in which a security actor's strategic culture is replaced with another, is unlikely and is usually in response to war or conflict. Meanwhile incremental change involves the reorientation of an aspect(s) of a strategic culture without its wholesale replacement (Longhurst 2004: 20). Whilst this framework is relevant to national strategic cultures, a European strategic culture is in the process of being created. In this respect windows of opportunity are even more critical in acting as a springboard for active political actors (including EU-level institutions) to shape how the EU views the use of force.

With a sub-optimal European strategic culture, Chappell and Petrov (2012: 47) underline that 'military missions that are too complex or too high in intensity, which could result in casualties, are unlikely to be agreed. In other words civilian operations are more likely to be deployed than military ones'. Whilst this subsequently impacts the type of military capabilities which Member States wish to develop, many of the capabilities which they lack are dual-use. Additionally military operations in other contexts, e.g. NATO's intervention in Libya, have highlighted significant shortfalls. These could also be acquired through EU initiatives. It is here that the EDA through P&S could play a role. Unlike the unsuccessful Permanent Structured Cooperation in Defence (PESCO), P&S focuses purely on capability development without the political contestations. Thus, in the context of the financial crisis, the EDA has the opportunity to become a motor in pushing P&S forward. This could result not only in increasing Member State capabilities but by extension could lead to the emergence of a European strategic culture and thus a more optimal CSDP. Nonetheless,

194   *L. Chappell and P. Petrov*

the task is far from easy. Bátora (2009: 1076) underlines that 'the EDA has been a flashpoint of institutional logics representing different visions of how various aspects of defense integration in the EU should be organized'. These divisions concerning how Member States approach the use of force have been hampering the acquirement of capabilities.

In relation to the acquirement of capabilities, we focus on two specific clashes of institutional logics (see Chappell and Petrov 2012: 48; Bátora 2009). The first relates to Atlanticist vs. Europeanist approaches, in which we investigate whether Member States consider the EU to be the most legitimate avenue to acquire capabilities. In particular this concerns whether Atlanticist countries, such as the UK, are more reluctant to work through the EDA to reduce defence capability shortfalls than Europeanist countries such as France. The second clash concerns defence sovereignty vs. pooled defence resources (Bátora 2009). We look at the extent to which Member States want to develop capabilities nationally, bilaterally or multinationally. Whilst there are those Member States who wish to remain self-sufficient, other Member States are prepared to work collaboratively at the EU level to pool capabilities.

Whilst other clashes between proactive vs. restrictions on the use of force and a global vs. regional approach to security (see Chappell and Petrov 2012: 48) are core to a creation of a fully developed European strategic culture which stipulates when, where and how the EU should use force, we posit that a European strategic culture is not developed enough to provide an overarching strategic direction. Indeed, certain Member States such as the UK and France have been looking towards national or bilateral initiatives rather than to the EU level. However, the economic crisis has created a window of opportunity for actors to step forward and act as motors to maintain and increase defence capabilities among EU Member States in the context of mainly static and declining defence budgets. With its bottom-up approach the EDA could provide precisely this platform to encourage Member States to engage in P&S projects to ensure they are able to fill capability gaps and in time find synergies. This bottom-up case-by-case process could lead gradually to common thinking and thus a strategic vision concerning the EU's role in the international security environment which can feed into a European strategic culture. Thus it is more useful to ascertain whether P&S will work practically which can then feed into this process. In this respect both clashes above could prevent the creation of capabilities.

## From permanent structured cooperation in defence to pooling and sharing

Defence cooperation in Europe has faced an uphill struggle. As Giegerich and Nicoll (2012: 54) underline in relation to an IISS Strategic Dosser published back in 2008 'it was clear that despite organisational efforts within NATO and the EU, numerous multinational military campaigns, and efforts at collaborative equipment programmes and industrial consolidation, defence in Europe remained very much a national rather than a cooperative endeavour'. This evidently impacts on what countries can do together, particularly important in an era where Member States can do little militarily by themselves. Despite this, the EU's various institutions have continued to pursue the idea of pooling capabilities, restricting the single market opt-out under Article 346 for defence equipment and improving the European defence industry. P&S is one of the latest tools in this pursuit for a more effective and capable European defence capability.

The first point to underline is that pooling capabilities is not new, with projects being conducted among two or more European countries in this direction, e.g. the Baltic Defence College. To understand how P&S came about we have to go back to its predecessor. PESCO was problematic from the outset because discussions came down to criteria which in turn dictated which Member States could (not) become part of the initiative. The inclusive/exclusive conundrum finally dealt a decisive blow to the concept. Additionally, as Giegerich and Nicoll (2012: 67) point out,

> cooperation and specialisation are likely to yield benefits in financial and capability terms, but these will come at the price of reduced national autonomy. Striking an acceptable balance – one that can be tolerated by governments worried about national security – poses large political challenges.

P&S better avoids these pitfalls by offering an *à la carte* solution or 'business as usual' (Simón 2012: 108) whilst setting out specific aims. At the same time, however, it also represents a downgrading of ambition.

The Ghent Initiative originated from a German/Swedish 'food for thought' paper in 2010. Its aim was to 'preserve and enhance national operational capabilities – with improved effect, sustainability, interoperability and cost efficiency as a result' (Germany/Sweden 2010: 1). Officially launched in December 2010 under the Belgian Presidency, P&S relates to three types of capability initiatives: the pooling of military equipment procurement, specialisation and sharing through some integration of force structures, e.g. joint units. Evidently, pooling already existing capabilities does not equate to a larger military capability although it does make using them more effective. Using P&S to create new capabilities would create such a momentum thus indicating that it will depend on how the initiative is used. For the Ghent initiative to work, however, requires greater political willingness to cooperate and, as Faleg and Giovannini (2012: 3) state, 'the effective liberalisation of the European defence market, leading to more competition among defence companies [...] and the Europeanisation of part of the defence budget'. At the same time, expectations need to be realistic, although for P&S to make any significant

196   *L. Chappell and P. Petrov*

impact there need to be signs that it is genuinely enabling EU Member States to fill important capability gaps. The question is whether P&S will go beyond project-by-project cooperation to create a truly capable CSDP.

In this vein, the EDA initiated a code of conduct on P&S which intends to ensure that P&S is integrated in Member States' decision and planning processes. This includes the following actions:

> 1. Systematically consider cooperation from the outset in national defence planning of Member States. 2. Consider Pooling and Sharing for the whole life-cycle of a capability, including cooperation in R&T, minimising the number of variants of the same equipment, to optimise potential savings, improve interoperability, and rationalise demand. 3. Promote where possible the expansion of national programmes to other Member States. 4. Share opportunities that could be open to Pooling and Sharing. 5. Consider the joint use of existing capabilities by Member States.
>
> (EDA 2012e)

Other areas include investment, coherence and assessment. A report on the code was produced towards the end of 2013 although it has not been made public. As reported prior to its completion, the Report will give a snapshot of progress within the P&S initiative including where work still needs to be done (EDA 2013c). This came at an opportune time considering that defence was on the European Council agenda in December 2013. In particular the European Council (2013: 7) tasked 'the European Defence Agency to examine ways in which Member States can cooperate more effectively and efficiently in pooled procurement projects, with a view to reporting back to the council by the end of 2014'. Additionally the European Council *inter alia* welcomed developments in AAR capacity as well as emphasising the importance of satellite communication and cyber security. The question is whether the EDA can provide the momentum for Member States to embrace P&S and move beyond stock-taking exercises. As previous mapping exercises have shown, pointing out capability gaps does not necessarily lead to their eradication. In this respect, two actors are key: the EU Member States and the EDA.

## Views from the Member States

The Member States will be key to the success of P&S – particularly the large ones. As with PESCO, deeper cooperation under P&S brings with it many advantages including economies of scale and interoperability. Nonetheless there are sensitivities. Thus P&S needs to avoid some of the pitfalls related to the conflict in institutional logics presented above. First, as Faleg and Giovannini (2012: 17) underline in respect to strategic heavy weapons systems, 'it is highly unlikely that M[ember] S[tates] will accept

*Making pooling and sharing work* 197

putting national defence capacities into a "common pot", which would result in an unacceptable loss of strategic autonomy'. Other areas such as non-strategic equipment are unlikely to be problematic depending on the definition of such equipment. Role specialisation could also be difficult, particularly for large and medium-sized countries due to sovereignty concerns. As Giegerich (2011: 190–191) highlights, there are two problematic possibilities: 'either to be entrapped into actions they would not deem appropriate from the perspective of their national interest, or to be abandoned by partners on whom they depend for successful conduct of operations'. This underlines the role of the EDA in assisting Member States in identifying non-controversial P&S projects. In particular, the EDA (2013a: 2) has been

> on one hand identifying and pursuing practical solutions towards delivery of quick wins and longer term operational projects and on the other hand providing an analytical overview, including the identification of potential obstacles to P&S and of enablers and incentives in response.

Hence it is in line with the EDA's (2012e) Code of Conduct which stresses the Agency's role in the process, particularly as a forum for information exchange as well as using its information provider function. The EDA's Capability Development Plan is also key insofar as it underlines future capability requirements and can be utilised as a way of identifying P&S projects.

Certain factors will make it either easier or more difficult to cooperate under the initiative. Similar strategic cultures will ensure that there is an understanding between those countries regarding the role of their militaries, which in turn will assist in trust concerning their respective capabilities. Second, Giegerich and Nicoll (2012: 67) suggest that 'Pooling and Sharing would be easier among countries whose forces were roughly similar in quantity and quality' to avoid burden-sharing issues or concerns over whether certain projects were really in a country's interest. Both these areas can in part be highlighted with the 2010 UK-French Lancaster House agreements, a theme addressed in Chapter 8. Whilst there are certainly differences concerning Atlanticism/Europeanism the fact that they are the most militarily capable countries in Europe with a proactive view on the use of force certainly helps.

However, when it comes to P&S through the EU, the UK is rather lukewarm, putting the EDA on probation (Interview with an official, Brussels, 2012; House of Lords 2012: 44). As highlighted above, British Atlanticism is in play which means that the UK carries out capability development more through NATO than the EU (Interview with an Official, Brussels, 2012) and is combining this with bilateralism (with France) as underlined by the Lancaster House agreement. Whilst the UK is participating in some

P&S projects (including the Helicopter Training Programme, the Maritime Surveillance Networking (MARSUR) and the European Satellite Communication Procurement Cell (ESCPC)) it is not taking the lead or suggesting projects to the EDA (EDA 2011, 2012d).

France, however, is focusing on capable and willing partners such as the British – and previously the Benelux countries – which in turn reflects frustration with the EU and by extension the EDA to produce results. The upshot is that France is not really taking the lead either, although it is participating in Maritime Surveillance Networking, the Helicopter Training Programme, the ESCPC and Medical Field Hospitals (EDA 2011; 2012d). It has also agreed to manage transport crew training and be one of the lead nations for AAR, although the Netherlands is in charge of the most successful stream. The problem for France is that it is one thing to say you promote capabilities in a multinational context, but when you get into precise projects – discussions at the national level – there are some nuances in the degree of commitment (Interview with Official, Brussels, 2013). In essence when discussing capability gaps, large Member States never start from scratch – there are existing programmes. In other words European processes can conflict with already existing national ones and the former do not necessarily represent savings in terms of time and money, particular at the beginning of the cooperation (Interview with an Official, Brussels, 2013). Therefore this combines both practical issues with cultural ones – underlining the defence sovereignty vs. pooled defence resources conundrum.

Germany, whilst being a co-initiator of P&S and thus politically supportive of it, is unlikely to take the lead in its development. This is due to the country's restrictions on the use of force combined with the impact of the financial crisis resulting in a lack of funds to put into pooling projects. Hence Germany's participation is similar to that of the UK and France – being involved in a few projects (e.g. Helicopter Training Programme, MARSUR and Medical Field Hospitals) but otherwise not leading (apart from AAR). It should also be noted that France and the UK have been similarly affected with both countries making cuts to their defence budgets. Poland meanwhile is politically a proponent of P&S. Former Defence Minister Bogdan Klich has described the project as 'one of the greatest European defence achievements of the last two to three years' (Klich in Butterworth-Hayes 2013: 12). Indeed Poland has been cooperating with other members of the Visegrad group (Czech Republic, Slovakia and Hungary) to provide an EU Battlegroup, amongst other initiatives. However, whilst it is participating in certain projects under P&S (e.g. MARSUR, ESCPC and AAR) it also is not leading, underlining its Atlanticist leanings. Thus France, the UK, Germany and Poland show differing levels of support but none are prepared to take the lead. This underlines the lack of importance of the Atlanticist/Europeanist divide at least as far as the larger Member States are concerned as they are not

*Making pooling and sharing work*  199

falling along these lines when it comes to being actively supportive of the P&S concept. What is surprising here is not the position of Atlanticist countries but that of the Europeanists.

However P&S is not just centred around the larger Member States. As outlined by Demetris Eliades (2012: 2), the Cypriot defence minister,

> since small Member States, like Cyprus, do not have a defence industry, cooperation ... was one of their top priorities. Thus thanks to the EDA, smaller Member States are given the opportunity to actively cooperate and contribute in a number of areas.

Another example is Sweden. As reported by Tom Wein (2012: 26), 'there is a legal requirement to procure jointly, or justify why they cannot. Finland has a similar system'. Meanwhile as far as Belgium is concerned 'pooled sovereignty means shared responsibility. It is far better to have collective capabilities rather than unsustainable or non-existent national ones' (De Crem, in Butterworth-Hayes 2013: 10). This emphasises the route down which the Member States will need to travel: the idea that pooling should be the norm rather than the exception (see Wein 2012: 26). It also highlights the support for P&S among a range of small and medium-sized Member States. Thus P&S could involve 'islands of cooperation' (Valasek 2011: 29) in which countries of a similar size and strategic culture could work more closely together to create and maintain military capabilities. The Nordic countries and Belgium/Netherlands certainly show the way forward in this respect. Unsurprisingly, the most active countries within P&S are the medium sized ones which have a culture of military cooperation, e.g. Benelux, Nordics (Interview with an Official, Brussels, 2013). This again highlights the defence sovereignty vs. pooled defence resources divide in that those countries who have already embraced the idea of the latter have fewer issues with P&S at the EU level than those who fall into the defence sovereignty camp.

So where does this leave Member State impetus for P&S? The House of Lords Report (2012: 57) underlines that

> we were told that, for successful pooling and sharing, 'clusters' of countries intending to cooperate should for preference have similar cultures, language, geography and history, as well as similar strategic cultures and attitudes to the use of force, compatible defence industrial policies and armed forces roughly similar in quality and quantity.

This has been underlined throughout this section. The question remains how these groups or islands of cooperation would then cooperate with each other. It is unlikely that specialisation would occur to the extent that countries would entrust certain capabilities to a regional cluster of which they were not a part (see Valasek 2011: 40). Thus burden sharing within clusters is more likely to yield results. Additionally the different islands may well want to acquire the same capability. Hence P&S needs to be done on a broader basis than the islands of cooperation idea suggests as well as motivating those countries who traditionally value their defence sovereignty to embrace P&S – particularly at the EU level. It is here that the EDA can come in.

## The EDA as a motor for capability development

Not long after its inception in 2004, the EDA demonstrated an active role by working closely with the Member States in setting up collaborative projects such as Future Transport Helicopter, European Air Transport Fleet and Software Defined Radio. P&S under the Ghent initiative continues this work and includes *inter alia* AAR, Multinational Medical Field Hospitals, ESCPC, Maritime Surveillance Networking, European Transport hubs, Smart Munitions and various training initiatives (EDA 2012, 2012a, 2013d). As such P&S has always been central to the EDA's rationale (EDA 2011, 2012a, 2013d).

Since its inception in 2004 the EDA has developed as one of the recognised players within the defence community in Brussels. It possesses relevant data and expertise crucial for providing strategic guidance on P&S initiatives. Reportedly, it has gradually established itself as trusted partner to the participating Member States (pMS) when it comes to providing information and advice in the context of collaborative projects (Interviews with officials, Brussels, 2012). Moreover, it is closely working with the Commission, developing a joint investment programme and being involved together with the European External Action Service in the Defence Task Force (European Commission 2013).

The role of the EDA is essential in the context of larger projects. AAR provides such an example, being one of the projects brought in under P&S, as emphasised above. All lessons identified from recent operations have highlighted AAR as a crucial force multiplier, allowing for the more effective deployment of forces, as well as the more efficient use of expensive and scarce fighter aircraft in crisis management operations. Today the necessity of AAR capabilities is clearly identified – the Council endorsed the EU Military Committee's recommendation that the AAR capability shortfall could have a very significant impact upon any EU-led operation (EDA 2013d). In particular only seven pMS contributed to AAR capability prior to this initiative: Germany, Spain, France, Italy, Netherlands, Sweden and UK. Their contribution makes up less than 30 per cent of the agreed requirement (EDA 2012b), which means that currently the Member States are far from achieving the identified target for this capability.

Thus far, the EDA has conducted a feasibility evaluation and has facilitated meetings attended by pMS. Four pillars have been identified and these act as foundations for coordinating work within the project which

*Making pooling and sharing work* 201

include 'short term solutions, including access to commercial AAR services; optimising the use of existing assets and organisations; increasing the A400M fleet AAR capability by acquiring more AAR kits; and increasing the strategic tanker capability in Europe by 2020' (EDA 2013a; see also EDA 2011, 2012a, 2013d). The most successful of these is the final pillar. Ten countries have signed a Letter of Intent for the procurement of strategic tankers in 2012 – Belgium, France, Greece, Spain, Hungary, Luxembourg, the Netherlands, Poland, Portugal and Norway, with the Netherlands taking the lead (EDA 2012c). However, the Member States' interests still play a role in determining the project's ambition and level of achievement. The AAR project demonstrates that 'national egoisms diminish the scope of what could have been done [...]. What we will get is again not sufficient to fill the shortfall although there will be improvements' (Interview with an Official, Brussels, 2013). Additionally, problems occur when a project is led by a smaller Member State. In the case of the Netherlands it is relying on Finnish expertise for the procurement of strategic tankers project and with such a small number of experts it is really struggling (Interview with an Official, Brussels, 2013). This once again highlights that those countries taking the lead are those which already have a history of pooling defence resources.

One of the most successful areas for P&S to date relates to training (Interview with an Official, Brussels 2013). In 2011 three P&S projects were announced (the Helicopter Training Programme, Pilot Training, Naval Logistics and Training) with a further two initiated in 2012 (NH90 and European Advanced Airlift Tactics Training Courses) (EDA 2013a). The Helicopter Training Programme stemmed from a lack of helicopter support during EU operations, including EUFOR Chad/Central African Republic. As highlighted by the EDA (2013b), 'several key strands were thought to contribute to this non-employability: a lack of training for the crews, a lack of technical equipment for the aircraft, and the difficulties of logistic support to deployed operations'. The initiative already existed prior to P&S, commencing back in 2009 with the aim of conducting training exercises but was then incorporated into the concept. Under P&S the initiative has been extended and now includes the Helicopter Exercise Programme (HEP), the European Helicopter Tactics Instructor Course, Helicopter Tactics Course and the Operational English Language Course. The first of these provides for two exercises per year. Portugal, Belgium, Germany, the Netherlands, Austria, Finland, Italy, Spain, Czech Republic, Slovenia, Sweden, UK, Hungary and France have all sent helicopters, while other countries have sent personnel. In addition to these countries, Luxembourg has acted as a coordinator of a multinational helicopter exercise – 'Green Blade' – which took place in Belgium in September 2012. Altogether 'a total of 123 helicopters, 794 aircrew, nearly 5,000 support personnel have been deployed to these exercises' (EDA 2013b).

The other three areas are new under P&S. The Helicopter Tactics Course involves six Member States and 'delivers helicopter tactics training for those nations who have an upcoming deployment, but who do not have sufficient operational experience to deliver this training organically' (EDA 2013b). In terms of the instructor training, this provides aircrew from participating Member States with the ability to deliver their own tactics training. A qualification would be obtained which should then be recognisable among the participating Member States, if not EU wide (EDA 2013b). Finally the English Language Course provides for specialised English language training. It is financed by Luxembourg and takes place in the UK. As the EDA (2013b) underlines, '35 students from 11 countries attended a four week residential course'.

From the above it is clear why such a programme works. Looking back to the German/Swedish 'food for thought' paper on P&S it listed three categories:

> Category 1: Capabilities and support structures that are deemed essential for individual nations and therefore maintained on a strictly national level limiting cooperation to find measures in order to increase interoperability. [...] Category 2: Capabilities and support structures where closer cooperation is possible without creating too strong dependencies. [...] Category 3: Capabilities and support structures where mutual dependency and reliance upon European partners is acceptable in an international role- and task-sharing framework.
>
> (Germany/Sweden 2010: 1)

Clearly training fits into Category 3. Thus, it poses no threat to countries' sovereignty as underlined by the fact that the UK and France are participating – both of which traditionally have a strong attachment to this principle. Its uncontroversial nature is also demonstrated by the fact that half of the Member States are participating in it. Indeed for P&S projects to work requires a large number of Member States, preferably including the big ones as this delivers economies of scale, efficiency and knowledge. Whilst training initiatives help to close a loophole, at the same time they do not involve Member States buying equipment to pool and/or share. Therefore the level of ambition is comparatively low. This is in contrast to AAR which can be categorised under Category 2. Here we can see that as the encroachment into defence sovereignty starts to materialise, the project whilst still feasible is not as successful as those which carry no risk in this regard, with large Member States failing to take the lead and fewer Member States participating overall.

Although it is too early to assess the actual success of the P&S initiatives for the development of new capabilities so far (as most projects are long-term), the EDA's latest annual report underlines that progress is relatively

Making pooling and sharing work    203

limited (EDA 2012a), which has been confirmed by officials in Brussels. Many projects have either achieved mixed results (as in the case of AAR), are only at the initial exploratory stages (such as Smart Munitions and European Transport Hubs), or have not even started, remaining only as an identified need ('Intelligence Surveillance Reconnaissance' and 'Future Military Satellite Communications') (EDA 2013d). The cases where the Member States have pooled resources more willingly are in less controversial areas (the various training initiatives and Maritime Field Hospitals). This shows that the Member States remain very pragmatic in choosing the level of their involvement, using the EDA mostly as a platform for information sharing and visibility for their initiatives. The EDA's ability to act as a motor for capability development has been limited by its minimal budget allocation and reliance on Member State political willingness to pool and share.

Overall, the EDA does not possess an overarching ability to champion the process of capability development on the EU level, by setting priorities or moulding Member States' preferences. However, it remains one of the important actors in this domain. The EDA is able to 'produce, in close cooperation with the EUMC and other EU actors, proposals on how European Pooling and Sharing could be taken forward, inter alia by identifying common operational requirements, areas and modalities with potential for substantial development' (EDA 2011: 1). This underlines that the EDA has the ability to partially set the agenda by making suggestions regarding potential projects as well as implementing those which the Member States agree to. As P&S progresses, this could provide momentum for shaping Member States' priorities as they become more adapt at working together. It can also be assisted by the fact that the EDA's steering board consists of pMS' Defence Ministers, ensuring that such initiatives as the Code of Conduct on Pooling and Sharing as mentioned previously get high-level support.

## Conclusion

Whilst some momentum behind P&S has been created, there are still issues, as reflected in the flashpoints of institutional logic. It is unlikely that P&S will lead to a PESCO-type process, insofar as the Member States are cautious and lack enthusiasm in developing larger collaborative projects. P&S can be partially successful in helping Member States close capability gaps. There is a danger that P&S may engage only small and medium-sized countries while the big ones shy away from leading collaborative projects. Small and medium-sized countries are playing the role of lead nation as underlined by the Netherlands (AAR), Finland (MARSUR) and Ireland (Naval Logistics and Training). However, ultimately the big Member States need to get on board and lead P&S projects for it to become a success due to the expertise, leadership and economies of scale they can provide.

204　*L. Chappell and P. Petrov*

Currently, although the EDA demonstrates relative weaknesses in setting priorities and pushing the Member States into agreeing to specific projects, it can suggest areas for cooperation. However, the decision concerning which projects should be pursued still depends on Member State agreement and action to make the project a success. The EDA has also set the precedent of collaborative project implementation which may demonstrate the added value of P&S in the long term. In this respect, P&S can provide momentum to push Member States from defence sovereignty to pooled defence resources. However, this will be a slow process, particularly considering countries such as the UK with its strong Atlanticist background. It is Atlanticism combined with defence sovereignty which is likely to act as the largest brake to this process for some Member States. This is also underlined by the level of ambition which the successful P&S projects reveal. In essence, as Toje (2008: 132) reveals in the context of European foreign policy, 'the trend is that the lower the level of commitment, the higher the likelihood of achieving consensus'. Overall P&S can provide some solutions to non-controversial projects which do not threaten defence sovereignty or conflict with certain Member States' Atlanticist orientations. It therefore reflects the current state of CSDP – a lack of political willingness from the Member States to fully commit to defence capability development at the EU level. With the defence market and capabilities a key aspect of the December 2013 European Council, momentum needs to come from Member States' political leaders before such initiatives as P&S can fully become a success.

## References

Bátora, J. (2009) 'European Defence Agency: A Flashpoint of Institutional Logics', *West European Politics*, 32(6): 1075–1098.

Baun, M. (2005) 'How Necessary is a Common Strategic Culture?', in A. Toje (ed.) 'A Strategic Culture for Europe: EU Security Policy after Iraq', *Oxford Journal on Good Governance*, 2(1): 33–38.

Biscop, S. and Norheim-Martinsen, P. (2011) 'CSDP: The Strategic Perspective', in X. Kurowska and F. Breuer (eds) *Explaining the EU's Common Security and Defence Policy: Theory in Action*, Basingstoke: Palgrave Macmillan: 63–85.

Butterworth-Hayes, P. (2013) 'The Two Choices Now Facing European Defence', *European Defence Matters*, 3: 8–11.

Chappell, L. (2010) 'Poland in Transition: Implications for a European Security and Defence Policy', *Contemporary Security Policy*, 31(2): 225–248.

Chappell, L. and Petrov, P. (2012) 'The European Defence Agency and Permanent Structured Cooperation: Are we Heading towards Another Missed Opportunity?'. *Defence Studies*, 12(1): 44–66.

Cornish, P. and Edwards, G. (2005) 'The Strategic Culture of the European Union: A Progress Report', *International Affairs*, 81(4): 801–820.

EDA (European Defence Agency) (2013a) 'EDA's Pooling and Sharing Factsheet'.

EDA (European Defence Agency) (2013b) 'Helicopter Initiatives'. Online. Available at: www.eda.europa.eu/projects/projects-search/helicopter-initiatives (accessed 31 July 2013).

## Making pooling and sharing work 205

EDA (European Defence Agency) (2013c) 'Pooling and Sharing Helps Filling Capability Gaps', *European Defence Matters*, 3: 26–27.

EDA (European Defence Agency) (2013d) 'Projects'. Online. Available at: www.eda.europa.eu/projects (accessed 18 June 2013).

EDA (European Defence Agency) (2012) 'How We Do'. Online. Available at: www.eda.europa.eu/Aboutus/Howwedo (accessed 1 August 2012).

EDA (European Defence Agency) (2012a) 'EDA Annual Report 2012', 12 March 2013.

EDA (European Defence Agency) (2012b) 'Air-to-Air Refuelling'. Online. Available at: www.eda.europa.eu/projects/projects-search/air-to-air-refueling (accessed 31 July 2013).

EDA (European Defence Agency) (2012c) 'Increasing Europe's Strategic Tanker Capability by 2020', 28 November 2012.

EDA (European Defence Agency) (2012d) 'European Satellite Communications Procurement Cell (ESCPC) Factsheet'.

EDA (European Defence Agency) (2012e) 'Code of Conduct on Pooling and Sharing', 19 November 2012.

EDA (European Defence Agency) (2011) 'EDA's Pooling and Sharing – Factsheet'.

Eliades, D. (2012) *Address of the Minister of Defence of the Republic of Cyprus Mr. Demetris Eliades at the Seminar on 'Innovative European Defence Co-operation – Pooling and Consolidating Demand'*, 19 September 2012, Brussels.

European Commission (2013) 'Defence Procurement'. Online. Available at: http://ec.europa.eu/internal_market/publicprocurement/rules/defence_procurement (accessed June 2013)

European Council (2013) 'European Council Conclusions', 19–20 December 2013, EUCO 217/13.

Faleg, G. and Giovannini, A. (2012) *The EU between Pooling and Sharing and Smart Defence: Making a Virtue of Necessity?*, CEPS Special Report 61.

Germany/Sweden (2010) 'Pooling and Sharing, German-Swedish Initiative Food for Thought', Berlin and Stockholm.

Giegerich, Bastian (2011) 'Memorandum by Dr Bastian Giegerich, Bundeswehr Institute for Social Sciences and International Institute for Strategic Studies', in House of Lords (2011) *EU Foreign Affairs, Defence and Development Policy Sub-Committee Inquiry into European Defence Capabilities: Lessons from the Past, Signposts for the Future. Oral and written evidence.*

Giegerich, B. and Nicoll, A. (2012) 'The Struggle for Value in European Defence', *Survival: Global Politics and Strategy*, 54(1): 53–82.

Gray, C.S. (1999) 'Strategic Culture as Context: The First Generation of Theory Strikes Back', *International Affairs*, 7(1): 49–69.

House of Lords (2012) *European Defence Capabilities: Lessons from the Past, Signposts for the Future*, European Union Committee 31st Report of Session 2010–12, London: House of Lords.

Johnston, A.L. (1995) *Cultural Realism: Strategic Culture and Grand Strategy in Ming China*, Chichester: Princeton University Press.

Longhurst, K. (2004) *Germany and the Use of Force*, Manchester: Manchester University Press.

Mawdsley, J. (2013) *A European Agenda for Security Technology: From Innovation Policy to Export Controls*, Brussels: Flemish Peace Institute.

Meyer, C.O. (2006) *The Quest for a European Strategic Culture: Changing Norms on Security and Defence in the European Union*, New York: Palgrave Macmillan.

Rynning, S. (2003) 'The European Union: Towards a Strategic Culture?', *Security Dialogue*, 34(4): 479–496.

Simón, L. (2012) 'CSDP, Strategy and Crisis Management: Out of Area or Out of Business?', *The International Spectator: Italian Journal of International Affairs*, 47(3): 100–115.

Toje, A. (2008) 'The Consensus-Expectations Gap: Explaining Europe's Ineffective Foreign Policy', *Security Dialogue*, 39(1): 121–141.

Valasek, T. (2011) *Surviving Austerity. The Case for a New Approach to EU Military Collaboration*, London: Centre for European Reform.

Wein, T. (2012) 'Making Cooperation the Norm not the Exception', *European Defence Matters*, 2: 26.

# 12 The EDA and the development of a European Defence Technological and Industrial Base

## Between nationalisation and globalisation

*Marie-Louise Chagnaud, Christian Mölling and Torben Schütz*

### Introduction

In 2007 the European Union (EU) Member States launched a strategy to support the European Defence Technological and Industrial Base (EDTIB). It aimed to ensure security of supply for EU countries through a Europeanisation of the landscape, i.e. the 'deepening' or 'widening' of the EU's relevance in national, intergovernmental and communitised politics and activities. To arrive at an EDTIB, the strategy envisaged the gradual integration of national DTIBs. The Europeanisation of policies and industries should lead to a less duplicative, more cooperative defence industrial landscape, supporting Member States' defence needs.

Building on the academic 'Europeanisation' approach, this article assesses what difference the EU has made to the European defence industrial landscape so far. It evaluates to what extent a Europeanisation of the policy field 'EDTIB' can be observed by assessing the influence the EU has through ideas, institutions and resources on the change in three dimensions: (1) politics: change in national and international policies towards and the polity of the EDTIB; (2) defence industry: change in the structure and qualities of the EDTIB; and (3) dependencies: changes in the supply chains and dependencies of industries and Member States. While we use Europeanisation as a guiding idea, the article especially contributes to the so far underdeveloped empirical knowledge regarding the characteristics of the EDTIB. As a result of this analysis, the article pictures potential paths to improve future activities towards the European DTIB.

208   *M.-L. Chagnaud et al.*

## EDA, Europeanisation and the EDTIB

### Theory: Europeanisation and defence (industry)

Europeanisation has been widely discussed as a concept to operationalise policy change and adaption between the national and the EU levels. Europeanisation is generally understood as an ongoing process that induces change on both the national and the European level. It can be largely defined as 'emergence and development at the European level of distinct structures of governance' (Caporoso *et al.* 2001: 3). The simultaneous 'processes of a) construction, b) diffusion and c) institutionalisation of formal and informal rules, procedures, policy paradigms, styles, "ways of doing things" and shared beliefs and norms' (Radaelli 2004: 3) are the key drivers of Europeanisation. Europeanisation leads to the definition of new 'European' interests and their implementation.

Three different forms of Europeanisation can be distinguished, on the basis of the direction at hand (Wong 2005; Radaelli 2004). First, 'uploading' is the introduction of preferences and political interests from the national level to the EU level, including the emergence of new structures of governance at the EU level. 'Downloading' concerns the adaptation of such ideas and preferences from the European level to the national level. This would become visible through national governance structures changing because of EU-level preferences. Third, 'crossloading' goes beyond the idea of only the EU-level offering the arena or induction for change. Instead it takes a 'cross country' dimension, where ideas, norms and ways of doing things are exchanged between Member States or other domestic entities (Stone 1999; Jacoby 2004). This again underlines the salient role of the actors (and their socialisation) in the area of security and defence policy that often acts as a transmission belt for change. Europeanisation takes place within a cooperation framework that may be part of or linked to the EU in general, and Common Foreign and Security Policy (CFSP) and European Security and Defence Policy (ESDP) in particular, but is not a formal EU-institution (Tonra 2003; Glarbo 2001). This third dimension is of great importance to the application of Europeanisation to foreign relations of the EU and to the defence sector. The initial concept of Europeanisation has been developed in the context of fully integrated, i.e. communitised, EU policies (Moumoutzis 2011). Against this, the intergovernmental nature of the defence policy area makes the classical direction of policy change, i.e. bottom-up, top-down, cross-load, difficult to identify (Major and Pomorska 2005).

The 2000s have seen a wave of Europeanisation studies in the areas of CFSP and ESDP/CSDP. More recent works, like Andreatta (2011: 35ff.), discuss and present the main theoretical approaches to the application to the CFSP and the integration of the 'military power' on the EU level. Jasper and Portella (2010) have addressed the question of EU defence integration with special regard to nuclear weapons. The different implications of Member States' approaches of the EU Battle group concept for the CSDP have been analysed by Chappell (2009). There has also been work covering the industrial politics (e.g. Hyman 2001). However, Europeanisation has not been applied to the intersection, i.e. the European defence industrial landscape, so far.

### Empirics: DTIBs as a policy field

Applying Europeanisation to the EDTIB has to respond to the distinct characteristics of the policy field in general, i.e. besides EU-specifics. The DTIB is the source for equipment and services for governments. It consists of research institutions and companies, as well as knowledge and skills related to products and processes, technologies, material, etc. The interaction of this ideational and material infrastructure enables armament as such. Hence, armament is a process that consists of three phases: (1) Research and Development (R&D); (2) industrial production; and (3) maintenance and modernisation of military equipment through service providers (Geyer 1984; Hartley 2011).

First, there are two ideal types of actors: states, on the demand side, and industries, on the supply side. States are demanders with a special interest in a DTIB that offers Security of Supply (SoS), i.e. ensures a constant flow of defence material and services to the armed forces in times of peace and war, and offers assurance against political risks (whereby another state blocks the delivery of means of warfare) or industrial risks (whereby contractors cannot guarantee supply as agreed). Companies aim to supply in the government's interest. However, being primarily economic actors, they are concerned about their business. As the business opportunities are limited due to restricted resources, their strategies aim to secure market shares against competitors and explore new business domains.

In practice, however, the dividing lines between the two actors are blurred as is the armaments process: the defence industrial field is uniquely politicised. While the official discourse is about economic issues, like competition, efficiency and customers, this area remains severely characterised by state intervention. Governments play the central role of both customers and regulators, undermining the economic rationale. Further, defence makes up one of the largest portions of public procurement in many countries; a process conducted by the state – and one single agency – the Ministries of Defence (MoDs) (Heidenkamp *et al.* 2013).

Policy-makers combine the objective of SoS with other aims they think can be achieved through defence industry as well, i.e. industrial, technological and social progress as well as political symbols, prestige, etc. Big ticket projects like the Joint Strike Fighter and the United Kingdom's aircraft carrier are social programmes as well as defence programmes. However, this inevitably leads to compromises being made on the defence

## 210 M.-L. Chagnaud et al.

programmes, as they get more expensive and deliver less capability than initially required.

Moreover, the defining issue in SoS is the tension between maximalistic national aspirations and the realities of DTIB on a global scale. Many states continue to aim for a strong national DTIB, which they consider key to their independence and sovereignty, and remain reluctant to rely on others for the supply of defence material. Yet, today's DTIBs are essentially international endeavours. Since the end of the Cold War, defence industries have increasingly become part of an international production and distribution process. They are no longer considered as uniquely national providers, and states, even the biggest ones, cannot escape this global dimension of the providers (see Bitzinger 2009: 1 for an excellent overview of the situation and challenges of the 1990s; Markusen and Costigan 1999; Guay and Callum 2002: 757–776; Hartley *et al.* 2008: 83–104). In addition, while western governments aim to keep control over defence industries, they do not offer the financial resources needed. As national markets are shrinking and production is globalised, the national defence industries are more and more dependent on the external dimension of DTIBs.

### Operationalisation: linking Europeanisation and the EDTIB

The EDTIB is thus a distinct form of a DTIB. However, there is no established definition. The EDTIB is first of all a political vision based on the broader idea of a more integrated European defence policy and the increasing pressures on Member States stemming from the changes in the defence industries in Europe. It aims to create congruence between the industrial and the defence political frames that exist in Europe. This vision has been outlined in the EDTIB Strategy 2007 by the EDA's participating Member States (pMS).

The adoption of the strategy already implies Europeanisation: the problem assessment and solutions have been uploaded by the pMS to the EDA level. Hence, our assessment focuses on the effect this strategy potentially had. As the strategy was not accompanied by a more detailed definition of EDTIB elements and a baseline assessment of the state of the EDTIB in 2006, our assessment can only offer a raw sketch on the developments since then.

The EDA's 2007 EDTIB strategy's problem assessment was quite clear and the Member States address the problems by declaring the need to:

> '[...] recognise that a fully adequate DTIB is no longer sustainable on a strictly national basis – and that we must therefore press on with developing a truly European DTIB, as something more than a sum of its national parts. We cannot continue routinely to determine our equipment requirements on separate national bases, develop them

through separate national R&D efforts, and realise them through separate national procurements. This approach is no longer economically sustainable – and in a world of multinational operations it is operationally unacceptable, too. We need therefore to achieve consolidation on both sides of the market in Europe: aligning and combining our various needs in shared equipment requirements; and meeting them from an increasingly integrated EDTIB'.

(EDA 2007)

Hence, the pMS where opting for a DTIB that should be more integrated, less duplicative, more independent, market-driven, moderated by policy consideration and more specialised on all levels of the supply chain. The strategy itself set out criteria or indicators for the operationalisation of Europeanisation on the policy and industry side and related to SoS or dependencies – the flipside of the SoS-coin.

First, the political dimension (demand side): Europeanisation in the political dimension would be visible on both the European and the national level: either on the supranational level or the intergovernmental level, policies would adapt European goals (download or crossload). Both options would be less orientated towards the national level than towards the European level. Europeanisation would lead to the development of more efficient and less duplicative National DTIBs. Furthermore, the integration and coordination of armaments and defence industrial policy would strengthen both the EDTIB and the Research and Technology (R&T) sector.

There are three dimensions in which Member States could influence the defence industrial structures: as a regulator, by harmonising rules and institutions, as an owner of defence companies or as a principal client, by pooling demand and research efforts, thus reducing costs. As a result, indicators for Europeanisation on the demand side are more cooperation, more common rules, national strategies based on the EU perspective, a consolidated demand, harmonisation of directives, more common armament and less national control in defence companies.

Second, the industrial dimension (supply side): Europeanisation on the industrial level would mean that the industrial structure is European and does not take into consideration national borders. It would be able to provide autonomous armament for the EU Member States, with the latter being totally free to decide over their military capabilities. The '3Cs' (Capabilities, Competences and Competitiveness) included in the EDTIB Strategy further circumstantiate this definition of Europeanisation.

In terms of capabilities, the EDTIB would provide SoS (design, production, maintenance, modernisation) for all capabilities, including complex solutions, as, for example, systems of systems. In terms of competences, the EDTIB would derive its products from R&T and ensure the technological and process development. Finally, in terms of competitiveness, as it

212   *M.-L. Chagnaud* et al.

would be more cost efficient, the EDTIB would contribute to economic growth with its exports and cooperation with non-EU partners. One effect of the Europeanisation on the supply side would be a consolidation of the market, i.e. less companies. These would be more specialised and at the same time would contribute to a larger range of products (division of labour).

Indicators for Europeanisation on the supply side can be summarised as follows: more integration, less duplication, more interdependency, centres of excellence through market-driven mechanisms, and a further integration into the overall industrial base of the EU, especially in the growing segment of dual-use commodities. The EDTIB is not only structured by companies, but by the production sectors these companies are active in and compete with each other, as well as with non-European companies. Moreover, the aerospace, land, naval and electronics sectors all show unique characteristics. Hence, an assessment of the 3Cs needs to be conducted along these sectors rather than along company lines.

In addition, regarding SoS, Europeanisation would mean fewer dependencies on non-EU suppliers and at the same time an increased interdependency among Member States. This is especially true for key technologies, in which Europe currently lags behind other competitors (e.g. Unmanned Aerial Systems (UAS)). As the EU-interdependency would be more regulated, its effects would be perceived less as negative. According to the EDTIB Strategy, the pMS were supposed to accept and to actively organise more mutual dependence within the EU-political framework.

## Europeanisation of EDTIB – the current state of EDTIB

### Political dimension: national and international policies

Against the declaration within the EDTIB Strategy, the pMS have prevented the development of a political and legal framework that would organise mutual dependencies. Instead, the long existing fragmentation of Europe into 28 defence markets with individual demand, regulations, standards and suppliers persists.

### International level

On the international level, traditional intergovernmental cooperation dominates the landscape. Such cooperation is ad hoc and appears mostly when single states lack the resources (funds, technology) to fill a capability gap. However, armaments projects realised in such a framework are regularly based upon the *juste retour* principle, ensuring a work share that equals the cost share of the countries participating, thereby neglecting market mechanisms which could help to consolidate the EDTIB or at least induce competition between suppliers (Hartley 2006, 2012; Darnis *et al.* 2007). While it has been agreed within the Organisation Conjointe de Coopération en matière d'Armement (OCCAR) to loosen the rules on *juste retour* (so-called global balance approach), there is no indication that this has been implemented.

Another traditional way to circumvent 'Europe' is the use of Article 346 of the TFEU. On the basis of 'national security interests', governments can choose their preferred supplier, thus neutralising the general obligation to apply public procurement procedures. While the Commission sought to seriously limit the use of this backdoor, Member States do not abide by the relevant Commission directive (European Commission 2013). Both principles contribute seriously to the steady cost increase of equipment because of duplication of efforts in R&D or production sites. They prevent cooperation and innovation through competition, and lead to long-winded negotiations over multinational projects, which all governments complain about as they lead to cost overruns and lower levels of capability delivered.

In order to institutionalise cooperation efforts, the European countries created a plethora of agencies, consisting of OCCAR and various NATO agencies, long before the EDA's EDTIB strategy. Besides, the six largest defence industrial countries in Europe signed the 'Letter of Intent' (LoI) in which they agreed upon coordination regarding the consolidation of their industry and future procurement programmes. However, neither the agencies nor the LoI created a huge political impact on the Member States' procurement. The EDA is the only agency founded after the new spirit that came with the creation of the ESDP in 1999. The idea has been to nudge the Member States towards industrial cooperation, and to focus that cooperation on the most urgently needed capabilities. EDA's task covers the whole spectrum of capability relevant issues: R&T, markets and industry, capability development and armaments.

In order to implement the EDTIB Strategy, the EDA has initiated numerous activities since 2007: the creation of a procurement portal, the Electronic Bulletin Board (EBB) and the Code of Conduct on Defence Procurement adopted in late 2005 have contributed to the growth of European cross-border procurement. The voluntary, legally non-binding 'Framework Arrangement for Security of Supply between subscribing Member States' and the web portal on SoS aim to be a further step towards a common understanding regarding SoS. Furthermore, the EDA has conducted a number of studies on EDTIB-related topics, e.g. on 'How to Measure Strengths and Weaknesses of the DTIB in Europe' (University of Manchester *et al.* 2008), on the 'Effects of Offsets on the Development of a European Defence Industry and Market' (Eriksson *et al.* 2007) and on the 'Ammunition Non-EU Dependencies' (BAE Systems *et al.* 2012). In 2013, the EDA presented its initiative for an increased support of Small and Medium Enterprises (SMEs).

214   *M.-L. Chagnaud* et al.

The limited outcome and impact of these initiatives is due to marginal support of the pMS. Their respective MoDs, in particular, seldom chose to take advantage of their agency.

Since 1996, the European Commission, as a supranational institution out of the direct reach of governments, sought to offer a coherent EU legal framework on issues like market, export and industry in the area of defence. However, the success is mixed. While its procurement directive aimed at limiting the use of Art. 346 came into force in 2009, Member States have simply circumvented it. Hence, EU rules and Member States' practice are two parallel worlds. More success came in areas where the Commission can offer funding, such as dual-use research.

The Lisbon Treaty introduced an innovative package that has real potential to improve the coherence of the overall institutional framework and could be applied also to armaments cooperation. The protocol on Permanent Structured Cooperation (PESCO) could in the long term bolster the link between the armaments framework and the capability development phase and, at the same time, enhance the role of the EDA. However, Member States were unable to agree on the precise criteria for participation in PESCO and on the role of the EDA. Eventually, infusing PESCO with life would have meant some investment, which was a non-starter since the fiscal crisis was just starting at that time.

*National level*

The international level only mirrors the divergent national realities and approaches. They have in common that they work against the creation of an EDTIB. The first reason is the diversity of defence industries.

The landscape of national DTIBs in Europe is unevenly divided: the six LoI countries (France, Germany, Italy, Spain, Sweden and United Kingdom) dominate the scene, holding about 80 per cent of the relevant DTIB in the EU. Within the other roughly 20 countries a DTIB exists only in some specific areas, as part of the globalised production chain (e.g. Netherlands – naval, air; Belgium – air, land; Austria – land), or to support national maintenance. The LoI DTIBs employ about 520,000 people. This represents only 0.024 per cent of the total workforce in the EU 27 (Eurostat 2011: 34; data does not include Croatia). The turnover of LoI may well account for 90 per cent of the defence industrial turnover in Europe – roughly €81 billion. This reflects the diverging industrial history and state attitudes towards the DTIBs. Thus, the size, ownership structure and role of defence companies in the national industry differ between Member States.

EU Member States also do not share a high degree of overlap regarding their armaments policies. This is because the differing strategic, political and economic and industrial traditions reflected varying attitudes towards freedom of markets and the importance of the industry for either the national sovereignty or the overall industrial landscape. States arrive at different conceptions of their sovereignty with regard to SoS, their strategic outlook – and thus the elements which they need in their DTIB – the relation between state and DTIB and structural and industrial effects of defence industry.

Because of the various differences, old, national procurement habits persisted in Member States (Mölling *et al.* 2014: 16). Nearly two-thirds of current procurement processes are either of national character, or include *juste-retour* paragraphs in multinational procurements. Furthermore, if Member States buy outside national or multinational projects (with their participation), they do not prefer European products, but buy at nearly the same share from non-European suppliers, mostly from the United States.

### Industrial dimension

#### Europeanisation on the supply side

After the end of the Cold War, the European defence industry went through a period of consolidation and integration. Large, multinational companies like EADS/Airbus are the symbol and result of this process. However, transnational consolidation was more or less concentrated on the aerospace and electronics sector, while the consolidation in the naval and land systems sectors ended at national borders. Furthermore, the decade of consolidation ended around 2002, leaving behind a fragmented landscape of small naval and land systems companies. Consolidation can be recognised by the concentration of defence industry, which is the percentage of a defined group of companies (e.g. Top 5, Top 10) on the total turnover of European defence companies. Measured by this factor, the EDTIB stagnated in recent years, with the top companies having a constant share of the total turnover. Between 2000 and 2012, the Top 10 European defence industrial companies made up between 75 and 80 per cent of the turnover (own assessment, based on SIPRI 1992 to 2014).

Duplication remains high in the EDTIB. Even with the described consolidation process in, for example, the aerospace sector, Europe developed and produced three fourth-generation fighter jets (Eurofighter, Gripen and Rafale). Thus, duplication of capabilities and capacities even exists in sectors regarded as highly consolidated. In the more fragmented land and naval sectors, the picture is even worse. Several companies and their respective products exist, offering a large number of different systems. Since Member States still often procure domestically, fragmentation – that is the relation of the number of different types of equipment to number of states – remains high.

With regard to interdependence among European defence companies, the network of companies comprising the EDTIB is deeply cross-linked, both vertically and horizontally. While vertical networks describe ever more complex supply chains, which often even lead outside Europe, horizontal networks are built through Joint Ventures (JVs) or the shareholding in other companies. However, this indicator of increasing interdependency is also true for connections of the EDTIB with companies outside Europe, not least due to offset-contracts, which require an entrance into the targeted market, often by cooperating with or buying local companies, e.g. the cooperation of the French DCNS with the Indian shipyard Mazagon Dock Limited on the construction of the Scorpene submarine.

Although there are clear centres of excellence for different sectors and products in Europe, these were not and are not shaped by market-driven mechanisms, but rather by historical prepositions, defence budgets, rising equipment costs, national defence industrial policies, industry supply-side adjustments via mergers/acquisitions and entry into foreign markets. They are concentrated in the major national defence industries, especially in France, Germany and the UK. These industries also have varying degrees of international competitiveness. Broadly speaking, France and Germany are competitive in land and naval systems, whilst the UK is competitive in the aerospace sector. Other Member States have varying elements of industrial capacities in their national defence industries (e.g. Italy, Spain, Sweden). Another symptom of this imbalance is the huge gap between Western and Eastern Europe. With the exception of Bumar, every European defence company listed in the SIPRI Top 100 arms producing companies list is based in Western Europe.

*Capabilities, competences and competitiveness*

The European DTIB shows varying degrees of the 3Cs. The land sector offers world-class products across the full range of capabilities. In the aerospace sector, the industry is highly capable. But the sector shows capability limits in Europe that will become more serious over the next years, especially in the field of larger UAS. Currently, every Medium Altitude Long Endurance (MALE) UAS in service with Member States' armed forces is based upon non-EU types. Not least due to the missing of a European alternative, France decided to procure US-made MQ-9 Reaper in 2013. In the naval sector, a comprehensive set of capabilities is available. However, they are spread across many companies. Moreover, the supplying industries deliver high quality components and subsystems such as sonars, guns, torpedoes and combat management systems. The electronics sector is capable of providing highest quality products and components according to current needs.

For all sectors, EU industries have the competence to manage the production process up to the level of system integration. Knowledge transfer from R&D and production chain management is working well in aerospace, due to the high level of dual-use. Knowledge transfer in the land segment works well, if the sectors in which the companies are active are interlinked in the battlefield (e.g. ammunition and guns). However, there is only limited transfer to the civilian domain. For naval knowledge and skills, the fragmentation of specific competences across many companies, the high degree of relevance related to the supplying companies, and the fact that companies are often active only in one single sector limits the knowledge transfers significantly. Moreover, for all sectors, the R&D funds are still spent nationally, and are also decreasing (EDA 2013: 14; Bekkers *et al.* 2009).

As for competitiveness, all sectors show excess capacities in production. This manifests itself with many small producers who are specialised in similar areas but do not compete against each other due to markets with high barriers for non-domestic suppliers. Moreover, the production lot itself is often small. This increases the price, limits economies of scale and learning, thus reducing competitiveness.

The land systems sector seems to be an area where the external markets can still absorb the excess capacities. Hence, the costs for the overcapacities do not feed directly back to the competitiveness. The naval industries have a very specialised market with only a few export segments, particularly for frigates, corvettes and conventional submarines. In order to maintain their competitiveness European companies include offsets into their export deals. These offsets comprise technological transfer or shares in the supply chain. One example is the Brazilian acquisition of Gripen fighter jets in 2013 (Rey Mallén 2013).

EU policies have apparently not shaped the sector and have failed to deliver with regard to their own objectives and benchmarks. Hence, the EU level has been ineffective in influencing the size, structure and performance of the EU's defence industries and the policies of national governments. Instead, as highlighted by the blocked EADS–BAE merger, Member States even actively inhibit further industry-driven consolidation.

*Dependencies*

The expected outcome of Europeanisation is a change to existing dependencies on all levels. Industrial production of defence related products relies on several dependencies (FOI *et al.* 2012). These include the availability of resources like components and raw materials and an economic reason to enter or stay in the business, thus an adequate demand. Furthermore, the defence market holds some specific characteristics, primarily an oligopolistic or even monopolistic structured supply and demand. To complete the picture of the current EDTIB, it is necessary to analyse these multiple dependencies, especially since most of the Member States rather see this as a problem for the industry than as one to work on at the political level.

218   *M.-L. Chagnaud* et al.

Import dependencies apply to both raw materials and components. Unfortunately, due to a very restricted information policy of defence companies regarding this matter, it is difficult to track and map which raw materials are imported from where and in which amount. Thus, only examples can be used to highlight this dimension. Rare earth materials, of which the People's Republic of China held 95 per cent of the world's production in 2010, gained the attention of the media after the People's Republic of China imposed export restrictions on these materials, thus creating shortages in the markets. This move ultimately led to the search for rare earth deposits in the Western world, even given the premise that extraction will be more expensive than importation. Another example is tungsten/wolframite, which is the basic material for armour-penetrating non-uranium munitions (e.g. for Main Battle Tank 120 mm smooth-bore guns). The main exporter of these materials is – again – the People's Republic of China.

In the case of import dependencies on components, there is not only the issue of availability to consider. While it is important to acknowledge that certain component productions are centred in a few countries (e.g. High Definition Devices production in Thailand), thus creating a high dependency, another dimension is security. Back doors, which can influence the performance of a component, and as such of the whole weapon system, pose a risk in imported components. Without any knowledge about the total supply chain, it is difficult ex-post to trace the sub-components (Committee on Armed Services United States Senate 2012). Moreover, Europe partly lacks not only the capacity to produce components, but also the capability. Especially the last point raises long-term dependencies on foreign suppliers.

Due to declining defence budgets and demand in Europe, European defence companies are more and more relying on the export of defence equipment to ensure the preservation of production lines and competitive market prices through economy of scale effects. Expansion strategies into non-EU markets differ considerably among Member States. Such developments follow long-established political relationships and profit from governmental support. Other main reasons for exports are long-term client-customer relations or traditional procurement habits. Companies increasingly establish Joint Ventures (JVs) or subsidiaries in non-EU countries to gain access to the market, transferring their EU-internal strategy to the global markets. At the same time, European exports only take place if they incorporate a significant level of technology transfer, thus reducing technological leadership and therefore the selling argument for future exports to these customers. Moreover, the export drive increases the competition among European companies and among companies and governments. European companies choose – sometimes because they have to, due to offset regulations – local companies as partners. Entering into JVs or buying them up allows access to domestic markets. At the same time, those companies compete against other European companies aiming at the same market. The potential export of fighter aircraft to India is one example for such intra-European competition in foreign markets. All three producers of European fighter jets applied for the Indian tender, competing against one another, thus enabling the Indian side to push for better conditions. Eventually, defence companies compete with their home countries' governments that would like to sell surplus equipment on these new markets as well. Export is already an important lifeline for national DTIBs in their current configurations and hence to all LoI countries. Export rates vary between 40 and 70 per cent of overall national defence industrial turnover. Thus, prices on the domestic market often depend more on the option to export than on national demand. Moreover, the main export destinations are changing. While traditionally North Atlantic Treaty Organisation (NATO) and EU allies have been the main recipients, markets are shifting towards Asia and the Middle East.

Defence dependence is the degree by which a company's turnover is dependent on its business in defence. While the productivity in defence is a constitutive element of a company's utility to military affairs, the same relationship also poses risks to the business and thus to the survival of the company. Especially given the expected decrease in defence business, reducing the defence dependence by diversification of companies into various civilian businesses is a potential element of defence industrial strategies that characterises the DTIB. The picture for European defence companies varies greatly in this regard, from companies totally dependent on defence, like KMW or DCNS, to companies in which their defence segment rather looks like an add-on, like ThyssenKrupp.

## Conclusion

While we use Europeanisation as a guiding idea, the chapter especially contributes to the so far underdeveloped empirical knowledge regarding the characteristics of the EDTIB. This sketch deserves further work in three dimensions: first, the application of the Europeanisation approach to the field of defence industry/DTIBs; second, the generation of data and its assessment from a time series perspective to give a richer picture and better micro foundation to the study of Europeanisation of DTIBs; finally, the distinctive interaction of state and industry, which is a key driver but difficult to integrate in the assessment of Europeanisation with regards to the ways ideas are exchanged between private and state actors.

### *No Europeanisation in sight*

As far as available information allows judgement, the EDTIB is stuck in the uploading phase of Europeanisation. Instead of a bigger role of EU concepts, institutions and resources, the EDTIB is a story of more of the same.

220   *M.-L. Chagnaud et al.*

Two main trends are even driving politics and industry further apart thus further questioning security of supply.

### Continued nationalisation

The EDTIB-related policies of Member States have traditionally been less driven by a European security policy or capability definition than by a mixture of national industrial and technological policies. This prolongs national DTIBs and ensures they remain incompatible with each other.

The landscape in the DTIB has not changed significantly compared to previous years. On the political side, the old habits of armaments cooperation prevail, enshrined in the principles of *juste retour* and Art 346 TFEU. At the same time, institutions and rules have proliferated on the EU level – the EDA, the European Commission, the Lisbon Treaty – with marginal policy impact, however. The national political level reflects the lack of influence of the EU level: the LoI Member States, who represent 20 per cent of the EU Member States, dispose of about 80 per cent of the EDTIB and are responsible for a similar split of defence investment turn-over. The diversity of the 28 national marketplaces and DTIBs, controlled by 28 national policies towards defence, technology, markets, procurements and exports, persists. As to the industrial structure, the EU did not deliver according to its own benchmarks and objectives related to the EDTIB. Europeanisation does not play a significant role in the industry's plans and its behaviour, national rules and international market opportunities shape it more than normative EU-centred political declarations. The top companies in the EU are global rather than European players. EU rules and regulations have played little role in forming the defence industrial landscape; cooperation patterns and institutions have evolved primarily outside the EU. Major consolidation has not happened or, as in the case of BAE–EADS, has been deliberately prevented. The industry shows varying degrees of competences, capabilities and competitiveness along the sectors. They all have in common that Europe does not play a significant role as an actor that frames developments. While the companies in the land and naval sector are often nationalised and highly specialised in one sector, they are globalised and often have more diversified portfolios in the aerospace and electronics sector.

### Increased globalisation

Dependencies have increased in two ways: the civilian basis for defence industry is growing and defence establishments have become more dependent on civilian supply chains. Moreover, as the civilian part of the business generates the majority of the turnover and income, it will become increasingly difficult and costly for the military to establish highly reliable supply lines. The other dependence comes with exports. While Member

States' dependence on non-EU platform suppliers has decreased, dependence has seriously diversified, especially in the industrial dimension, both on exports and imports. While their role in the EDTIB is shrinking, the SoS the EDTIB can deliver is under new sources of pressure. States primarily focus on military supply. Yet they miss the strong link between the military and industrial SoS, e.g. the possibility that the industrial supplier itself runs out of supplies, e.g. components and raw materials.

### Outlook

The current state and likely development of defence industrial activities make it increasingly improbable that the Member States and the EU implement the official vision of the EDTIB. Europeanisation based on a joint political vision has lost contact with the individual political and industrial reality of the growing export orientation of European suppliers. In addition, SoS depends ever more on the influx of civilian and defence goods as well as on raw materials from beyond Europe's borders. The future of a EDTIB is dependent on national and global DTIB developments: national demand is declining as well, while global demand is growing, pointing towards a further globalisation of DTIBs by market shifts and the internationalisation of production for the coming years. As a consequence, Europeanisation becomes less likely because the national DTIBs may become more integrated into the global DTIB. Purely national DTIBs risk becoming increasingly difficult to sustain. These circumstances, together with the existing and predictable budget austerity, beg the question how Europe can maintain a DTIB that effectively delivers the needed spectrum of military capabilities. In contrast, a new paradigm for SoS is emerging: instead of national independence, Member States will have to aim for managing critical global supply chains. This will be even more important if the EU becomes a bigger importer.

As the basis for the creation of an EDTIB is changing drastically, the Member States, EDA, European Parliament and the European Commission have to add new solutions to the already existing recommendations from the last years. The entire EU has to find new ways in managing its defence sector as a whole and the relations among the relevant actors. A key step would be a revision of the 2007 EDTIB Strategy to create a new vision for Europeanisation. This has to be based on the new realities, both in terms of what a European DTIB means today and in the future, and the means available to achieve such an EDTIB. In core, it means to shift from a geopolitical to a functional approach regarding the EDTIB.

A second element would be to establish continuous defence industrial monitoring and a regular assessment of risks and opportunities to the EDTIB. Far beyond specific defence aspects, national governments and EU institutions should develop an understanding about industrial priorities in times of austerity and thus find a formula for a more coordinated

222    *M.-L. Chagnaud et al.*

European industrial policy in relation with the EDTIB. Here, a Defence Sector Council would be necessary to get the political mandate from the heads of states and governments. Such a Council should first take a comprehensive look at the State of the EU defence sector and second develop a Military Headline Goal and an Industrial Headline Goal for the 2030 horizon that sets out common priorities for the European armed forces' procurement and the EDTIB.

Notwithstanding future visions of defence, current reality implies that EU Member States should immediately engage in greater consolidation of demand through joint R&T projects and through bundling demand for shared capabilities, for example by harmonisation of demand, synchronisation of procurement, cooperative or common procurement. In this context, Pooling and Sharing is particularly important and deserves a step change.

For all these tasks, Europeanisation may imply first of all a closer institutionalisation among the classical intergovernmental and communitised actors and instruments, as the latter reflects the growing importance of the civilian area for the EDTIB. Hence a closer cooperation of EDA and European Commission is indicated. Recent actions like the framework agreement and the reorganisation of the EDA are only first steps towards managing a set of tasks that are truly European. Besides furthering cooperation through joint workflow planning and programmes, both need to engage with the key stakeholder in European defence: the Member States.

## References

Andreatta, F. (2011) 'The European Union's International Relations: A Theoretical View', in C. Hill and M. Smith (eds) *International Relations and the European Union*, Oxford: Oxford University Press: 21–43.

BAE Systems, Nexter, Diehl BGT Defence, Expal, Rheinmetall Defence and MBDA (2012) *Ammunition Non-EU Dependencies*, EDA Study, Brussels.

Bekkers, F., Butter, M., Eriksson, E.A., Hartley, K., Hoffmans, D., Leis, M., Lundmark, M., Masson, H., Rensma, A., van der Valk, T. and Willemsen, G. (2009) *Development of a European Defence Technological and Industrial Base*, Report to the European Commission, DG Enterprise and Industry, Brussels.

Bitzinger, R.A. (ed.) (2009) *The Modern Defense Industry: Political, Economic, and Technological Issues*, Santa Barbara: ABC-CLIO.

Briani, V., Marrone, A., Mölling, C. and Valasek, T. (2013) *The Development of a European Defence Technological and Industrial Base (EDTIB)*, European Parliament, DG for External Policies, Policy Department EXPO/B/SEDE/2012/20, Brussels.

Caporaso, J., Cowles, M.G. and Risse T. (2001) 'Europeanisation and Domestic Change: Introduction', in J. Caporaso, M.G. Cowles and T. Risse (eds) *Transforming Europe: Europeanisation and Domestic Change*, Ithaca, NY: Cornell University Press: 1–20.

Chappell, L. (2009) 'Differing Member State Approaches to the Development of the EU Battlegroup Concept: Implications for CSDP', *European Security*, 18(4): 417–439.

Committee on Armed Services United States Senate (2012) 'Inquiry into Counterfeit Electronic parts in the Department of Defense Supply Chain'.

Darnis, J.-P., Gasparini, G., Grams, C., Keohane, D., Liberti, F., Maulny, J.-P. and Stumbaum, M.-B. (2007) *Lessons Learned from European Defence Equipment Programmes*, Occassional Paper 69, Paris: EU Institute for Security Studies.

Defense News Journal (2012) 'TOP 100 Defence Company Listing': 14–16.

Direction Générale de l'Armement (2012) *Calepin international des principales entreprises travaillant pour la défense*, Paris.

European Commission (2013) 'Commission Staff Working Document on Defence Accompanying the document Communication Towards a More Competitive and Efficient Defence and Security Sector', COM (2013) 0542 final.

EDA (European Defence Agency) (2013) 'Defence Data 2012'.

EDA (European Defence Agency) (2007) 'A Strategy for the European Defence Technological and Industrial Base', 14 July 2007.

EDA (European Defence Agency) (2005) 'Code of Conduct on Defence Procurement of the EU Member States Participating in the European Defence Agency', 21 November 2005.

Eriksson, E.A., Axelson, M., Hartley, K., Mason, M., Stenérus, A. and Trybus, M. (2007) *Study on the Effects of Offsets on the Development of a European Defence Industry and Market*, EDA Study.

EUROSTAT (2011) *Key Figures on European Business with a Special Feature on SMEs*, Brussels: European Commission.

Featherstone, K. and Radaelli, C. (eds) (2003) *The Politics of Europeanization*, Oxford: Oxford University Press.

FOI, ONERA and RAND (2012) *Addressing Key European Defence Technology and Industrial Dependences – Executive Summary*, EDA Study.

Geyer, M. (1984) *Deutsche Rüstungspolitik: 1860–1980*, Frankfurt am Main: Suhrkamp.

Glarbo, K. (2001) 'Reconstructing a Common European Foreign Policy', in T. Christiansen, K.E. Jørgensen and A. Wiener (eds) *The Social Construction of Europe*, London: Sage: 140–157.

Guay, T. and Callum, R. (2002) 'The Transformation and Future Prospects of Europe's Defence Industry', *International Affairs*, 78(4): 757–776.

Hartley, K. (2012) *White Elephants? The Political Economy of Multi-National Defence Projects*, Brussels: New Direction.

Hartley, K. (2011) *The Economics of Defence Policy: A New Perspective*, London: Routledge.

Hartley, K. (2006) 'Defence Industrial Policy in a Military Alliance', *Journal of Peace Research*, 43(4): 473–489.

Hartley, K., Bellais, R., and Hébert, J.-P. (2008) 'The Evolution and Future of European Defence Firms', in J. Fontanel and M. Chatterji (eds) *War, Peace and Security (Contributions to Conflict Management, Peace Economics and Development)*, vol. 6, Emerald Group Publishing: 83–104.

Heidenkamp, H. Louth, J. and Taylor, T. (2013) *The Defence Industrial Triptych: Government as Customer, Sponsor and Regulator*, RUSI Whitehall Paper 81.

Heuninckx, B. (2008) 'A Primer to Collaborative Defence Procurement in Europe: Troubles, Achievements and Prospects', *Public Procurement Law Review*, 17(3): 123–145.

Hill, C. and Smith M. (eds) (2005) *International Relations of the European Union*, Oxford: Oxford University Press.

224   *M.-L. Chagnaud* et al.

Hyman, R. (2001) 'The Europeanisation – or the Erosion – of Industrial Relations?', *Industrial Relations Journal*, 32(4): 280–294.

Jacoby, W. (2004) *The Enlargement of the European Union and NATO: Ordering from the Menu in Central Europe*, Cambridge; New York: Cambridge University Press.

Jasper, U. and Portella, C. (2010) 'EU Defence Integration and Nuclear Weapons: A Common Deterrent for Europe?', *Security Dialogue*, 41: 145–168.

Major, C. and Pomorska, K. (2005) 'Europeanisation: Framework or Fashion?', *CFSP Forum*, 3(5): 1–4.

Markusen, A.R. and Costigan, S.S. (eds) (1999) *Arming the Future: A Defense Industry for the 21st Century*, New York: Council on Foreign Relations Press.

Mölling, C., Chagnaud, M.-L., Schütz, T. and von Voss, A. (2014) *European Defence Monitoring (EDM)*, SWP Working Paper FG 03, No. 01, January 2014.

Moumoutzis, K. (2011) 'Still Fashionable Yet Useless? Addressing Problems with Research on the Europeanization of Foreign Policy', *Journal of Common Market Studies*, 49(3): 607–629.

Radaelli, C. (2004) 'Europeanisation: Solution or Problem?', *European Integration Online Papers*, 8(16). Online. Available at: http://eiop.or.at/eiop/texte/2004-016a.htm (accessed 17 October 2014).

Rey Mallén, P. (2013) 'Brazilians aren't Happy about $4.5 Billion Purchase of Saab Gripen Fighter Jets', *International Business Times*, 19 December 2013.

SIPRI (Stockholm International Peace Research Institute) (1992–2014) *SIPRI Yearbook*, vols 1992 to 2014, Stockholm.

Stone, D. (1999) 'Learning Lessons and Transferring Policy across Time, Space and Disciplines', *Politics* 19(1): 51–59.

Tonra, B. (2003) 'Constructing the CFSP: The Utility of a Cognitive Approach', *Journal of Common Market Studies*, 41(4): 731–756.

Wong, R. (2005) 'The Europeanization of Foreign Policy', in C. Hill and M. Smith (eds) *International Relations of the European Union*, Oxford: Oxford University Press: 134–153.

University of Manchester, University of York, CNRS/GREDEG and Instituto Affari Internazionali (2008) *Study on How to Measure Strengths and Weaknesses of the DTIB in Europe*, EDA Study.

# 13 The EDA and defence offsets
## Trailing after the Commission

*Peter Platzgummer*

## Introduction

This chapter discusses the efforts of the European Defence Agency (EDA) to decrease the fragmentation of the European Defence Technological and Industrial Base (EDTIB) by coordinating offset practices of its Member States. It uses a historic, descriptive analysis in order to assess how successful the EDA has been in overcoming the negative effects of offsets, considering the fragmentation of the EDTIB.

The chapter begins with a short discussion of the effects of offsets and an overview of the development of offset practices in the European Union (EU) since the end of the Cold War. Additionally, the efforts of the European Union and several Member States towards a common EDTIB before the foundation of the EDA are discussed. The next section deals with the endeavours of the Industry and Market (I&M) Directorate, particularly the introduction of the 'Code of Conduct on Offsets' (CoCO). The last section concentrates on the time since the introduction of Directive 2009/81 EC, which constricted offsets definitively to the area of defence and had game-changing effects on national policies.

The prime argument of the chapter runs as follows. The EDA has thus far played a marginal role in coordinating offsets. While offset practices have seen major changes, especially in the last few years, they have mainly been influenced by the European Commission's objective to increase free trade. The chief outcome of the EDA's efforts, the CoCO, almost became obsolete with the introduction of the European Commission's 'Defence and Security Procurement' (DSP) Directive. As a result, offsets may be changed, even 'gradually' reduced (O'Donnell 2009: 3), but, due to the positive effects still perceived by some countries, offsets will not entirely disappear (Kimla 2013: 7–16). The EDA should therefore concentrate its own efforts on the provision of best case practices and feasible tools for countries to use these protectionist practices for a common EDTIB.

## Protectionist practices and the European Defence Industrial Base

Much of the work of the EDA involves areas affected by decisions in the first and the second pillars of the EU. This is particularly the case for tasks of the European Synergies and Innovation (ESI; the former I&M) Directorate. While economic or industrial interests in other directorates are often subordinate to Headline-Goal-based military objectives, a common EDTIB is subject to decisions that were made outside rather than inside the EDA. The strongly fragmented European defence market is the result of a process driven as much by national security interests as by other factors, such as the decline of military budgets over the last few decades, unemployment numbers, regional distribution between Member States, and globalisation (Briani *et al.* 2013: 13–17). Discussions about an EDTIB are not so much about the collective development of future military capabilities, but mainly about defending the status quo of a country's own industry (Mölling *et al.* 2014: 19).

With declining national defence budgets, countries have to decide if they would still like to have weapon systems produced domestically, or buy them off-the-shelf from foreign companies. A domestic production has the advantage of having a positive effect on employment rates, and also gives the opportunity to develop a system specific to the needs of the country's own armed forces. However, due to often low economies of scale, it is likely to be significantly more expensive than a pre-developed product from a foreign vendor. The effects of importing a weapons system include a decrease of knowledge and employment within the domestic defence industrial base (Nambiar *et al.* 1999: 424), and are to that extent the same as those of a top-down Europe-wide restructuring process (Briani *et al.* 2013: 60). As a result, countries have tried to use remaining armament procurements in a way that their own industry can profit from, at least partially, even when the military system is imported. Especially before interoperability became a major topic for armed forces, domestic companies often heavily adapted foreign off-the-shelf products to their own soldiers' needs.

An alternative is the usage of *juste retour* regulations in joint-system development, where the domestic industry gets a share of the production that is proportional to its own government's financial contribution to the system. This approach, in particular, has led to situations in which an unrealistically high procurement commitment was made in order to gain a larger portion of the production (DeVore 2014: 421).

Over the last few decades, the fastest growing option has been reciprocal trade agreements (Anderson and Moores 2013: 5), most often called offsets or industrial compensation, where

> governments require compensations from defence contractors as a condition for purchasing defence articles or services. These compensations

can cover a wide range of activities directly related to the defence project object of the procurement contract (direct offsets). Indirect offsets, in turn, can be defence related or non-defence related.

(Schmitt 2005: 16)

Offsets are conceived by policy-makers aiming not only to increase employment rates, but also to shift the main objectives towards giving the domestic defence industrial base the export volume necessary to sustain budget cuts, along with the knowledge to maintain or even advance the weapon systems at home. In reciprocal trade agreements, the foreign military-supply producing company must work directly with domestic companies to fulfil offset obligations based on a previously determined offset policy. A specialised national agency specifically defines the industrial fields or technologies where offsets are allowed to take place, and supervises these efforts.

The effects of these protectionist practices are severe. Europe's Defence Technological and Industrial Base is nowhere near what was envisioned in the EDA's EDTIB 2007 strategy. It consists of a group of LoI countries with large, often government-controlled national champions representing only 20 per cent of the Member States but at the same time 80 per cent of the EDTIB, and another group comprises the remaining Member States with either only a handful of small producers and suppliers or no industry at all. Even though these two groups are completely different, they are both influenced by the same two drivers: nationalisation and globalisation. National security policies have generated industrial bases that are almost incompatible and have led to an extreme situation where a government is either procuring at home or on a global scale. A preference for European producers is non-existent in European defence procurement (Briani *et al.* 2013: 9). With reduced market in Europe, European companies are more and more dependent on global exports (Mölling *et al.* 2014: 20) and, with cost pressures at home, they are also sourcing their suppliers on the more competitive global market (Briani *et al.* 2013: 10).

Offsets not only sustain the existing fragmentation, but also in some ways accelerate it. One way, for example, is in the manner that direct offsets force a domestic company into the current supply chain of the purchased system from a foreign supplier (Eriksson *et al.* 2007: 53). However, while critics highlight the inefficiency and additional costs of offsets, others see them as a possibility for facilitating industrial and technological development (Martin 1996: 38–39). From a European point of view, offsets could ensure a better security of supply by increasing the incentives for producers to source their suppliers within Europe. Also, by using a sophisticated offset policy, they could support the development of centres of excellence (Briani *et al.* 2013: 20). For example, Turkey became one of the world's top 20 defence exporters by strategically using offsets since 1984 to promote its own industry (Hoyos and Amann 2013).

228   *P. Platzgummer*

With a volume of more than €5 billion in Europe in 2006 (Eriksson *et al.* 2007: 4), and a specialised offset agency in almost every country, offsets and the attempts to regulate them have had considerable one-of-a-kind effects on the EDTIB. A successful coordination of offsets by the EDA should therefore enforce the positive effects of remaining offsets and not be restricted to overcoming the negative effects.

## The beginning of offsets: a fast growing use of protectionist practices

The 'birth' (Hébert 1996: 139) of offsets began in Europe in the mid-1970s almost in parallel in different countries but in very diverse ways. Offsets were offered by non-European producers to increase their chances in competitive tenders, or were required 'as a form of additional *quid pro quo*' (Udis 1996: 322) to strengthen a country's industrial base. However, the majority of these first offset agreements were not part of a larger strategic plan, but rather ad-hoc decisions included in the procurement process (Neuman 1985). Until the end of the 1980s, offsets were just another form of countertrade, and as such were not questioned, as countertrade was often the only possibility to maintain any kind of stable trade relations with weak-currency countries.

Offsets became a real problem in the 1990s when, with the fall of the Iron Curtain, countertrades began to rapidly increase. 'By 1992, a total of 130 countries had some form of countertrade/offset policy' (Martin 1996: 16). However, the increase in numbers was not the only determining factor: First, because of decreasing military budgets after the Cold War, armed forces shrank and therefore asked for fewer quantities of a system. Tight budgets forced governments to ask for cost-efficient systems, often going for cheaper foreign off-the-shelf purchases instead of choosing their own developments (Neal and Taylor 2001: 351). Also, in many cases, governments decided to increase the offset obligation from the moderate 25 per cent to 75 per cent in earlier years to, most often, 100 per cent of the contract volume. Second, the defence industry faced two trends: while larger defence companies were often state-owned up until the late 1980s, governments started to privatise the industry in the 1990s (Dunne and Surry 2006: 394). This, combined with a movement towards globalisation, led to a reduction of the domestic defence industry, especially in smaller countries. Third, the growing attention to interoperability favoured the defence industry of larger nations, as their product was more often used as the international standard (Neal and Taylor 2001: 349). And fourth, technological changes made it more difficult to involve small companies in a weapons system's pre-existing supply chain. For example, with the introduction of computerised aircraft maintenance test systems, which replaced members of the workforce, and the fact that changing entire sub-systems was often cheaper than just regularly changing spare parts (Sandberg and Strömberg 1999), direct offsets no longer had the employment impact they once had. Overall, these factors changed the position of the large exporters. Producers not only had to sign more contracts with more importing countries, but were also confronted with larger offset obligations in these contracts, coupled with a weaker domestic industrial base that could not easily take over the production of essential parts.

Also, the 1990s put security back onto the agenda of the EU. The Maastricht Treaty established the EU with an intergovernmental second pillar for Common Foreign and Security Policy (CFSP) that involved close cooperation with the Western European Union, and eventually the adoption of the Petersberg tasks. By 1996, the EU had already launched its first Communication on a defence industrial issue. Just a year later, the Commission called for the establishment of a European defence market. Even though these initiatives never really progressed, there were several intergovernmental policies and agreements, such as the LoI Framework Agreement or the Coherent Policy Document, which can now be considered important for the foundation of a common EDTIB (Schmitt 2005: 13). While offsets were not specifically addressed, they all introduced measures to enhance transparency and competition, and aimed at increasing cooperation and defence industrial consolidation. The Commission and Member States with large defence suppliers were aware of the fragmented defence industrial base and its negative effects for military capability building, but were not ready to take the actions necessary to achieve the objective of a common EDTIB. The exemption of areas 'necessary for the protection of the essential interests of (the) security' of an EU Member State, as defined in Article 296 of the EU Treaty, was still not brought into question by the Commission. The academic literature (see, for example, Weiss 2013: 39) often mentioned the Case C-414/97, Commission vs. Spain interpretation of the European Court of Justice in 1999, which supported the appraisal of the Commission, stating that Article 296 does not automatically permit that exemption for all defence procurement. However, this was in this case irrelevant, as the main focus in this court case concerned questions of taxation, and the argument of exemption was brought up at a very late point by Spain and was immediately refused by the court. Up until almost a decade later, the article may have been used in political discussions, such as the argumentation in the Commission's interpretative communication on the application of Art. 296 in 2006, but the Commission never went so far as to lay a charge against a Member State based on it. Offsets were at most a side issue and were often ignored by European policy-makers. The Commission lacked any kind of coordinative effort as offsets were still seen as a purely national area of interest.

## The establishment of the EDA: a first phase of awareness building

In June 2003, the Italian Presidency of the EU announced the initiation of the EDA. The establishment was approved based on 'Council Joint Action

230    *P. Platzgummer*

(2004/551/CSFP) of July 12th, 2004' as a support authority for CSFP and ESDP 'in the field of defence capabilities development, research, acquisition and armaments'. The EDA and its directorates were structured around these fields, with the addition of a separate Defence Industry and Market Directorate. The existence of this functional directorate is interesting, as in a way it constitutes a hybrid between a classic military armaments agency and an economic agency. This is due to the realisation that Europe's military capability 'could not' be developed without the existence of an adequate European Defence Technological and Industrial Base (Alfonso-Meiriño 2010b: 173), as well as the uniqueness of a defence market in contrast to traditional markets. In some regards, this ambiguous structure also led to a vague flagship project for the I&M Directorate. While all other operational directorates had relatively concrete projects defined for them (e.g. Research and Technology Directorate: long endurance Unmanned Aerial Vehicles (UAVs)), the Steering Board assigned the I&M Directorate the 'launch of initiatives leading to the creation of a truly European defence market and the strengthening of the EDTIB' (Alfonso-Meiriño 2010a: 39). The main objective was to analyse the options defined by the EC in its Green Paper on Defence Procurement and identify possible EDA initiatives based on these options (Grigoleit *et al.* 2005: 18). Taking Article 296 as the borderline between supranational EC and intergovernmental EDA work, the I&M Directorate had two different options. On the one hand, it could start general initiatives that would include areas that would otherwise be part of the Commission's responsibility; on the other hand, it could define the borderline more precisely and come up with initiatives where an intergovernmental approach would clearly be necessary.

One of the first actions of the newly founded EDA was to accept the Organisation for Joint Armament Cooperation's (OCCAR) principles; among them the abandonment of the mostly inefficient *juste retour* system in arms collaboration projects (Mawdsley 2008: 377). For offsets, the situation was somewhat different. Except for a small sentence on the use of offsets as award criteria for tender processes and a short discussion about how offsets add to the complexity of arms acquisition programs, the 2004 Green Paper on Defence Procurement did not address the issue of offsets. With the adoption of the EDTIB Strategy by the Steering Board in May 2007, the EDA offered the first glimpse of its own position towards offsets. According to the strategy, offsets could provide opportunities for individual Member States and would be an acceptable practice under the current market conditions, but should not be used as an award criterion in defence competitions. The strategy also stated that, while a common EDTIB would most probably render offsets irrelevant in the future, the short-term goal was to mitigate negative effects within competitions and the current EDTIB (Eriksson *et al.* 2007: 9).

The first specific initiative that started parallel to the development of the EDTIB Strategy can be seen as an attempt to define the borderline of

*EDA and defence offsets* 231

Article 296 more precisely and collect information necessary for further steps. Due to lack of internal resources, the I&M Directorate commissioned in 2006 an external report with the objective of mapping offsets quantitatively and qualitatively, and of measuring the current effects of offsets and their impact on the future development of a common EDTIB and EDEM (Eriksson *et al.* 2007). The report was inconclusive, showing that due to lack of transparency and coherent data, the effects and the legal national framework could not be precisely depicted. Still, it confirmed former academic assumptions (e.g. Martin 1996) that had been made about the positive and negative effects of offsets. The report's authors were able to estimate that the additional costs of offsets for Member States ranged between 5 and 10 per cent of the contract volume. They also revealed that negative effects were less severe the more competitive and capable the offset-requesting country's domestic defence industrial base was. The report was also the first to estimate the distribution of direct (40 per cent), indirect military (35 per cent) and indirect civil (25 per cent) offsets. More important is the legal interpretation of Article 296 in the report. There, the authors were more biased than the Commission, the EDA or even opposing countries at that time. The report came to the conclusion that it is difficult to justify any kind of offset on the basis of Article 296, which conflicted with an Interpretative Communication the Commission published at the same time, one that considered only indirect civil offsets to be a legal problem (Eriksson *et al.* 2007: 76). The strict, literal interpretation of Article 296 was foreseen by some critics, arguing that the commission of a Swedish government agency could lead to a report that favours the interests of LoI states (CTO 2007: 2).

These were very interesting results as they came at a time when, on the one hand, the use of offsets by some Member States was rising to questionable heights, making it almost impossible to accomplish demands while, on the other hand, the Commission was in the middle of a process leading to a stricter handling of offsets. For example, Austria, under political pressure to stop the acquisition of a new multi-role combat aircraft, demanded offsets worth €4 billion for a procurement price of not even half that sum (Tiron 2002). Smaller countries hoped that the economic effects would be seen as a great incentive for the public to be in favour of a procurement (de Vestel 1995: 45). By the 2000s, Eastern European countries overall were becoming aware of the economic effects of offsets. With the enlargement of NATO and the positive economic developments within the area, countries started to proactively request offsets of often 100 per cent or more of the contract volume in most of their defence procurements. For example, in the early 2000s, Hungary was not only increasing the amount of European imports from 16 per cent to almost 90 per cent (Eriksson *et al.* 2007: Annex 2) but was also asking for offsets of between 100 and 180 per cent of the contract volume (Friedli *et al.* 2009: 52). The hope of supporting one's own industrial base was stronger than any consideration

232    *P. Platzgummer*

towards a common EDTIB, as the example of Poland trying to boost its own naval industry against all European consolidation trends shows (Briani *et al.* 2013: 44). During this time, media attention on offsets was growing. The Swedish Saab and British BAE Systems companies were confronted with severe allegations of corruption in South Africa (Platzgummer 2013: 11) that led to many debates concerning the transparency of defence procurement, especially in regards to offsets.

The best-known initiative of the EDA regarding offsets was, in some senses, a response to the attention raised by the public, the Commission and the Member States. With approval by the Member States of a proposed Code of Conduct on Offsets (CoCO) on 24 October 2008, the EDA reached a first goal 'in the process of finding a strategy dealing with defence offsets that is acceptable to all EDA countries' (Alfonso-Meiriño 2010b: 183). The CoCO was intended as a gentlemen's agreement on how to use offsets in a moderate and effective way regarding both the supranational EU legislative framework and the intergovernmental regime within the EDA. The CoCO, which was signed by all participating Member States (pMS) of the EDA except for Romania, had two main goals: First, to increase transparency between all Member States by making the national legal framework for offsets publicly available. And, by transmitting data on offset deals for the EDA to statistically analyse as benchmarks for all Member States. Second, having countries voluntarily vow to not demand offset practises that would have negative effects on the creation of a common EDTIB. Additionally, the benchmarking was supposed to lead to the identification of best-case practices of the positive effects of offsets for a commonly optimal EDTIB.

The CoCO may be seen as an absolute minimum objective for the EDA, but it took four years for this intergovernmental organisation to devise a proposal that could be approved by all Member States. This is certainly the result of scarce resources within the EDA, where offsets may have been seen as important, though this was never reflected in the number of employees specifically working in the Directorate, bearing in mind that even basic studies had to be outsourced. But the fact that a regulation, however innocuous, was finally approved may also be the result of some countries' realisation that existing requests were nearly impossible for the foreign vendor to accomplish, compounded by their own defence industrial base's inability to fulfil government claims. However, the CoCO did lead to a slight increase in transparency, especially after the establishment of the offset internet portal, and the publication of all Member States' offset policies. Unfortunately, the EDA decided to keep the benchmarking data closed to the public (CTO 2010: 5–6), which in a way contradicted its own transparency efforts.

In 2010, two years after the introduction of the CoCO, with the exception of Cyprus, France, Malta and Latvia, all EDA Member States maintained an offset policy, and asked for offsets within most of their defence acquisitions. It is apparent that a division of the pMS purely based on the

*EDA and defence offsets* 233

size of the national defence industrial bases was not highlighted in the policies (Platzgummer 2011). For example, the UK had a policy most similar to Luxembourg, Poland, Italy, Greece, Bulgaria and Estonia. This group had a relatively liberal approach, with few specific restrictions, and was not directly supporting its own industry with abatements (where countries 'swap' offset obligations) or special requests for Small and Medium Enterprises (SMEs). But all the countries in the group used offsets as an award criterion within their procurement process, and offsets were most often restricted to areas of defence or security. Spain, Belgium, Czech Republic and Germany also had a rather liberal approach and were, at least according to their policies, not using very strict steering mechanisms as guidelines on the foreign vendor's interaction with the domestic industrial base. In contrast to these two groups, the Nordic countries and the Central European countries had policies that were stricter, in that they explicitly defined industrial areas of interest. But, while the Nordic countries seemed to have a relatively 'realistic' view of offsets with fairly high threshold values – meaning that offsets were only agreed upon when the volume was large enough to balance out the transaction costs, and the proactive use of abatements in order to decrease offset obligations of their own industry with foreign governments, the main commonality among Central European countries was their demand for the maximum offsets possible. Here, the CoCO likely had the biggest impact as it decreased offset requests of the members of this group to the postulated 100 per cent. But the EDTIB was not severely affected by this group, as these countries had already shifted their claims into the civilian market. It seems that a country with significant defence imports asks for offsets irrespective of the size its defence industrial base. However, the smaller a country's defence industrial base is, the more likely indirect civil offsets are demanded due to the 'limited absorptive capacity' (Eriksson *et al.* 2007: 77) of their defence industry.

The division of responsibilities for offsets is also of importance. While countries that use offsets more as an overall industrial promotion tool tend to make decisions through their Ministries of Economics (MoE), only countries with a clear focus on areas of defence and security hold an agency within their Ministries of Defence (MoD) for this purpose. For example, Italian's offset agency at the MoD was dealing with offsets completely restricted to the area of defence, while the Dutch, having an agency within the MoE, did not restrict offsets to civil areas (Platzgummer 2011: 9). This is important, since the EDA's structure focuses almost exclusively on decision-making processes with representatives of MoDs.

The period between 2004 and 2010 constituted a phase of awareness building. Member States underwent a process of rationalisation, realising that offsets could have negative effects for their own defence industry. However, the overall use of offsets was not questioned, as the positive effects outweighed transaction costs in most countries. It seems that this

234   *P. Platzgummer*

was especially the case when the transaction costs were included in the MoDs' budget, while offsets and their effects were steered by other, more influential ministries – perhaps due to their size. For the EDA, this first phase following its establishment was chastening. Considering its limited resources, the introduction of the CoCO can be seen as a success, yet the effects seem marginal. While the CoCO increased transparency, providing an overview of policies and annual volumes, the same policies did not always reflect the de facto position of a country. For example, while Spain and Germany are in the same group of countries regarding their policies, Germany, overall, has a very negative approach of offsets and sees them more as an absolute exception. In comparison, Spain has been one of the most actively demanding countries, with very strict requirements during the offset process (Molas-Gallart 1998).

Also, while some countries may have hoped that an intergovernmental organisation would be advantageous when their own offset interests were conflicting with the EC's interests, this has not been the case. In fact, the I&M Directorate made it clear from the very beginning that the final objective would be to abandon offsets and their negative effects. The EDA made a seemly clear distinction between the role of the EC and its own somewhat subordinate role. The Commission faced no opposition, since the CoCO was mainly considered an effort 'within the legislative framework of the EU' (Alfonso-Meiriño 2010b: 183) to increase the information of offsets for the EDA's Steering Board. It appears that the EDA never intended to hold a fundamental debate on the use of offsets but, instead, waited for a final decision taken within the first pillar of the EU.

## The introduction of the Commission's procurement directive: a new focus on defence

2011 marked what was probably the most important change for offset practices in Europe thus far. From 20 August 2011 onwards, the EU Member States have had to adopt laws or regulations based on the DSP Directive which, without specifically mentioning them, had two direct implications on offsets. First, it prohibited discrimination on the grounds of nationality, based on Article 18 TFEU, meaning that a country cannot solely ask foreign vendors for compensation obligations, but needs to ask a potential domestic vendor for similar compensations. Most commentaries believe that this is against 'the very nature of offsets' (Weiner 2012: 17) as tender practices contradict this principle. While this may be true, it is a rather small problem as long as countries only ask for a specific amount of domestic production for the purchased product, and therefore ask for equal requirements from all vendors. Second, it restrained the security-related justification, based on Article 346 TFEU, the former Article 296 of the Nice Treaty, by emphasising that economic justifications for offsets are not accepted and that countries using offsets need to prove the essential security interest and necessity of every specific measure. Up until that point, Member States had been using Article 346 TFEU as an argument for the exemption of almost all procurements in the area of defence. From 2011 onwards, the use of the exemption had to be based on specific cases and 'the question of whether or not the provisions contained in Article 346 TFEU are fulfilled may be decided in court' (Weiner 2012: 17). Eventually, this should lead to the abandonment of indirect (civil) offsets, and at the same time reduce the use of direct offsets to few specific cases, therefore limiting debauched usage.

While former regulations and interpretations by the EC already stressed the problematic usage of the exemptions, the DSP Directive is the first output of the EC with game-changing potential in the area of defence offsets. Interestingly, the official reaction of the Member States and the EDA was neither a fast nor a coordinated effort to appropriately address these new rules. While one would have guessed that countries in favour of offsets would proactively defend their own interests, a real examination of the effects of the directive did not start before 2011. By August 2011, only ten countries had officially transposed the directive into national legislation, so in 2012 the Commission issued reasoned opinions to several countries that did not implement the directive satisfactorily (Furter 2012: 27–28). Countries where offsets had been used as award criteria and countries that opened their offsets to the civil sector especially began to oppose the Commission's efforts, and hoped for a clarification in their favour from the court (CTO 2011: 1).

There are two possible explanations for this hesitant reaction by the Member States: First, during the consultation phase of the European Commission's Green Paper on Defence Procurement, some Member States stated that the issue of offsets should be discussed within the EDA, and that the activities of the Commission should not lead to 'prejudicially forestalling' (BKA 2005: 5) the activities of the EDA. In 2007, a Commission staff working document discussed the option of not mentioning offsets in a future DSP Directive, as the topic of offsets would go beyond the objectives of the initiative and, because of Article 346 TFEU, would also concern areas exempted from EU law. 'Expecting EC procurement rules to solve the offset problem would thus be mistaken and could even endanger the initiative (given the sensitivity of the issue)' (European Commission 2007: 48). One could say that maintaining silence about offsets in the Commission's directive 'lulled' countries defending offset practices into a false sense of security, implying that only the EDA would be responsible for offsets. This could have led to a division of responsibilities within the countries, with public officials responsible for offsets focusing their attention on discussions of the CoCo with the EDA, with officials responsible for the main aspects of defence procurement focusing their attention on the directive and the Commission. Second, for the development of the DSP Directive, the Commission had several consultations with the EDA. The

236   *P. Platzgummer*

aforementioned structural problem of the EDA, namely that decision-making processes occurred almost exclusively within MoDs, possibly led to a situation where the representatives of MoDs were aware of the negative effects of the directive on indirect civil offsets, but were also aware that these same effects would lead to a concentration on direct offsets, thereby not misusing their own tight budgets for industrial promotion activities outside of the area of defence. Countries that tended to accept civil offsets were especially likely to have agencies responsible for offsets within their MoEs (Friedli *et al.* 2009: 52). This could mean that the reaction was not really hesitant but that instead, due to an inter-institutional rivalry between ministries, government agencies responsible for offsets either were not informed enough or could simply not agree internally on a common opinion. Also, the defence industry representatives involved in the consultation phase consisted mainly of large manufacturers who may have seen the DSP Directive as an opportunity for limiting excessive use of offsets, especially in civil areas outside their core businesses. Their initiation of counter measures on a national level would have, in this case, led to unfavourable outcomes.

While the EDA has seen itself as a 'catalyst, [...] facilitating the coordination of Member States from the perspective of the Defence Ministries' (Alfonso-Meiriño 2010b: 200), its own initiatives have done little to accelerate the change process over recent years. Besides the development of the offset portal and the important but less visible offset benchmarks for all Member States, the main new initiative was a proposal for a Europe-wide abatement process. Here, the objective was to facilitate the exchange of offset obligations between two or more countries, which would have led to an immediate decrease of individual obligations and would have been especially alleviating for large European suppliers with obligations in these countries (EDA 2010: 14). At least officially, the EDA has been very uncritical towards the EC and the DSP Directive.

Except for Greece and – on paper – the UK, most countries did not abandon offsets because of the DSP Directive, but in the future will instead ask for more specific offsets in the area of defence. Here, the EDA underestimates the negative effects of this change, as European vendors will on the one hand have to provide more defence related offsets, which often presume higher technological capabilities from the domestic defence industrial base than civil ones, and, on the other hand, large producers will still have to provide offsets to countries outside Europe without the advantage of receiving reciprocal offsets as part of the industrial base of a buyer country. A consortium of research institutions was awarded a study on the effects of this last point by the EDA in early 2013 but this study, as well as a study commissioned in the same year by the Commission to measure the impact of the DSP Directive, have not been made open to the public. According to CTO (2013b: 1–4) the authors struggled to measure the effects because of an unwillingness of the European defence industry to cooperate. Also, the study did not only reveal positive effects of the DSP Directive but also discussed *inter alia* the problems some SME's from Member States with a smaller industrial base could have with a phasing out of offsets.

## Conclusion

Since the creation of the EDA, national interests have been hanging like the sword of Damocles over one of Europe's main goals, the establishment of a common EDTIB. Offsets are one of the tools Member States with decreasing defence budgets use to strengthen their domestic defence technological and industrial bases, but they can contribute to a further fragmentation of the European defence market. As offsets are often not part of EU legislation, due to exemptions based on Article 346 TFEU, it has been the EDA's task as an intergovernmental agency to deal with the use of offsets by its Member States.

Offsets rose dramatically following the end of the Cold War due to decreasing military budgets and an increasing globalisation of defence procurement. With the constitution of the EDA, Europe had, for the first time, an agency responsible for coordinating these protectionists practices, and the efforts of the Agency helped to increase – at least within the Steering Board – the transparency and information about offsets. Still, this chapter comes to the conclusion that the EDA has had a rather marginal role in coordinating offsets so far. While offset practices have seen major changes, especially over the last few years, they have largely been influenced by the European Commission objectives to increase free trade. The main outcome of the EDA's efforts, the Code of Conduct on Offsets, became practically obsolete with the introduction of the DSP Directive by the Commission. By delimiting offsets to the area of defence, the DSP Directive could have the positive effect that the responsibility for offsets will be within the realm of MoDs and will therefore be better coordinated by the EDA's ESI Directorate. But, while civil offsets at least had no negative effects on the fragmentation of the EDTIB, a focus on defence offsets could have a negative effect on the fragmentation of the defence industrial base. Offsets may change forms, but will not disappear. In fact, the 17th Annual Report to Congress on the Impact of Offsets in Defence Trade (BIS 2013: 4) shows that more countries than ever before ask for larger and larger offset contracts, and the Commission sees its 'bids to ban offsets failing' (CTO 2013a: 2). The change process, initiated with the introduction of the DSP Directive, is not yet finished, and discussions of new opportunities, such as the shift from offsets towards subcontracting, or the introduction of 'European offsets' (Weiner 2012: 18), are already beginning. While European offsets – offsets received by all EU Member States when requested by a single country – do not seem to be a viable future option as the purchaser would still have to pay additional

## 238 P. Platzgummer

transaction costs, demand for direct offsets and subcontracting requirements will probably grow.

In May 2014, the EDA declared the working group on offsets 'dormant, apparently on the assumption that Directive 2009/81 EC has made its work redundant' (CTO 2014a: 3). This seems to be a very questionable decision as neither national interests of Member States and, therefore, protectionist practices such as offsets will vanish overnight, nor will the DSP Directive lead to an end of offset obligations of European producers requested by countries outside Europe. Instead, the EDA should concentrate its own efforts on the provision of practicable tools in order for countries to use these protectionist practices in the best possible way for a common EDTIB. So far, this has not been the case, with the exception of the – momentarily closed – offset portal. With the EC refusing to define 'national interests' indicated in Article 346 any further (CTO 2014b: 2), the EDA could step into the breach and clear up the confusion that Member States as well as the defence industry have at the moment. Also, the EDA could collect and offer best case practices that could not only be used to build up excellence centres within Europe, but also to support the European defence industry on how to deal with the increasing amount of offset obligations from abroad. If this were to come about, the EDA could strengthen its own role as a facilitator between Member States and the Commission, instead of being the catalyst of a process not all Member States agree on.

## References

Alfonso-Meiriño, A. (2010a) 'Establishment of the European Defence Agency', in Centre for National Defence Studies (eds) *European Defence Agency: Past, Present and Future*, Spain: CESEDEN, Ministerio de Defensa: 19–60.

Alfonso-Meiriño, A. (2010b) 'The Defence Market and the Strengthening of Europe's Defence Technological and Industrial Base', in Centre for National Defence Studies (eds) *European Defence Agency: Past, Present and Future*, Spain: CESEDEN, Ministerio de Defensa: 173–204.

Anderson, G. and Moores, B. (2013) *The Growing Offset Burden: What A&D Businesses Need to Know*, London: IHS White Paper.

BIS (Bureau of Industry and Security) (2013) *Offsets in Defense Trade. Seventeenth Study*, Washington, D.C: U.S. Department of Commerce, Bureau of Industry and Security.

BKA (Bundeskanzleramt der Republik Österreich) (2005) 'Grünbuch "Beschaffung von Verteidigungsgütern"; Stellungnahme der Republik Österreich (BKA-671.801/0078-V/A/8/2004)'.

Brauer, J. (2004) 'Economic Aspects of Arms Trade Offsets', in J. Brauer and J.P. Dunne (eds) *Arms Trade and Economic Development: Theory, Policy and Cases in Arms Trade Offsets*, London: Routledge: 54–65.

Briani, V., Marrone, A., Mölling, C. and Valasek, T. (2013) *The Development of a European Defence Technological and Industrial Base (EDTIB)*, EXPO/B/SEDE/2012/20, Brussels: Directorate-General for External Policies of the Union, Directorate B.

CTO (CTO Data Services) (2014a) 'EDA Loses Interest in Offsets', *Countertrade and Offset*, 32(10): 3.

CTO (CTO Data Services) (2014b) 'The Defence Directive: Burkard Schmitt Sanctions Unsolicited Offers', *Countertrade and Offset*, 32(7): 1–2.

CTO (CTO Data Services) (2013a) 'EC's Bid to Ban Offsets is Failing', *Countertrade and Offset*, 31(13): 2.

CTO (CTO Data Services) (2013b) 'Special Report: European Commission Struggles to Measure the Impact of the Directive', *Countertrade and Offset*, 31(20): 1–4.

CTO (CTO Data Services) (2011) 'Poland Declares War: First Test Case Looms over the Directive', *Countertrade and Offset*, 29(12): 1–2.

CTO (CTO Data Services) (2010) 'EDA to Address Abatements', *Countertrade and Offset*, 28(3): 4–6.

CTO (CTO Data Services) (2007) 'Partiality Questioned of EDA Study on "Impact of Offset Practices within the EU"', *Countertrade and Offset*, 25(9): 2.

de Vestel, P. (1995) *Defence Markets and Industries in Europe: Time for Political Decisions?*, Chaillot Paper 21, Paris: Western European Union Institute for Security Studies.

DeVore, M.R. (2014) 'International Armaments Collaboration and the Limits of Reform', *Defence and Peace Economics*, 25(4): 415–443.

Dunne, J.P. and Surry, E. (2006) 'Arms Production', in *SIPRI Yearbook, 2006: Armaments, Disarmament and International Security*, Oxford: Oxford University Press: 387–418.

EDA (European Defence Agency) (2010) *Abatements: A Pragmatic Offset Tool to Facilitate the Development of the European Defence Equipment Market*.

Eriksson, E.A., with contributions by Axelson, M., Hartley, K., Mason, M., Stenérus, A.-S. and Trybus, M. (2007) *Study on the Effects of Offsets on the Development of a European Defence Industry and Market*, Stockholm: FOI, S.C.S.

European Commission (2007) 'Annex to the Proposal for a Directive of the European Parliament and of the Council on the Coordination of Procedures for the Award of Certain Public Works Contracts, Public Supply Contracts and Public Service Contracts in the Fields of Defence and Security', Staff working paper.

Friedli, T., Neumüller, K. and Platzgummer, P. (2009) *Nachhaltige Offset-Ansätze für die Schweiz*, St. Gallen: CSET-IPW-HSG.

Furter, L.D. (2012) *Update on the EU Directive and its Impact on Industrial Partnership in the European Arena*, presented at the DIOA GOCA Fall 2012 Conference, Brewster, US, 11 September 2012.

Grigoleit, S., *et al.* (2005) 'European Defence Agency (EDA) im europäischen Kontext', INT-Bericht; 185/1, Euskirchen: Fraunhofer-Institut für Naturwissenschaftlich-Technische Trendanalysen.

Hébert, J.-P. (1996) 'Offsets and French Arms Exports', in S. Martin (ed.) *The Economics of Offsets: Defence Procurement and Countertrade*, Amsterdam: Harwood Academic Publishers: 139–162.

Heuninckx, B. (2008) 'Towards a Coherent European Defence Procurement Regime? European Defence Agency and European Commission Initiatives', *Public Procurement Law Review*, 17(1): 1–20.

Hoyos, C. and Amann, A. (2013) 'Turkey Builds Domestic Defence Industry', *Financial Times*, 9 October 2013.

Kimla, D. (2013) *Military Offsets and In-country Industrialisation – Market Insight*, Warsaw: Frost & Sullivan.

## 240  *P. Platzgummer*

Martin, S. (1996) 'Countertrade and Offsets: An Overview of the Theory and Evidence', in S. Martin (ed.) *The Economics of Offsets: Defence Procurement and Countertrade*, Amsterdam: Harwood Academic Publishers: 15–46.

Mawdsley, J. (2008) 'European Union Armaments Policy: Options for Small States?', *European Security*, 17(2–3): 367–385.

Molas-Gallart, J. (1998) 'Defence Procurement as an Industrial Policy Tool: The Spanish Experience', *Defence and Peace Economics*, 9(1–2): 63–81.

Mölling, C., Chagnaud, M.-L., Schütz, T. and von Voss, A. (2014) *European Defence Monitoring (EDM)*, Working Paper, Berlin: SWP.

Nambiar, R.G., Mungekar, B.L. and Tadas, G.A. (1999) 'Is Import Liberalisation Hurting Domestic Industry and Employment?', *Economic and Political Weekly*, 34(7): 417–424.

Neal, D.J. and Taylor, T. (2001) 'Globalisation in the Defence Industry: An Exploration of the Paradigm for Us and European Defence Firms and the Implications for Being Global Players', *Defence and Peace Economics*, 12(4): 337–360.

Neuman, S.G. (1985) 'Coproduction, Barter and Countertrade: Offsets in International Arms Market', *Orbis*, 29 (Spring 1985): 183–213.

O'Donnell, C.M. (2009) *The EU Finally Opens up the European Defence Market*, CER Policy Brief, London: Centre for European Reform.

Platzgummer, P. (2013) 'Arms Trade Offsets and Cases of Corruption: The Usage of Anti-Corruption Tools in Special Forms of Arms Acquisitions', *International Public Management Review*, 14(2): 14–38.

Platzgummer, P. (2011) *Small States and Defense Offsets: When Size Doesn't Matter*, Paper presented at the International Studies Association (ISA) Annual Convention, Montreal, Canada, 16–19 March 2011.

Sandberg, A. and Strömberg, U. (1999) 'Gripen: With Focus on Availability Performance and Life Support Cost over the Product Life Cycle', *Journal of Quality in Maintenance Engineering*, 5(4): 325–334.

Schmitt, B. (2005) *Defence Procurement in the European Union: The Current Debate*, Report of an EUISS Task Force, Paris: EU Institute for Security Studies.

Tiron, R. (2002) 'Eurofighter Battling for Foreign Sales', *National Defense*, 87(588), November 2002.

Udis, B. (1996) 'US–Swiss F-5 Transaction and the Evolution of Swiss Offset Policy', in S. Martin (ed.) *The Economics of Offsets: Defence Procurement and Countertrade*, Amsterdam: Harwood Academic Publishers: 321–336.

Weiner, K. (2012) 'Towards European Preferences? Implications of Directive 2009/81/EC on Domestic Preferences in Defense Procurement', *The Procurement Lawyer* (Spring 2012): 16–20.

Weiss, M. (2013) 'Integrating the Acquisition of Leviathan's Swords? The Emerging Defence Regulation within the EU', in P. Genschel and M. Jachtenfuchs (eds) *Beyond the Regulatory Polity: The European Integration of Core State Powers*, Oxford: Oxford University Press: 27–45.

# 14 The EDA's inroads into space

*Frank Slijper*

## Introduction

Space has become a cornerstone of the European Union's (EU) security and defence policies and thus a focal point for the European Defence Agency (EDA). According to its chief executive:

> developing the right tools to act is out core mandate. Space is an obvious part of this objective as it has become a vital element of any security or military action. [...] Space is now embedded in practically everything we do, in our everyday lives, but also in security operations, from intelligence gathering to flying a drone.
>
> (ESA 2013c)

In close cooperation with the European Space Agency (ESA), the European Commission and national capitals, Europe's military space agenda has been developed since the beginning of this century. Also, the Commission considers space as a key area to foster its military–industrial agenda, stressing increased synergies between civilian and military activities. Both in terms of research funding and major EU-led space programmes, the European industry in turn has a clear interest in nurturing Europe's (military) space ambitions.

While there used to be a clear distinction between the ESA's civil space agenda and the predominant national military space programmes, over the past decade the ESA has moved more and more into the military field. Mostly under the banner of 'security' it is involved in a number of space projects with dual-use (i.e. military and civilian) aspects. Many officials stress that the fusion of these characteristics is natural and logical, but others warn for the negative consequences of ignoring key characteristics of military space programmes. After all, it cannot be ignored that after the Cold War we have witnessed a major increase in the military's use of space. With increased use, as well as changing geopolitical relations, the potential of conflict in space is not illusory.

As will be outlined in this chapter, the key role of the EDA consists of connecting national military organisations, European institutions and industry. Structural problems (political, financial, as well as organisational) have so far limited progress, but since both space and military policies are relatively new areas of EU policy, this is not surprising. However, with the EDA tasked to engage in space activities, the ESA working on military programmes and the incorporation of space in European military policies, the EU is clearly further raising its military posture. Given the contentious connection of space and its military use, as well as limited public knowledge, it is argued here that it is of imminent importance to monitor the evolution of Europe's Space Policy, the strategic mission of which is based on 'the peaceful exploration and exploitation of outer space' (EC 2013c). Against that background, this chapter describes how the Commission, the EDA and the ESA, together with the industry, are shaping the space component of the EU's military policies.

## EU space policy: military aspects

The European Commission describes the importance of space as part of the EU's security and defence policy as follows:

> Space-based systems are making an increasingly important contribution to the security of Europe, and to the Common Security and Defence Policy (CSDP), in particular. Europe faces constantly evolving security threats that are now more diverse, less visible and less predictable than in previous decades. [...] Space assets provide a significant contribution to confronting these threats through global monitoring, communication and positioning capabilities.
>
> (EC 2013d)

In more general terms it also asserts that

> Space systems are clearly strategic assets that demonstrate independence and the ability to assume global responsibilities. To maximise the benefits and opportunities that they can provide to Europe now and in the future, it is important to have an active, co-ordinated strategy and a comprehensive European Space Policy.
>
> (EC 2013a)

Indeed, over the past decade Europe has put space high on its agenda. The European Space Policy, setting out a vision and strategy for the space sector, is relatively new. Jointly drafted by the Commission, the ESA and Member States, the policy paper was released in 2007, following up on preparatory 'Green' and 'White' papers in 2003, the 2004 'ESDP and Space' document and other Commission communications. It is a break with the past, when the EU and the ESA had always carefully avoided any clear involvement in the military dimensions of space, at least formally (Smid 2007; Tigner 2007).

Still, article II of the ESA Convention states that 'the purpose of the agency shall be to provide for and to promote, for exclusively peaceful purposes, cooperation among European states in space research and technology and their space applications'. While the ESA insists that peaceful purposes do not rule out military applications (Morsillo 2010), the reality is that the military potential of space systems in which the ESA participates allows for facilitating and enabling military interventions, including those aiming at regime change or justified under the flag of combating terrorism. No matter the justification, such involvement certainly cannot be called peaceful.

On 'security and defence' the European Space Policy states:

> The Member States in the Council have identified Europe's generic space system needs for military operations and stressed the necessary interoperability between civilian and military users. [...] Within the framework of existing EU principles and institutional competencies, Europe will substantially improve coordination between its defence and civil space programmes, while retaining primary end-user responsibility for funding.
>
> (EC 2007)

At a hearing by the European Parliament a few days prior to the release of the policy document, a top official at the EC's Directorate-General for Enterprise and Industry had said: 'We all agree that there is no security [in Europe] without space. If we want to be independent, Europe must use space as an asset and it must offer a mixture of civil and military applications' (Tigner 2007).

In more general terms, space policy was subsequently integrated in the 2009 Treaty of Lisbon which under article 189 states:

> To promote scientific and technical progress, industrial competitiveness and the implementation of its policies, the Union shall draw up a European space policy. To this end, it may promote joint initiatives, support research and technological development and coordinate the efforts needed for the exploration and exploitation of space.

The European Space Policy was the first such joint document addressing all dimensions of space activities, compiled after consultations with member countries, as well as industry and others. Key to that consultation process was the work of the so-called Panel of Experts on Space and Security, contributing in 2005 its vision on how space was relevant in areas of military and security policies. The experts were largely drawn from the

Commission, space organisations (including the ESA and the EU Satellite Centre), military structures (the European Capabilities Action Plan (ECAP); Space Assets Group; Organisation Conjointe de Coopération en matière d' Armement (OCCAR)) and industry, represented through its EU lobby group Eurospace, which has since merged with ASD. The newly established EDA had an observer status.

Expert groups feature dominantly in EU policy making and have been criticised for their lack of transparency and business-domination (Slijper 2005; Vassalos 2010). Especially with the Enterprise and Industry directorate of the Commission in charge of space policy (as well as defence industry policy), such a focus of the Panel of Experts on Space and Security may even be less surprising. One of the key findings of the expert group was that Europe needed to change its relationship with the military use of space:

> Europe must establish a new balance between the civil and military uses of space. There is little point in concentrating on purely civil applications and ignoring the military requirements or vice versa. Striking this balance effectively will require continued effort as international events unfold.
>
> (EC 2005)

That echoed similar alarmist notions in the European Security Strategy (ESS) presented by the Commission in 2003. However, that document at least acknowledged in its introduction that 'Europe has never been so prosperous, so secure nor so free. The violence of the first half of the twentieth century has given way to a period of peace and stability unprecedented in European history' (EC 2003). This of course contradicts the rhetoric of increased and unpredictable threats, necessary to garner sufficient support for expanding security policies. The panel of experts further noted that 'due to their inherent large-scale investment, and their common interest, security and defence programmes in particular represent a unique way to foster greater efficiencies at European level and a well developed programme for space and security can help achieve this goal' (EC 2005).

The shift towards a more inclusive security concept – claiming that boundaries between internal and external security have blurred, and 'thus' that distinguishing between military and other security has become merely artificial – was reflected in this and other Common Security and Defence Policy (CSDP)-related reports emerging from the late 1990s onwards.

Strategically, for EU planners such a vision enables putting forward potentially controversial military projects, which likely receive less resistance when labelled as security projects. With anything that could possibly suggest a development towards EU armed forces or a military union and the potential loss of national sovereignty still highly controversial, labelling anything 'military' as 'security-related' has become the convenient way to smoothen potential resistance against such plans (Slijper 2005).

The ambiguity towards the militarisation of space is clearly reflected by the support of EU Member States for United Nations initiatives to prevent an arms race in space (such as the Outer Space Treaty and the Conference on Disarmament-led Prevention of an Arms Race in Outer Space), while at the same time their militaries have become increasingly reliant on space infrastructure to support military missions. However, obscuring the military elements of space programmes executed under EU auspices comes close to disinformation. With much of today's warfare inextricably linked with space systems – from communications and surveillance, to navigation for the guidance of missiles – it is necessary to be clear about the military potential of such systems.

Practically, it also enables easier access to EU funding, traditionally off-limits for military work, but allowing for 'dual-use' security areas, covering both military and non-military applications. For example, research funding has been allocated under both the area of 'space' and 'security' under the 2007–2013 Seventh European Union Framework Programme for Research and Development (FP7). That may change from 2014 as FP8, or Horizon 2020, will likely open funding opportunities for military research (EC 2013b).

## Interlinking actors: the EDA–ESA–Commission nexus

As much of the European Space Policy is relatively new, so are relations between the EDA, the ESA and the Commission. Some activities and projects are developed in common, some separately – but always stressing the synergies of the different initiatives. For example, the 2010 Space Policy Resolution of the Council invites the European Commission, the Council of the European Union, the EDA, the Member States and the ESA to

> explore ways to support current and future capabilities for crisis management through cost-effective access to robust, secure and reactive space assets and services (integrating global satellite communications, Earth observation, positioning and timing), taking full advantage of dual-use synergies as appropriate.
>
> (cited in EDA 2011a)

Cooperation takes place at various levels, including the Space Council, the Structured Dialogue on space and security, as well as bilateral exchanges.

### EC/ESA cooperation

In November 2000, the ESA and the Council of the European Union met together for the first time and endorsed the setting up of a cooperative

246   *F. Slijper*

structure to bring together the ESA Executive and the European Commission: a high-level joint taskforce. The EC/ESA Framework Agreement, providing the legal basis, entered into force in May 2004. 'The Framework Agreement recognises that both parties have specific complementary and mutually reinforcing strengths, and commits them to work together to avoid duplication of effort' (ESA 2012). Under this agreement the European Commission and the ESA coordinate their actions through the Joint Secretariat. Meetings of the Council of the European Union and the ESA Ministerial Council, known as the 'Space Council', were a practical result of the Framework Agreement. Member States representatives prepare the Councils in the High-level Space Policy Group (HSPG). The European Space Council first came together in November 2004 and has met more or less annually since.

While both sides applaud the progress made since, it is not always a happy couple. A few contentious issues have arisen recently (De Selding 2012). With the ESA also having non-EU members (Norway and Switzerland) and an associate (Canada), the European Commission (2012) voiced an 'acute problem when it comes to security and defence matters' in a November 2012 communication. The same document also mention diversions about the way industry gets contracts: while the ESA awards national industries according to the amount of its members' contributions, the Commission operates from a value-for-money point of view. Finally the EU considers the ESA's 'missing political accountability' as problematic, as decision-making generally takes place behind closed doors. To resolve these difficulties, the EU proposed that the ESA be brought under EU authority, one way or another.

Subsequent council conclusions diplomatically watered down the concerns – not even mentioning security concerns – and proposed to solve these issues through close cooperation between the Commission and the ESA (Council of the European Union 2013), recognising their mutual dependencies. While the Commission considers ESA as a 'technical manager' for its space programmes, the ESA 'views the commission's space budget as force multiplier [...] at a time when its own budget is relatively flat' (De Selding 2013).

### Enter the EDA

Regular exchange of views and coordination takes place through the Structured Dialogue on space and security, bringing together the relevant European Commission services, the Secretariat-General of the Council, the European Satellite Centre (EUSC), the EDA and the ESA. According to an EC/ESA paper it is an 'increasingly effective instrument to exploit inter-institutional synergies [and] should be used more intensively for an enlarged range of topics' (EC/ESA 2010).

As the paper (EC/ESA 2010) further outlines:

European security services should rely on existing and available national and European assets, thereby avoiding unnecessary duplications. These assets are in many cases under military control. This will require close coordination with Member States owning relevant assets and capabilities and discussion on the terms and conditions under which they can be made available to Europe.

A priority issue 'in this highly sensitive area' is partnering European actors and Member States' authorities 'to better exploit synergies between relevant European and national dual-use or military space security space activities and assets', including the potential of replacing national assets with European assets (EC/ESA 2010).

While the Commission together with the ESA has been leading most of the security and military related space initiatives – notably Galileo and Global Monitoring for Environment and Security (GMES) – the EDA has taken up specific military (components of) space programmes, often in tandem with the ESA and/or the Commission.

Space is one of the EDA's key priorities. Its 2006 'Long-Term Vision' already noted that 'the preparation and conduct of future EU led operations will require continued consideration of space related aspects, such as communication, and the detection and identification of potential threats in advance of an appropriate answer' (EDA 2006). At the 2009 'Space for Security and Defence' conference, the EDA stressed the need to integrate space systems in the wider Intelligence, Surveillance, Reconnaissance (ISR) and network-enabled capabilities (EDA 2009b). The following year's event – both part of the Structured Dialogue – highlighted the common interests in surveillance programmes such as GMES and Space Situational Awareness (SSA) (ESA 2010).

At the 'Critical Space Technologies for European Strategic Non-Dependence' workshop in September 2008, the Commission, the ESA and the EDA agreed to work together on the development of critical space technologies in Europe, with the aim 'to ensure that Europe can rely on a technical and industrial capacity for accessing space, in particular in the area of the manufacturing of satellites and launchers' (ESA 2008). The meeting's list of speakers included almost all key European officials and industry representatives in the area (Congrex 2008). The EC, the EDA and the ESA identified a number of 'urgent actions' to be addressed (EC/EDA/ESA 2012).

At its November 2012 steering board meeting, EU ministers of Defence tasked the EDA to 'federate defence-related requirements, identifying civil–military synergies in preparation of demonstrators and by providing support to critical space technologies for European non-dependence' (EDA 2012h).

The EDA is also involved in the European Framework Cooperation (EFC) for defence, civilian security and space-related research.

248   *F. Slijper*

> The EFC aims at systematically coordinating research investments by the EDA, the European Commission and the European Space Agency, focusing in particular on areas of dual-use for civilian security and military users. The overall aim is to prevent duplication between defence and civilian research to save resources, and to improve civil–military interoperability and standardization.
>
> (EDA undated)

At the launch of the EFC in 2011, the EDA highlighted its relevance 'for future cooperation under Horizon 2020. I believe that it would be beneficial for both civil and military when we could co-finance the dual-use technologies that both constituencies need for their applications' (Sowa 2011). Indeed, this is a development that has been strongly pushed by the EDA, the Commission and industry, as what they consider a logical next step after the introduction of a fully fledged security research programme under FP7 (Tigner 2014a, 2014b).

### EDA and ESA

In 2011, the EDA and the ESA signed an Administrative Arrangement concerning the establishment of cooperation between the two agencies and to enable joint projects, aiming in particular: to identify capability gaps or shortfalls that could be filled by space assets in support of relevant EU policies; to investigate whether capability requirement can be shared/supported by both agencies; to investigate synergies between existing and future EDA and ESA programmes; to coordinate research, technology and demonstration activities; and to explore synergies and coordinate activities in support of industrial competitiveness and European non-dependence (EDA 2011a). Other common areas of work identified include ISR; civil–military synergies in earth observation; satellite communications; SSA; and critical space technologies for European non-dependence (EDA 2011a).

Such activities were also highlighted by ESA head Giuseppe Morsillo, one of the main speakers at the annual EDA conference in 2010 (Morsillo 2010) and again in an interview in July 2013 with then-chief EDA Claude-France Arnould and ESA director at the time Jean-Jacques Dordain. In that interview cyber defence was mentioned as a 'novel cooperative avenue' which needed to be incorporated (EDA 2013). 'Space has become a major enabler for the military, without which it cannot do critical missions', according to an ESA official:

> The threats to that enabler are real. They can occur against ground stations and radar sites, and before a satellite is launched by planting malicious software during its development. Once you launch it into space, it is very difficult to deal with an embedded virus.
>
> (Tigner 2012b)

The Commission, the EDA and the ESA are exploring how to exploit the Horizon 2020 budget in favour of cyber projects benefiting both civil and military users.

## Space budgets, Galileo and Copernicus

Europe's largest military and security related space programmes are the Galileo satellite navigation system and Copernicus, the earth observation programme formerly known as GMES. With funding for the 2014–2020 Multiannual Financial Framework under pressure, the EU cut Galileo funding by 10 per cent, to €6.3 billion, with the Copernicus budget slashed 35 per cent, down to €3.78 billion for the same period (De Selding 2013).

Through the EU's FP7, space research projects were funded with an average €200 million annually between 2007–2013 (EC 2014). Under Horizon 2020, space is expected to get a nominally similar amount: €1.35 billion (De Selding 2013). A lot of the research will relate to Copernicus, SSA and critical technologies for non-dependence.

The ESA's 2013 budget was €4.3 billion, with roughly three-quarters coming from individual Member States and less than a quarter from the EU (ESA 2013a). This latter part is mainly for work on Galileo, Copernicus and SSA. The EDA has no specific space budget and is largely dependent on individual Member States for contributions on specific themes, including space-related ones.

### Galileo

Galileo's programme management is controlled by the EC and the ESA; it should be fully operational in 2018. Due to many delays Galileo has lost much of its precision advantage vis-à-vis its US rival Global Positioning System (GPS). Still, the European space community considers Galileo to be an essential element of an independent space policy.

The desire for European military autonomy was an important reason for the EU to proceed with Galileo and thus it is clearly set to become a crucial asset in future military operations. An unnamed diplomat cited on an EU news portal suggested that 'everybody knows that there is no business case for Galileo. We only need a European system of our own, because at a militarily very critical moment we can't trust the GPS to be available' (Euractiv. com 2012). With many missiles today being guided by navigation satellites, Galileo is thus set to become Europe's preferred system to guide bombs and missiles against any target perceived as a threat.

### Copernicus (GMES)

In 2001 the European Council decided on 'establishing by 2008 a European capacity for global monitoring of environment and security'. This

250   *F. Slijper*

became known as GMES, set up in 2005 by the European Commission and the ESA. It has since changed its name to Copernicus. According to the ESA (2013d),

> Copernicus is the most ambitious Earth observation programme to date. It will provide accurate, timely and easily accessible information to improve the management of the environment, understand and mitigate the effects of climate change and ensure civil security.

Data received from satellites and ground-based information will be coordinated, analysed and prepared for end-users, including the 'security' community.

Originally, its main purpose was in the area of disaster prevention and protection of the environment, Copernicus has increasingly become a typical dual-use project with military dimensions (Slijper 2012). As such the system of systems is set to become an important source of information to support military operations:

> Reflecting on current political dynamics, GMES stakeholders are now taking initiatives to strengthen the 'S' in GMES by creating synergies between civilian and military actors. The 2008 EU Council Conclusions on GMES call on the Commission to foster the implementation of GMES security related services to support the related European Union policies. Border surveillance, maritime surveillance and support to EU External Action have been identified as priority areas for action.
>
> (EC/ESA 2010)

## Supporting the space industry

The space industry has grown rapidly over the past decade, with Europe's space industry concentrated in a few major companies, including Thales-Alenia Space and Airbus Defence and Space (formerly EADS Astrium). The industry is represented in Europe through the ASD (AeroSpace and Defence Industries Association of Europe) lobby umbrella, which took part in the Panel of Experts on Space and Security. Its 2005 report stressed the need to give priority to the security applications of space and called for new projects 'in order to maintain the level of European industry at a competitive state of the art' (Oikonomou 2007).

That exactly has happened over the past years, and has been re-established by the Commission's July 2013 Communication 'Towards a more competitive and efficient defence and security sector'. Despite financial constraints, the Commission proposes an action plan to make the military industry more efficient and competitive, emphasising the importance of space technology. Under the header 'Space and Defence', the Communication reads: 'Although some space capabilities have to remain under exclusive national and/or military control, a number of areas exist where increased synergies between civilian and defence activities will reduce costs and improve efficiency' (EC 2013b).

The action plan outlines three areas considered key to such cooperation, including the protection of space infrastructure (such as Galileo and Copernicus) through Space, Surveillance and Tracking (SST). The Commission proposes to support the emergence of a European SST service built on existing national assets, and which 'should be available to public, commercial, civilian, military operators and authorities' (EC 2013b).

A second area is Satellite Communications (SATCOM) used by military and civilian security actors, where the 'Commission will act to overcome the fragmentation of demand for security SATCOM. In particular, building on the EDA's experience, the Commission will encourage the pooling of European military and security commercial SATCOM demand' (EC 2013b). A month earlier, during the Paris Airshow, the EDA had organised a seminar, proposing that European countries pool their Military Satellite Communication (MILSATCOM) assets (UPI 2013), as part of the wider EDA agenda on Pooling and Sharing (P&S).

Finally, the Commission considers building an EU high-resolution satellite capability as key to support the common security and military policies.

> EU access to these capacities is crucial to perform early warning, timely decision making, advanced planning and improved conduct of EU crisis response actions both in the civilian and military domains. [...] The European Commission together with the European External Action Service and the EDA will explore the possibility to develop progressively new imaging capabilities to support CFSP and CSDP missions and operations.
>
> (EC 2013b)

Regular meetings and events, where officials from industry and European institutes can exchange views and ideas, function as back up for such policy support. Besides previous mentioned occasions, one of such key events is the annual conference on EU space policy, the fifth of which was held in Brussels in January 2013. At that event European Commission vice-president Tajani, also Commissioner for Industry and Entrepreneurship, stressed that space played a vital role in strengthening the EU's competitiveness. 'Space activities are a source of highly skilled jobs, bring innovation, open new business opportunities and improve the well-being and safety of citizens', he said (*European GNSS Agency* 2013). Tajani added that a European Commission communication on space industrial policy would be published soon and would propose a series of actions to fulfil the space industry's potential to drive innovation and generate growth.

In practice industry appears either less convinced or unable to reap the fruits planted with EU support. Speaking in Brussels to European industry

252   *F. Slijper*

representatives, a EU official said with a sense of understatement: 'Market development activities, along with policies, are fundamental if we want to capture the benefits of all this EU investment. There are big opportunities out there that we are not yet fully exploiting' (Guttierez 2013). According to EU figures, there should be €90 billion in benefits to be reaped by industry as a result of Europe's €11 billion investment in Galileo. Such data put in doubt other claims of potentially huge economic opportunities, such as the 83,000 jobs Copernicus would create in Europe by 2030, as boasted by Commissioner Tajani at the European Space Solutions conference, another annual business-bureaucracy get-together (EC 2012b).

Nevertheless it is apparently lucrative enough for Europe's industry to get involved in lucrative low-risk, subsidised space projects with military and security dimensions. Exemplary is the leaked US cable quoting German OHB-System's chief-executive Berry Smutny as telling US diplomats: 'I think Galileo is a stupid idea that primarily serves French interests', and, in particular, French military interests (cited in Amos 2011). He was further reported as saying that Galileo was 'doomed for failure' or would 'have to undergo drastic scalebacks for survival'. OHB is part of the consortium that builds Galileo's spacecraft. Although Smutny has denied the cable's contents, OHB removed him from his post after the revelation.

## The EDA in space

Space is part of the EDA's Capability Development Plan and is labelled as a 'core enabler for defence-related capabilities' and of direct relevance to a wide range of military operations (EDA 2011a). Oikonomou (2012) distinguishes the EDA's involvement into: (1) project development; (2) collaborative projects; and (3) definition of strategic requirements and orientation. The EDA has been involved in a number of projects in this field, mostly on space-based imaging, SSA, UAS (Unmanned Aerial Systems) and space, and SATCOM.

### *Space-based earth observation: MUSIS*

In 2009 the EDA agreed with the governments of Belgium, Germany, Greece, France, Italy and Spain to make their MUSIS (Multinational Space-based Imaging System) initiative an EDA project, setting up a procurement unit and liaising with the ESA and the Commission (Tigner 2009). Poland and Sweden have since decided to join the MUSIS programme.

MUSIS is also an example of growing EDA cooperation with OCCAR, as a so-called 'federated common programme' under the auspices of OCCAR (EDA 2012d). In addition, the EDA also represents the MUSIS nations' interests in any institutional forum where defence and security issues related to space capabilities are discussed and synergies between civil and military EU Space capabilities are addressed (EDA 2012f).

MUSIS was initiated by these six countries to ensure continuity of some of their military space-based imaging capabilities beyond the current generation systems (EDA 2012f). MUSIS is based around a federation of systems: space components (optical and radar) and a common ground user segment to access any space component. The €1.3 billion system is scheduled for completion by 2014–2015. In 2009 then EDA Head Javier Solana said on MUSIS:

> Space-based related assets are critical to improve European military capabilities, including for information gathering. The approved project will be critical to ensure this capability in the longer-term and I welcome very much the initiative of the six EU Member States to bring it to EDA.
>
> (EDA 2009a)

The EDA has been seeking opportunities to connect with the Copernicus programme and the ESA's European Data Relay System (EDRS), from the idea that future generations of earth observation systems are likely characterised by large heterogeneity in terms of ownership (national, bilateral, European), type (civil, dual-use, military) as well as assets (satellites, UAS, planes). The EDA and the ESA currently run a project aimed at networking earth observation systems to maximise their overall performance in the future. Within this 'System of Systems' concept, as it is called, the EDA focuses on military and dual-use systems and the ESA on civil and dual-use ones (EDA 2011b). Together with the European Council and the Commission they documented 'Civil–military synergies in the field of earth observation' (EU/EDA/CSG/ESA Joint Task Force 2010).

### Space situational awareness

Surveillance of space has been a priority of the ESA since it started working on defining a SSA system in 2008, with its military needs specified by the EDA (De Selding 2008). In this area there is also cooperation with the US Pentagon (ESA 2013b). 'SSA was conceived as a dual-use program from the beginning, meant to serve institutional, commercial and scientific end-users, but most importantly military end-users' (Nardon and Venet 2011).

Built into an expanded network it would give Europe a space-monitoring capability alongside that of the US and Russia. According to space journalist Amy Butler (2007),

> SSA refers to understanding what objects are in space and what capabilities they have. Accurate SSA is required to know for certain if a satellite's operations have been intentionally affected by an adversary. Talk of SSA and space control only began to show up in speeches

254   *F. Slijper*

given by senior political officials and the uppermost echelons of the military brass after China destroyed one of its own aging weather satellites in a dazzling anti-satellite test in January 2007.

It has since has become more palatable to openly discuss the issues of space situational awareness and the more politically sensitive areas of offensive and defensive space operations, according to the American general William Shelton (Butler 2007).

Practically, in an EU context, there are a number of hurdles on the road. As a German official put it: 'You have to think about how this would be organised and who provides what products to whom, and then you get into the very sensitive questions of data policy and governance' (Svitak 2013). The Commission's earlier mentioned SST support programme is meant to contribute to a more comprehensive EU SSA capability (European Parliament 2013).

### Satellites for UAS operations

The EDA and the ESA work together on the role of satellite communications and satellite navigation within the wider infrastructure for UAS operations (EDA 2012e). A 2009–2010 project on command and control over satellites was their first joint project (EDA 2012b), followed in 2011 by a common demonstration project (Demonstration of Satellites enabling the Insertion of RPAS in Europe, DeSIRE), as part of a 'Joint Roadmap for UAS' (EDA 2012c). DeSIRE has undertaken a series of test flights to demonstrate the role of satellite communications in UAS operations in civil and military airspace, as current legislation does not provide a harmonised framework in Europe for enabling them to fly in civil airspace.

Both the EDA and the ESA are also involved in another UAS related project: Emerging System Concepts for UAS Command and Control via Satellite (ESPRIT). Thales Alenia Space won a contract in 2011 to lead a study seeking satellite communications solutions for UAS. ESPRIT focuses on providing communication capacity for command-and control links to military UAS flying through civilian airspace.

It is slightly confusing that the EDA is doing similar work with the Commission in a separate project. A workshop in February 2012 concluded though 'that more needs to be done, and preferably in a coordinated way, if Europe wants to develop civil and military UAS capacity' (EDA 2012a). Apparently that is easier said than done. Adding to the confusion, the Commission-initiated 'European RPAS Steering Group', also including EDA and ESA officials, as well as industry umbrella group ASD, launched its 'European RPAS Roadmap' at the Paris Airshow in June 2013 (Van Blyenburgh 2013). RPAS here stands for Remotely Piloted Aerial Systems (RPAS), which can be considered as similar to UAS.

## EDA's inroads into space   255

### Military Satellite Communications (MILSATCOM)

The UK, France, Germany, Italy and Spain are currently Europe's only nations operating MILSATCOM. With these assets all due for replacement between 2018–2025 the EDA has embarked on a project to stimulate P&S on a Europe-wide basis through leasing use of communication satellites. The EDA's European Satellite Communication Procurement Cell (ESCPC) has been specifically set up for that purpose. The ESCPC was launched to enable collective purchases of commercial SATCOM services, saving money over individual contracts. 'This is a test case for the military in the satellite sector', said an EDA official, 'But it has to prove its political and economic worth first' (Tigner 2012a). If it proves to be an effective instrument the EDA hopes it will grow into bigger collective purchases, such as military satellite hardware. Exceptionally for the UK in EDA projects, it plays a leading role in the ESCPC, 'due to the way it has consolidated its commercial SATCOM service through the public-private Skynet 5 partnership' (Tigner 2012a).

### Micro-satellite cluster technology

Probably the oldest EDA-led space technology project was around 'micro-satellite cluster technology', aiming at lower-cost satellites for situational awareness. This initiative was inherited from the Western European Armaments Group (WEAG), which started it in 2004 and transferred it to the EDA in 2006; it was completed in May 2007. A proposal for a follow-up project has been prepared (EDA 2012g).

## Conclusion

Until recently the EU used to emphasise the civilian potential, while disguising the military dimensions of Europe's space initiatives. However, since space has emerged as a key EU policy area and a cornerstone of Europe's security and defence policies, these military dimensions have come more clearly to the fore. The Treaty of Lisbon envisions the progressive development of Europe's military capabilities, taking forward Europe's space policy, as well as nurturing the defence industrial base. It is no coincidence that the EDA – itself a product of the Treaty of Lisbon process – plays a crucial role in fulfilling these agendas (Oikonomou 2012).

Though tangible results have so far been limited to setting up project groups, writing road maps and executing small-scale demonstrations, the EDA functions as a useful bridgehead connecting with both national military organisations, European institutions and industry. On the other hand, despite dominant rhetoric on exploiting synergies, many different structural problems (political, financial, organisational and other) have hampered progress on a larger scale, which more ambitious EU visionaries

256   *F. Slijper*

might have hoped for. With space a relatively new aspect of EU military policies – themselves a relatively pristine area – this is not surprising.

Especially in times of economic problems there seems to be a strong case for increased cooperation in the area of (military) space projects. Without doubt, the space industry employs many highly skilled people, contributing to innovation and economic progress. However, the economic arguments raised to justify extremely expensive projects so far have hardly been backed up by facts. Galileo is the clearest such example.

The emerging military dimensions of the EU's space policy fit in a global pattern. Space has become inextricably linked with military use and warfare, with Global Positioning System (GPS) – guided missiles and satellite information used for war planning just two examples of what has become the norm. A few years ago a US Air Force Major stated that 'NATO is now fighting its first space war', referring to the war in Afghanistan, supported by satellite communications, GPS-guided weapons and command and control systems (Barrie 2008). Europe's push to jump on that very same train, setting up its own navigation and surveillance satellites with the very same potential, has made it part of the growing risk of a highly militarised space. Without an answer yet to the growing risks of rivalry in space, this could eventually lead to military confrontation.

It is doubtful whether EU citizens are well enough aware of these implications. Against that background the issue of corporate influence on decision-making, as well as the lack of transparency in such processes should top agendas aimed at reforming the EU. Without such change it risks political backlash sooner or later, undermining the very existence of the Union. With all relevant European institutions – most notably the Commission, the EDA and the ESA – narrowly involved in such a contentious area, the expected growth of Europe's military footstep in space deserves close and critical scrutiny.

## References

Amos, J. (2011) 'Wikileaks: "Galileo boss" Smutny removed over cable row', *BBC News*, 17 January 2011.

Barrie, D. (2008) 'Empty Space', *Aviation Week and Space Technology*, 22 September 2008.

Butler, A. (2007) 'Bush Memo Orders Space Situational Awareness', *Aerospace Daily and Defense Report*, 12 October 2007.

Congrex (2008) *Agenda, 'Critical Space Technologies for European Strategic Non-Dependence'*. Online. Available at www.congrex.nl/08c37/agenda.asp (accessed 2 September 2013).

Council of the European Union (2013) 'Draft Council Conclusions on "Establishing appropriate relations between the EU and the European Space Agency"', 11 February 2013.

De Selding, P. (2013) 'Resolution Underscores Complications in ESA-EU Partnership', *Space News*, 19 February 2013.

De Selding, P. (2012) 'Battle Brewing between ESA and EU over Space Policy, Budget Authority', *Space News*, 30 November 2012.

De Selding, P. (2008) 'France To Keep Pushing for New EU Space Policy', *Defense News*, 14 July 2008.

EU/EDA/CSG/ESA Joint Task Force (2010) *Civil–Military Synergies in the Field of Earth Observation*, 26 November 2010.

Euractiv.com (2012) 'Galileo', 28 May 2012. Online. Available at www.euractiv.com/science/galileo/article-117496?display=normal (accessed 3 September 2013).

EC (European Commission) (2014) 'Seventh Framework Programme (FP7)', 5 May 2014.

EC (European Commission) (2013a) 'Bringing Space down to Earth (second part)', 5 February 2013.

EC (European Commission) (2013b) 'Towards a More Competitive and Efficient Defence and Security Sector', 27 July 2013.

EC (European Commission) (2013c) 'European Space Policy', 13 August 2013.

EC (European Commission) (2013d) 'Space and security', 13 August 2013.

EC (European Commission) (2012a) 'Establishing Appropriate Relations between the EU and the European Space Agency', 14 November 2012.

EC (European Commission) (2012b) 'GMES: Good for Environment, Good for Jobs!' 3 December 2012.

EC (European Commission) (2007) 'European Space Policy', 26 April 2007.

EC (European Commission) (2005) 'Report of the Panel of Experts on Space and Security', March 2005.

EC (European Commission) (2003) 'A Secure Europe in a Better World – European Security Strategy', 12 December 2003.

EC/ESA (2010) 'Space and Security', February 2010.

EC/ESA/EDA (2012) 'Excerpt from Critical Space Technologies for European Strategic Non-Dependence – List of Urgent Actions for 2012/2013', June 2012.

EDA (European Defence Agency) (2013) 'EDA-ESA Bilateral at ESA's European Space Research and Technology Centre', 17 July 2013.

EDA (European Defence Agency) (2012a) '5th Joint Workshop on R&D on Unmanned Aerial Systems Hosted by EDA', 13 February 2012.

EDA (European Defence Agency) (2012b) 'ESA/EDA 3rd User/Stakeholder Workshop on Unmanned Aircraft System', 8 March 2012.

EDA (European Defence Agency) (2012c) 'Third EDA/ESA Workshop User/Stakeholder Workshop on Unmanned Aircraft Systems', 14 March 2012.

EDA (European Defence Agency) (2012d) 'EDA & OCCAR Build Links, Seeking Efficiencies through Cooperation', 27 July 2012.

EDA (European Defence Agency) (2012e) 'ESA-EDA Demonstration on the Use of Satellites for UAS Operations', 23 August 2012.

EDA (European Defence Agency) (2012f) 'Multinational Space-based Imaging System', 23 August 2012.

EDA (European Defence Agency) (2012g) 'Micro-satellite Cluster Technology', 24 August 2012.

EDA (European Defence Agency) (2012h) 'Interaction between Defence and Wider EU Policies', 19 November 2012.

EDA (European Defence Agency) (2011a) 'EDA and Space – Fact Sheet', 17 June 2011.

258   *F. Slijper*

EDA (European Defence Agency) (2011b) 'Kick-off of the Networking Earth Observation Systems (NEOS) Project at EDA', 9 December 2011.

EDA (European Defence Agency) (2009a) 'New EDA Project on Space-Based Earth Surveillance System', 5 March 2009.

EDA (European Defence Agency) (2009b) 'Space for Security and Defence: Towards Increased Synergies among European Stakeholders', 21 September 2009.

EDA (European Defence Agency) (2006) 'An Initial Long-Term Vision for European Defence Capability and Capacity Needs', 3 October 2006.

EDA (European Defence Agency) (undated) 'Civ–Mil Synergies', Online. Available at www.eda.europa.eu/aboutus/how-we-do-it/Civmil (accessed 26 August 2013).

European GNSS Agency (2013) 'Tajani: Space Boosts European Jobs and Growth', 7 February 2013.

European Parliament (2013) *Working Document on the Proposal for a Decision of the European Parliament and of the Council Establishing a Space Surveillance and Tracking Support Programme*, 12 August 2013.

ESA (European Space Agency) (2013a) 'Budget 2013 as Presented during DG Press Conference', 24 January 2013.

ESA (European Space Agency) (2013b) 'About SSA', 1 April 2013. Online. Available at www.esa.int/Our_Activities/Operations/Space_Situational_Awareness/About_SSA (accessed 3 September 2013).

ESA (European Space Agency) (2013c) 'Claude-France Arnould, Chief Executive of the European Defence Agency: "Space is Now Embedded in Practically Everything we do" ', 22 July 2013.

ESA (European Space Agency) (2013d) 'Copernicus Overview', 13 August 2013. Online. Available at www.esa.int/Our_Activities/Observing_the_Earth/Copernicus/Overview3 (accessed 2 September 2013).

ESA (European Space Agency) (2012) 'European Milestones', 24 January 2012. Online. Available at www.esa.int/About_Us/Welcome_to_ESA/European_milestones (accessed 21 August 2013).

ESA (European Space Agency) (2010) 'Conference Highlights Deepening Connection between Space and Security', 11 March 2010.

ESA (European Space Agency) (2008) 'Critical Space Technologies for European Strategic Non-Dependence', 19 September 2008.

Guttierez, P. (2013) 'EU Calls Out European Industry on GNSS Opportunities', 18 June 2013. Online. Available at www.insidegnss.com/node/3605 (accessed 10 December 2014).

Morsillo, G. (2010) *ESA AND SECURITY – Increasing Responsiveness for Civil and Security Actors. The Space Dimension in Support of Crisis Management*, 9 February 2010.

Nardon, L. and Venet, C. (2011) 'Space Weather and NEO's in the European Space Policy', *Actuelles de l'Ifri*, August 2011.

Oikonomou, I. (2012) 'The European Defence Agency and EU Military Space Policy: Whose Space Odyssey?', *Space Policy*, 28: 102–109.

Oikonomou, I. (2007) *The European Arms Industry as a European Security and Defence Policy Actor: A Historical Materialist Theory of EU Military Integration*, unpublished PhD Thesis, University of Wales Aberystwyth.

Slijper, F. (2012) 'Space: The High Ground of the European Union's Emerging

EDA's inroads into space   259

Military Policies', in K. Gouliamos and C. Kassimeris (eds) *The Marketing of War in the Age of Neo-Militarism*, New York: Routledge: 145–169.

Slijper, F. (2005) *The Emerging EU Military–Industrial Complex: Arms Industry Lobbying in Brussels*, Amsterdam: TNI and Campagne tegen Wapenhandel.

Smid, H. (2007) 'Europese Militaire Ruimtevaart: Het taboe doorbroken?', *Ruimtevaart*, 3.

Sowa, A. (2011) *Keynote Speech at EFC JIP-CBRN Workshop*, 15 September 2011.

Svitak, A. (2013) 'Eye on the Sky', *Aviation Week and Space Technology*, 5/12 August 2013.

Tigner, B. (2014a) 'EDA to Boost Defence Industry Access to EU Structural Funds', *Jane's Defence Weekly*, 1 January 2014.

Tigner, B. (2014b) 'Europe Eyes Benefits of Direct Funding of R&D', *Jane's Defence Weekly*, 19 March 2014.

Tigner, B. (2012a) 'EDA Set to Ink Key SATCOM Arrangement', *Jane's Defence Weekly*, 18 July 2012.

Tigner, B. (2012b) 'EU Must Focus on Cyberspace, Officials Say', *Jane's Defence Weekly*, 31 October 2012.

Tigner, B. (2009) 'EDA Set to Oversee MUSIS Collaboration', *Jane's International Defence Review*, April 2009.

Tigner, B. (2007) 'Space Policy Rises on EU Radar', *Defense News*, 7 May 2007.

UPI (2013) *EDA Proposes Wider-Sharing of SATCOM Assets*, 21 June 2013.

Van Blyenburgh, P. (2013) 'European RPAS Roadmap is Published and Available Online', *UAS Vision*, 24 June 2013.

Vassalos, Y. (2010) 'Expert Groups: Letting Corporate Interests Set the Agenda?', in H. Burley, W. Dinan, K. Haar, O. Hoedeman and E. Wesselius (eds) *Bursting the Brussels Bubble*, Brussels: Alliance for Lobbying Transparency and Ethics Regulation in the EU.

# Conclusion

## Future trajectories and a new research agenda

*Nikolaos Karampekios and Iraklis Oikonomou*

### Future trajectories

This edited volume has attempted to analyse the European Defence Agency (EDA), as the leading European armaments agency, ten years after its foundation. And, if there is a common thread that runs through the contributions to this volume, it is the idea that European Union (EU) armaments policy in general, and the operation of the EDA in particular, are replete with contradictions. The persistence of these contradictions renders locating and elaborating the future trajectories of the Agency and the policy it serves a rather difficult task. What the EDA will look like, or what its aims and objectives will be in the next ten years should be the focus of another volume; however, it is worth delineating the factors that may influence its development, not as another theoretical exercise, but rather as a theoretical account with serious practical implications.

In attempting to forecast what the future has in store for the fascinating story, or stories, told in this volume, a range of parameters have to be taken into account, which have the potential to influence any given trajectory, either towards the EDA becoming the dominant institution, setting and managing entirely the conceptualisation-to-production process of EU armaments policy – and thus 'weaponising' the Common Security and Defence Policy (CSDP) – or towards the EDA dissolving in favour of other alternatives. These parameters include: the shift of the United States' (US) strategic priorities and the future shaping of the transatlantic relationship; the future growth of the European economy and its capacity to sustain a large defence-oriented segment of the economy; the potential rise of Euroscepticism and other forms of critique against the European consolidation of armaments policy; the heightening of conflict within the European continent and the fate of CSDP; the unfolding of the complex relations among core Member States, namely the United Kingdom, France and Germany, and their urge to enter into bi-, tri-, or multi-lateral armaments initiatives that run counter to the logic of the EDA; and, finally, the potential for further industrial consolidation.

*Conclusion*  261

To begin with, the US has been undergoing a major shift on its global geopolitical and foreign policy priorities. The 'strategic pivot' or rebalancing, launched at the end of the previous decade, is based on the assumption that a large portion of the political and economic history of the twenty-first century will be written in the Asia-Pacific region. The geopolitical dynamism and economic growth of China and the need to uphold existing bilateral commitments has streamlined US interests to this particular area. Having exited Afghanistan after a more than decade-long engagement, US policy-makers will attempt to 'pivot' by drawing from existing resources situated in other regions of the world, rather than committing extra ones. This conveys a message the Europeans are sure not to miss: that the projected vacuum will have to be filled by the Europeans who are called upon to assume responsibility for the collective security of their continent, in addition to being able to project, or co-participate in related tasks in distant theaters. The EDA will be pivotal for developing the tools necessary for taking up those tasks. The same is true if one follows the scenario of the intensification of transatlantic competition politically and economically. The quest for European technological and military autonomy relative to the US and the interrelated quest for the competitive survival of the European arms industry vis-à-vis its US counterpart has been and will be a constant source for the strengthening of the role of the EDA.

The issue of economic growth in Europe has the potential to shape the EDA's future as well. Given the sluggish – at present – growth rate, where to spend public funds or for which public domains to place industrial orders will become an issue of acute political contention. Supporters of further defence policy federalisation will find it increasingly difficult to advocate higher EU spending in a context of austerity. Increases in Research and Development (R&D) expenditure for military purposes may appear a luxury, not only to the eyes of the European peoples, but also to other, productive sectors of the economy. However, there can be no clear-cut answer regarding the potential for a militarisation of the economy as a response to the current crisis, and whether such a response shall utilise national or EU/EDA resources. Dan and Ron Smith (1983: 100–101) have provided an excellent reminder of the complexity of such a question and, in fact, of every question relating to military spending:

> Military spending is a complex and contradictory process. It erodes what it maintains; it buttresses what it undermines. No simple functionalism or economic determinism can be adequate to explain it, either in general or in detail. Instead, to explain the economic phenomenon of military spending it is necessary to refer to the social, ideological and political fabric of advanced capitalism. Its complexities and contradictions derive from the complexities and contradictions of the social system which produces it and in which it functions.

Furthermore, 'domestic' political developments, in the form of the rise of political forces capable of mobilising the European peoples against further concentration of power at the hands of EU or quasi-EU institutions, may also prove significant. Occupying a notable number of seats, not only in national parliaments but also in the European Parliament, Eurosceptic political parties increasingly question the validity of the European experiment, exploiting a range of issues from the EU-wide anaemic economic growth to un-elected executive EU authorities, and counter-proposing a return to the nation-state as a most welcome answer. While the issue of empowering Europe militarily has not become an issue of contention by those parties – only because a multiplicity of other issues to choose from are so easily available – this is certain to be so in the future. Organisations/agencies that stand against the return to the nation-state and are committed to the deepening of EU military collaboration are sure to face stiff resistance. Coming from a different starting point, i.e. that the EU should preserve a peaceful character and refrain from militarisation, similar criticism could be voiced by political forces of the Left that are critical of the EU's military empowerment.

On the other hand, public opinion findings concerning a common foreign, security and defence policy of the EU indicate a constant flow of public support. Not only do a majority of citizens stand in favour of a common EU foreign, and defence and security policies – at 64 and 74 per cent respectively – (European Commission 2013a: 85), but they also support 'enabling such a policy to face up to international crises' (28 per cent, ranked fourth out of a total of 12 policy areas) (European Parliament 2012: 4). Given that the EDA is such an enabler, one may expect EU policy-makers to capitalise upon it in order to garner public support for further integration.

Then, there is the issue of war returning in the European continent. The Russian-Ukrainian conflict is telling in this respect. Not since the 1990s, with the war in Yugoslavia that ended in the country going six ways, has a conflict revealed, in a realist sense, that the European near-abroad environment is violent and harsh. Recognising that countries do have national interests, which they quite literally can fight for, is a sharp reminder of a past, not so long ago, which Europe thought it could skip. Military integration, a stage for which the EDA is critical, would be further complicated given the still-open question of how to fuse diverging national interests into a common European one.

The need to produce a general interest out of the several partial, societal and national ones takes us to CSDP as the overarching project that fuelled the legitimacy of the Agency's establishment. The imperative of European military–industrial competitiveness would have not dominated the practice and discourse of EU institutions without the prior existence of CSDP, aiming at the projection of EU politico-military power abroad. Through CSDP, the partial, sectoral interests were translated into a general interest, anchoring the vision of a strong European arms industry into a broader project of power projection and strategic autonomy. The development of CSDP is indistinguishable from the development of EU armaments cooperation. The dichotomy between the 'strategic' (operations, capabilities) and 'economic' (procurement, budgets) aspects of CSDP is relevant solely for academic and analytical purposes. Procurement, R&D, budgetary developments all touch upon both the strategic and the socio-economic nature of European military policy. Moreover, the overcoming of different national standards and operational requirements among Member States belongs to both areas. Armaments cooperation is possible and meaningful only when similar operational requirements are needed, and CSDP has been the main homogenising force of these requirements. To cut a long story short: CSDP has been a prerequisite of EU-wide armaments cooperation; and the future direction of this policy – its strengthening or weakening, its coherence or fragmentation – will prove key to the direction of armaments cooperation, especially through the EDA.

Another factor casting its shadow on the EDA is related to the aspirations of Member States. Here, the same Member States that spearheaded EDA's foundation have launched a number of initiatives that go against the role of EDA. This list of bi-, tri- or multi-lateral initiatives on capability initiatives include the Anglo-French Defence Cooperation, the Weimar Triangle of France, Germany and Poland, and the Ghent initiative on Pooling and Sharing. Whether such initiatives discredit the role of the EDA, and signal a return to country-to-country type of agreements, is to be seen. Yet, these signs exhibit an imperviousness to the progress achieved by the EDA, and indeed nullify the financial and other resources already spent in the latter – if national governments do not wish to be portrayed as inconsiderate of citizens, tax payer's money should also be wisely allocated.

Finally, the industrial factor should not be underestimated. Due to the transformation in the structures of arms production – through privatisation and international consolidation – EU arms-industrial actorness acquired an internationalised scope, particularly visible since the late 1990s, and helped build the conditions that allowed for the setting-up of the EDA. However, the internationalisation of European military–industrial capital has been partial and incomplete, generating new contradictions between and within different fractions of arms-industrial capital. Crucially, it did not lead to the emergence of genuine transnational mergers, not even in the case of EADS. Students of EU armaments policy do use the term 'European arms industry', but this is just an ideotypical abstraction for analytical purposes, since in practice no single European arms industry exists. In addition, the effects of internationalisation have been mediated by the continued dominance of state authority within the EU when it comes to defence matters, and the lack of a genuine supranational, EU-wide, state-like arrangement

## 264  N. Karampekios and I. Oikonomou

for the management of military–industrial affairs. The persistence of these conditions could compromise the power and effectiveness of the Agency.

## Towards a new research agenda

This book has already pointed out certain topics that may prove fertile ground for further research. For example, Chapter 4 addressed the range of capability development projects as prioritised by EDA, by offering an up-to-date account of the progress – and hindrances. Providing a systematic determination of each project's worth and merit, also in relation to its technological spillover potential to other industrial, i.e. civilian, fields, could well be such a topic. This is linked to topics neighbouring those addressed in Chapter 6, such as smart specialisation and defence-related regional clusters. Seeking to create economies of scale with a strong innovation potential, EDA will have to touch more on the actual synergies between civil and military sectors. This brings us to a third interesting topic, EDA's relations with the Commission, a theme addressed in Chapter 10. Issues of institutional turf war notwithstanding, evaluating the security- and space-related projects in the 7th European Framework Programme for Research and Development (FP7) in terms of their technological output can be used as a stop-gap measure of the pending shortfalls of EDA's European Capability Action Plan. This is equally true for Horizon 2020, where the EDA and the Commission are actively engaging in tailoring in tandem the two research themes (security, space), as well as holding discussions about incorporating defence as a distinct R&D priority (European Commission, 2013b). The degree to which the two institutional actors will cooperate, as well as whether the EDA, capitalising on its role as an armaments' agency, can shape the outcomes to fit its own agenda, remains to be seen.

Concerning the military use of space (Chapter 14), the EDA is making headway. For example, efforts to pool and share the next generation of governmental satcom assets (European Satellite Communication Procurement Cell (ESCPC), now EU Satcom Market), and set the tone for the future agenda (Post-2025 Satcom Capabilities Agenda) have become EDA's priorities. Yet these issues are destined to cause frictions between the EDA and national governments. How the EDA's pro-integrative point of view in satellite communications will cope against a national, strategically autonomous view is an open question. In terms of pooling resources and managing purchases, something addressed in Chapters 5 and 11, the more countries will start to realise that economies of scale can be achieved through the EDA, as opposed to going it alone, the more deals like the one with SAAB Dynamics for the supply of the 84mm anti-tank ammunition will be delegated to be managed by the EDA (Fiorenza 2014). Whether this economic assertion will go down easily in every such occasion is an open question. Perhaps the EDA should quantitatively

Conclusion 265

evaluate such practices – corroborating its case, also, with the use of counter-factual examples. Lastly, drawing from Chapters 7 and 13, offsets will persist being a thorny issue, in the sense that scrapping their use on the EU level will conflict with the fact that a number of domestic defence industrial bases are financially – almost exclusively – sustained by such practices. Providing empirically based assessments of their impact is needed in combination with the study of the degree to which the formation of a European defence equipment market is proceeding, inside and outside the EDA.

Turning to the more general topics that stem from an emerging, EDA-related research agenda, one is offered a broad menu of choice. EU armaments policy – as is the case with any other policy of the EU – is influenced by certain interests, mediated by certain institutional actors, and framed through certain ideas and concepts. These interests, actors and ideas deserve further attention, as they are unfolding hand-in-hand with the preferences of the Member States. Indeed, the interaction between states, non-state actors – such as firms, the Agency, and other EU institutions provides an environment that is full of challenges for the researcher as well as the policy-maker, irrespective of his/her theoretical predisposition.

To put it simply: the EDA and EU armaments policy are not just about advanced weapons, detailed technical specifications, weird acronyms and complex technologies. The way the EU and its Member States will decide to handle their armaments affairs in the future, including military spending, capabilities development, R&D, weapons procurement, the military–industrial base, and the strategic orientation and priorities that armaments will be called upon to serve conceptually, is a profoundly political, strategic and ideological question. If more students of European political economy and security decide to tackle this question, in the direction of safeguarding global peace and prosperity, then this book will have served its purpose.

## References

European Commission (2013a) *Standard Eurobarometer 79, Spring 2013; TNS Opinion and Social*, Brussels/Luxembourg: European Commission.

European Commission (2013b) 'EU, National and Industry Officials Mull how to Promote Stronger R&D Links between Civil Society and Defence Sectors', *News Report*, 22 March 2013, Brussels/Luxembourg: European Commission.

European Parliament (2012) *Special Eurobarometer; Parlemeter EB78.2*, Brussels/Luxembourg: European Parliament.

Fiorenza, N. (2014) 'European Defence Agency Pools Carl-Gustav Ammo Procurement', *Aviation Week*, 9 July 2014.

Keck. Z. (2014) 'Europe Needs to Get Serious about its Defence', *National Interest*, 24 June 2014.

Smith, D. and Smith, R. (1983) *The Economics of Militarism*, London: Pluto Press.

# Index

7th European Framework Programme for Research and Development (FP7) 114

A400M 140, 150, 151
AeroSpace and Defence Industries Association of Europe (ASD) 37, 38, 53, 56, 176, 177, 244, 250, 254
Airbus Defence and Space 250
Air-to-Air Refuelling (AAR) 99, 191
Alliance security dilemma 6, 156, 159, 160, 164–5, 167
Arnould, Claude-France 248
Article 346, 89, 122, 125, 131, 157, 181, 195, 213, 234–5, 237–8
atlanticist 41, 71, 73, 194, 198–9, 204

BAE Systems 31, 46, 53–6, 151, 163, 232
balance of power 6, 158–61
balance of threat 159, 162
bandwagoning 156, 159–60, 162, 167
battlegroups 4, 7, 21, 23, 66, 70, 164, 191
Belgium 88, 96, 112, 199, 201, 214, 233, 252
bilateralism 166, 197
Britain 5, 17, 21, 32, 139, 140, 143–52, 157, 159–61, 165
Budgetary Committee of the Bundestag 163–5
Bundeswehr 164, 167

Canada 75, 145, 246
Capabilities, Competences and Competitiveness (3Cs) 211–12, 216
Capability Development Plan (CDP) xvii, 47, 72, 94, 107, 185, 197
Capability Development Mechanism (CDM) 74

capability gap(s) 65, 67, 69, 98, 149, 174, 180, 183, 185, 192, 194, 196, 198, 203, 212, 248
Capability Technology Areas (CapTech) 103, 105, 107–11
Catherine Ashton 32, 37
CDU/CSU Bundestagsfraktion 166
Chancellor's Office 166
Code of Conduct on Offsets 7, 35, 122, 125, 180, 182, 225, 232, 237
collaborative procurement 6, 49, 85–6, 94, 123, 132, 165
Common Foreign and Security Policy (CFSP) 12, 66, 208, 229
Common Security and Defence Policy (CSDP) xv, 1, 27, 39, 46, 65, 94, 102–3, 140, 156, 192, 242, 244, 260
consolidation xvi, 6, 27, 35, 43, 45, 48, 52–3, 58, 88, 130, 146–7, 151, 195, 211–13, 215, 217, 220, 222, 229, 232, 260
constructivism 27–8, 36
convergence 6, 18, 23, 51, 78, 90, 93, 115, 141, 146–7, 156, 160, 162, 193
Copernicus/GMES 249–53
crisis management xvii, 18, 20, 31–4, 65–8, 70, 87, 89, 174, 200, 245
critical constructivism 27–8, 36

de Maizière, Thomas 164–6
Defence and Security Procurement Directive (Directive 2009/81/EC) 5, 7, 225, 238
defence budget 7, 31, 33–4, 39, 73, 79–80, 86–7, 105, 120, 140, 145, 155, 157, 160, 173–4, 183, 185, 191, 194–5, 198, 216, 218, 226, 237
defence industry 7, 30, 35, 37, 43, 48, 54, 56, 74, 86, 88–90, 107, 116, 144,

162–3, 165, 195, 199, 207, 209, 213, 215, 219–20, 228, 230, 233, 236, 238, 244

Defence Ministers 21, 23, 50, 70, 88, 148, 162, 203

defence offsets (offsets) i, 5, 7, 35, 122, 125, 126–9, 134, 180, 182, 184, 213, 217, 225–38

defence sovereignty 194, 198–200, 202, 204

Defence Technological and Industrial Base (DTIB) 7, 38, 163, 207, 209–11, 213–16, 219–21

discourse/discourse analysis 2, 4, 27–32, 34, 36–9, 141–2, 144, 146, 209, 262

Dordain, Jean-Jacques 248

dual-use 59, 109, 113–14, 116, 172, 193, 212, 214, 217, 241, 245, 247, 248, 250, 253

EADS 31, 33, 52, 54–6, 151, 163, 215, 217, 220, 250, 263

economies of scale 31, 49, 53, 85, 130, 196, 202–3, 217, 226, 264

EDA Industry and Market Directorate 157, 230

European Defence Technology Industrial Base (EDTIB) xvi, 7, 50, 94–5, 104, 107, 157, 207–17, 219–22, 225–33, 237–8

EDTIB Strategy xvi, 207, 210–13, 221, 227, 230

EU armaments policy 1–2, 6, 44–6, 58, 189, 260, 263, 265

EU Military Committee xv, 34, 56, 68, 200

EU Satellite Centre 244

Eurofighter 86, 146, 215

Eurogroup 144, 175, 178–9

European Advanced Airlift Tactics Training Courses 201

European agencies 3, 11–13, 21–2

European Capabilities Action Plan (ECAP) 20, 68–71, 89, 244

European Commission ('the Commission', EC) xvi–xvii, 2, 5–8, 12–13, 21, 32–5, 38, 45, 48, 54–8, 77–8, 102, 104, 113, 121, 123, 127–9, 131–4, 147, 150, 158, 171–2, 175–7, 180–5, 200, 213–14, 220–2, 225, 229–32, 234–8, 241–2, 244–56, 262, 264

European Court of Justice 158, 180, 229

European Defence Market 38, 86, 89, 92, 98, 121, 127, 184–5, 226, 229, 237

European Defence R&T Strategy (EDRTS) 107, 116

European External Action Service (EEAS) 73, 78

European Framework Cooperation (EFC) 32, 38, 103, 110–11, 113–16, 247–8

European Helicopter Tactics Instructor Course 201

European Parliament (EP) 17, 55, 57, 121, 221, 243, 262

European Satellite Communications Procurement Cell (ESCPC) 77, 198, 200, 255, 264

European Security and Defence Policy (ESDP) 34, 51, 68, 70, 89, 94, 99, 118, 206, 213, 230, 242

European Security Strategy (ESS) 67, 244

European Space Agency (ESA) 8, 77, 102, 104, 113–15, 241–50, 252–6

Europeanisation 7, 37–9, 118–19, 160–1, 171, 195, 207–12, 215, 217, 219–22

Europeanist 71, 73, 194, 198–9

financial crisis/economic crisis 7, 73, 78, 80, 91, 191, 193, 198

financial cuts 33

framework agreement 54, 88, 90, 129, 140, 147, 150, 229, 246

France 5, 19, 21, 32, 35, 50–1, 66–7, 74, 79, 88, 96, 111–13, 121, 139–51, 157, 159–61, 165–6, 194, 197–202, 214, 216, 252, 255, 260, 263

Galileo 247, 249, 251–2, 260

General Inspector of the Bundeswehr 165

German Defence Industry 162–3

German–Dutch Memorandum of Understanding on Defence Cooperation 166

Germany 6, 18, 79, 88, 96, 111–12, 121, 130, 140, 143, 145, 151, 155–67, 195, 198, 200–2, 214, 216, 233–4, 252, 255, 260, 263

Ghent initiative 7, 74, 79, 191, 195, 200, 263

globalisation 6, 46, 207, 220–1, 226–8, 237

Greece 52, 96, 112, 182, 201, 233, 236

268 *Index*

Green Blade 201
Group of Personalities 33
Guidance, Energy and Materials (GEM) 108

Helicopter Exercise Programme (HEP) 201
Helicopter Tactics Course 201
Helicopter Training Programme 96, 198, 201
Helsinki Headline Goal (HHG) 66, 68–9
Horizon 2020 111, 113–15, 248–9, 264

Independent European Programme Group 87, 99, 144
Industry and Market Directorate 157
Information Acquisition and Processing (IAP) 108
internationalisation 4
interoperability 39, 50–1, 70, 73–4, 76, 114, 130, 157, 176–7, 183, 191, 195–6, 202, 226, 228, 243, 248
ISAF xiv, 77
islands of cooperation/clusters xvii, 199–200, 264
Italy 50, 53, 77, 88, 96, 112, 121, 143, 150, 181, 200–1, 214, 216, 223, 252, 255

Joint Investment Programme (JIP) xvii, 97, 103–4, 106, 108, 111–12, 115, 157, 164, 200
juste retour xvii, 88, 93, 111, 147, 212–13, 215, 220, 226, 230

Lancaster House Treaties/Agreement 6, 140, 150, 166, 197
Letter of Intent (LoI) xvi, 50, 76–7, 88, 90, 103, 106, 109–11, 113, 120, 183–4, 201, 213–14, 219–20, 227, 229, 231
liberalisation 30–1, 33–5, 37, 195
Lisbon Treaty/Treaty of Lisbon 4, 13, 66, 73, 92, 99, 103, 114–15, 181, 214, 220, 243, 255
LoI Framework Agreement 90, 229
Long Term Vision (LTV) xvii, 21, 71, 247

Maritime Surveillance Networking (MARSUR) 77, 97, 198, 203
medical field hospitals 198, 200
Morsillo, Giuseppe 248

nationalisation 207, 220, 227, 263
Naval Logistics and Training 201, 203
neoclassical realism 158, 162, 167

neorealism 158, 167
Netherlands 76, 112, 198–201, 203, 214
norms 14–15, 21, 29, 36, 180, 192–3, 208
North Atlantic Treaty Organisation (NATO) xvi, 4, 6, 8, 20, 23, 56, 68, 71, 74, 75, 80, 85, 87–8, 130, 142–5, 147–9, 156, 159–61, 164, 171–81, 183–5, 191, 193, 195, 197, 213
Norway 75, 112, 148, 201, 246

OHB-System 252
Operation Unified Protector 166
Organisation Conjointe de Coopération en matière d'Armament (OCCAR) xvi–xvii, 20, 22, 49, 88, 90, 93, 120–1, 130, 133, 140, 147, 150, 165, 174, 213, 230, 244, 252

Panel of Experts on Space and Security 243
Peace Project 193
Permanent Structured Cooperation (PESCO) 2, 7, 74, 193–6, 203, 214
Petersberg Tasks 18, 68–70, 229
pilot training 201
pivot toward Asia 65, 79–80, 155–6, 167
Poland 79, 96, 112, 198, 201, 232–3, 252, 263
pooled defence resources 194, 198–9, 204
Pooling and Sharing (P&S) xvii, 2, 6–7, 34, 71, 74, 76, 79, 84, 97, 130, 151, 156, 160, 162, 165–6, 185, 191–204, 222, 251, 255, 263
privatisation 140, 146–7, 263

reformed bandwagoning 156, 159–60, 162, 167
Research & Development (R&D) 5, 34, 37, 48, 50, 54, 56, 78, 85, 111, 114, 116, 123, 132, 134, 163, 172–3, 179, 209, 211, 213, 216–17, 245, 261, 263–5
Research and Technology (R&T) xv–xvii, 3, 5, 20, 27, 32, 47–8, 50–1, 53, 70, 86–8, 91, 93, 102–16, 155, 157, 196, 211, 213, 222, 230, 243
Ruehe, Volker 162

Scharping, Rudolf 162
Schockenhoff/Kiesewetter Paper 166
Security of Supply (SoS) 7, 34, 49, 88, 122, 128–9, 132, 134, 207, 209–13, 215, 220–1, 227

## Index    269

Security Studies 29
Smart Defence 71, 156
Spain 88, 96, 112, 122, 133, 181, 200–1,
    214, 216, 229, 233–4, 252, 255
strategic culture 7, 140–1, 150, 162–3,
    191–4, 199
supply chain 6–7, 35, 107, 122, 124–5,
    140, 180, 207, 211, 216, 217–18,
    220–1, 227–8
Sweden 88, 96, 112, 176, 200–1, 214,
    216, 252
Switzerland 176, 246

Tajani, Antonio 251–2
technology domains 103–4, 108
Thales 54–5
Thales Alenia Space 250, 254
Treaty of Amsterdam 18–19, 31, 35,
    50–1, 66–7, 71, 74, 79, 88, 112, 122,
    139–40, 145–51, 160–1, 166, 194,
    197–8, 200–2, 204, 216, 233, 236, 255

United Kingdom (UK) 66–7, 88, 111,
    121, 209, 214, 260, 19
United States of America (USA) xvii,
    30, 65, 78, 79–80, 86, 90, 120, 139,
    143, 147, 155–6, 171, 173–5, 215, 218,
    260
Unmanned Aerial Systems (UAS) 92,
    212, 252

Walt, Stephen 158–9
Waltzian neorealism 158
Western European Armaments Group
    (WEAG) xvi, 20, 22, 87–8, 90, 103,
    109, 120–3, 173–4, 176, 255
Western European Armaments
    Organisation (WEAO) xvi, 20, 22,
    87–8, 90, 120, 140, 179
Western European Union (WEU) xvi,
    18, 85, 87–8, 120, 143, 146–7
Witney, Nick 49, 51–2, 148, 155

# eBooks
## from Taylor & Francis

Helping you to choose the right eBooks for your Library

Add to your library's digital collection today with Taylor & Francis eBooks. We have over 50,000 eBooks in the Humanities, Social Sciences, Behavioural Sciences, Built Environment and Law, from leading imprints, including Routledge, Focal Press and Psychology Press.

**Choose from a range of subject packages or create your own!**

Benefits for you
- Free MARC records
- COUNTER-compliant usage statistics
- Flexible purchase and pricing options
- 70% approx of our eBooks are now DRM-free.

Benefits for your user
- Off-site, anytime access via Athens or referring URL
- Print or copy pages or chapters
- Full content search
- Bookmark, highlight and annotate text
- Access to thousands of pages of quality research at the click of a button.

**Free Trials Available**

We offer free trials to qualifying academic, corporate and government customers.

## eCollections
Choose from 20 different subject eCollections, including:
- Asian Studies
- Economics
- Health Studies
- Law
- Middle East Studies

## eFocus
We have 16 cutting-edge interdisciplinary collections, including:
- Development Studies
- The Environment
- Islam
- Korea
- Urban Studies

For more information, pricing enquiries or to order a free trial, please contact your local sales team:

UK/Rest of World: **online.sales@tandf.co.uk**
USA/Canada/Latin America: **e-reference@taylorandfrancis.com**
East/Southeast Asia: **martin.jack@tandf.com.sg**
India: **journalsales@tandfindia.com**

**www.tandfebooks.com**